DATE DUE			

DIPLOMACY AND STRATEGY OF SURVIVAL

British policy and Franco's Spain, 1940–41

This book analyses Britain's diplomatic efforts to preserve the non-belligerency of Franco's Spain, during the period between December 1940 and the end of 1941: Spanish participation in the Axis war effort would have increased considerably the strategic odds against Britain in its already unequal struggle for survival with Hitler's Germany, fresh from its triumph over France. Making extensive use of recently available British and Spanish (governmental and private) documentary records, and material gathered from published and unpublished sources in six European languages, Denis Smyth explains how Britain's uphill struggle to secure Spanish non-belligerency had been rewarded with success by December 1940. This diplomatic goal had been attained in spite of Franco's own readiness to enter the war against her in return for satisfaction of his territorial desires, and despite Hitler's interest in recruiting Spaniards into the active ranks of the Axis camp. Rather, the economic weakness of post-Civil War Spain, and the failure of Berlin and Madrid to agree on the terms and the timing of Spanish participation in the war, stabilised Franco's neutrality by the close of 1940, in the absence of any apparently irreparable injury to the British cause. The various means which Britain employed to encourage Franco's Spain to remain at peace – measured economic support, political blandishment and even bribery of Spanish generals – are also studied.

Ironically, however, British policy-makers were unaware of the early success of their efforts to persuade Franco to avoid joining the fight against them. So they remained alert throughout 1940–1 to the danger of sudden Spanish support for, or acquiescence in, a German move across their territory against Gibraltar. London's vigilance often took the form of a concern to anticipate a possible German move against the Rock by seizing alternative naval bases in the Spanish or Portuguese Atlantic Islands. Such preventive military action would have automatically provoked Franco's belligerency, the very contingency which British policy-makers sought to avoid. Only the cautionary counsel of Britain's Foreign Secretary, Lord Halifax, in 1940, and its Ambassador to Spain, Sir Samuel Hoare, in 1940–1, as well as Churchill's own capacity for second throughts on the wisdom of a pre-emptive strike against Iberian territory, rescued the British on several occasions from precipitating Spain's entry into the war.

In order to emphasise the uniqueness of the diplomatic challenge posed to British policy-makers by Franco's Spain, the principles which had governed British policy towards the Spanish Civil War of 1936–9 are also analysed and assessed. Again, by way of underlining the long-term significance of the respective diplomatic attitudes ultimately assumed by Britain and Spain towards each other in 1940–1, the conclusion notes how Spanish neutrality helped the British endure 'their finest hour' and the Franco regime survive the destruction of its former Fascist and Nazi patrons.

'Trouble in the Wings', a cartoon by Low from *The Evening Standard*,
21 November 1940. (Cartoon supplied by permission of *The Standard*.)

DIPLOMACY AND STRATEGY OF SURVIVAL

British Policy and Franco's Spain, 1940–41

DENIS SMYTH

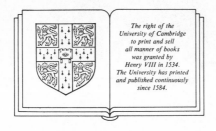

The right of the
University of Cambridge
to print and sell
all manner of books
was granted by
Henry VIII in 1534.
The University has printed
and published continuously
since 1584.

Cambridge University Press

Cambridge
London   New York   New Rochelle
Melbourne   Sydney

Published by the Press Syndicate of the University of Cambridge
The Pitt Building, Trumpington Street, Cambridge CB2 1RP
32 East 57th Street, New York, NY 10022, USA
10 Stamford Road, Oakleigh, Melbourne 3166, Australia

First published 1986

Printed in Great Britain at the University Press, Cambridge

British Library cataloguing in publication data

Smyth, Denis
Diplomacy and strategy of survival : British policy and Franco's Spain,
1940–41.
1. Great Britain – Foreign relations – Spain
2. Spain – Foreign relations – Great Britain
3. Great Britain – Foreign relations – 1936–1945
4. Spain – Foreign relations – 1939–1975
I. Title
327.41046   DA687

Library of Congress cataloguing in publication data

Smyth, Denis, 1948–
Diplomacy and strategy of survival.
Bibliography: p.
Includes index.
1. World War, 1939–1945 – Diplomatic history.
2. Great Britain – Foreign relations – Spain.
3. Spain – Foreign relations – Great Britain.   I. Title.
D750.S57 1986   940.53′22   85–15138
ISBN 0 521 22819 0

For my wife, Margaret,
and in memory of my parents

Well,
To the latter end of a fray and the beginning of a feast
Fits a dull fighter and a keen guest. [Falstaff]

Shakespeare, Henry IV Part One, Act IV, Scene II

Contents

Preface

Perhaps even more than other forms of historical investigation, diplomatic history is inevitably a collective enterprise, for all that one person is usually acknowledged as the individual author of a particular study. The group of archivists, librarians, scholars, students, typists and friends who contribute to the production of any work of history is multiplied for the diplomatic historian by the number of different countries which attract his professional attention. Although sometimes inhibited from immersion in the historical culture of a particular country, to the extent possible for the domestic historian of a given society, by the need to ascertain simultaneous developments on 'the other side of the hill', the international specialist does have his compensations. The variety of his intellectual diet and cultural experience, as he studies – often at source and *in situ* – states with varying principles and policies at play in the 'great game', expands his mind but can also enrich his whole experience. Individuals and cultures become accessible, almost in an accidental way, as the international historian conducts his researches in a succession of cities and countries.

Therefore, the intellectual indebtedness of any diplomatic historian, and of this one in particulr, to many people and places is often pronounced. Such debts can hardly be repaid – the creditors are too numerous, too dispersed and always too generous to want any sort of reimbursement – but they may be acknowledged. Formal recognition of the interest invested and the energy expended by colleagues and contacts in a research project which eventually becomes one's own published work is but token recompense for many kindnesses and services rendered. However, it remains a pleasure and privilege to express my gratitude to the following individuals and institutions.

To Professor T. Desmond Williams, of University College, Dublin,

I am grateful for stimulating my interest in international history in his inimitably inspiring fashion. My thanks are also due to Professor F. H. Hinsley of the University of Cambridge for his patient and highly professional supervision of the doctoral thesis which constituted the original nucleus of this work. To Professor J. J. Lee of University College, Cork, I express my gratitude for both gainful employment and an academic working environment conducive to the pursuit and completion of this body of research and writing.

I am glad to avail of the opportunity, too, to express my heartfelt gratitude to Paul and Gabrielle Preston for providing me with hospitality and friendship on my visits to London. Indeed, Paul Preston has helped in a variety of invaluable ways, facilitating indispensable research contacts, proffering prudent scholarly advice and luring me into expanding my collection of books on Spanish history to a size so swollen as to resemble, but not seriously rival his own unique private library in this area.

Professor Angel Viñas has interrupted his busy schedule, during my sojourns in Madrid, to extend me many academic services and social courtesies for which I was, and am, very grateful.

I wish to thank the Masters and Fellows of Peterhouse for their support during my years in Cambridge and Mr Maurice Cowling, in particular, for his assistance and advice during my days as a postgraduate student in that college.

I am also grateful to the Faculty of Arts at University College, Cork for some financial support which enabled me conduct part of the research for this book.

William Davies of Cambridge University Press deserves special mention for not baulking at the prospect of contracting an Irishman to write on an aspect of Spanish history. He bore the protracted gestation of this book with considerable patience. I am also extremely grateful to my heroic and utterly exploited typists, Norma Buckley and Charlotte Wiseman.

The courteous and efficient services of the staffs of the following archival centres and libraries are gratefully acknowledged: The Public Record Office, London and Kew; The University Library, Cambridge; The Archival Section, Ministerio de Asuntos Exteriores, Palacio de Santa Cruz, Madrid; The British Library; The British Library of Economics and Political Science; The Archives' Centre, Churchill College, Cambridge; York Public Library; The Boole Library, University College, Cork; The Library, Trinity College, Dublin; The House of Lords Record Office; The Franklin D. Roosevelt Library, Hyde Park, New York.

The archivist of the Alba collection in the Palacio de Liria, Madrid, was extremely helpful in facilitating my access to the Papers of the 17th Duke of Alba, the first time that these latter documents had been opened to an historical researcher. Sr Manuel Arroyo and Paul Preston, again, combined to provide me with this unique archival opportunity. I am very grateful to the Duke of Alba for his permission to consult and cite the papers of the 17th Duke.

Permission to quote from the Templewood collection was granted by P. E. Paget, Esq.

Permission to quote from the Dalton Papers was granted by the British Library of Economics and Political Science.

Quotations from Crown copyright material appear by permission of the Controller of Her Majesty's Stationery Office.

Finally, I want to record my most profound debt of gratitude, unrepayable in kind because of the quantity and quality of assistance afforded me in my labours on this book, to a former member of the staff of the University Library, Cambridge. This book is dedicated to her and it is a gesture which only inadequately expresses my gratitude to Margaret for her support and solidarity.

Naturally, in spite of my indebtedness to the individuals and institutions mentioned above, any faults and flaws to be found in this book are all my own work.

Cork, September 1984. DS

Introduction

Countless and inestimable are the chances of war. Those who read the story, and still more those who share the dangers, of a campaign feel that every incident is surrounded with a host of possibilities, any one of which, had it become real, would have changed the whole course of events.[1]

Britain's grand strategists indulged understandably in a form of 'whistling in the dark' during the period of their country's desperate struggle for survival in 1940–1. The three-pronged strategy which they elaborated to effect the destruction of Nazi Germany by way of bombs, blockade and 'bolshevism', may have derived more from their own psychological necessity to conceive some path to victory than from any objective assessment of their real military, economic and political possibilities in the fight with the Axis. Certainly, British strategic thought had come to stress, well before the outbreak of war in 1939, the advantages of enervating aggressive German power by such indirect means, as against the frightful cost of direct military confrontation with the Wehrmacht. The lethargic Anglo-French search for oblique avenues of assault against Germany during the 'Phoney War' exemplifies this aversion to engaging in frontal combat.[2] However, the resolution with which British strategists formulated, after the collapse of France, a grandiose plan for the reduction of German power by economic strangulation, aerial bombardment and popular subversion inside the Nazi-occupied countries, suggests that they were making a virtue of necessity. For, they founded their scheme exclusively on those strategic devices apparently still available after the defeat of their continental ally and the expulsion of British troops from the European mainland.[3] Yet the elimination of the French Army inevitably undermined the effectiveness of any British offensive design. Without the defensive buffer of the French force, there was nothing to contain and confine Germany's striking power indefinitely while the programme of attrition by air, sea and internal disruption steadily sapped its strength. Britain's grand strategists in 1940–1 were motivated by faith rather than hope. Belief in

1

victory, somehow, someway, was an expression of their will to survive.

Winston Churchill was, during the Second World War, as he had been during the first, a protagonist of various versions of the indirect attack on Germany. Nonetheless, in the period 1940–1, although formally subscribing to the strategy proposed by his Chiefs of Staff, he was perhaps less in need of any psychological solace which it provided than his colleagues.[4] To him, resistance was its own justification. He found it enough to fight on and to wait for something to turn up, to turn the tide eventually. As he acknowledged to a conference of Commanders-in-Chief in London, on 31 October 1940:

No more than anyone else did he see clearly how the war was going to be won . . . for four years in 1914–18 nobody could foretell the final collapse of Germany, which came so unexpectedly at the end, and in an unexpected way. All we could do for the present, as during the Great War, was to get on with it and see what happened – our chief weapons at the moment being the blockade and air bombardment.[5]

No matter how British military planners might envisage the long-term prospects of their cause, the British battle, throughout the eighteen months from the fall of France until the entry of the United States into the war, was to endure. If the dominant theme in German strategy in 1940–1 was the preparation and launching of a massive drive for *Lebensraum* in Eastern Europe, Britain was engaged, at the same time, in a sustained fight for breathing-space.

It was precisely in the context of this struggle for survival that Franco's Spain assumed great importance for Britain's grand strategists. For Spain's strategic location astride maritime, imperial and inter-continental lines of communication made its attitude towards the war crucial for the British fight to survive. Even if the fortress of Gibraltar could have withstood attack longer than the few days within which the Germans reckoned they could conquer it, the vital naval, and valuable air bases on the Rock would have been rendered unusable by a few hours' air and artillery bombardment.[6] The loss of control over the Strait of Gibraltar would clearly have an immediate impact upon the British position in the Mediterranean, 'the pivot of their world Empire', to use the German Admiral Raeder's phrase.[7] Direct communications with Egypt and the Suez Canal would be throttled and, perhaps, severed completely. British pressure on the weaker Axis partner, Italy, would be relieved and Britain's Eastern Mediterranean friend, Turkey, cowed. As Churchill wrote, 'Spain held the key to all British enterprises in the Mediterranean'.[8]

British dependence upon overseas sources of food and raw

materials only accentuated the critical character of Spain's international stance for a Britain at war. Italian entry into the war had blocked easy access to Middle East oil and the resources of the British and Dutch Asian Empires by making the passage via the Suez Canal route too risky, but even the 'long haul' round the Cape would be jeopardised by the expulsion of the British Navy from Gibraltar. For, with British war-ships driven north to home bases and south to Freetown, and German surface and submarine craft operating from Spanish – and probably Portuguese – ports, Britain's ability to conduct maritime traffic in the central and south Atlantic would be severely, maybe even fatally, damaged. The operational radius offered to the German Navy by Spain's strategic situation is indicated by the fact that, even before the fall of France, German submarines, clandestinely refuelled in Spanish harbours, were able to operate off the north Brazilian coast.[9] The range of German air attack and reconnaissance on British shipping would also be extended by the use of Spanish airfields. Recognising these dangers, and that Britain and the Empire depended for their survival on the security of the sea-lanes, Basil Liddell Hart, as early as 1938, advised the then War Minister, Hore-Belisha, that in wartime 'a friendly Spain is desirable, a neutral Spain is vital'.[10]

After the French defeat, Spain's position as Europe's gateway to Africa also assumed great significance. As British hopes and German fears came to focus on the possibility of renewed French resistance based on their North African Empire, the Spanish artery to Morocco became the common factor in their counter-calculations. Thus, the British Joint Planning Staff engaged, in February 1941, upon assessing the feasibility of assisting a possible revival of French belligerency under Weygand in French North Africa, concluded, thus:

The greatest threat to our interests would arise from a German occupation of Spain and Spanish Morocco, as this would reduce our control in the Western Mediterranean and gravely jeopardise our sea communications with French North African ports. It would also menace General Weygand's supply lines through Casablanca and so threaten his whole position in North Africa.[11]

Once over the Spanish bridgeway, of course, the way would be open for German forces to West Africa and the port of Dakar, affording still greater opportunities for domination of the Atlantic sea-lanes, and even of threatening America. French North Africa, geographically in Spain's shadow, was also the most convenient point of entry for United States' forces into the Eurafrican war. Both Churchill and the British Ambassador in Spain, 1940–4, Sir Samuel Hoare, grasped the importance of the Hispano–North African region for future American operations long before Operation 'Torch' of November 1942.[12]

Spain's reaction to the war could well determine, too, the ultimate accessibility of the vast economic resources of the Mediterranean and African regions, to which it could open or bar the way. All in all, as Churchill again wrote, 'Spain had much to give and even more to take away.'[13]

The purpose of the following chapters is to define the course, crises and consequences of the process by which a British policy, to meet the dangers emanating from Spain, was formulated and sustained during the period from June 1940 until December 1941. In 1940, that policy was largely the function of a policy-making partnership between two ex-members of the discredited Chamberlain Cabinet, Sir Samuel Hoare and Lord Halifax. For, if Hoare found himself as British Ambassador 'on Special Mission' in Madrid, at the beginning of June 1940, Halifax remained Foreign Secretary until late in December of that year. Hoare, in fact, articulated a policy for Britain towards Spain which, with Halifax's support, in large part determined the nature of its diplomacy and strategy towards the latter in 1940, and even into 1941. This policy success for two of the 'Old Gang' was all the more remarkable in that that policy could be labelled by both contemporary critics and at least one modern historian, as 'in effect, appeasement once more'.[14]

Based on the assessment, perhaps the assumption, that Franco wished to remain outside the European conflict, and might be weaned away from the Axis orbit, a policy emerged designed to satisfy Spanish economic needs, and demonstrate British sympathy and, or support for Spain's territorial ambitions. It was hoped that this double-barrelled policy would offset both the intimidating proximity of German forces on the Pyrenean frontier, and the influence exercised by the apparently invincible German military machine over Spanish minds. This scheme was stunted less by domestic British opposition than by Spanish recalcitrance, stemming from their fear of the Germans. The gradually disclosed unwillingness of the United States Government to co-operate in furnishing substantial economic aid and credits to Spain, also greatly reduced the scope of economic help with which Britain could tempt the Spaniards. Despite Hoare's repeated efforts, British economic policy towards Spain tended to impress negatively, rather than positively: Britain's power to starve Spain through its naval blockade of Nazi-dominated Europe, was more evident than any effort to feed the hungry Spaniards.

It was in its negative aspect, indeed, that the Hoare–Halifax policy-line on Spain would prove most significant. This was not only a consequence of the fact that Hoare had to spend so much time defending his policy against its critics and opponents. This tendency of the negative, restraining, rather than the positive, prescriptive side of Hoare's policy to predominate, was probably inherent in Britain's perilous strategic position in 1940–1. For although Britain's rulers were naturally anxious not to multiply the enemies or difficulties which they faced in their desperate circumstances, one of their most urgent concerns was to discern new sources of potential danger, and to forestall or anticipate them. The way the Germans had managed to seize the initiative throughout the earlier phase of the war only reinforced the British determination not to be wrong-footed yet again. 'Must we always wait until a disaster has occurred?', Churchill asked his Foreign Secretary, in July 1940.[15] Britain could no longer afford to respond to German surprises after the event. Churchill, as is explained in chapter two, was worried at that time about British vulnerability at Gibraltar, so open to attack from Spain. Spain, indeed, was to become throughout the remainder of 1940 and 1941 a constant object of British fears and anxieties. It could present so many new threats by its active enmity, or merely by acquiescing in a German move through its territory. Thus it was that the Prime Minister, despite his earnest desire that Spain should remain at peace – 'I want Spain to keep neutral as long as possible', he told Hugh Dalton in March 1941 – came to contemplate initiating military action against Spain on several occasions in 1940–1.[16] The evidence at certain times seemed to suggest to him and, or to others that Franco had definitely gone over to the Axis: so why not anticipate the inevitable loss of Gibraltar by striking first and seizing alternative bases, say in Spanish Morocco or the Portuguese and Spanish Atlantic Islands?

In the event, the Prime Minister's particular fears proved unfounded, and he was only too happy to revert to his preferred policy of peace with Spain. Had he acted on his initial impulses, however, it would have been too late and Britain would have precipitated Spanish belligerency, the very contingency which British policy-makers sought to avoid. It was exactly at this point that the moderating influence of Halifax or Hoare, and their Spanish policy, proved decisive. For by personal intervention and counter-interpretation they were able to assuage Churchill's apprehensions and alarm and to defuse these dangerous crises. Ironically, Hoare did not know just how crucial was his role in preventing a British attack on Spain as he was not privy to the grand strategic deliberations at the critical moments. However, resolve these crises Hoare and Halifax did, in more ways than one. Because their policy-line on Spain seemed to have achieved some success, with the passage of time and without any change in Spanish non-belligerency, Churchill was inclined to listen to them in an emergency, even when his strategic instinct sensed danger. So the actual momentum of the Hoare–Halifax Spanish policy created an atmosphere of wariness and reflection for policy-making on Spain, even at times of crisis. It was in this context of caution that the personal interventions of Halifax or Hoare served to inhibit any dramatic reversal in policy. The very durability of the Hoare–Halifax line on Spain was also the major factor in converting a leading sceptic, Anthony Eden, Halifax's successor as foreign Secretary in late 1940, into a grudging supporter of the policy.

The most salient feature of the following chapters will be an exposition of the way in which the positive aspects of the policy advocated by Hoare, large-scale economic aid and some expression of support for Spanish territorial ambitions, tended to wither away for several reasons, leaving the negative facet of the policy to exercise a vital check on those over-anxious to get their retaliation in first, as it were. If Britain could not draw Spain away from the Axis, it must, at least, abstain from such actions as a military assault or a total economic blockade, which were bound to provoke Spanish belligerency. Although Hoare tenaciously persisted in trying to mount a coherent and elaborate British effort to tempt Spain into the British orbit throughout 1940–1, Spanish sensitivity to German wrath and American suspicion were too great. Nevertheless, in his efforts to prevent an intolerable economic blockade of Spain and to calm his Government's nerves in times of peril, he was outstandingly successful – much more so than even he realised. In doing so, he was helped sometimes by luck with apparently favourable Spanish developments, and always by the Prime Minister's surprising willingness to listen, and to let himself be dissuaded from aggressive action.

For if Churchill could impress as being 'a wild tactician, certainly; frequently a crackpot strategist', what is striking about his role in the successive crises in Anglo–Spanish relations during 1940–1, is the capacity which he revealed for reflection and reappraisal.[17] So, in spite of his reputation for letting enthusiasm outweigh calculation when the prospect of a fight loomed, the Prime Minister manifested, where Spain was concerned, an ability to reassess and reverse projected courses of action. Churchill's open-mindedness became even more decisive in maintaining an attitude of forebearance towards

Spain in the course of 1941. Then, the removal of Halifax from the Foreign Office, and the growing suspicion amongst Britain's grand strategists that the Spaniards were likely to be drawn into the Axis war effort, meant the virtual elimination of influential voices consistently advocating caution concerning Spanish affairs in the inner circles of the British Government. Hoare's pleas from Madrid for circumspection would have been futile without a receptive listener at 'the centre of the web' in London.

The essence of the subsequent chapters will be an analysis of the whole of the foregoing process, highlighting the major crises in Anglo-Spanish relations during the period 1940–1.

However, what is attempted is not simply a contextualisation of crisis diplomacy. An effort will be made to display the full significance and complexity of Anglo-Spanish relations in 1940–1. It is possible, from a juxtaposition of American, British, German, Portuguese and Spanish sources, to sketch some dimensions of the domestic, economic and political scenes in Spain and to comment on certain aspects of Spanish policy. Thus, it will be observed that Franco, though treading very warily, did entertain the idea of entering the war in the latter half of 1940. A seasoned survivor, Franco recognised that the feeble Spanish economy and his own delicate political position would not withstand the shock of a sustained war effort. If he had to avoid getting embroiled in a long war, however, Franco was equally concerned not to let Hitler win without his intervention. That might be just as dangerous to his survival in power as premature entry into the war. It certainly would prevent the Spanish leader from using the instrument of German victory to realise his designs on French North Africa by making a token and tardy contribution to it. It will be explained in the second and fifth chapters how Franco evinced a definite interest in belligerency on the side of the Axis powers in June and again in September 1940, when he considered them to be on the threshold of triumph. British stamina and the unsympathetic German response to these initiatives did not, at first, deter Franco from the attempt to tie his country to Germany and Italy in a diplomatic association which would bring Spain into the war, at a future moment of his own choice, in return for the Axis-aided acquisition of those North African territories – principally Morocco and the Oran region of Algeria – which he coveted. However, Hitler's aversion to jeopardising the uncertain Vichy French hold on their North African Empire by promising parts of it to a Spanish Government, which he felt was sure to divulge such a commitment and thus provoke a movement towards de Gaulle in that area, was evident by November 1940. The German refusal to satisfy him on this essential point alienated Franco from contemplating any but the most reluctant and belated war effort. From the early winter of 1940 onwards, Spanish non-belligerency was effectively stabilised in the absence of any apparently irreparable injury to the British cause, such as the loss of Suez. This new stability in Spain's international position was by no means evident to the watchful British. Indeed, the irony is that all their real frights about Spanish policy post-date the *démarche* by Franco in the autumn of 1940.

However, that British statesmen and grand strategists occasionally misread the signs of Spain's international intentions during 1940–1, is not surprising. For Franco's Spain presented them with diplomatic and strategic problems of a character without precedent in Anglo–Spanish relations in modern times. In order to emphasise the novel nature of the difficulties posed by Francoist Spain to British policy-makers, from June 1940 to December 1941, an analysis is made in chapter one of the main purposes and priorities shaping Britain's policy towards the Spanish Civil War, 1936–9. That policy was founded on what seemed to be a secure set of expectations concerning Spain's international position. For the facts of Spain's geopolitical situation, with the counry encircled by British sea, and French land, power appeared to condemn it to the position, however reluctantly adopted by the Francoist state, of Anglo-French satellite. Spain's economic dependence on London and Paris was also reaffirmed by the destructive impact of a three-year-long civil war. However, the process of post-civil war reconciliation between Britain and Franco's Spain which, in fulfilment of London's confident expectations, was well under way by the spring of 1940, was rudely interrupted by Germany's western offensive. France's capitulation to its German conquerors, in June 1940, seemed to remove the basis for Anglo-Spanish *rapprochement*. Released from Anglo-French confinement, the Franco regime was at liberty to consort with the Nazi forces as they reached the Pyrenees. British policy-makers could no longer assume that Franco would meekly accept the role of diplomatic client of the democracies. Diplomatic ingenuity and strategic improvisation were now employed in a desperate bid to retain Britain's influence in a country where, previously, the reality of Anglo-French power had sufficed to ensure, almost automatically, the primacy of their interests.

With Britain engaged in a life-and-death struggle against Hitler's Germany, and the Franco regime confronted with a crucial choice for external war or peace as the means of internal political consolidation, both London and Madrid found that their foreign policies inevitably concentrated on the most basic issue in international relations: survival or extinction. The long-term significance of the policies pursued by Britain and Franco's Spain, in 1940–1, for the subsequent survival of their respective political systems and national sovereignties is assessed in the conclusion.

1

Britain and the birth of Franco's Spain, 1936–39

On 19 June 1940, a Labour member of Britain's new wartime co-alition government, Hugh Dalton, conferred with Rear-Admiral T. S. V. Phillips, Vice-Chief of Naval Staff. During the course of their conversation concerning Britain's blockade of Nazi-dominated mainland Europe, the admiral was moved to denounce the political blunders which had placed his country in such mortal danger by successively antagonising Germany, Japan, Italy and Spain. Phillips was particularly critical of British policy towards the recent Spanish Civil War:

To have Spain as an enemy would jeopardise the whole of our control both of the western Mediterranean and the Atlantic sea routes. It is unthinkable that we should have been brought to such a point. We backed the Bolsheviks in Spain in 1936 and '37 against the only man who, in modern times, has been able to make Spain strong.[1]

The admiral was mistaken in both assertion and assumption. Far from favouring the Republican camp in 1936–7, or afterwards, the British Government were almost all sympathetic towards the Spanish Nationalist cause.[2] However, unsure as to the ultimate victor in the contest, and cautious lest precipitate action should prejudice British interests on its termination, His Majesty's ministers refrained from any spectacular support for Franco. They sought security in non-intervention, thereby hoping to ensure that whichever side won it 'should not enter upon its inheritance with any serious grudge' against Britain.[3]

By its very inaction, however, the British Government rendered vital services to the Nationalist civil war effort.[4] Britain's adherence to the international Non-Intervention Agreement of August 1936 relieved its Government of the need to confess openly its unwillingness to allow Republican Spain to purchase war *matériel* within its jurisdiction.[5] The signatories of the Non-Intervention Agreement

10

pledged themselves to close their war materials markets to the Spanish belligerents, thereby depriving the Republican Government of its right, as the properly constituted executive of Spain, to buy arms abroad.[6] This denial of the legitimate Government's freedom to acquire the means to suppress the military rebels was, in fact, a 'very effective intervention in the internal affairs of Spain', as the Spanish Ambassador in Paris complained.[7] After witnessing the implementation of non-intervention for nine months, the President of the Spanish Republic, Manuel Azaña, was not only sure that it operated to his regime's disadvantage, he was also certain as to the power responsible for this systematic bias. He identified the culprit in his diary entry for 31 May 1937: 'Our greatest enemy until now has been the British Government. All the schemes devised for non-intervention . . . have damaged the Government of the Republic and favoured the rebels.'[8] Britain's aversion to becoming involved in the Spanish imbroglio produced other instances of official inaction or lethargy similarly injurious to Spanish Republican interests. The Royal Navy was employed only grudgingly to break the attempted Francoist naval blockade of Bilbao in 1937, and British air and sea power not used, in 1938, to protect British maritime commerce with the starving Republican city of Barcelona against illegal Nationalist attack.[9] The tenor of British policy throughout the Spanish Civil War was assessed by the Chief Diplomatic Adviser to the Government, Sir Robert Vansittart, in January 1939, thus: 'the whole course of our policy of non-intervention – which has in reality, as we all know, worked in an entirely one-sided manner – has been putting a premium on Franco's victory . . .'[10]

The benefits that accrued to the Nationalist insurgents in Spain from Britain's stance were not merely the result of British passivity, however. British influence on France at crucial junctures in the evolution of the Spanish Civil War definitely, and maybe even decisively, boosted Franco's fortunes. The Francoist diplomatic agent accredited to the British Government, the Duke of Alba, was directed by his Foreign Ministry, on 25 April 1938, to impress upon his hosts that only French support for the Spanish Republic obstructed a 'sincere and loyal' *rapprochement* between Nationalist Spain and Britain. The British could avail themselves of the forthcoming meeting with members of the French Government to urge the closure of the recently re-opened Pyrenean frontier across which flowed the 'sole tonic' that sustained the Republic, in the wake of the Nationalists' successful Aragonese offensive.[11] Alba presented the official Nationalist request for British action to this effect to a non-committal

Sir George Mounsey, Assistant Under-Secretary of State at the Foreign Office, on 28 April.[12] As British ministers met their French counterparts on the morning of that day for the first session of their inter-governmental talks, the only one during which the Spanish problem was discussed, Alba's formal representations were apparently too late to affect these deliberations. However, Spanish Nationalist disquiet over the matter does seem to have been communicated to the British representatives in time to influence their attitude at the Anglo-French conference.[13] For, Britain's Foreign Secretary, Lord Halifax, used the occasion of the conversation with the French ministerial team, on the morning of 28 April, to deprecate the 'difficult, dangerous and melancholy situation' in which 'the minute one side in Spain made an advance, support to the other side was immediately increased'.[14] Again, the Prime Minister, Neville Chamberlain, cited Alba as his source for the information that France had recently permitted the trans-shipment of 300 Soviet aircraft across its territory into Spain.[15] Moreover, the British certainly did press the French in subsequent weeks to reseal their frontier with Catalonia.[16] So Alba was able to report home in May that the British were 'endeavouring to have the French border closed to shipments of war *matériel* to the Reds', at a time which his own Foreign Minister, General Gómez Jordana, recognised could be 'a very important turning point in the Spanish Civil War'.[17] London kept up the pressure on Paris, as Halifax's Private Secretary, Oliver Harvey, noted in his diary on 5 June: 'In Spain the [British] Government are praying for Franco's victory and bringing all the influence they can bear on France to stop the inflow of munitions to Barcelona.'[18] The reluctant French Premier, Edouard Daladier, was eventually prevailed upon to reseal France's frontier with Republican Spain, on 13 June 1938, a date which a contemporary commentator described as 'perhaps the most fatal day for the Spanish Government'.[19] The British connection had proved decisive, as Vansittart observed on 27 June:

The French . . . were apprehensive of closing their frontier before the scheme of the Non-Intervention Committee (to end foreign involvement in the Civil War) became effective – even if that instrument could work with even hand; but they have been brought to believe, as several Frenchmen of authority have informed me, that Anglo-French relations can only be preserved in their fullness by facilitating the victory of Franco.[20]

Officially the British Government had only requested its French counterpart, on 7 June 1938, to agree to reseal its Pyrenean frontier if and when London had succeeded in establishing an armistice between the Spanish combatants.[21] However, even after the failure of

Britain's armistice proposal, with its rejection by the Italians, the British Government exerted its influence to keep the French–Catalan border closed.[22] Indeed, there were actually French politicians who were only too glad to receive, and even invite, such advice from London. France's Foreign Minister, Georges Bonnet, concerned to effect appeasement abroad and avoid any encouragement of revolutionary leftist aspirations at home, was thus prepared to 'welcome any *régime d'ordre* in Spain'.[23] He informed the British 'very privately and confidentially', on 23 June 1938, to 'lay great stress with Daladier' on the desirability of 'the Pyrenees frontier remaining closed'.[24] On 30 June, the British Ambassador in Paris, Sir Eric Phipps, did inform Daladier of 'the absolutely vital importance that his Majesty's Government attached to the continued closure of the Pyrenees frontier in order to give reasonable time for the British non-intervention plan to come into operation'.[25]

Moreover, that the British had more general diplomatic reasons for wanting the continued closure of the French–Catalan border was revealed when the plan for the withdrawal of 'volunteers' from both sides in Spain, which they had steered through the Non-Intervention Committee, came to grief in August 1938.[26] Franco's rejection of this laboriously evolved scheme, then, prompted his Republican opponents to remind London and Paris that the Pyrenean frontier had only been sealed 'to facilitate the creation of an atmosphere propitious to the acceptance and execution of the plan'.[27] However, the urgent plea of the Republican Minister of State, Julio Álvarez del Vayo, that the border be reopened was heeded in neither democratic capital.[28] The British Government believed that the reopening of France's frontier with Republican Spain would prolong the Civil War and thus obstruct Anglo-Italian *rapprochement*, thereby 'holding up appeasement among the Mediterranean Powers generally and in turn retarding any progress towards a wider European settlement'.[29] This rationale induced the British, and the French, to ignore such warnings as that voiced by the Spanish Republican Ambassador in London, Pablo de Azcárate, on 26 August 1938:

All that ... will cause a profound effect in Spain; the government and public opinion consider the present moment to be the decisive test; all that does not draw the natural consequences from [Franco's] negative, any attempt to prolong further the game of non-intervention will be considered in Spain as an active collaboration by France and England in Italo–German aggression against Spain.[30]

Chamberlain, however, had priorities other than upholding Britain's reputation among Republican Spaniards. As relayed by Lord

Plymouth, British Parliamentary Under-Secretary of State for foreign affairs and chairman of the Non-Intervention Committee, to the Italians in early September 1938, they were 'to defuse the Spanish question, and meantime to gain time in which it can be resolved in the way that is most favourable to the interests of Europe and of Italo–British understanding'.[31] The French were not much more responsive to Spanish Republican cries for help. Only Franco's drive towards Barcelona, begun on 23 December 1938, and powered by German *matériel*, induced the French to re-open the Pyrenean avenue of supply to the outgunned defenders of Catalonia. But this was too little, and definitely too late, to salvage the Spanish Republican cause.[32]

Indirectly, therefore, Britain contributed to Nationalist victory and Republican defeat in Spain. For all the resentment among the Francoists against Britain's failure to grant them 'belligerent rights' to intercept, on the high seas, ships suspected of transporting war materials to the Republicans, or to lend the rebels other overt support, there was a realisation among Nationalist leaders of the advantageous effects of British policy upon their position. In early October 1938 General Jordana privately acknowledged that the Chamberlain Government's attitude towards the insurgents was one of 'relative and benevolent neutrality'.[33]

Moreover, Admiral Phillips was wrong in apparently assuming that a Spain reinvigorated by Franco's rule would be readily compatible with Britain's national interest. A strong Spain would constitute a strategic menace to Britain where a weak country had left the British undisturbed in their possession of Gibraltar and unmolested in their Atlantic commerce and communications. In the early days of the Spanish Civil War, the Chiefs of Staff Sub-Committee advised their political masters that 'the possession by a hostile Power of harbours on the Atlantic seaboard in Spanish territory would imperil our communications by way of the Atlantic'. The Chiefs of Staff highlighted another area of British vulnerability: 'Our position at Gibraltar has for many years been based on a continuation of friendly relations with Spain.'[34] Experience of the ensuing years of civil conflict in Spain did not alter British grand strategic opinion. The First Lord of the Admiralty, Lord Stanhope, informed a Cabinet colleague on 19 May 1939, that 'ever since the long-range gun was invented, our whole position in the Mediterranean has been dependent on a weak or friendly Spain'.[35] Gibraltar's harbour lay on the landward side of the Rock, fully exposed to bombardment from any heavy batteries situated on a twenty-mile stretch of Spanish coast commanding the royal naval base.[36] Spanish infirmity was the best guarantee that they would continue to tolerate the British presence at Gibraltar. A weak, and consequently an acquiescent, Spain was a condition of Britain's Mediterranean and Eastern Atlantic security.

The various right-wing and reactionary interests which combined to challenge Spain's Republican Government by open rebellion, in July 1936, were motivated primarily by domestic concerns and conflicts. However, the long-standing rightist aspiration to revive Spain's imperial greatness and restore its international stature was an inspiration to all, and a crucial commitment for some.[37] The very man who came to lead the Nationalist rebellion, Francisco Franco, had defined, years before, his greatest ambition thus: 'That Spain become as great again as she was of old.'[38] The pre-civil-war leader of Spain's fascist Falange, José Antonio Primo de Rivera, proclaimed his political purpose in these terms, in 1934: 'And that is what we can struggle to achieve. Not to be a middling country; for either we are a vast country fulfilling a universal mission, or else we are a meaningless and degraded people. Spain must be given back the ambition to recover her leading role in the world.'[39] The Falange's programme also emphasised a commitment to empire: 'We declare that Spain's historical fulfilment is the empire. We demand for Spain a prominent position in Europe. We will not tolerate either international isolation nor foreign interference.'[40] José Antonio appears to have been particularly concerned with regenerating communal cohesion within Spain, and with ensuring international recognition of a regained national virility.[41] Nevertheless, his admiration for Mussolini's imperialist war against Ethiopia led him to assert that colonisation was the mission of a cultured people, and empire its fulfilment.[42] Other Spanish fascist ideologues were more explicitly certain that a successful counter-revolutionary project would have to take the form of actual physical expansion. Only an authentic imperialist enterprise could eliminate the class struggle and recreate the social solidarity and national unity that they wanted.[43]

Whether imperial yearnings sprang from rightist nostalgia for Spain's past glories, or from the rationale of counter-revolutionary ideology, there was agreement as to the powers responsible for Spain's previous decline and decadence. According to Ramón Serrano Suñer, brother-in-law of Franco's wife and the Generalissimo's intimate political adviser in the later stages of the Civil War, Britain and France had long scorned Spain's 'natural and historic right'. He assessed the impact of these states' policies on Spain in recent centuries, thus: 'The Anglo-French group dominant during our worst political phases had sentenced Spain to be a people of the third order, a mere satellite, a market, a source of scarce raw materials.'[44] The authors of an officially sponsored tract, cataloguing Spain's imperial territorial claims, published in the early years of Franco's rule, condemned the Republican regime which the Nationalists had over-thrown as an 'instrument of Anglo-French domination over the dying Fatherland'.[45] Britain was often singled out for special abuse. Nationalist Spain's party newspaper, *Arriba*, indicted England in August 1940, as the 'most direct interruptress of our destiny'.[46] Such resentments were not confined to the fascist or chauvinistic factions of Nationalist Spain. Even the Anglophil Spanish Ambassador in London, the Duke of Alba, defined Britain's 'traditional policy' for his minister in 1940, as 'consisting in fomenting a weak Spain'.[47]

The British retention of Gibraltar was alone sufficient to earn the enmity of a Nationalist regime intent on rescuing Spain's interna-tional reputation and resuscitating its national pride. José Antonio Primo de Rivera had seen in Spain's inability to oust the British from the Rock a shameful symptom of its general 'debility' and 'servility'.[48] The official publicists of Spain's imperial claims in 1941, de Areilza and Castiella, maintained that Spain without Gibraltar was a 'mutilated [and] incomplete' nation, describing the Rock as an 'inexhaustible source of hatred against England welling up from the very heart of our people'.[49]

Of course the Franco regime, which conducted such public propa-ganda against the British, on its accession to full control of Spain, was not exclusively dominated by fascist politics or programmes. Indeed, the Caudillo of the 'New' Spain was neither inclined by intellect nor temperament towards fascism. He was a conservative officer with simplistic patriotic sentiments and authoritarian instincts.[50] Although he had no specific ideological inspiration, Franco was opportunistic enough to employ fascist façades and formulae when he deemed them useful or necessary. As his long-serving military aide and cousin, Francisco Franco Salgado-Araujo, perceived, however, Franco was not a true Falangist, but a 'Francoist above everything . . . one hundred percent Francoist'.[51] Indeed, Franco had demonstrated his political eclecticism, within the broad spectrum of the Spanish right, by forcibly uniting the Falange, the traditionalist Carlist communion and other anti-Republicans into an ideologically incoherent political movement, the Falange Española Tradicio-nalista y de las Juntas de Ofensiva Nacional–Sindicalista (F.E.T.), under his leadership in April 1937. The imposition of political uniformity ensured a united front on the Nationalist side for the duration of the Civil War and was made the easier by the convenient death of José Antonio at Republican hands.[52] Franco did require the organisational and propaganda resources of the F.E.T. to control the political energies and tensions accumulating in the Nationalist camp, but he served notice in the first weeks of his nation-wide rule that he would brook no charges of ideological deviation from Falangist principles in his conduct of the affairs of state. He informed the F.E.T.'s National Council, on 5 June 1939, that the 'constant interpretation' of the twenty-six points of the Falange's programme was an 'irrefutable and exclusive imperative of the *caudillaje* (chieftaincy)'.[53] Franco would determine what was Falangist.

Certainly, it was not fascist principle which imbued Franco with imperialist ambitions. These were gathered from the reflex rightist veneration of Spain's past grandeur and his personal involvement in the country's last colonial war in north-west Morocco. He acknowledged both these influences in an interview with an Italian journalist soon after clinching his Civil War victory. Observing that his success implied 'a revival of Spain's historic mission', Franco added that 'Spain was busily occupied in Morocco, where she had a future'.[54] Personal impulses and political imperatives alike ensured that an assertive foreign policy was among the priorities of the new state.[55] However, the Civil War leader whose pedestrian generalship had so annoyed some of his Axis assistants was not going to endanger his recently-won hold on power at home by impetuous action abroad.[56] Franco's pursuit of territorial aggrandisement would be pragmatic rather than programmatic. As he told a Portuguese diplomat, his foreign policy would be 'geographical', not ideological.[57]

However, geographical factors were more than sufficient to focus the hostility of the 'New' Spain upon the democratic great powers. French possession of the bulk of Moroccan territory which Franco coveted, and his claim against the British over Gibraltar, ensured that his regime would gravitate naturally towards political alignment with the revisionist Powers, Italy and Germany. The Italo–German drive to redraw European boundaries and redefine spheres of influence coincided with Francoist Spain's own inclination, a community of interests already demonstrated by Nazi and fascist support for the Nationalist civil war effort. By a secret agreement of 28 November 1936 with Italy, Nationalist Spain promised to adopt 'an attitude of benevolent neutrality' towards, and to provide all communications and commercial facilities for, Italy if the latter was engaged in military or economic conflict with one or more powers.[58]

In July 1939, Franco reiterated his 'intention of maintaining very favourable – even more than very favourable – neutrality towards Italy', should Mussolini go to war.[59] Spain's adherence to the Anti-Comitern Pact on 27 March 1939, and the conclusion of the German–Spanish Treaty of Friendship, of 31 March 1939, further embodied this trend towards co-operation among the dictator powers.[60] By Article Six of the latter compact, Germany and Spain agreed to 'avoid anything in the political, military, and economic fields that might be disadvantageous to its treaty partner or of advantage to its opponent' should either state 'become involved in warlike complications with a third power'.[61] The obligations, which Spain had thus contracted during the course of the Civil War to adopt a position of benevolent neutrality towards the Axis Powers in any future European conflict, might seem to signify the total failure of British policy-makers to protect one of the primary strategic interests that they had defined at the outset of the Spanish contest. For the Chiefs of Staff had counselled the Foreign Office, on 24 August 1936, that one of the vital British concerns in the Spanish crisis must be the 'maintenance of such relations with any Spanish Government that may emerge from the conflict as will ensure benevolent neutrality in the event of our being engaged in any European war'.[62] Notwithstanding this setback, however, it appears, on closer examination, that the British foreign policy line towards the Spanish Civil War was fashioned with some skill and was rewarded with some success.

The outbreak of the Spanish Civil War, in July 1936, exacerbated an already troubled international scene for Britain. The emergence of restless regimes in Central Europe, the Mediterranean and the Far East exposed the strategic vulnerability of an overstretched and underarmed British Empire. The civil conflict in Spain threatened to subvert the grand diplomatic design which the British were pursuing, in the summer of 1936, to restore the international consensus that was essential for their own security: the negotiation by the main Locarno Powers of a revised western pact that might lead, in turn, to 'the general settlement of those problems [whose] solution [was] essential to the peace of Europe'.[63] The Spanish *Kulturkampf* promised to precipitate the consolidation of the European Powers into those opposed ideological blocs whose formation would prevent any continental settlement.[64] Ideologically inspired war in Spain might even draw the rival powers into active confrontation and initiate another world war, precisely the issue that the British were striving to avoid. The British were fearful, at first, that the Non-Intervention Agreement proposed by the Popular Front Government in France, might be a stratagem to involve them in a moral commitment to support the Spanish Republic.[65] However, as the need to assist those elements in the French administration opposed to France's intervention on behalf of the Spanish Republic impressed itself on the British, they rallied to the project.[66] Although aware that the agreement was violated continually by the Axis Powers and Portugal on the one side, and by the Soviet Union and, occasionally, France on the other, British policy-makers came to regard it as 'an extremely useful piece of humbug'.[67] Non-intervention kept foreign backing for the Spanish combatants to a level unlikely to provoke full-scale international conflict, for all that it failed to stop the flow of foreign supplies to the rival camps in Spain. As Chamberlain candidly admitted to the House of Commons on 21 December 1937, the essential object of non-intervention was not to cut off the warring Spaniards from external sources of support, but 'to prevent the conflict spreading beyond the borders of Spain'.[68] By confining the fight to Spanish soil, non-intervention allowed the Chamberlain Government to pursue its aims of diplomatic reconciliation with Mussolini's Italy and appeasement of Hitler's Germany.[69]

Increasing doubts, based on principled or pragmatic grounds, came to be voiced inside British politics about the Government position on Spain. Dissent was revealed right at the heart of the Government itself, in February 1938, when Anthony Eden resigned from the Foreign Secretaryship in protest at Chamberlain's intention to negotiate an Anglo-Italian accord without obtaining, in advance, any material token of Mussolini's willingness to disengage from Spain.[70] Eden and his closest counsellors had been certain for some months that the Spanish problem was central to the Anglo-Italian impasse.[71] However, Eden's cabinet colleagues rejected his suggestion that this 'impossible complication' should be removed 'both for its own sake and as a test of Italian performance' before *rapprochement* was attempted.[72] Certainly, Chamberlain and Eden had come to differ on several aspects of British politics and policy by early 1938, but Spain may have been more than merely the occasion for the latter's resignation from high office.[73] Anyway, Britain's Spanish policy was cushioned by governmental adherence to the Non-Intervention Agreement against such political shock tactics. British subscription to non-intervention rendered the Government relatively invulnerable to domestic political criticism of its policy-line on Spain. Neither dissident Conservatives nor opposition Labour and Liberal members of Parliament could penetrate the penumbra of political prestige and moral principle attaching to non-intervention.[74]

The Labour movement's response to the crisis in Spain was conditioned by the pre-existing splits within its ranks between moderates and militants. Party and trade union deliberations on the Spanish Civil War also inevitably raised other vital issues of the day, like possible political alliance with Communists and/or Liberals, and the appropriate response to the Government's policy of national rearmament. Again, the positions assumed on these matters often reinforced the contrary inclinations of those ready or reluctant to help Republican Spain.[75] When, more rarely, ideologically incongruent attitudes were held on domestic and international politics, the line taken towards Spain could become rather tortuous. Thus, Herbert Morrison, although a partisan of Repubican Spain, opposed the proposal, discussed by the National Executive Committee of the Labour Party in 1938, to hold a special conference on Spain, because it would provide a platform for the advocates of a 'People's Front' to preach their united progressive crusade.[76] As an inveterate anti-communist and party disciplinarian, Morrison set domestic political interest above his radical leaning in foreign policy and solidarity with the Spanish Republic.[77] Indeed, whatever the sympathy of Labour's rank and file for Republican Spain, the reformist leadership was wary of any campaign on its behalf which could open the party to Communist infiltration. Labour Party leader, Clement Attlee, revealed one parochial concern in his retrospective consideration of the Civil War: 'The Spanish struggle was the occasion for a very determined attempt by the Communist Party to get into the Labour Movement by devious methods, but the majority of the party were too experienced to fall into the trap.'[78] Although Attlee, himself, was to express his support for the Spanish Republican cause in private and public, during and after the Civil War, some of his senior colleagues were less disposed to speak or act in its favour.[79] This proved to be an enduring dichotomy in the response of even Labour's leaders to Spanish affairs. Thus, in November 1944, when Attlee (as a member of Britain's wartime coalition government) pressed his Cabinet colleagues to boycott the Franco regime economically in the hope of bringing about the Caudillo's downfall, his fellow Labour minister, Ernest Bevin, urged a different priority: 'It would be very undesirable to encourage the [Spanish] Left Wing to think that they had more support in this country than might be the case, and so perhaps to provoke them to unwise and precipitate action'.[80] In spite of individual affinities among Labour's leaders for the Republican side during the Spanish conflict, collectively they manoeuvred very cautiously through the complex problems which it presented. Grass-roots pressure and the flagrant Axis breaches of non-intervention did soon induce them to call for the restoration of the Spanish Republican Government's right to purchase arms abroad and, later, to withdraw their support for the international agreement.[81] However, the Labour leaders nearly all shrank from any advocacy of positive British intervention in the Spanish Republican interest, perhaps not least because it would expose them to an electorally injurious Conservative charge of being war-mongers.[82] They were thus bereft of any active alternative to the Non-Intervention Agreement which the Government could always brandish as compelling evidence of its bona fides to rebut Labour accusations of connivance at fascist interference in Spain.

Nevertheless, critics of British policy were correct in detecting a deep aversion to the Spanish left and all its works within government ranks. The first concern of the British Prime Minister, Stanley Baldwin, in the early days of the Spanish Civil War, was to avoid being drawn 'in to a fight on the side of the Russians' over Spain.[83] The First Lord of the Admiralty, Sir Samuel Hoare, also preferred a position of absolute detachment for Britain, a stance which he defined in these singular terms, on 5 August 1936:

When I speak of 'neutrality' I mean strict neutrality, that is to say, a situation in which the Russians neither officially or unofficially give help to the Communists. On no account must we do anything to bolster up Communism in Spain, particularly when it is remembered that Communism in Portugal, to which it would probably spread and particularly in Lisbon, would be a grave danger to the British Empire.[84]

The man who succeeded to the Prime Ministership in May 1937, Neville Chamberlain, did not want to see Franco's cause 'messed up' by 'the Bolshies' who were 'the limit'.[85] Moreover, Eden, while still British Foreign Secretary, admitted to Juan Negrín, Republican Spain's Prime Minister, during a conversation in September 1937, that Chamberlain feared 'communism would get its clutches into western Europe' through the Spanish crisis.[86] Ironically, in so far as fear of Communist influence in Spain may have prompted Britain's commitment to non-intervention, and the British Government's tacit anti-republicanism, this attitude proved counter-productive. Denied sustenance by the democracies, Republican Spain had to rely, from 1936 onwards, on Soviet aid to maintain its fight for survival, a dependence which allowed the Partido Comunista de España (a relatively minor group in the pre-civil-war period) to compete on advantageous terms with the large anarcho-syndicalist and socialist movements in the internal political struggles of the Republican zone.[87] It was appreciated in the British Foreign Office that the

Kremlin, far from engineering the outbreak of the Spanish conflict, initially regarded it as an unwelcome complication of an already menacing international scene in Europe.[88]

However, what one historian has described as generic anticommunism, that is, a general antipathy towards radical leftism as represented by the Spanish Republic, was the essential influence shaping mainstream British Conservative reaction towards events in Spain.[89] Spain's Republican Government might or might not be a creature of the Comintern, but its revolutionary aura was enough to alienate British Tories who were as ready as their domestic political opponents to believe that the Spanish conflict was 'the class war played out on an international scale'.[90] For many Britons, inside and outside Parliament, it was solidarity with their social counterparts in Spain that swayed sentiment towards one side or the other. The Labour radical, Aneurin Bevan, condemned Chamberlain's ministers, in 1938, for 'throwing away important strategic advantages in Spain' for 'selfish class interests'.[91] Yet, class consciousness, diplomatic priority and strategic concern might converge in determining policy. Thus, the Nyon Agreement of September 1937, establishing international naval patrols to counter piratical attacks by Italian submarines on ships trading with Republican Spain, was vaunted as a timely show of Anglo-French force against fascist aggression. Nonetheless, the then British Foreign Secretary and a primary architect of the Nyon arrangement, Anthony Eden, was mainly anxious, during its negotiation, on 10–11 September, to avoid the appearance of creating 'an Anglo-French–Soviet bloc on an ideological basis'. He was gratified that the democracies had been able to 'make themselves felt in Europe' by deploying their naval powers to police the Mediterranean but felt that 'perhaps most important of all we managed to keep the Russians out' of that sea. On some points at least, then, Eden's attitudes coincided with those of his Prime Minister, Chamberlain, and other Cabinet colleagues. These had maintained, at a meeting only two days before the Nyon Conference opened, that Russia must be kept out of Mediterranean waters and that no anti-Axis ideological grouping aligning Britain with France and the Soviet Union should result from the powers' deliberations.[92]

However, for all the instinctive and strategically-inspired anticommunism informing British governmental attitudes towards the Spanish Civil War, Britain's pragmatic policy-makers were not usually inclined to analyse the international scene in exclusively ideological terms or to assess it according to excessively ideological preferences.[93] They more readily interpreted international behaviour by reference to notions of national interest and to alleged personal or national characteristics. This latter tendency only served to reinforce the implicit bias in British policy towards the Francoist camp during the Civil War. For, it was generally assumed in London that both Spain's objective need to cultivate economic links with Britain and the Spaniards' own innate determination to preserve their national freedom would prevent any permanent Spanish subjection to the Axis.[94] Sir Robert Hodgson, Britain's agent to the Francoist administration, from November 1937 until March 1939, made this latter point in an internal Foreign Office memo, on 1 February 1939:

should Germany and Italy have done what their detractors assert they have done and profited by Spain's weakness to impose their will upon her, they have been guilty of a miscalculation revealing a strange contempt for the teachings of history. If there is one lesson that history should have taught them, it is that any attempt to coerce Spaniards to do that which they do not want to do is foredoomed to failure. If there is one thing which is a fetish to Spain it is her independence.[95]

Neville Chamberlain, for one, was confident, in the same month, that Franco would resume freedom of international action, once the Civil War was over, to establish 'excellent relations' with Britain.[96] There was a sound basis for this judgement. For, within a few months of the end of the Spanish conflict, Foreign Minister Jordana privately communicated to the Duke of Alba his own exposition of Francoist foreign policy, with which he claimed the Caudillo was in fundamental agreement, which shows that the New Spain was not irrevocably wedded to the fascist states:

They [i.e. the Powers] all make love to us and it is necessary to flirt for a while because it suits us neither to surrender ourselves to anybody, not even at a good price, nor to offend completely all our seducers so as to prevent us from being in a position to incline ourselves at the opportune moment to the side which is most convenient for us, or so as to spoil any deal of the many which we have in hand and which are dependent on foreign (good) will.[97]

Moreover, the British were sure that they had the means with which to win the international competition for Spain's diplomatic affection and strategic favours. A confident Lord Plymouth had explained to a sceptical Soviet Ambassador, Ivan Maisky, in 1937, that the prospect of a Francoist victory held no terrors for Britain. For a devastated, post-civil-war Spain would have to seek foreign financial aid. As Nazi Germany and Fascist Italy had no substantial capital reserves to fund reconstruction in Spain, then the victor in the struggle there would have to turn to London, according to Plymouth: 'Whoever leads Spain after this war, he will have to come to our banks

... That is when our hour comes ... We shall be able to come to terms with the future government of Spain on all the things that interest us: financial compensation, and political and military guarantees as well ...'[98] Indeed, Britain had remained restrained in the face of large-scale German penetration of Spain's foreign commerce in raw materials, and particularly the strategic minerals, iron ore and pyrites.[99] Again, it was reckoned in London that Britain's availability as the sole significant source of European capital to finance post-civil-war reconstruction in Spain would ultimately ensure respectful treatment for its economic interests there.[100]

It is true that General Franco did denounce in a speech, delivered on Spanish radio on 20 May 1939, any foreign economic encirclement of his country undertaken for the political purpose of subjecting Spain, once more, to the previously predominant interests which allegedly had reduced it to a dependent international status.[101] However, his declaration was prompted not by resentment at an offer from Britain of financial assistance for reconstruction but from apparent frustration at some British policy-makers' temporary reservations about the wisdom of permitting large loans, amidst a deteriorating international situation, to the new Spanish state until it had proven its independence of its patrons in Berlin and Rome.[102] On the Spanish side, internal political divisions between pro and anti-German elements within the new regime, its anti-capitalist inclinations and its administrative inefficiencies, also contributed to delaying economic *rapprochement* between Britain and Franco's Spain until six months after the outbreak of the Second World War.[103] However, on 18 March 1940, three Anglo-Spanish economic agreements were signed. These comprised a trade and payments agreement establishing a clearing system to effect the repayment of commercial debts already owed to British firms and to support renewed Anglo-Spanish trade, a loan agreement granting the Franco regime £2 million to spend within the sterling area, and a war-trade agreement allowing Spain to import certain commodities through the Anglo-French naval blockade of Nazi Germany, on condition that these items would not be re-exported without authorisation by the Allies.[104] The Allied economic blockade of the Third Reich had already drasticlly reduced the volume of Hispano-German trade built up during the Civil War. Thus, German imports of Spanish iron ore fell from 499,000 metric tons in 1938 to 1,000 metric tons in 1940. British trade with Franco's Spain, on the other hand, grew in 1940 as against 1939.[105]

The commercial consequences for Spain of the onset of the Second World War combined with the economic aftermath of the protracted

Civil War to return Spain to an apparently inescapable dependence on, and subjection to, the Anglo-French bloc by the spring of 1940. British credit and commerce, with France's backing, now appeared set to complete the restoration of Anglo-French strategic domination over a Spain which Britain's carefully constructed civil-wartime policy, and the subsequent outbreak of war in Europe, had already made amenable or vulnerable to pressure from London and Paris. For all Franco's imperial yearnings, the three-year long resistance of the Spanish working class to his bid to impose an authoritarian regime on his country, had seemingly robbed him of the means even to contemplate an adventurous foreign policy and left him instead with a fragile hold over an exhausted land and people.

However, within weeks of the Anglo-Spanish economic reconciliation in March 1940, there occurred a strategic earthquake of such proportions as apparently to open whole new vistas of diplomatic possibility even to a state with economic and military resources as depleted as Franco's Spain. The collapse of France before German invasion in May–June 1940 vitiated, at a stroke, all the assumptions which had governed Britain's policy towards Spain during the previous four years. Now, far from possessing substantial resources with which to entice Spain back to its traditional, subordinate position in the Anglo-French sphere of influence, Britain hardly disposed of the means to conduct its own desperate struggle for survival with Hitler's Germany. Again, far from resting secure in the knowledge that the strategic subjection of Franco's Spain to the democratic powers was ensured by the preponderance of Anglo-French economic and military might in its vicinity, Britain was now confronted with the establishment of a direct land frontier between German-occupied France and the Francoist state. Finally, no longer able to count on Spanish incapacity to challenge the British position at Gibraltar, London had to recognise that even a country with Spain's limited striking power could inflict serious injury on Britain's over-stretched war effort in the Atlantic and Mediterranean theatres in 1940, and into 1941. It is the purpose of the following chapters to analyse British efforts to counteract these threats presented by Franco's Spain to their survival in 1940–1.

2

Defining a policy

Conflicting ideological belief, political opportunism and strategic insight impelled Winston Churchill through a succession of varying attitudes towards the Spanish Civil War.[1] By 1938, however, he had come to a characteristic conclusion. Had he been Spanish, he told an Argentinian journalist, he would have supported Franco, who, as a patriot and a defender of Europe against the Communist danger, had right on his side. Yet as an Englishman, he continued, he preferred the 'others' to triumph, since Franco, unlike them, could menace and disturb British interests.[2] Such a candid declaration readily lent itself to effective anti-British propaganda in Spain, during Churchill's wartime premiership. This propaganda emphasised the callousness and cynical self-interest of the British Prime Minister in his dealings with Spain.[3] As Prime Minister, Churchill naturally did continue to give priority to furthering British interests in Anglo-Spanish affairs, but he no longer felt that this necessarily entailed friction or conflict with Franco. For, after replacing Chamberlain, in May 1940, Churchill soon revealed his anxiety to prove his earlier judgement wrong and to come to terms with Franco. His concern to do so was clearly connected with the increasingly massive rout of the Anglo-French armies in France, and he rapidly dispatched one of the recently discharged Cabinet Ministers, Sir Samuel Hoare, to Madrid as British Ambassador, 'to keep the Spanish Government neutral'.[4]

The motives inspiring the offer of the Madrid embassy to Hoare may have been as ambiguous as his reasons for accepting it. Indeed, Robert Bruce Lockhart, who later in the war became Director-General of the Political Warfare Executive, was puzzled as to why the existing ambassador to Spain, Maurice Peterson, whom he regarded as 'one of the few strong men in [British] diplomacy' should be removed to make way for 'a man like Sam Hoare' whose only qualification for the job appeared to be 'political failure'.[5] Halifax

26

considered that a senior public personality might boost the British diplomatic effort in Spain, even while France was falling, but Sir Alexander Cadogan, Permanent Under-Secretary of State at the Foreign Office, also discerned an anxiety to be rid of an embarrassing political liability whose record as an appeaser was notorious.[6] Hoare's reputation had never really recovered from his co-authorship of the infamous Hoare–Laval proposals to deliver part of Ethiopia over to Mussolini's tender mercies. Churchill, though temporarily willing to tolerate the survival in high office of other prominent appeasers, had been thoroughly antagonised by Hoare in the past, and was conscious of the popular animus towards the latter as one of the guilty men of Munich.[7] Hoare's image as an appeaser was so solid that Hitler even saw him as a possible *capitulard* successor to Churchill, in the event of a failure of the British will to fight on.[8] The opportunity to remove such an unloved figure from the British political scene probably played a part in his appointment to the Madrid post.

If the motives behind the offer of the Spanish mission to Hoare were mixed, his response was, similarly, less than wholehearted. Smarting 'like a bear with a sore head' from his political fall, he grudgingly accepted the Madrid position under the impression that he would merely have to fill in time for a few months there, before attaining his real heart's desire, the Viceroyalty of India.[9] We may discount Cadogan's rancorous charges in his diary – that Hoare was frantic to flee the country, like the proverbial rat deserting the sinking British ship of state – and not only because of the latter's initial reluctance to take up the appointment. Hoare revealed rather the opposite concern before embarking for Spain, in pleading with Halifax to ensure his rescue should any upheaval threaten his safety.[10] Cadogan's very *Schadenfreude* at the 'good chance of S.H. being murdered' by one of the many Germans or Italians in Madrid, also contradicts his notion that Spain was a secure refuge.[11] Anyway, the political and personal ill-will involved in Hoare's assumption of the endeavour, as Britain's 'Ambassador Extraordinary on Special Mission', to 'hold the position' in Spain hardly augured well for the enterprise.[12]

However, the disastrous turn of military events in France appeared even more ominous in its implications for Hoare's mission. The angry exasperation aroused in Cadogan by Hoare's departure moved him to voice one penetrating query, 'and what the Hell can he do anyway in Spain?'.[13] What Hoare could do was something which only the future could reveal. What he was to attempt to do, on the other hand, seemed obvious enough. It was succinctly stated in a Foreign

Office memorandum supplied to Churchill, for his use in a meeting with Hoare about the latter's mission to Spain:

It is hoped that . . . the appointment of Sir Samuel Hoare as Ambassador on special mission will greatly contribute to the realisation of our objective in Spain. This is to keep Spain neutral [and] to support and strengthen the elements in Spain desiring to maintain neutrality and now represented by the present administration . . .[14]

In the same vein, Lord Halifax informed a Spanish journalist, on 20 May 1940, that the British Government desired friendly relations with Spain and that Britain would respect the Spaniards' neutrality as long as it was respected by others. He cited as an example of Britain's goodwill for, and ability to aid, Spain, the Anglo-Spanish economic agreements of the previous 18 March.[15] This economic support was, indeed, in the prevailing Foreign Office view, the only concrete inducement which Britain could offer Spain at this juncture.[16] Hoare, then, could simply implement Britain's existing policy, the maintenance of Spanish neutrality by economic aid to Franco's regime.

Nevertheless, official policy might often appear to have more substance in London, than amongst the actual men in the field. Certainly, the Naval Attaché at the British Embassy in Madrid, Captain Alan Hillgarth, regarded his country's policy towards Spain as ill-defined and tentative. Hillgarth was a personal acquaintance of Churchill and the latter regarded him as a 'very good' man and 'equipped with a profound knowledge of Spanish affairs'.[17] Hillgarth, though recognising his newly-arrived Ambassador to be 'a disappointed politician', gave him the benefit of his counsel. He advised him, on 2 June 1940, that to prepare for all eventualities, even the 'rather remote possibility' that Spanish neutrality could be preserved, Britain 'must adopt a consistent, clear and unmistakable official policy that no one can deny'.[18] British policy was no more tangible to another foreign member of the diplomatic community in Madrid. Portuguese Ambassador, Pedro Theotonio Pereira, affirms in his memoirs that Britain 'did not have anything that could be called a policy' towards Franco's Spain prior to Hoare's arrival in Madrid.[19] Sir Samuel Hoare did accept, as a priority, the definition of policy goals and methods for Britain's relations with the Franco regime, in his early days in Madrid.

Still, what Cadogan's scornful question implied was that diplomatic manoeuvring was irrelevant, in view of the French catastrophe. For what changed radically on Hoare's arrival in Spain was the context of possible diplomatic action. With the magnitude of the French defeat becoming apparent, Hoare's mission appeared increasingly abortive. So daunting did the situation seem that Hoare was extremely reluctant to return to Britain the aircraft on which he travelled to Madrid. He wanted to be ready for a quick getaway. He only parted with it on the formal assurance that another would be forthcoming in case of an emergency.[20]

Indeed, Hoare candidly admits, in his memoirs, that his first impressions of the rumour-ridden and tension-filled Spanish capital left him severely shaken and even concerned for his personal safety.[21] He reported to Halifax, on 3 June 1940, that he was working in Madrid in 'a framework of a very rickety kind and the picture is a picture of instability, risk and sudden surprise'.[22] He was no more at ease, three days later, when he wrote to inform Brendan Bracken, Churchill's confidant, of his situation:

. . . I have found myself in a bewildering turmoil of futility, intrigue and . . . risk. I mean by the futility that we have little or no influence in Spain, the Germans having dug themselves in everywhere and that the Embassy machinery is absolutely hopeless . . . As to the risk, I cannot show my head outside my hotel or the Embassy without an army of unattractive looking gunmen around me.[23]

Given Hoare's reputation for pusillanimity, his mission may have risked being stillborn. However, even someone like David Eccles, the Ministry of Economic Warfare's representative in the Iberian Peninsula, who was repelled by what he saw as Hoare's sporadic 'bouts of physical and moral cowardice', was also willing to acknowledge the latter's considerable political talents: his skill in negotiation, his administrative competence, his impressive professional demeanour and his capacity for comprehension of a subject 'after a minimum of briefing'.[24] It is the last quality which seems to have helped him recover his nerve in Madrid, in June 1940. For, included in the advice which the new Ambassador received from his Naval Attaché, Hillgarth, was an urgent warning that the Embassy which he had come to lead was 'defeatist'. Not only its inefficiencies and disorganisation, but also its morale required remedial action: 'There are among us too many signs of panic. There is no need for it, though there is need for resolution and action.'[25] According to his lights, Hoare set about rekindling among his staff a belief in what Hillgarth termed their country's 'ultimate invincibility'.[26] He led by example, moving into a house right next door to the German Ambassador's residence on the Castellana in order 'to create an atmosphere of British indifference to alarms and excursions'.[27] He also obtained from London the authority to overhaul, and render more secure, the operation of his Embassy in its demanding and dangerous setting.[28]

Still, however much Hoare tried to keep his head amidst what he, himself, described a little later as the 'atmosphere of the Mad Hatter's Tea Party', he was not, at first, very hopeful that Spain could be persuaded to remain at peace.[29] He informed Lord Halifax that he felt he should try to induce Spain to adhere to its neutrality, even though there was but an outside chance of succeeding in the endeavour.[30] Halifax, too, thought that the effort was at least worth making, though conceding that it was rather 'a forlorn hope'.[31] Again, Kingsley Wood, the Chancellor of the Exchequer, was reluctant to sanction expenditure on such an apparently lost cause, when Hoare sought additional funds to finance his political and diplomatic activities in Spain.[32] Indeed, Hoare had been in Spain hardly a fortnight when he counselled the British Government to adopt a 'go slow' attitude on economic assistance to Spain, which would enable Britain to wait upon developments without any apparent change in its Spanish policy. His advice was accepted with alacrity.[33]

The chances of his diplomatic rearguard action succeeding were even slighter than Hoare could perceive. For, unknown to the British, on 19 June 1940, the Spanish Government offered to join the war on the Axis side in return for substantial territorial concessions in North Africa (French Morocco, the Oran region of Algeria and the expansion of Spanish Sahara and Spanish Guinea) and extensive deliveries of economic and military supplies.[34] One member of that Government has since testified that whatever reservations some Spanish ministers entertained subsequently about the wisdom of going to war, all of them succumbed to a 'great warlike enthusiasm' to join the fight against Britain in the wake of the successful Nazi *Blitzkrieg* against France, not least because hostilities seemed about to end.[35] Hitler saw no need to pay for services which might never have to be rendered and the German reply, on 25 June 1940, merely stated that the Reich Government had 'taken cognizance' of Spain's North African territorial desires, and promised further consultation upon the clarification of the international situation. The Führer had equally avoided any specific commitment to promote Spain's imperial ambitions, in conversation with Franco's personal representative, General Vigón, Chief of the Supreme General Staff of the Spanish armed forces, on 16 June. German indifference to Spain's self-interested offer of active military alliance bitterly antagonised Franco, but it did save him from embroilment in a war which he, apparently, mistakenly thought Germany had already won. Nevertheless, according to the memoirs published after Franco's death by Serrano Suñer, the Spanish leader continued to maintain a 'blind faith' in the inevitability of Nazi victory after this disappointing episode, hoping to exploit Germany's triumph to his country's advantage, via friendship or alliance with Hitler.[36] Franco, thus, played a role, for much of the latter part of 1940 other than that of consistent champion of Spanish neutrality, in which some British observers were inclined to cast him. The Spanish ruler's attitude towards participation in the war during the vital autumn–winter period of that year is subjected to close scrutiny in chapter five.

Fortunately, perhaps, the new British Ambassador did not get wind of this Spanish *démarche* which, had he become aware of it, might well have finally convinced him of the futility of his mission. Instead, even amidst the shock of acclimatisation, Hoare's very pessimism came to be cast in such a form as to assume the necessity, and feasibility, of a determined British attempt to preserve Spain's neutrality. His doubts about the effectiveness of such an effort derived less from any feelings of the inevitable hostility or unreliability of Franco's Government, than from his scepticism about their ability to maintain control of their country in the developing strategic context. Hoare felt that they were acutely vulnerable to overthrow through Axis-instigated agitation. Thus, even if Franco proved resolute enough to resist Axis threats, Germany and/or Italy could easily capitalise on the numerous and intense Spanish discontents to destroy his fragile regime, as a means of achieving eventual Spanish belligerency. Therefore, Hoare went on to argue, it was vital for Britain 'to do everything in ... [its] ... power to maintain the Government that upon the whole desires neutrality'.[37] So, though the War Cabinet was informed, on 13 June 1940, that Hoare had serious doubts about the durability of the Spanish Government, it was not a counsel of despair. In Hoare's view, rather, was this all the more reason to try to strengthen Spanish nerves in and out of government.[38] In the same way, when Franco abandoned orthodox neutrality in favour of Italian-style non-belligerency, on 12 June 1940, the new Ambassador interpreted it as a call to action rather than a cause for gloom.[39] By declaring non-belligerency Franco, Hoare felt, was positioning himself to join the Axis powers if the French collapse proved to be irrevocable. Once again, Hoare called upon the British Government to rally the anti-war forces in Spain.[40] Given a Spanish context characterised by a substantial German presence, by the approach of a seemingly invincible German army to the Pyrenean frontier, and by the devastating aftermath of the Civil War, a vigorous British effort to consolidate the influence of the Franco Government was necessary. For every Spanish difficulty and dissension provided an opportunity for foreign intervention:

I am convinced that any change of Government in Spain at this moment would at once open the door to German and Italian intervention. Judged by our standards, General Franco's Government may be incompetent. None the less it is solidly in favour of non-belligerency, and for us non-belligerency, even with all its unpleasant associations, is better than war. It seems to me essential that we should keep the Atlantic ports of the Iberian Peninsula out of German hands . . .[41]

Hoare, then, even in his earliest weeks in Madrid, articulated a fundamental theme of his Spanish policy: that Franco's regime was the best, indeed the only, possible instrument for ensuring the continuance of Spanish neutrality. Hoare did inherit a belief in Franco's trustworthiness from the line pursued by the Chamberlain Government towards Spain, but its reaffirmation as a policy-premise in the new situation produced by the French defeat represented a fresh, and vital vote of confidence in the Spanish administration. He doggedly clung to this basic identification between the survival of the Nationalist regime and the maintenance of Spanish neutrality for the rest of the period under review, and beyond. If, as will be seen, Hoare could consider Franco's replacement in 1941 by a grouping apparently more sympathetic to the British cause, the proposed alternative government was to be based on precisely the same elite which underpinned Franco's personal rule: the generals of the Spanish Army. In terms of Spanish Civil War loyalties, Hoare chose to rely on the Nationalist victors, not the Republican vanquished.

Hoare's policy was founded on something firmer than mere presumption. For he recognised the rigid limits imposed upon Spain's freedom of action by the decrepit post-civil-war Spanish economy. He emphasised this point to Lord Halifax, on 26 July 1940: 'Franco's very existence depends upon keeping Spain out of the war. If Spain enters the war, an economic crisis would inevitably make trouble in the country and trouble in the country is bound to react adversely against Franco and his friends.'[42] Hoare certainly did not go to the same length as his predecessor in Madrid, Maurice Peterson, in asserting that any British policy for Spain was in a sense irrelevant, in that Spain was so prostrate that Britain could never provoke its active enmity.[43] Nevertheless, he must have been encouraged by the way in which prominent Spaniards proclaimed Spain's sheer incapacity to go to war. Thus the Infante Alfonso of Bourbon-Orleans, Commander of Spain's Second Air Region, informed the British Ambassador that he always responded to those advocating Spanish entry into the war with the terse question: *'con qúe?'*, 'with what?'.[44] Similarly, General Orgaz, Captain-General of Catalonia, answered the anxious query of the Rector of a Barcelona religious order as follows: 'Father, you have no doubt studied Logic – I will give you a premise: To wage war successfully a nation must have money and food; have we money? have we food?'[45] Other observers of the Spanish scene were reaching the same conclusion. A German Army study of the Spanish Army, in August 1940, noted that the internal weakness and external dependence of Spain, forced it to adopt 'a reserved attitude'.[46] The categorical nature of the assurances that Spain would keep out of the war and resist aggression from any quarter, which the Spanish Minister for Foreign Affairs, Colonel Juan Beigbeder Atienza, gave Hoare in the hectic June weeks must have been equally reassuring. Thus, Hoare was able to inform London, on 20 June 1940, that Beigbeder 'repeated over and over again with increasing force his conviction that on no account and nowhere would General Franco allow the violation of Spanish territory'.[47] Beigbeder, too, coupled Spain's determination to avoid getting embroiled in the war, with Spanish inability to do so in any case. He pointed out to Hoare, on 11 June 1940, that Spain lacked all the essentials for conducting a war effort.[48] Franco, personally, informed Hoare of his desire for good relations with Britain, on 22 June 1940, and even the politically powerful and fervently anti-democratic Minister of the Interior, Ramón Serrano Suñer, told Hoare on 15 June 1940, that Spain would definitely avoid any 'premature action'.[49] So, on 24 June 1940, Lord Halifax felt able to inform the War Cabinet that whilst he could give no cast-iron guarantees, Britain should not expect any immediate trouble from Spain.[50]

Hoare, then, began to report what he interpreted as tangible shifts in favour of Britain, despite the arrival of German troops at Spain's northern frontier on 27 June 1940. Thus, his vigorous protests over an official reception planned for German troops in San Sebastian, near the Franco-Spanish frontier, led to the cancellation of the affair and to the local Spanish military commander's suspension.[51] The results of this affair may have had more to do with internal Spanish political and military discipline, than with any necessarily pro-British shift. But Hoare chose to read it as a British victory. He was likewise encouraged by the dismissal of the pro-Falange Air Minister, General Yagüe, and the arrest of some of his adherents around the same time.[52] Again, this affair, as the Germans recognised, was also probably mainly the result of intra-regime rivalry, with Yagüe falling from political grace due to his 'strong opposition' to Serrano Suñer who seemed to exercise 'decisive influence' on Franco at this juncture.[53] Indeed, Hoare had himself, at their first meeting, recognised in

Yagüe qualities that marked him as a potential leader of an opposition to Franco.[54] However, prompted by Hoare, London attributed Yagüe's political demise to indiscretions concerning foreign affairs, as the Chiefs of Staff reported to the British Cabinet, in early July 1940: 'General Yagüe was suspected of supporting a German suggestion that Spain should attack Portugal, and his outspoken comments that Spain should enter the war so as to share in the booty raised a storm of protest from those who still desire peace, and led to his downfall . . .'[55] Hoare was equally ready to interpret the Additional Protocol, of 29 July 1940, to the Spanish–Portuguese Treaty of Friendship, providing for mutual consultation for self-protection, in a favourable light.[56] No doubt, he felt justified in doing so, since it had originated, at least in part, from an initial *démarche* of Lord Halifax to Salazar, in May 1940.[57] Halifax, himself, told the War Cabinet, on Wednesday 31 July 1940, that he thought the Protocol was a move in the right direction.[58] It was this developing tendency which Hoare purported to discern in Anglo-Spanish relations, that made him inform Churchill roundly, on 22 July 1940, that if Britain played its hand correctly, it could prevent Spain from joining the Axis.[59]

Hoare, nevertheless, still occasionally admitted his reluctance to express his opinions as to future events, caught as he was in 'the Spanish labyrinth'.[60] He did for instance, on 26 July 1940, mention the possibility that Spain might after all enter the war against Britain, but only to go on to argue that, even if that were to happen, it would surely be prudent to postpone the fateful day as long as possible. Time could not, in his view, but work to Britain's advantage. He specifically sought the guidance of the Chiefs of Staff on this point and concluded with a summary of the basic policy line which he was advocating:

The policy does not mean approval of Franco and the methods of his Government. My friends of the Left are fully entitled to continue to hold their views on this issue. It means one thing and one thing only; namely, the most effective way of keeping Spain out of the war altogether if possible, and if that is not possible, for as long a period as we can.[61]

What Hoare was seeking was absolute approval, upon the firmest grounds of national security, for his policy. He got it. Halifax replied in the most positive fashion, declaring that he whole-heartedly shared Hoare's view that even every week gained was of value.[62] The Chiefs of Staff, too, fully accepted, on 7 August 1940, even this most negative formulation as official policy for Spain: in the event of it proving impossible to prevent Spain entering the war, it was British policy that its entry should be delayed for as long as possible.[63] Hoare would greatly rely upon this verdict by Britain's grand strategists, on the necessity for careful treatment of Spain, in later advocacy and defence of his policy. He did not, however, immediately abandon his misgivings about Franco's intentions. For, on 7 August, he wrote to Lord Beaverbrook, expressing his feeling that the Spaniards were waiting upon events, so that if England or Egypt collapsed, they could join Britain's enemies and gain Gibraltar and the North African territories which they so desired.[64]

Again, Hoare might have been less enthusiastic over the Protocol of 29 July 1940, to the Spanish–Portuguese Treaty of Friendship and Non-Aggression, had he known that Spain was allowed liberty of action against Britain, in the matter of Gibraltar and that Hispano–Portuguese contacts had been welcomed and encouraged by the Germans.[65] Indeed, Beigbeder repeated the Spanish offer to enter the war on Germany's side, on the previously specified conditions, to the German Ambassador, von Stohrer, on 20 August 1940.[66]

Hoare did recognise the impact on Spaniards of what he termed the 'incredible fact' of a German military presence upon the Franco-Spanish frontier.[67] He testified to the totally intimidating effect which it had upon Spain.[68] Lord Halifax informed Hoare that it was realised in London that his most skilful diplomatic manoeuvres would be set at nought should the German divisions be ordered across the border.[69] He had already acquiesced in Hoare's demands for a liberty of action not normally accorded an Ambassador and special funds to bolster Britain's waning influence in Spain. In practice, this meant permitting Hoare to expend large sums of money on 'subsidising' or bribing prominent individuals, who were probably all Spanish generals, in an attempt to rally the anti-war forces within the Franco regime. The details of this operation, which was the brainchild of Captain Hillgarth, are obscure but Juan March, the Spanish financier who backed the Nationalist rebellion of 1936, was employed to distribute large sums among ten of the most important Spanish generals (including, it seems, General Aranda). Apparently, half the money was paid as cash down in regular instalments and half placed in blocked bank accounts in Argentina and/or New York.[70] Some idea of the scale of these activities may be gleaned from the fact that British officials, in the autumn of 1941, were trying to 'unblock' ten million dollars (lodged in bank accounts frozen by United States Government action) which had been paid to Spaniards 'for a consideration'. They were acting on Churchill's exhortation: 'We must not lose them now after all we have spent – and gained. Vital strategic issues depend on Spain keeping out or resisting.'[71] Looking back on the affair, after the war, one Briton who played a part in it, was sure that the combination of the personal inclination of the major Spanish military figures involved, and the British financial 'inspiration' offered to, and accepted by them, ensured that their opposition to Spanish belligerency on the Axis side was 'loyally maintained'.[72]

The purpose of this clandestine British operation, it seems, was to exert pressure on Franco through his own professional comrades to keep Spain neutral, and if he refused to listen to them, to have a ready-made military nucleus upon which to base an armed monarchist conspiracy against the Caudillo. It was also probably expected that the generals in receipt of British money would lead Spanish resistance to a German military incursion into Spain, if Franco allowed, or yielded to, such a move. However, the influence literally bought by Britain within the Spanish military elite was probably of limited value. Certainly, Hoare was occasionally inclined to ascribe an apparently favourable development in Spain's internal politics, or its external policies, to Britain's covert bribery operation, his contention sometimes being given credence in London.[73] Thus, Hoare seemingly believed that Yagüe's dismissal as Spanish Air Minister, already mentioned above, was due to the influence of pro-British elements who now had a vested interest in Spain's remaining at peace with their paymaster.[74] But, as also noted above, there were obvious internal political reasons for Yagüe's removal from ministerial office. Moreover, as is emphasised in what follows, neither the real possibility of Franco's intervention in the war in 1940, nor British anxiety in 1940–1 over such an eventuality, were seriously diminished by Britain's bribery of the Spanish generals.

However, aside from the problematic influence afforded by such covert methods on the ultimate direction of Spanish foreign policy, the political position which the British attempted to uphold in Spain in the summer of 1940, was slight in comparison with that which their enemies had managed to establish. The Germans actually had their own agents working inside the Spanish police force, and the press was greatly under the sway of the Chief of the Press Division at the German Embassy, in Madrid, Hans Lazar. He had bought or intimidated into subservience to his country's propaganda a substantial section of the Spanish press corps.[75] In addition, as Minister of the Interior and Chairman of the Political Committee of the Falange – Spain's radical nationalist state party – Serrano Suñer had a dual power to censor and influence the press.[76] From whatever mixture of deference for, and devotion to, Germany, Serrano Suñer ensured that the press took a heavily pro-German line. Indeed he reminded those attending a German press exhibition in Madrid, in March 1941, that the Spanish press had followed an unswervingly pro-German line during his three-year period of control over it.[77] The most notorious paper from the British point of view was the Falange party organ *Arriba*, which, when it was not inveighing against 'putrid liberal topics, sentimentalism, blasphemous liberal voices', expressed the most spectacularly pro-Nazi and anti-British opinions.[78] On 13 August 1940, in an article entitled 'Spain Attacked', *Arriba* accused Britain of starving Spain through its blockade measures and of actually sabotaging oil stores at Alicante.[79] Although the Spanish Government did officially repudiate the latter charge, it was predictable that a country in Spain's unenviable proximity to German military power should pay lip-service, at least, to the Spanish–German Treaty of Friendship.[80] Hitler was pleased enough with the sycophantic Spanish chorus to declare, 'the Spanish press is the best in the world!'[81] An additional factor dictating such an obsequious Spanish attitude, was the apparently ample opportunity Germany had for fifth-column activities in Spain, through the large numbers of its citizens – reckoned in one rather exaggerated British estimate to be as high as 80,000 – in the country.[82]

It was in this intractable environment that Sir Samuel Hoare settled down to elaborate a policy to preserve Spanish non-belligerency. The policy which he produced was, in its economic aspect, an exension of that already begun under Chamberlain. But even this aspect of the policy was novel, given the fundamentally altered circumstances in which he had to operate. As noted above, despite the completely changed conditions, the foundation-stone of the new policy also remained the same as in the old one: Franco could be depended upon to keep Spain out of the war. This conclusion, according to Hoare was based not on an act of faith in the Caudillo but on a judgement that Franco had really no choice but to steer clear of the war. The speed with which Hoare had formed that judgement, notwithstanding his depressing surroundings, suggests that he may have been influenced in doing so by his sympathy for the Nationalist cause in the Spanish Civil War.[83] Whatever the subjective and objective factors in Hoare's assessment that Franco could be trusted in practice, if not in principle, he was fortified in defining his policy by the Chiefs of Staff's express declaration that Spain should be kept neutral as long as possible. However, it has been noted already, and will be stressed again below, that Franco's actual position on Spanish neutrality, rendered him – at least for some of the period under review – a less than reliable agent to effect its continuance.

If British policy was to keep Franco in power, then, the converse was to avoid relations with elements opposed to him, however ideologically sympathetic to the British cause they might be. Thus, Hoare rebuffed an approach, in early August 1940, from a Spaniard whom he described as 'the leader of the Left Wing malcontents'. He made it clear that he would have nothing to do with groups attempting to overthrow a Government anxious to keep Spain out of the war, and the Chiefs of Staff again concurred.[84] He also sent off alarm-signals to London whenever he found any hint that a British secret service organisation might be involved with left-wing groups opposed to Franco.[85] Hoare had been an intelligence operative, himself, in Russia during the revolutionary upheavals there and had formed firm views on the need to subordinate espionage to diplomacy. Upon his arrival in Madrid he imposed strict limits on the activities of the local Secret Intelligence Service (S.I.S./M.I.6) Head of Station, Hamilton-Stokes. Although permitted to run an intelligence-gathering network of about 168 agents and sub-agents throughout Spain, Madrid Station was almost completely prevented by ambassadorial veto, supported by London's authority, from engaging in an active espionage campaign, especially one employing opponents of the regime, against either Axis or pro-Axis elements on Spanish territory, which could have antagonised Franco.[86] Kenneth Benton, S.I.S.'s Section V (counter-espionage) officer in Madrid, did breach Hoare's ban on active intelligence operations on one occasion, in order to ascertain the extent of the threat posed by the agents being run in Britain by Angel Alcázar de Velasco, a Spanish spy-cum-adventurer who was acting in the German interest. However, the burglary of Alcázar de Velasco's safe in Madrid, facilitated by the bribery of his secretary, proved that the Spaniard was having to fabricate reports about Britain for the Germans to compensate for the inadequacies of his espionage organisation there. Thus, he was left unmolested to exercise his imagination at the Germans' expense.[87] Indeed, those agents that Alcázar de Velasco did manage to infiltrate into England were controlled, directly or indirectly, through the British 'double-cross system' and so used, either as conscious collaborators or unknowing dupes, in the strategic deception of Britain's enemies.[88]

Hoare was no less adamant that the Special Operations Executive (S.O.E.) which had been created in July 1940 to promote popular subversion of, and resistance to, the Nazi occupation of mainland Europe, should abstain from any active preparations (again employing Spanish Republican elements) for organised guerrilla warfare in Spain against a possible German military entry into that country.[89] Churchill himself, backed Hoare's objections to clandestine activity which could provoke the Franco regime. So, he warned the Ministry of Economic Warfare (which controlled S.O.E.) in a prime ministerial minute, of 2 January 1941, of the danger of inciting Spanish 'Reds' to stir up revolution in Spain. The Minister of Economic Warfare, Hugh Dalton, replied in conciliatory fashion, five days later:

I think that you will find that any lingering suspicions which the Madrid Embassy may have had that S.O.E. was pursuing a policy at variance with the policy of the Government have now been effectively dispelled, as a result of the talks which Hillgarth has had with myself . . . and other responsible officials.[90]

Indeed, from early in 1941, until he left for Asia in 1943 to become Chief of Intelligence, British Eastern Fleet, Captain Hillgarth was empowered to supervise and co-ordinate the activities of S.I.S., S.O.E. and the Naval Intelligence Division (N.I.D.) in Spain.[91] Enthusiastic advocate as he was of the Hoare policy-line on Spain, he applied himself to ensure that these agencies refrained from covert operations likely to offend the Franco Government. However, Hillgarth, as N.I.D. representative in Spain, was able to maintain a watchful team of agents throughout Spain's ports whose vigilance limited instances of the re-supply of Axis (mainly German) submarines in Spanish harbours to twenty-three or twenty-four.[92] These British agents could exert an inhibitory influence simply by making their presence felt. Thus, in October 1941, while U 564 was being surreptitiously refuelled in Cádiz, flares fired by Hillgarth's men, illuminated the scene and impressed upon both the Spaniards and Germans present that their collusion in violating Spanish neutrality was not going undetected.[93] Still, the restrictions which Hoare managed to place on the policies and practices of the British secret services in Spain did prevent them seriously embarrassing his efforts at Anglo-Spanish *rapprochement*.[94] However, this British self-denying ordinance in the sphere of espionage and covert operations was merely a negative expression of British policy towards Spain. Hoare felt that positive action was also necessary to effect Francoist Spain's reconciliation with Britain.

Britain, in Hoare's view, possessed two positive powers for influencing Spanish policy in the new strategic context of 1940. It should, he believed, make Spain aware of British naval and economic resources which could sustain or strangle the decaying Spanish economy, and also express its sympathy for Spanish desires for territorial aggrandisement, especially at the expense of the French North African Empire. Hoare argued, as early as 26 June 1940, that since Franco and Beigbeder were set on keeping Spain out of the war, Britain should support them to the hilt, and that that support should be twofold. Firstly, given the fear and imminence of famine in Spain, Britain should embark upon a policy of firm and consistent economic help to Spain to stave off starvation.[95] Equally, he felt that since Franco and Beigbeder had such an intense desire for a Moroccan Empire, Britain could well benefit by showing sympathy with Spanish aspirations for replacing France in Morocco. He concluded by telling Halifax that since he was forced to play 'an almost impossible game' the former would have to be willing to act as his partner in managing his meagre hand.[96]

As regards economic relations, however, the initial priority of the British Government was to reinforce their economic warfare against Germany. So, Lord Halifax's first intervention on behalf of Spain in the field of economic policy was occasioned by the extension of Britain's economic blockade of Nazi-occupied Europe. For as one of the few remaining 'adjacent neutrals' on the European continent, Spain became a primary target for the newly tightened blockade: it must not be allowed to act as a channel for German exports, or for imports of vital extra-European strategic war materials. Equally, since Spain could be forced into the war at any time, it must not be permitted to stockpile reserves of strategic commodities which could come into Nazi possession. The new blockade measures consisted mainly in establishing a system of compulsory 'navicerts' (commercial passports for ships' cargoes permitting them to pass through the blockade) and compulsory rationing of adjacent neutrals (to eliminate stockpiles temping to the Germans).[97] Having been informed of these measures, Hoare asked that their announcement to the House of Commons by Hugh Dalton, the minister concerned, be postponed, in order to give him more time to explain them to the Spanish Government. Halifax put pressure on Dalton to agree to a postponement, and the latter, anxious at that time to remain friendly with the Foreign Secretary, complied, against his better judgement and desire, deferring his declaration until 30 July 1940.[98] Hoare, in fact, was to find himself engaged for a long time to come in arguing over, and applying, British blockade measures to Spain, rather than securing new and large-scale British material support for the tottering Spanish economy. However he did, at least, have the satisfaction of shepherding through the Anglo-Spanish–Portuguese Agreement, on 24 July 1940, which had originated from a direct British proposal to Dr Salazar, the Portuguese Head of Government in May 1940. This tripartite accord supplied Spain with British credit to enable it to purchase Portuguese colonial products, and through extensions and amendments provided it with some, though hardly an extensive, measure of economic relief.[99]

Donald S. Detwiler, an analyst of German policy towards Spain in this period, links the decision of the British to apply the blockade to Spain with their alleged concern over the dangerous tendencies in Spanish policy indicated in General Franco's speech, of 17 July 1940, commemorating the Nationalist uprising, begun on that date in 1936.[100] In that speech Franco declared that Nationalist Spain's tasks were as yet unfinished. 'We have to form a nation and create an empire', he exclaimed, and defined the legacy of the Spanish nation as consisting in 'the mandate of Gibraltar, the vision of Africa and political unity'. He also reminded his listeners that Spain had two million soldiers ready to fulfil this programme, the political testament of Queen Isabel.[101] In associating the application of Britain's blockade measures to Francoist Spain with the Caudillo's provocative public declarations of 17 July, Detwiler is influenced by a report made to Madrid by the Anglophil Spanish Ambassador in London, the Duke of Alba, who described the reaction of certain circles in London to Franco's speech, thus:

Elements free from direct (governmental) responsibility, but influential on, and exponents of, public opinion, as well as sometimes of the official point of view, have ascribed great significance to His Excellency's [i.e. Franco's] words and they try to present our claim on Gibraltar, since it is expressed by the highest representative of the state, as irrefutable proof that our policy is similar to that followed by Italy right up until its entry into the war and they strive to convince those who believe the contrary that England should consider Spain as an enemy and act accordingly, preparing military plans for possible offensives and exercising stricter vigilance over our (overseas) supplies, thereby preventing us from accumulating reserves for when we are belligerents or when we serve as a transit country for Germany and Italy.

However, Alba also informed Beigbeder that the British Government, itself, had refrained from 'all commentary' on, and was maintaining the 'most absolute reserve' towards the Caudillo's recent discourse.[102]

In fact the British Government had not been very alarmed by Franco's speech. So, Lord Privy Seal and Labour Party Leader, Clement Attlee, was not dissembling when he told the House of Commons, on Wednesday 31 July 1940, that the British Government did not regard Franco's discourse as implying any change in Spanish policy and that therefore, no special British official reaction was required.[103] Hoare and the Foreign Office were equally unimpressed by it. In any case, the War Cabinet had already decided to implement the new blockade measures, on the general grounds mentioned above, four days before General Franco made his speech.[104] In addition, the American Government's action restricting oil supplies to Spain had been sought by the British as early as the previous month.[105] Hoare, certainly, did not help the interpretation of this affair by claiming in his memoirs that he had seriously viewed the speech as an accurate reflection of Spanish intentions.[106] However, Hoare's memoirs are not always the most reliable source, especially when the matter at issue might reflect the extent to which he advocated support for Franco. Hoare's real view, as expressed in a letter to an English newspaperman, in September 1940, was that Franco had said 'the least possible that any Spaniard could'.[107]

There was a point at which the two aspects of the policy advocated by Hoare, the territorial and the economic, touched. For one particularly irritating feature of the British blockade system in Spanish eyes, was the fact that their ships were often detained or seized in Gibraltar which they regarded as a Spanish port. A Spanish journalist, Manuel Aznar, declared in *Arriba* of 31 May 1940, that Gibraltar ran like a shadow between England and Spain, and that a position of 'honourable intransigence' had been adopted by Spain concerning its return. Aznar had allegedly written earlier articles, and perhaps this one also, at Franco's request, to express the Caudillo's views on the Gibraltar question.[108] Aznar was, anyway, undoubtedly articulating Franco's feelings when he said that Spaniards were pained to the depths of their soul to see Gibraltar in foreign hands.[109] Hoare's arrival in Madrid was the occasion for street demonstrations with the popular slogan being 'Gibraltar Español'. In fact, a public campaign concentrating on the Spanish claim for the return of the Rock, which was obviously inspired in at least some official quarters, continued for some months. Always prone to taking a hint, Hoare requested guidance from London on his response, should the Spanish Government broach the topic of Gibraltar with him, adding a personal caution that the British attitude on the matter might 'well prove decisive in certain circumstances as to the future policy of Spain'.[110] The War Cabinet decided, after consideration on 18 June, that Hoare should answer any such request by stating that he had to seek his Government's instructions. Their answer, in that eventuality, would probably be that, whilst the British Government was not prepared to discuss Gibraltar during the war, it was prepared to discuss questions of common interest to Spain and Britain, as matters primarily interesting themselves, after the termination of hostilities.[111] The account of this question given in the published, official history of British foreign policy during the Second World War concludes misleadingly at this point, merely stating that the Spaniards never raised the topic.[112] But the subject was far from closed, even if the initiative did not come from the Spanish side.

Churchill, subsequently, had serious doubts about even an offer of future peacetime discussions on Gibraltar. He minuted to Lord Halifax on 21 June 1940, thus:

Do you think there is much use in preparing to discuss the cession of Gibraltar to Spain after the war? The Spaniards know that if we lose they will get it anyhow, and they would be great fools to believe that if we win we shall mark our admiration for their conduct by giving it to them. The news that we were willing to entertain the idea of giving up Gibraltar will do no end of harm.[113]

Halifax, on the other hand, was inclined to make some conciliatory gesture towards the Spaniards on the issue. He explained his reasoning to Churchill, on the same day:

The question as I see it is largely one of tactics, for I agree with you in your statement of the realities. If we lose there will not be much discussion and if we win we can discuss on our own terms or not at all.

The immediate objective is to keep Spain out of the war, if not permanently, for as long as possible.

If we say flatly now that we can never discuss Gibraltar, I should think we might be giving some unnecessary ammunition to those who want to make mischief for us now.[114]

The matter rested with this exchange of views, until three days later, when Hoare appealed from Madrid for leave to introduce into a 'general discussion', with the Spanish Minister for Foreign Affairs, a British promise to discuss Gibraltar with Spain when the war was over.[115] This request prompted the Prime Minister to reiterate his objections to any such stratagem. He wrote to Halifax on 26 June in this vein:

I am sure we shall gain nothing by offering to 'discuss' Gibraltar at the end of the war. Spaniards will know that if we win, discussions would not be fruitful; and if we lose, they would not be necessary. I do not believe mere verbiage of this kind will affect the Spanish decision. It only shows weakness and lack of confidence in our victory, which will encourage them the more.[116]

It was the full text of this last minute which Churchill issued, in May

1954, amid renewed Anglo-Spanish controversy over Gibraltar, to rebut a Spanish charge that they had been promised the return of the Rock at the end of the war, if they remained neutral during it.[117] However, he was being rather less than candid in replying in this manner to the post-war Spanish allegations. For, Halifax had challenged the Prime Minister's view, on 29 June 1940, arguing that Hoare as the man 'on the spot' should be allowed 'to judge the wisest tactics to adopt'. He reminded the Prime Minister that the issue was tactical and, indeed, 'academic' for the very reasons advanced by Churchill. He fully backed Hoare's request: 'I feel myself that we should give him the latitude that he desires to use in his language about Gibraltar.'[118] Churchill yielded to the persistent pleading of his Foreign Secretary, commenting, 'I cannot press my point further.'[119] So, Hoare was able to inform the Spanish Minister for Foreign Affairs, in a 'general' but private discussion of the British willingness to engage in post-war talks over Gibraltar.[120]

Yet, the foregoing record of this offer of post-war discussions does not support the Spanish claim, made in 1954, that they had been promised Gibraltar in return for wartime neutrality. Britain had merely offered to talk and had, in fact, no intention of making any significant concessions in negotiation. The above account does, however, substantiate the more qualified accusation, expressed in the reply by the Spanish Ministry of Foreign Affairs, of 21 May 1954, to Churchill's denial of a wartime deal, which stated that 'the British Government . . . offered to discuss with the Spanish Government, should Spain remain neutral, the return of Gibraltar once the war ended'.[121] Whatever may be the importance of this episode in the long history of the Anglo-Spanish dispute concerning Gibraltar, it could hardly have been crucial in Spain's decision for war or peace. Britain's wartime promise of post-war negotiations probably smacked too much of 'jam tomorrow' to influence Spanish minds at the critical moment.

Still, Hoare had managed to give at least a tentative indication of Britain's sympathy with Spain's irredentist claim. Gibraltar would emerge, again, as a factor in British policy-making for Spain in the rather dramatic days of late September and early October 1940, as will be seen. Nevertheless, it was Spain's claims against France, rather than Britain, which constituted the most suitable material from which to fashion an Anglo-Spanish understanding, according to Hoare.

Geographically, Morocco was a natural focus of Spanish imperial ambitions. However, Spain's imperial designs on Morocco had deeper roots amongst its political and military elites than merely geopolitical ones. For Morocco had been the military and political crucible of many of the top military men of Nationalist Spain, and the campaigns against the Rif rebels in the small Spanish Moroccan territory had generated an *esprit de corps*, a consciousness of Hispanic–Muslim historical relations, and a sense of imperial mission amongst them which singled them out as a definable group: *los africanistas*, the 'Africans'. Most prominent of the *africanistas* was the Caudillo himself, Francisco Franco. It was his ability in the Moroccan campaigns which enabled him to rise so rapidly as to become, reputedly, the youngest general in the Europe of his day, and it was from Morocco that Franco led into Spain the most formidable force in the rebellion against the Spanish Republic, the army of Africa. In January 1939, he asserted that it was in Africa that 'the possibility of restoring Spain's greatness was born'.[122] Serrano Suñer, political intimate and member of his family circle, recognised Franco to be 'above all an African'.[123] Franco's Foreign Minister, Beigbeder, was an 'African' in a broader sense than his chief. Franco's obsession with the region sprang from his professional experience and a specifically Spanish patriotism. Beigbeder, who had been Nationalist Spain's High Commissioner in Morocco for most of the Civil War, was steeped in the Muslim cultural tradition and was an enthusiastic Arabist. 'We are all Moors', he once declared to Sir Samuel Hoare, including even the Ambassador in his description, and he could suddenly break into chants from the Koran to prove his point.[124]

The collapse of the French raised Spanish hopes regarding fulfilment of their designs on Morocco.[125] The Spaniards did have an historical claim to some territorial transfers from the large French Zone to their own small north-western coastal strip in Morocco, but their appetite increased with France's collapse, and, as already mentioned, they had approached the Germans, in June 1940, to secure their good offices in this regard. Actually two days before formally consulting the Germans, the Spaniards had demanded the cession of two Moroccan provinces from France, but it was not until the end of September 1940, that the Vichy Government made definite offers of some Moroccan territory to the Spaniards, and then only because of alarm at their apparently increasing intimacy with the Germans. The Spaniards, by then, had become entangled in such a web of diplomatic pressure and counter-pressure with Britain and Germany that such an offer was largely irrelevant.[126] However, the Spaniards did occupy the internationally administered city of Tangier, an enclave within the Spanish Moroccan Zone, on 14 June 1940. Beigbeder had assured

Hoare, however, that the occupation was merely a temporary measure to ensure law and order and there was no immediate attempt to abolish the institutions of international administration. Notwithstanding these assurances, however, the Spanish military occupation of Tangier was intended, as Serrano Suñer has since admitted, to be the first step in a total takeover by Spain there. Events in Tangier, later in 1940, dealt with in chapter seven, would also reveal Spain's possessive designs on Tangier.[127] The British were not too ruffled by this Spanish move as they had already been pressing the French to make a gesture to Franco by offering him further representation in the control of Tangier, and the French did negotiate with the Spanish Government prior to the occupation.[128]

Sir Samuel Hoare had emphasised the importance of the Moroccan question in Spanish eyes to the Foreign Secretary, as early as 26 June 1940, as already noted. Halifax replied in a slightly restrained fashion, on July 8 1940, that he fully realised the desirability of being as sympathetic as possible towards Spanish designs on Morocco, without getting embroiled with the French.[129] However, Hoare repeated his views strongly, a few weeks later and summarised his argument, in a letter to Lord Beaverbrook on the same day (23 July 1940), no doubt hoping to persuade the truculent Minister of Aircraft Production, a former benefactor and political crony, to side with him:

If, however, we are to keep them [i.e. the Spaniards] in our imperial and maritime orbit, we must be forthcoming to them over the Mediterranean and North Africa. I believe myself that I could do a deal with them over these questions ... we ought to have some *modus vivendi* over Morocco. You cannot imagine what Morocco means to the new Spanish generation and particularly to the present Spanish leaders. Franco, Beigbeder and many others made their careers in Morocco and they are much more interested in Morocco than they are in Europe. Is there any chance of the French Empire continuing in Morocco? I am very doubtful. If this is so, is it not worth using Morocco as the bridge over which we can bring the Spaniards from the Berlin side to our own ...

He conceded that there existed the obvious difficulty of appearing to be involved in partitioning the French Empire, but thought that a suitably cautious approach would circumvent this snag.[130] Hoare's relative insouciance about the dismemberment of France's Empire stemmed, according to a contemporary colleague, David Eccles, from the former's low opinion of the French and all their works. Eccles summarised Hoare's views on this topic in a letter home, on 27 September 1940:

Sam has very definite ideas about the French Empire. He has always hated the

French. I can find no solid reason for his aversion; it seems to spring from professional jealousy, as between slick politicians. He says the French Empire must disappear – that it is an artificial creation without guts to live on its own. France will relapse into an agricultural third-rate power and her empire fall to pieces. He would therefore have no compunction about bribing Tom, Dick and Harry with promises of bits of the French Empire.[131]

However, apparently unaware of the motivation behind Hoare's proposal to coax Spain into the British sphere of influence with expressions of London's sympathy for Francoist ambitions in Morocco, Halifax was persuaded, on this occasion, by the cogency of the Ambassador's argument. For he communicated Hoare's suggestion to the Cabinet, the very next day, and expressed his own opinions as follows: his first inclination was to regard the Moroccan problem as primarily a matter of Spanish and French concern. However, the Spanish Government should be told that if French authority there crumbled, Britain would welcome Spanish intervention to restore law and order, and that the future of the territories could be defined by post-war negotiation. Whilst Britain should not over-commit itself in the matter, it was also 'important to encourage Spanish consultation and co-operation with us'.[132] Hoare was, it seems, allowed to relay this rather muted British acknowledgement of Spain's interest in Morocco to the appropriate quarter, in late July.[133]

However, there was danger, as well as opportunity for Britain in Spain's ambitions in French Morocco. For, as Hoare reported, whilst Colonel Beigbeder did not consider that Gibraltar need be a *casus belli* between Britain and Spain, the Spanish Minister was very anxious lest the two countries get embroiled over Morocco. Beigbeder's anxieties over Morocco, Hoare said, had gone through two phases. In the first, Beigbeder had repeatedly expressed his expectations of a rising of the Moroccan tribes, and the disintegration of French authority in the country consequent upon the French collapse before Germany. Spain would then, according to Beigbeder, be forced to intervene to restore order.[134] However, what Beigbeder chose to express as fears of a French collapse and ensuing Spanish intervention, were really Spain's hopes for the area. For not only did Beigbeder express the same 'fears' to von Stohrer, the German Ambassador, at this time, but the latter had informed Berlin, on 25 June 1940, that the Spanish Government had apparently decided to invade French Morocco, as soon as the disarmament of the French Air Force there had taken place.[135] Moreover, the Spaniards also actively explored the possibility of inciting a rebellion by the indigenous inhabitants of

French Morocco against the authorities there, which would have given them the excuse they wanted to march into France's Zone.[136] However, the French managed to maintain relatively powerful air and ground forces in Morocco during the following months, so Spain had to abandon any notion of conquering 'her African vital space' by force of her own arms.[137] These French forces were sufficient to deter either an attempted local Spanish military assault on, or subversion of, French authority in Morocco. Hoare, indeed, recognised that Spain's inaction was explicable by the locally predominant French military presence in Morocco.[138] No wonder, then, that the Spanish Government should request the Italian Government, on 29 June 1940, through its position in the Armistice Commission, to effect a reduction in the 'excessive' French forces in Morocco.[139] Again, Serrano Suñer later constantly warned Germany of the perils of French treachery in North Africa, offering, at the same time to assume the role of guarantor of stability and peace there.[140] The Germans, like their Italian partners, however, were unwilling to aid Spain's imperial ambitions at this stage. Germany and Italy, of course, had North African ambitions of their own, and, more important, Hitler was not going to commit himself in any definite way to North African complications, until he could discern whether Britain's power was, or could be directly, broken. Baron von Stohrer was thus enjoined in June, and again in July 1940, to maintain 'complete reserve' on the Moroccan question.[141] Again, Franco's desire for Moroccan spoils communicated, on 15 August 1940, to Mussolini merely evoked a mild reminder that Spain would have no 'moral justification' for demanding its African *Lebensraum* without joining the war.[142]

The second phase of Beigbeder's anxieties regarding Morocco found expression in his fear that a British-aided French resistance movement, inspired by de Gaulle, would inevitably embroil French and Spanish troops, even if it should, as was likely, fail. This would give Germany the opportunity for intervention under the guise of protecting Spain's endangered Moroccan aspirations. The Spanish Government could hardly reject German intervention in such circumstances, where Britain would appear to be consolidating its hold on the Straits at the expense of Spain's vital interests.[143] Beigbeder's analysis was as incisive as it was candid. Hitler, by September, especially after the abortive Dakar venture, had become increasingly aware of the opportunities available to Britain for interference in the French North African Empire, as will be noted in chapter five. The Dakar expedition indicated, too, that Beigbeder was quite right to be fearful of British action amongst French North African colonies. For the British–Free French attempt to seize Dakar, in late September 1940, had not been conceived of as an inherently self-contained operation. Thus, the Prime Minister had minuted to the Chiefs of Staff, on 1 September 1940 the day after the Dakar expedition had set sail, as follows:

It would seem that as soon as De Gaulle had established himself there [i.e. at Dakar] . . . he should try to get a footing in Morocco, and our ships and troops could be used to repeat the process of Menace [code-name for the Dakar operation] . . . immediately and in a more important theatre.[144]

The function of the Dakar expedition was, in effect, to rally the French Empire to de Gaulle, and therefore, to Britain, and as Beigbeder had perceived Morocco was a primary target for any further joint British–Free French effort to promote this purpose.[145]

However, on 27 August 1940, Hoare had advised Churchill of the 'Africanist' character of Spain's new rulers. 'Morocco is a central fact in the Spanish outlook', he declared.[146] As soon as he got wind of the way policy was developing in London with regard to the French colonies, Hoare began to warn his Government of the 'special position and peculiar dangers of Morocco' with regard to Anglo-Spanish relations. In an important despatch of 13 September 1940, sent directly to Churchill, he traced the development of Beigbeder's thoughts in connection with the problem, and emphasising that 'Morocco is now the centre of the Spanish picture', he counselled against any incursion into Morocco unless Britain was sure of its military position there. For an abortive move would be disastrous, and a successful one should be accompanied by the immediate cession of the disputed border-areas to the Spanish Zone of Morocco.[147] He related a new warning by Beigbeder of the risks of Moroccan complications, to Halifax, on 16 September.[148] In a co-ordinated manoeuvre, Hillgarth, sent the Prime Minister a note on the Spanish situation, on 13 September 1940, stressing the 'vital importance' of Morocco in Spanish eyes, and that Morocco was the real danger-point in Anglo-Spanish relations. He pointed out that any move by the British Government and/or de Gaulle over Morocco, which did not take account of Spanish susceptibilities would play straight into Germany's hands. This would be particularly unfortunate in his view, as German influence was waning in Spain. Churchill was clearly impressed by this analysis, as he circulated it to his colleagues as a War Cabinet paper.[149]

This combined assault by Hoare and Hillgarth on grand strategic opinion in London had its effect. Indeed, even the Prime Minister's military advisers were swayed by the advice from Madrid. For, the Joint Planners and the Chiefs of Staffs had been prompted by Churchill, earlier in September, to counsel attempted British landings in Morocco in the wake of an easy success at Dakar, and subject to there being 'a sufficiently favourable political atmosphere' in the French north-west African colony.[150] However, given pause for thought by Hoare's warnings, the Chiefs of Staff, on 19 September, requested the Joint Planning Staff to reconsider the problem, and had their reservations confirmed. For, the Joint Planners pointed out, the following day, that there were now serious strategic objections to proceeding with the Moroccan project, Operation 'Threat':

Since the previous decision was taken, there has been a change in the political situation. It now appears likely from telegrams from Sir Samuel Hoare that the establishment of Free French Forces in Morocco, particularly if with direct British backing, will lead either to a direct clash with Spain in Morocco, or to a German demand for the passage of German troops through Spain, a demand which Spain would not be able to resist. The visit of Senor Suñer to Berlin lends support to this view.[151] [dealt with in chapter five.]

Now, the Joint Planners advised against any attempt to execute Operation 'Threat', even if 'Menace' were an 'unqualified success'. For, Britain could not lend sufficient forces to the Free French to ensure that they held Morocco against all comers. Neither could Britain's over-stretched forces prevent the loss of Gibraltar, nor seize alternative bases to the Rock amongst the Iberian Atlantic Islands if they were engaged in supporting the Free French in North Africa.[152]

The convergence of cautionary diplomatic and military counsel persuaded Churchill, too, to back away from action which could provoke a confrontation and, perhaps, even conflict with Franco's Spain. Thus, he informed (the then) General Smuts, on 22 September 1940, that Britain did 'not intend to disturb Morocco at present on account of the German pressure on Spain and Spanish interests there'.[153] Now Hoare was instructed to reassure the Spaniards that the Dakar expedition was intended to be a self-contained operation, which was 'not intended to be followed by a similar *coup* in Morocco', even though it was possible that its success might inspire a spontaneous Free French takeover inside Morocco. Moreover, Churchill personally authorised Hoare to explain to the Spanish Government that British actions were in no sense hostile to Spain, and that Britain would favour the establishment of an acceptable *modus vivendi* on the Moroccan Zones at issue between France and Spain.[154] So Hoare now received sanction to express a somewhat more substantial sympathy for Spain's Moroccan ambitions than he had apparently been granted two months before. Beigbeder, however, when given the British assurances, remained adamant that Morocco had to be kept quiet, and that a spark there would start a general conflagration involving Spain.[155] Actually, of course, the Dakar operation of 23–5 September 1940 was a failure, and there was no knock-on effect on Morocco. So a dangerous circumstantial threat to Hoare's policy-line disappeared, although the *débâcle* did dent further Britain's already battered image among Spaniards.[156]

However, the dangers generated by the Dakar project demonstrate clearly how the negative, restraining facet of Hoare's policy tended to come to the fore. Thus, although Hoare wanted his Government to court Spain's favour by actively sympathising with its territorial designs, he had to exert himself fully to try and thwart British action bound to alienate Spain, and maybe even provoke its belligerency. In Britain's straitened strategic circumstances in 1940–1, its Government was constantly on the lookout for new dangers or opportunities. The British search for new strategic openings might cut across their desire to 'let sleeping dogs lie' in Spain, as easily as their anxiety over a Spanish or German move. Either way Hoare would be forced on to the defensive, and his attempt to mount a concerted British effort to influence Spain would be deflected and endangered. The Dakar episode was also an example of the manner in which the hope, or spectre, of renewed French resistance might complicate efforts to secure an understanding with Spain. This was a recurring difficulty in both British and German policy-making towards Spain, as will be emphasised below.

The foregoing chapter described Hoare's definition and elaboration of a British policy for Spain and the conditions immediately affecting that procedure. Prominence has been given to Hoare's role as he was the catalyst, under the influence of his locally-based advisers, in policy formulation. As Halifax acknowledged, the subject of Spain had been largely lost to view in the welter of perils which beset Britain in the summer of 1940. Hoare, then, was to a great extent left to his own devices in his early period in Madrid.[157] However, owing to the recently and intensely controversial nature of Spanish affairs in British politics, it was inevitable that opposition to Hoare's policy-line would emerge. The next chapter examines the forms and bases of the opposition which developed.

3

Opposition

At the beginning of November 1940, Sir Alexander Cadogan, with a bureaucratic sense of detachment from the passions of politics, commented, thus, upon an apparently perplexing aspect of British political behaviour: 'Any Spanish topic makes the politicians go all hay-wire and Attlee, otherwise a dormouse becomes like a rabid rabbit. Why?'[1] However, if Cadogan had forgotten already the emotions aroused by the Spanish Civil War, then many British politicians had not. Churchill himself, had testified, on 5 April 1938, to the fundamental cleavage in British political life caused by the Spanish struggle: 'As between Spanish Nationalists and Republicans, British sympathies are divided. Strong elements in the Conservative Party regard the cause of Franco as their own. All the Parties of the "Left" feel outraged by its triumph.'[2] But it was naturally amongst Labour and radical circles that vestigial civil wartime loyalties remained most vital, sustained as they were by resentment at the defeat of their Spanish comrades. Prominent members of the Labour movement, of course, were now part of Churchill's National Coalition government, and they might be expected to feel uneasy about the Hoare–Halifax policy for Spain. All the more so, when this policy bore the marks of the despised and discredited appeasement. Halifax reminded Hoare, on 24 September 1940, that large sections of British parliamentary and public opinion rejected, or only accepted very grudgingly, 'our present policy towards Spain'.[3] In the House of Commons on 20 August 1940, a Labour M.P., F. S. Cocks, expressed the hope that 'no futile policy of attempted appeasement' was being applied to Spain by Hoare, who had such diplomatically inauspicious associations with Laval and the Anglo-German Naval Agreement.[4] The *News Chronicle*, of 30 September, argued that the aim of British policy towards Spain should be to organise the scattered Republican movement, not to hobnob with reactionary generals. A *Daily Express* article, of 19 July 1940, entitled 'If Franco Wants War He's In For Trouble', called upon Britain to use the Republican prisoners and the Spanish people against Franco to 'dynamite his whole regime from within and smash one end of the Axis' should the Caudillo be foolhardy enough to fight Britain. Translations of this article were distributed by the Spanish Government, the Republican underground, and the Germans amongst the Spanish people as an alleged embodiment of Britain's real attitude towards Spain. The Franco Government also used it as convenient propaganda for frequent dissemination by press and radio.[5] Hoare repeatedly emphasised to London that the most effective German propaganda line in Spain was that a British victory in the war would mean the end of Nationalist Spain and Franco.[6] Churchill and Halifax both often intervened in press circles to prevent or, at least, moderate press attacks on Franco, but with indifferent success.[7] Thus Halifax sought the aid of Sir Archibald Sinclair, Liberal Secretary of State for Air, on 29 July 1940, to curb the anti-Francoism of the *News Chronicle*, since Britain's interest lay in 'strengthening those elements in Spain which are determined to maintain Spanish neutrality', i.e., the Franco Government. He did have to inform Hoare, however, that the British Government could not legally prevent the publication of such anti-Franco material.[8] Hoare regarded such recrudescent Civil War partisanship as 'as much out of date as pacifism and appeasement'. The overthrow of Franco, in his view, would not produce a new Spanish Republic, merely internal chaos and immediate German intervention.[9]

However, there was an added dimension to anti-Francoism after the fall of France. For taking Churchill's dictum that this was 'a war of peoples and of causes' at face value, many socialists, radicals and those simply appalled at the terrible peril which Conservative statesmen had brought on their country, began to argue that British resistance to Nazism should be cast in a new mould. Reckoning, like George Orwell, that Hitler was 'the leader of a tremendous counter-attack of the capitalist class', they concluded that 'any real struggle means revolution'.[10] The *Daily Express*, of 23 July 1940, summarised the logic behind this argument, thus, in supporting it vigorously: 'Our allies are ordinary people, not Fascist dictators. And since the ordinary people of Europe are now ruled by Fascists we must organise revolutions.'

The *News Chronicle*, too, believed that Britain's war for the liberation of Europe was 'essentially revolutionary'.[11] The Labour Party's leading socialist intellectual, Harold Laski, believed that

Britain should inspire by revolutionary example, voluntarily trans-
forming its own economy and society, to win the hearts and minds of
Europe's masses for the fight against fascism. He summarised his
message in a book, first published in September 1940:

To defeat the menace of the dictators it [is] essential to appeal to the dynamic
of democracy. To appeal to that dynamic it [is] necessary to make the war
against the dictators in the fullest sense a people's war. But to make the war a
people's war it [is] necessary to ask for their sacrifices on the supreme
condition that they [are] not to be used merely to preserve the *economic and
social status quo*. A democracy that is to wage totalitarian war must end
economic and social privilege as the price of victory. It must, that is to say,
take large steps towards the transformation of the capitalist basis of its
economic foundations to a socialist basis.[12]

A campaign was, in fact, organised by the publisher, Victor Gollancz
and left-wing members of the Ministry of Economic Warfare, like
R. H. S. Crossman, inside Britain to persuade its people and politicians to raise revolution against Europe's fascist oppressors.[13] Victor
Gollancz published a book entitled *100,000,000 Allies – If We
Choose*, in the summer of 1940. Its co-authors, under the *nom de
plume*, 'Scipio', were Crossman and Kingsley Martin, editor of the
left-wing weekly, the *New Stateman*. They argued, in this work, that
if Britain was to prosecute an 'uncompromising and ungentlemanly'
people's war against the Nazi 'New Order' then what was required
'above all' was 'a picture of the new order which we shall build in this
country and shall help the peoples of Europe to build in theirs'. They
provided their own sketch for the required portrait of post-liberation
Europe in these words:

So our message to Europe should be this. Hitler has been destined to be the
whirlwind which has swept away an old and corrupt order. His ruthless
conquests have at least done one good thing – they have exposed the
defeatists and the capitulators in the ranks of democracy and forced us to
discard outworn institutions and effete privileges. To fight him, we have had
to pull ourselves together, to admit the error of our ways and to begin to scrap
our present social inequalities. Since we could only hope to defend them by
capitulating to Hitler, we are discarding them and thereby fitting ourselves to
become what we once were, leaders in the cause of freedom. We do not ask
you to accept our leadership because we are a rich, imperial people. On the
contrary, we invite you to join in our war against tyranny because we are now
going to sacrifice those riches in that cause of freedom which we all have in
common. You ask us what we have to offer you when the battle is done? We
reply 'Freedom and work – on equal terms for all. Freedom to think, to
practise our own religion – or irrelegion, to study, to form Trade Unions in
defence of our working rights, but not freedom to exploit others, to bully
them or to obtain privileges which injure our neighbours. Work, to repair the
ravages of war and revolution, to build the thousands of miles of roads and

railways which commerce needs, the millions of houses for those who have no homes, the hospitals and schools and universities for the millions who cannot learn. There will be no lack of work if we look not to the individual profit but to the need of all.' . . . It will not be an easy life for any individual or any class. We shall all be poor compared to the comfortable minority in pre-war days, and we shall probably make many mistakes in our social planning which will bring us hardship and want. But in the planned freedom of the New Europe we shall all be able to express our criticisms and suggestions, though we may not have parliaments and political parties on the old lines.[14]

Indeed Aneurin Bevan called on Britain to espouse a programme of radical war aims, in the House of Commons, on 5 November 1940: 'we must have a deeper and wider social purpose. You must give the people of Europe some idea of the sort of Europe to which we are wading and fighting, and . . . for which we are bleeding.'[15] Again, the *Daily Herald*, on 5 October 1940, had characterised the declaration of war aims, which it wanted Britain to enunciate, as 'the code of those revolutionary movements in the enemy and occupied countries which might so dramatically hasten the end of the war'.

However, there were more right-wing individuals within British government circles who feared the post-Dunkirk 'slide to the left in foreign politics', believing that it would be 'disastrous to ally . . . with the dregs of Fronts Populaires'.[16] Thus, even Lord Halifax's draft paper on war aims, with its emphasis on general moral and political principles (it was described by Churchill as 'a vague paper four-fifths of which was from the Sermon on the Mount and the remainder an Election Address') did not please his Permanent Under-Secretary, Sir Alexander Cadogan.[17] For, Cadogan thought that to proclaim a British crusade for 'democracy' and 'liberty' would allow Germany to allege that Britain was bent upon restoring the 'Front Populaire' in France and the 'Red' Government in Spain which he claimed he and millions of Europeans detested.[18]

The proponents of the people's war concept certainly did advocate that Britain take up the Spanish Republican cause as an integral part of its revolutionary struggle for social and national liberation in Europe. William Forrest devoted particular attention to the Spanish Republicans in the *News Chronicle*, of 18 July 1940: 'These are our allies in this war of peoples and causes. They have fought and suffered in a cause which we now realise to have been OUR cause – the cause of OUR people.'[19] He demanded that the restoration of the Spanish Republic be included in Britain's war aims. Bevan connected the issues in his Commons' speech just cited. 'Scipio' also reminded his readers how many potential partisans remained in Spain, awaiting employment against Hitler's Spanish Gauleiter, the Caudillo: 'In

spite of daily executions, General Franco has been unable to exterminate the revolutionary elements in Spain. There are thousands of
dynamite-miners in the Asturias, of Catalan and Basque nationalists,
and of revolutionary workers and peasants all over Spain.'[20] Whilst
Charles Duff, in his *A Key to Victory: Spain*, also published by
Gollancz in 1940, singled out that country as the most secure base
from which to launch a British-led crusade for social and political
liberation from Nazidom:

In a state of Europe so confused as the present, Spain is the safest horse we can
back. In spite of the complexity of its internal politics, it is perhaps the only
country of which one can be absolutely sure of an active response to any
attempt on our part to liberate the people from the totalitarian yoke. The
geographical proximity of the Peninsula, and our domination of the sea,
render success as certain as anything can be in such operations.[21]

Attlee, too, when voicing his doubts about Britain's Spanish policy to
Halifax, stated his view that 'the active forces to be mobilised against
Hitlerism must be those people who are devoted to the ideals for
which we stand'.[22] Hoare maintained, on the contrary, that his policy
did not entail sympathy for a dictator. It was 'simply elementary
prudence at a very dangerous moment in the national life'.[23]

Actually the very depth of the crisis which brought Labour into the
Government and called forth the people's war-concept naturally laid
a premium on unity of purpose. This militated against rocking the
ship of state too much on any particular issue, such as Spain. So the
Labour Cabinet Ministers did not insist on Britain's adopting a
revolutionary set of war aims as the price of their continued participation in the management of the British war effort. A Cabinet sub-
committee was established to formulate war aims but its mildly
progressive conclusions were ignored by Churchill.[24] For the Prime
Minister believed that a British declaration of general war aims
would lack substance to attract any real support at home or abroad,
while a more precise programme could create many individual problems.[25] As regards the particular case of Spain, the Labour Party had
already demonstrated during the Spanish Civil War, and even when
in opposition, a readiness to curb ideological zeal in the interests of
Britain's national security.[26] R. A. Butler, Parliamentary Under-
Secretary for Foreign Affairs, perceptively grasped both the significance of the Spanish question for British politicians and their readiness to restrain party passions concerning it, as best they could,
during the dangerous days of later 1940: 'The feeling about Spain
remains extremely acute, since it is all bound up with the division
which all sections here feel is inevitable in English society and

politics. But this division is appreciably less now that the menace of invasion is near.'[27]

The Hoare-Halifax line on Spain, therefore, was not likely to be disturbed by a simple intellectual challenge. Where it could encounter serious difficulty was when some set of diplomatic or military events in Anglo-Spanish relations united with the intellectual scepticism about Britain's Spanish policy, in and out of Government, to yield the conclusion that imminent strategic danger threatened from Spain. The major purpose of the following chapters is an analysis of the course of British diplomacy and strategy towards Spain in the period September 1940 to August 1941, when precisely this combination of specific suspicion and general strategic worry sporadically produced perceptions of impending threat from Spain. However, it may prove informative to cite a brief example here, of the way in which even a relatively minor issue in Anglo-Spanish relations could rouse political tempers in Britain.

Hoare informed London on various occasions of Spanish resentment at the way Britain granted asylum to such Republican refugees as Dr Juan Negrín, late President of the Council of Ministers of the Spanish Republic. Negrín, in particular, was the *bête noire* of the Francoist authorities, who made frequent protests through Hoare and their own Ambassador in Britain about his presence there.[28] Hoare indicated how Negrín's presence in Britain lent substance to the German charge that the British aimed to replace Franco's Spain with a new Republic. He urged that 'in the interests of high policy he should be got out of England as soon as possible'.[29] Halifax had brought the matter before the War Cabinet as early as 2 July 1940, and though he found the Labour War Cabinet members, Attlee and Greenwood, 'rather ticklish' and the former in particular 'disposed to make difficulties', Attlee was eventually induced by the Foreign Secretary to try and persuade Negrín to leave the country. Negrín said he would go if he could announce that he had been asked to leave which clearly did not suit Attlee. Negrín also told the Soviet Ambassador, Maisky, of the affair, who in turn, informed prominent Labour men like Dalton who put counter-pressure on their leader. Negrín did agree to go to the United States but President Roosevelt, personally, decided against allowing him in. The War Cabinet resolved, on 30 July 1940, not to force him to leave.[30] Hoare kept up a steady rhythm of complaint in the following weeks, getting the B.B.C. to deny in a Spanish broadcast in the autumn that Britain had any intention of returning Negrín to power after the war.[31]

The climax of the episode came in November. For, by then, as is noted in chapter five, Beigbeder had lost his position as Spanish Foreign Minister to Serrano Suñer, and had established clandestine contact with Hoare, to prepare military resistance to what seemed an imminent German move into Spain. Hoare seized his opportunity and told his Government that, if they were to stimulate an army-led movement of Spanish national resistance to the Germans' entry into their country, it was essential to drive Negrín from England. The question, he argued, was now 'one of high policy upon the settlement of which may depend very big issues'.[32] Attlee however believed, on the contrary, that the state of the Spanish people and economy were the only factors that might keep Spain out of the war. He conceded, in a letter to Halifax, that Hoare had worked hard at keeping Spain neutral, but also advocated that Britain should not sacrifice its Spanish friends to appease its real enemies.[33] In Cabinet, Halifax pointed out that the only hope of Spanish resistance to a German incursion lay in the army, whose leaders were unlikely to move if they considered Britain was intriguing with Spanish revolutionaries. He admitted it was difficult to withdraw Negrín's right of political asylum, but also declared the following: 'Our object in this matter had nothing to do with internal Spanish affairs, but turned on the best way to win the war. For this purpose we wanted to keep Spain out of the war and to keep the leaders of the Spanish Government friendly to us.' Attlee, again, emphasised to his Cabinet colleagues that he was convinced that Spain's decision for war or peace would hinge on its own assessment of its own interests, not on the fate of a few political refugees. He continued in this vein: 'the action suggested would have a most discouraging effect on the people, the world over, who believed that we were fighting for democracy, and on those who might otherwise carry on disruptive activities in the occupied territories.' The 'people's war' concept clearly informed this argument. Sinclair, the Liberal, thought a compromise might be possible. Churchill felt that to keep Negrín in Britain was to impose 'a further strain on this country', but since it probably did not involve a 'moral hurt' and the Cabinet could not agree, a compromise should be attempted. It was decided that Halifax and A. V. Alexander, the Labour First Lord of the Admiralty, should try to get Negrín to leave, but if they failed, there was 'no present intention of compelling him to go'.[34]

They could not persuade him to leave voluntarily and the Government was seriously embarrassed when Claud Cockburn's *The Week* newsheet, among others, exposed their covert approaches to Negrín.[35] A question was put down by a Labour M.P. about the affair and Attlee flatly refused R. A. Butler's request that he 'square' it in advance.[36] The result was what Halifax called 'a first-class political row in Parliament'.[37] One Labour M.P., Emanuel Shinwell, asked for an assurance that no Labour members of the Government were associated 'with this discreditable attempt to induce Dr Negrín to leave this country'.[38] Another Labour M.P. told Cadogan that it was clear that British public opinion would not tolerate any further action of this kind.[39] There were protests from left-wing, trade union and anti-fascist groups.[40] Halifax informed Hoare that nothing, then, could have made the Cabinet agree on expelling Negrín, especially when Canada, the only other country to which he was willing to go, refused him a visa.[41] So, if Hoare was singularly successful in inducing the British Government to accept his general views on Spain, the Negrín affair was a warning that there were certain limits beyond which he trespassed only at risk to his whole policy. Spain remained a potential flash-point in wartime coalition politics in Britain, as a chastened Halifax realised (in terms remarkably similar to those employed by Cadogan, cited at the start of this chapter) after his Cabinet confrontation with Attlee: 'It is very remarkable how all political parties here manage somehow to agree upon most social controversies but, as soon as the microbe of Spain enters into the discussion, the patient immediately falls into a high fever.'[42]

One formidable opponent of the Hoare line on Spain was Dr Hugh Dalton. For not only was Dalton a Labour M.P., but also, as Minister of Economic Warfare, he had responsibility for applying the British economic blockade to Spain, and was therefore professionally interested, as he noted, in keeping 'Spain so short that she cannot re-export and is not worth pillaging'.[43] It was perhaps inevitable that Dalton and Hoare, with their widely different professional perspectives and priorities, should disagree over the application of Britain's blockade to the Spanish economy. Dalton was a self-styled 'extremist' on the blockade, and conceived his duty to be 'to light the fires and let the F.O. extinguish them if they must'.[44] Emphasising the Spanish failure to apply for navicerts (to enable them to import through the blockade), their apparent disinclination to accept British wheat, and the intense anti-British tone of the Spanish press, he argued, thus, in late August 1940:

I would rather that we both kept Spain out of the war and prevented her from being a channel of supply to the enemy. If, however, this cannot be, it is not clear to me that we would do better by allowing Spain to be such a channel for some time, and then have her as an enemy, all the same, than by letting her come in against us naked and starved, even if a little sooner.[45]

The Minister of Economic Warfare, then, was prepared to entertain the idea that Spanish belligerency might be inevitable. He accused the M.E.W. official, David Eccles, of advocating, along with Hoare, an economic policy for Spain which went 'far beyond appeasement'. It was, he asserted, 'sheer abasement'.[46] The Commercial Counsellor at the British Embassy in Madrid in 1940–1, Sir John Lomax, claims in his memoirs that the Labour members of the British Cabinet were appalled at the idea of conciliatory economic treatment of Spain and that Hugh Dalton's animosity, in particular, 'unnecessarily soured ... blockade enforcement'.[47] David Eccles also maintains that Dalton was so personally and ideologically antagonistic to the Franco regime that he thought it right to starve Spain into inanition.[48]

Hoare, on the other hand, had been advised by Hillgarth, Churchill's friend, the day after his arrival in Spain, that Britain should absolutely avoid appearing to threaten Spain with its ability to supply or cut off vital commodities, since the Spaniards were subtle enough to appreciate British power, but sensitive enough to be alienated by intimidation.[49] Hoare heeded this advice and on 16 July 1940, for instance, he counselled Halifax against adopting a rigid blockade policy towards Spain. He contended that the correct policy was first to guarantee Spain essential supplies and then to seek the guarantee against re-export required for blockade purposes.[50] Interestingly, Dalton had adopted a rather similar approach, in his initial imposition of the new blockade upon Spain, which the War Cabinet approved.[51] However, much hinged upon the general attitude with which it was intended to apply such a policy. Thus, Hoare was quite willing to tolerate small leakages of goods, obtained by Spain through the British blockade, into Germany, if that indulgence helped to secure the incomparably more valuable prize of Spanish neutrality.[52] On the other hand, just a few days later in July, Hoare was convinced that Dalton and the Ministry of Economic Warfare were determined to starve Spain.[53]

Of course, attitudes on the blockade and economic policy were themselves contingent upon a political assessment of Spain's likely future action concerning the war. There was an unfortunate, and painfully recent, analogy to hand, Italy. For Italy, like Spain now, had assumed a status of non-belligerency before its entry into the war on Germany's side, and the British effort to induce Mussolini to refrain from active hostilities by a restrained application of the blockade, and some measure of economic attraction, had failed. The proponents of a tough economic policy towards Spain had the Italian example prominent in their minds, especially as they felt that Mussolini had been allowed to accumulate large stores of strategic war material which were now in use against Britain. Dalton jotted down, before a meeting on policy towards Spain, 'I remember Italy; so does H. of C. and country'.[54] Hoare retorted by maintaining that Mussolini always intended to go to war, whereas 'Franco definitely wishes to keep out'.[55] Hoare's assessment of Italian policy aside, his answer does underline the crucial point: ultimately the decision about what kind of economic policy to apply to Spain had to be based upon a political assessment of the future of Spanish neutrality. When that goal was deemed achievable it followed that a method of warfare like the blockade and/or economic support should be so used as to render that aim all the more attainable, by strengthening the Spanish adherence to peace. So, Britain's economic policy towards Spain only became really severe when there were serious doubts about the continuance of Spanish neutrality, and a political decision that firmness might be needed, at least temporarily, to consolidate such neutrality. In mid-August 1940, Hoare articulated the premise of all the arguments over economic policy towards Spain: 'we must at once make up our minds as to whether we are going to treat Spain as a potential friend or as a certain enemy'.[56] It is not surprising, then, that the official historian of Britain's economic blockade in the Second World War, should conclude that all through the war in regard to Spain, 'political considerations forced the Ministry (of Economic Warfare) into decisions on other than economic grounds'.[57]

Both the primary features of the new British blockade measures of 1940, compulsory navicerting for ships' cargoes passing through the blockade, and compulsory rationing of the commodities so imported, aroused antagonism in Spain.[58] Hoare argued that Spanish incompetence and indolence, rather than intent to deceive, were alike responsible for their repeated failure to apply for navicerts, and for their irregular methods when negotiating the permitted quotas for the rationed commodities. He wanted to avoid a legalistic system which could end in alienating Spain. It was much better to adopt a friendly and flexible policy which could be applied for short periods and so be contingent upon Spanish good behaviour. A trusting attitude in negotiations over quotas, and a flexible and speedy naval blockade system which would avoid delaying ships excessively, were his requirements.[59] Dalton felt that if Hoare had his way, 'there would soon be no blockade left', and found him more troublesome than any other British diplomat over the blockade.[60] Hoare and Dalton, indeed, both accused each other of attempting to call in question official British policy as laid down by the Cabinet.[61]

However, Halifax made sure that their squabble was kept within limits. In general, he gave strong support to Hoare. He continually intervened 'to moderate some of the political thoroughness of the robust Dalton', and asked Churchill to do the same.[62] He constantly brought Hoare's complaints to the attention of Dalton.[63] He had a series of discussions about the blockade and Spain with the Minister of Economic Warfare, from 3–6 September 1940, and told Hoare that Dalton was certainly not unappreciative of the latter's 'invaluable work'.[64] The Foreign Office, at every opportunity, urged that for reasons of high policy the Spanish should not be severely treated in the working of the blockade.[65] On the other hand, Halifax ensured that when the Ministry of Economic Warfare proved co-operative, news of this was conveyed to Hoare and the Foreign Secretary, also, underlined how unreasonable the Spanish Government were being over blockade measures.[66] In fact, there was substance in Halifax's reassurances concerning the Minister of Economic Warfare's willingness to make some concessions on blockade policy towards Spain. For, though refusing to submit to Hoare's 'blackmail', Dalton exhorted his men, on 23 August 1940, in relation to the blockade and Spain, thus: 'Root out needless delays everywhere.'[67]

Actually Hoare's case was strengthened by the fact that the Ministry of Economic Warfare's own men in Spain, tended to support his policy-line. For instance, the Spanish Government asked for an import quota for oil, on 16 July 1940, after joint British–American action had restricted supplies due to alarm at estimated Spanish oil-stocks. An official of the Ministry, Mark Turner, was sent out, at the Foreign Offices suggestion, to ascertain true Spanish needs and stocks. He confirmed Hoare's analysis that inefficiency, rather than intention to deceive, characterised the administration of the Spanish oil monopoly company, Campsa. Another M.E.W. official, David Eccles, who also campaigned for lenient treatment of Spain – and influenced Hoare towards doing so as well – visited Dalton to present the case for a sympathetic attitude to the Spaniards. These approaches had a cumulative effect on Dalton, who was persuaded that Britain must not push its 'policy of restriction too far' and who agreed to allow Spain a petroleum ration sufficient to satisfy normal demand and maintain fuel stocks at a level equivalent to two and a half months' national consumption, a quota which the Spaniards seemed ready to accept. But they baulked at the last hurdle, refusing to guarantee that they would not impose further restrictions on domestic oil consumption and, thereby, possibly again build up

Spanish stocks beyond the agreed limit. This impasse may well have resulted from pressure from the Germans and anti-British sections of the Franco Government over such attempted British interference in internal Spanish affairs. Anyway, Hoare withdrew the British condition, on his own initiative, which resulted in immediate acceptance of the agreement by the Spaniards. The agreement, of 7 September 1940, provided for the reduction of Spanish stocks of petrol products by regular rationing from 224,000 to 160,000 tons by the end of 1940, and their maintenance at that level. The Spaniards promised, in return for this guaranteed fuel-ration, not to re-export any imported oil. Colonel Beigbeder, the Spanish Minister for Foreign Affairs, claimed that he and fellow anti-Germans had been saved from disaster by Hoare's action, and later asserted that the agreement assuring Spain of this vital fuel-supply, was a real turning-point in Anglo-Spanish relations.[68]

On 1 October 1940, when Dalton drew up his brief for a meeting with the Foreign Secretary on blockade policy towards Spain, he summarised the pattern of argument up to then: 'He [Hoare] wants to keep them sweet; I want to keep them short. Constant differences of views, and I have conceded reluctantly a great deal.'[69] Dalton was, doubtless, emphasising his concessions in order to avoid having to make more. For the Spaniards did yield, however ungraciously, to the system of compulsory rationing of imports via quota agreements with the British, and the compulsory navicerting of ships' cargoes. Still, Hoare won his case, both in principle, that Spain should not be treated as irretrievably hostile and, consequently, subjected to a total blockade and in practice, that the blockade should not be applied to Spain so hamfistedly as to incite its active hostility. Naturally, Hoare's success on the question of principle was bound to be somewhat more complete than its application in practice. This may be deduced from Dalton's candid letter to Halifax of 4 October 1940, in which he said of Hoare and himself, the following:

... I quite believe that our objects are identical – namely to make the blockade as effective as possible – while at the same time maintaining Spanish neutrality and endeavouring to improve our political position there. I cannot pretend that I think his methods are always those best calculated to achieve this dual object, but I expect he would say the same of me.[70]

Indeed, despite the apparent *rapprochement* between Hoare and Dalton, in early October 1940, on the blockade and Spain, for which see below pp. 96–7, Hoare could complain to Halifax only a few weeks later: 'A letter that I have received from Dalton makes me think that he still wishes to starve Spain. If this is really his policy and it is accepted in Whitehall, this Mission had better pack up bodily and come home at once.'[71]

However, the tenor of British blockade and economic policy in general remained predominantly conciliatory rather than coercive throughout the period 1940–1. A temporary stiffening of economic policy towards Spain only occurred, as in December 1940, when an altered assessment of Spanish political intentions challenged its basic assumption of Franco's bona fides. When, as will be seen, the original appraisal of Spanish motives was reverted to, economic policy was quickly liberalised. In fact, British economic policy towards Spain was always dependent on, and subordinate to, political and strategic evaluations. It was the priority given to the maintenance of Spanish neutrality in British Government circles, especially amongst the Chiefs of Staff, which ensured that basic British policy towards Spain would be as Hoare desired. Thus, in an important appreciation on 'Future Strategy', of 4 September 1940, the Chiefs of Staff Committee argued that ever-mounting economic pressure on Germany should be the foundation of British strategy, and that therefore British economic policy concerning Spain and Portugal must prevent those countries being used as a supply route by Germany. The report went on, however, also to say of Spain and Portugal, that 'nevertheless, it is so important that they should not be forced to join our enemies that we should be prepared in the last resort to make certain relaxations in the economic blockade . . .'.[72] Churchill accepted the paper's main conclusions in mid-October.[73] Again, Dean Acheson, from late 1940, American Assistant Secretary of State, has described the peril of the Spanish joining the Germans as 'the most elusive political imponderable to confuse economic warfare calculations'. He contends that the British Government never lost their 'obsessive fear' of such an eventuality, which inspired them to hinder, successfully, United States attempts to weaken Franco's Spain by economic pressure.[74]

Another factor tending to make for acceptance of Hoare's views on Spanish economic policy was the fact that his mission to Madrid began to appear more and more like a remarkable success, as the months of Britain's strategic isolation slipped by, and Spain did not join the fight against it. Beaverbrook called Hoare's work in Madrid a 'fine edifice of achievement' and a 'triumph'.[75] Halifax, of course, was equally pleased with Hoare's performance.[76] Churchill too, felt, as he told Halifax, that Hoare was 'doing very well in Madrid'.[77] It was not simply a matter of prestige. Since Hoare seemed to be getting results with the policy which he was advocating, there seemed good reason to accept his demands and arguments.

Also, contrary to Lomax's assertion that Hugh Dalton was maliciously anti-Spanish, the Minister of Economic Warfare's confrontation with Hoare sprang from professional rather than personal or ideological motives.[78] Dalton had not been an enthusiastic supporter of the Spanish Republican cause, and had deliberately refrained from speaking in debates on the Spanish Civil War in Parliament. His civil-wartime opposition to Franco had been purely pragmatic: if Franco won he would be an ally of Britain's enemies, therefore, he should be opposed – a line similar to that eventually taken by Churchill. He asserts in his memoirs, retrospectively conceding Hoare's argument during the Second World War, that a Republican Government in Spain would have prompted a German occupation, whereas Franco was able to keep Spain neutral.[79] So, Dalton was not fired by any great crusading zeal in his arguments with Hoare. He could be, and was, persuaded by colleagues and officials to defer to Hoare's persistent pleas. Their differences were of policy rather than of political principle and therefore amenable to solution by intra-governmental politics. In the latter process Hoare had powerful allies, as already indicated.

Nevertheless, again it will be noted that the Ambassador had to expend much energy in preventing British blockade policy towards Spain assuming forms likely to antagonise the Spaniards irrevocably. His success in securing relatively gentle blockade treatment of Spain was vital, since its economic plight was such as to imply that a really rigorous blockade would have entailed its active enmity. Yet again, the negative side of Hoare's policy was most prominent. For, as is described in chapter six, although Hoare's advocacy of a positive programme of economic support for Spain was soon regarded favourably in London, American reluctance to complement it so reduced its scale as to deprive it of great influence. The blockade, though, would retain its power to impress.

Finally, there was another powerful person who might subvert Hoare's policy-line on Spain, the Prime Minister. For, although Churchill supported Hoare's policy strongly, for the most part, his position as Britain's warlord made his perspective on Spanish developments and dangers necessarily different from Hoare's, and even Halifax's.[80] He had to span the whole range of possible threats or advantages opening up to Britain, and he was acutely aware that Spain's belligerency might result from, or in, the realisation of any number of strategic developments. Britain's margin of error in strategic calculation was too contracted now, to allow Germany to pre-empt it once more. Anticipation, even preventive retaliation, came to seem important features of Britain's strategy for survival, and Spain was consistently at the centre of British speculation about possible new German moves and threats in 1940–1.

Moreover, Churchill as a 'child of genius' had a certain tendency to act somewhat impulsively in foreign and strategic policy.[81] Churchill's relation to foreign policy was described by Cadogan as that of 'a rather too oppressive thundercloud overhead'.[82] This metaphor implied both a readiness to intervene, and to disrupt rather arbitrarily, a policy that had been carefully and patiently fostered. Churchill did, for example, draft actual telegrams for dispatch, 'loving his own power of the English language, and his own close grip upon a mobile situation', as Halifax observed.[83] In relation to Spain, there was an early example of the Prime Minister's talent for spontaneous intervention. At the same Cabinet meeting, on 24 June 1940, at which Halifax had said that a move by Spain against Britain was not likely in the near future, Churchill had expressed the view that to keep valuable ships in Gibraltar under Spanish guns offered them excessive temptation.[84] It was the same concern over his precious battleships which caused Churchill to intervene spectacularly in the area of policy for Spain, a few weeks later.

The incident occurred in the context of the significance attached by the Chiefs of Staff Committee to denying the Iberian-ruled Atlantic archipelagos – invaluable as naval bases and transatlantic cable stations – to the enemy, and to securing their strategic advantages for Britain. Axis possession of bases in either the Portuguese Cape Verde Islands or the Spanish Canaries, would force the British to make costly detours westward in their vital south Atlantic sea-borne trade, a re-routing which would be expensive in terms of time, fuel, merchant ships and naval escorts. Given the re-direction westward of Britain's Atlantic traffic which even Spanish belligerency would entail, it was equally essential to ensure that the Portuguese Azores would not furnish the enemy with a forward position from which to assail it.[85] In addition, a seizure of Atlantic Islands was seen as the appropriate response to Gibraltar being rendered unusable, for otherwise Britain would have no naval base between Plymouth and Freetown.[86] The search for an alternative base to the Rock was inspired less by the hope of exercising control over the Strait of

Gibraltar and thus, the entry to and exit from the Mediterranean, from afar, than by the need to secure a substitute *point d'appui* which would afford some protection for British maritime trade, and maintain the effective disposition of the naval patrols which sustained the economic blockade of the European mainland. The occupation of the Canary Islands was regarded as unlikely to enable the British to retain dominance of the Strait, after the loss of Gibraltar, and was, therefore, deemed an excessively expensive enterprise since it would require a heavy investment of Britain's overtaxed resources, without clear assurances of strategic return.[87] So the main British effort to obtain Atlantic stations would have to be directed against the Portuguese Azores, which offered prospective naval and air bases. Such action would simultaneously deny these facilities and the cable station at Horta to the enemy, while a parallel move against the Cape Verdes would prevent realisation of their potential for oceanic warfare by hostile forces, and safeguard the cable station at St Vincent.[88] To circumscribe the geographic advantages which might accrue to German naval warfare from intervention in the Iberian area, the British were ready to strike pre-emptively at the territory of their 'oldest ally'.[89] Churchill contrives to convey the impression in his memoirs, that the Portuguese islands would only have been occupied with Lisbon's consent but this was not so.[90] The War Cabinet approved the Chiefs of Staff Committee's recommendation, on 22 July 1940, to seize the Azores and Cape Verdes should *either* Spain or Portugal join the war against Britain or, indeed, if it were 'clear beyond reasonable doubt that either of these Powers intended to intervene against us'.[91] Thus, if Spain did move against Britain, or seemed bound to do so, the British response would be to occupy the Portuguese Atlantic Islands.

However, nervous as he was of Britain's naval vulnerability at Gibraltar, Churchill soon began to contemplate an actual preventive occupation of the islands, although he admitted such an act might bring about the very contingency which the Atlantic Islands project had first been designed to meet. Churchill minuted to Halifax two days after the above mentioned Cabinet meeting, as follows:

All my reflections about the dangers of our ships lying under the Spanish howitzers in Gibraltar lead me continually to the Azores. Must we always wait until a disaster has occurred? I do not think it follows that our ocupation temporarily, and to forestall the enemy, of the Azores, would *necessarily* precipitate German intervention in Spain and Portugal . . . Moreover once we have an alternative base to Gibraltar, how much do we care whether the Peninsula is overrun or not? If it is not overrun at the present moment, that is only because Hitler shrinks from Germany becoming embroiled in a war with the Spanish people. It does not follow that it would be a bad thing for us if he were so embroiled, as was Napoleon before him. There is much to be said on the other side, but I am increasingly attracted by the idea of simply taking the Azores one fine morning out of the blue . . .[92]

The flaw in Churchill's argument lay in his assumption that the Spaniards would be passive spectators of a British occupation of the Portuguese Atlantic Islands and only respond to a German invasion of their own country. The Additional Protocol to the Luso-Spanish Treaty of Friendship and Non-Aggression had been signed on 29 July, only five days after Churchill broached the problem of the Azores with Halifax. By this diplomatic instrument, Portugal and Spain bound themselves to reach agreement on the best means of safeguarding their mutual interests, whenever circumstances threatened 'to compromise the inviolability of their respective metropolitan teritories' or endangered 'the security or independence of one or other of the Parties'.[93] When questioned by London some months later as to the likely Spanish reaction to a pre-emptive assault by British forces on the Portuguese Atlantic Islands, Hoare acknowledged that a legalistic interpretation of the condition relating to 'metropolitan territories' might conceivably exclude the application of the Protocol in such a case, but he doubted it. He was sure that the Spanish Government would regard such a move as an attack on the Iberian Peninsula.[94] At the very least, Churchill was surely over sanguine in expecting a vigorous Spanish resistance to a German entry into their country which had been precipitated by British action. Hoare certainly felt, in December 1940, when the tide of opinion in Spanish military circles was running much more strongly in Britain's favour than in July, that resistance to Germany would hardly materialise in such circumstances.[95] It was even less likely the previous summer. Indeed, even before the conclusion of the Additional Protocol, the Spanish Ambassador to Portugal, Franco's brother, Nicolás, relayed to Salazar, on 13 July 1940, the Caudillo's assurance that he was prepared to help 'with all his forces' to repel any British demand upon, or abuse against, Portuguese territory which would endanger the Peninsula.[96]

However, Halifax followed his own advice on how to deal with Churchill: 'Always stand up to him. He hates doormats'.[97] He spoke to Churchill the same morning that he received the minute, and wrung from him the admission that he was not completely convinced of his own argument for immediate action but wished the matter to be examined. A week later, Halifax, having marshalled the support of the Central Department of the Foreign Office (which dealt with Spain) behind him, minuted to the Prime Minister that, though taking full account of the latter's views, he should counsel against any immediate action, especially as there had been a definite improvement in the Spanish and Portuguese situations of late. Halifax also sent the Prime Minister minutes by Foreign Office men to back up his case. One, R. M. Makins – an acting Counsellor particularly concerned with policy towards Spain – pointed out that the action Churchill contemplated would completely destroy the policy pursued to date with some success, and Cadogan contended that any hope of a substantial Spanish resistance to a German incursion would be swept away by British action. Even Sir Robert Vansittart, Chief Diplomatic Adviser to the Government, who had long preached wariness of German diplomatic and strategic designs, counselled waiting upon events. He was unhappy when the Admiralty admitted that, due to naval shortages, they would be unable to maintain a close patrol of the Azores which would ensure some measures of advance warning of a German move against them, but he still advised that Britain must stay its hand for the foreseeable future. The continuing British inability to keep such a close watch over these islands due to other pressing demands on their naval resources would lead some of Britain's grand strategists again, in late 1940, to consider seizing them preventively, as is described in chapter seven. However, presented with the unanimous view of the Foreign Office, Churchill did not contest the matter further, at this juncture.[98]

This may have been in character to an important extent. In line with Cadogan's lurid metaphor cited above, Churchill certainly did unleash a continuous barrage of his so-called 'prayers' ('Pray do, etc.') at his Government colleagues and civil servants, a flood of provocative minutes and memoranda which might elevate or exasperate, energise or antagonise their recipients. Controversy raged amongst Churchill's contemporaries, as it has amongst subsequent commentators, as to whether the Prime Minister's catalytic role in Britain's war effort was ultimately more constructive or destructive.[99] But one possible interpretation of Churchill's tendency to shower verbal instructions, advice and inquiries in all directions is of interest, as highlighting a facet of his character which was of vital significance in the evolution of British policy towards Spain. Early on in Churchill's period as Prime Minister, after a rambling Cabinet meeting dominated by his voluble truculence, Halifax observed, 'I am coming to the conclusion that his process of thought is one that has to operate through speech.'[100] By direct extension, Churchill's mass-production of official missives may be regarded as equally embodying the process of overt expression by which his mind was finally made up on a given point. It seems possible that this was, in part, a dialectical exercise in which others' opinions, assenting or dissenting, facilitated his own ultimate conclusion on a particular issue, however apparently resolute his initial commitment to a position – which he might, in the end, uphold or abandon.

In any case, however one interprets Churchill's mental processes, the relevant fact is that he could be dissuaded – with great or little difficulty, with more or less ill-grace – from a projected course of action, as the example described above illustrates.[101] His willingness to listen, and to reconsider, would increase in importance as the intensity of the crises in Anglo-Spanish relations grew apace in 1940–1. Nevertheless, this episode also showed that the very strategic exigencies which made Britain's grand strategists so anxious to preserve Spanish neutrality, might also induce them to consider anticipating, and so precipitating, Spanish belligerency rather than be caught off guard. Preventive attack came, in certain circumstances, to appear to be the best form of defence. It was this consideration that led the British to hold an increasingly substantial expeditionary force at short notice for eighteen months, to seize the Atlantic Islands. As is described in chapter nine, the Spanish Canary Islands became, from April 1941 onwards, the main potential target, with a large force of troops and sea transports, along with the necessary naval and air support, designed to execute the operation. When, in September 1941, the Minister of War Transport, Lord Leathers, complained to the Prime Minister about the 'indefinite immobilisation' of important personnel and cargo-vessels involved in holding this force ready, Churchill retorted, thus: 'We have to pay the price, or be caught unawares.'[102] However, this very state of preparedness was an additional source of menace to continued peace with Spain. With the gun already cocked, a nervous hand might so easily fire it. It would be the vital role of Hoare and Halifax in 1940, and the Ambassador alone in 1941, to calm such dangerously apprehensive nerves. Churchill's open-mindedness and ability for reappraisal would be even more crucial in this context of advanced preparedness.

The preceding chapter, then, was concerned with defining the various foci of opposition, actual and potential, to the Spanish policy of Halifax and Hoare. It is explained in chapter seven, below, how the various strands of this opposition were driven together by the development of strategic and diplomatic events to constitute the first major crisis for that policy, in December 1940. Before embarking upon an analysis of that crisis, it is necessary to describe two aspects of the Spanish domestic scene – the political and economic – which had great bearing on the development of events, and British policy, and to chart the diplomatic manoeuvrings of Britain, Germany and Spain in the crucial autumn–winter phase of the war in 1940.

4

The Spanish scene

On 30 October 1940, Colonel-General Franz Halder, Chief of the German Army's General Staff, had a discussion with his staff-intelligence officer, General Kurt von Tippelskirch, and the German Military Attaché in Madrid, Colonel Walter Bruns, about the Spanish situation. Halder was told of the many cleavages which had already appeared in Franco's Civil War coalition. The Army and the Carlists were opposed to the young Falangists, as were the older Falangists. Serrano Suñer was supported only by the young members of the Falange and by Franco. Halder was further informed that Franco's Spain was riven with antagonisms, social dissensions being the sharpest, and nowhere could the renewal of old, or the emergence of new forces be discerned.[1] The very cumbersome title of Francoist Spain's only party, the Falange Española Tradicionalista y de las Juntas de Ofensiva Nacional-Sindicalista (F.E.T.) reflected its hybrid composition.[2] The main institutional groupings in the 1937 merger were the fascist-style Falange and the Carlist Traditionalists, inveterate enemies of modernity. If they were unlikely political partners, they were increasingly joined by even more bizarre associates as more and more Republican territory fell to Franco in the Civil War, and membership of the F.E.T. seemed the only way for ex-anarchists, communists, socialists and democrats to avoid the bloody Nationalist revenge in the conquered zones. By 1940, the result was such an eclectic mélange that Hillgarth could tell Churchill that the F.E.T. was not so much 'totalitarianism but a muddle that baffles description'.[3]

However, as Halder was told, the divisions in Spanish political life were not confined to the F.E.T. A contemporary American journalist noted a four-way division of state power amongst the Army, the Government, independent commissions, with full or limited autonomy from the control of Government departments, and the

72

Falange.[4] Again, differences on policy and principle cut across these institutional lines of cleavage, so that the German Ambassador too, was led to speak, in July 1940, of 'the muddled state of the present political situation'.[5] Thus the potentially most important single political group, the monarchists, had no coherent organisational existence. They, too, were divided. The Carlists, the minority who had supported their pretender from their Navarre stronghold for decades, were notionally members of the F.E.T. but they had left it *en masse* at the close of the Civil War. The mainstream Alfonsist monarchists were well represented in the ranks of the Spanish ruling class but lacked a popular base. Conservatives of all particular nuances were wary of the socially radical aura of the Falange. Hillgarth, and the German Ambassador, von Stohrer, singled out the army as the one stable element in the kaleidoscope of Spanish politics.[6] It certainly was the real power-base of Franco's regime but it, too, was divided on matters of policy and principle, and by personal rivalries.[7] Traditional provincial loyalties, despite the victory of Franco's anti-separatist crusade, and the brutal Nationalist vendetta against their defeated Republican opponents, compounded the picture. Increasing economic enervation and international danger did not help to lend stability to the fragile equilibrium of Spanish politics. Indeed, Nazi Germany's Minister for Propaganda and Popular Enlightenment, Goebbels, was so negatively briefed about Franco's Spain, in November 1940, that he was persuaded to discount its value as a belligerent ally to Germany.[8] His diary entry for 1 November 1940 reads, thus:

Read a very pessimistic report on the present situation in Spain. According to this, the whole country is still in a wild, almost anarchic state of disorder. Franco is not at all in control, and the country is restless, wracked by internal spasms. Symptoms of senility in a former world empire. The present system did not develop organically, but has been imposed.[9]

It was inevitable that the world war would have its impact upon the internal political dissensions of Spain, and that they would assume significance for the belligerent powers. Again there was agreement between both the British and German Ambassadors as to the salient political division in Spain in the months after the fall of France, namely, the rift between Colonel Juan Beigbeder Atienza, Spanish Minister for Foreign Affairs, and Ramón Serrano Suñer, Minister of the Interior (Gobernación), Chairman of the Political Committee of the Falange. Beigbeder had originally been something of a political protégé of Serrano Suñer's, but his apparent enthusiasm for Falangism soon evaporated and they became, as Ministers, bitter rivals. Von

Stohrer explained to the Reich Foreign Ministry that such was the depth of enmity between them that any action attempted by the German Embassy without the prior approval of both Ministers would lead to active obstructionism by the one not consulted.[10] Hoare, too, encountered consistent obstructionist tactics from the Ministry of the Interior when he tried to work through the Ministry of Foreign Affairs.[11]

Conflicting interpretations of the duration and likely result of the war, and consequently, the appropriate Spanish attitude to adopt towards it, became a major factor in defining their political differences. Serrano Suñer, according to his own testimony, believed that a German victory was inevitable, after France fell, and his rival also charged him with holding that the German triumph would come quickly, after a short struggle with the British. Spain, therefore, had to display absolute friendship to Germany, as strict neutrality in such circumstances was at best irrelevant and, at worst, lethal. Appropriate adjustment to Germany's new European order could attain for Spain a more privileged position – for example, by securing the return of Gibraltar and Moroccan expansion – than had been its lot when Britain and France dominated Europe.[12] Beigbeder seemed rather less sure of the imminence, and perhaps even the inevitability, of German victory. He was impressed by a report from the Duke of Alba in late July, stressing British resilience.[13] It was alleged later that he had decided, by the end of June 1940, that a long war was going to ensue. Moreover he appeared pessimistic about the consequences which a German success would entail for Spain.[14]

What is certain is that he rapidly developed a remarkably intimate relationship with Hoare, and within weeks the latter's visits to him had become daily occurrences.[15] Beigbeder had an altercation with Serrano Suñer over the telephone in Hoare's presence during the latter's protest about the *Arriba* press allegations against Britain, of 13 August 1940, mentioned in chapter two. He concluded their meeting by attacking the anti-Christian policy of the German Nazis and denouncing the militant Falangists as 'a gang of ignorant adventurers' using Nazi methods. Next day he told Hoare that there was still a civil war going on in Spain, but in this new kind of civil war a group of Spanish Nazis backed by Ribbentrop opposed the majority of the Council of Ministers, including himself, who were determined to keep Spain out of the war.[16] On the other hand, hardly a week later Beigbeder was assuring the German Ambassador of rampant defeatism in Britain, and renewing Spain's offer to enter the war on Germany's side.[17] However, the weight of evidence seems to suggest that this latter was an example of Spanish diplomatic dissimulation. Indeed, Beigbeder reminded Hoare, on 3 September, that 'we have a monster on our frontier . . . il faut ménager ce monstre'.[18] Beigbeder's Anglophilism appeared to grow increasingly flamboyant. He literally paraded it by strolling arm in arm with Hoare through crowded Madrid streets early in September, and they finished their walk by having a drink at a hotel frequented by many Germans.[19] It was such reckless exhibitionism that led Serrano Suñer later to call him 'mad'.[20] On 27 August 1940, Hoare, describing Beigbeder as 'an emotional romantic', informed Churchill of the relationship which he had managed to establish with the Spanish Foreign Minister, thus:

he [Beigbeder] seems to have taken a great liking for me and appears at any rate to tell me all his innermost thoughts. This is not only my impression. It is what he is telling his staff and his friends in Madrid. He talks to them always of 'Don Samuel' and says openly that he and I understand each other and that we are each dependent on the other. When I go to see him, he shows me the most confidential papers and tells me not only of his conversations with Franco but also of his conversations with the Germans and Italians.[21]

Hoare did admit that Beigbeder had the 'faults of his qualities' and was 'extremely difficult to hold down to any decision'.[22] Nonetheless, he was impressed by Beigbeder's argument that, if Britain only sustained Spain economically, there would be as great a somersault in Spaniards' opinions as had occurred between 1805 and 1808 to transform them into England's allies in the Peninsular War. So Hoare asserted that, even if the Minister for Foreign Affairs could not always control Spanish policy, he was 'at least a good historian'.[23] By 20 September, Hoare was telling Halifax that Beigbeder had almost certainly gone over to the British.[24] There would, apparently, be dramatic confirmation of this view the very next day, as is described in the next chapter. Certainly, it seems that, by mid-September 1940, Beigbeder had become firmly opposed to Spanish belligerency in the Axis interest. Thus, around that time, he told Vichy France's Ambassador in Madrid, Comte Renom de La Baume, of his opposition to the armed intervention of Spain in the war and of his strong hope that such Spanish involvement in the conflict would not occur.[25]

Hoare's first impression of Serrano Suñer was that he was a fanatic, though not necessarily the total partisan of Germany and Italy that he was reputed to be.[26] In fact Serrano was pro-Italian but his German-ophilism seems to have been much more calculated.[27] He certainly was anti-British, and he believed that the alleged failure of the British Embassy to grant his brothers asylum in Republican Madrid, during the Civil War, had been responsible for their deaths.[28] He was ideologically also opposed to the democracies, inveighing against both 'western corruption' (capitalism) and 'asiatic barbarism' (communism). He favoured a kind of authoritarian Catholic corporatism which would endow Nationalist Spain with a juridical foundation, which a simple dictatorship could not supply.[29] Serrano's political skill was admitted by most observers, including both Hoare and von Stohrer.[30] His position as Minister of Gobernación and his dominance in the Falange gave him, under Franco, an unrivalled power-base, with a virtual monopoly on the internal government of his country. However Spanish wits, with an acute insight into the real basis of his power, dubbed him *Cuñadísimo* (brother-in-law-issimo, mimicking Franco's title of *Generalísimo*), for it was his personal relationship with Franco (he was married to the Caudillo's sister-in-law) that was the decisive factor in his pre-eminence. Franco certainly had great need of his political acumen, in his task of producing a viable equilibrium amongst the contradictory and fluid political elements of the 'New' Spain. According to von Stohrer, Serrano had more influence with Franco than any other Spanish politician even though he did not entirely dominate him.[31] The relationship between Franco and Serrano Suñer clearly was never one-way only, but Serrano's very success in enervating the Falange's fascism and whipping the other disparate factions into line rendered him politically vulnerable. The latter function combined with his driving ambition and political zeal to make him extraordinarily unpopular in Spain. Again, British and German sources bear witness to his immense unpopularity, and one historian contends that the only thing uniting the Spanish Generals was their common detestation of Serrano Suñer.[32] Indeed, Admiral Canaris, Chief of the German Abwehr (military security service), told General Halder, on 2 November 1940, that Serrano Suñer could be aptly described as 'the most hated man in Spain'.[33] Moreover, Franco ensured that Serrano Suñer never built up an effectively independent power-base.[34] In a real sense, therefore, Serrano Suñer was a court favourite, a political dependant, for all his ability and apparent power, and when the moment came – as it did in 1942 – even the *Cuñadísimo* could be jettisoned by Franco, despite his vital services in the past. Nevertheless, the British came to regard him as the most dangerous Spanish war-monger in their long struggle to maintain Spain's non-belligerency.[35]

However opportunistic and fruitful Franco's relationship with Serrano was, it may well have been counter-productive. Captain Hillgarth informed Churchill in September 1940 that, in his view,

Franco was considered to have 'betrayed Spain, by complacency rather than by treachery, and to be so much in the power of his brother-in-law as to be past hoping for'.[36] In August, Admiral Canaris, something of an expert on Franco's Spain, told General Halder that Franco had the generals and the clergy against him. In November, he told Halder that Franco had nothing behind him, and that the Caudillo's position was worsened by his involvement with the detested Serrano Suñer.[37] Indeed, the Archbishop of Valladolid, an intimate of General Franco, admitted to an official of the British Embassy in Madrid, that the Caudillo's prestige was definitely on the wane, and that his biggest mistake had been to endow Serrano Suñer with excessive power.[38] Hoare, too, described, in early October 1940, how Franco's 'super royal isolation' was contributing to a decline in his influence.[39]

On the other hand, Hoare needed less than a year in Spain to reach this perceptive conclusion about the Spanish leader's extraordinary instinct for political survival:

General Franco is the Brer Rabbit of dictators. He lies very low, often so low and so long that people think that he is dead or asleep. Then suddenly, when no-one is expecting it, he bobs up and gives evidence of unexpected agility . . . it looks as if he is only forced into active movement when he is in actual danger of being trodden underfoot.[40]

Indeed, as early as July 1940, Hoare had been impressed enough by Franco's resolute action, during the dramatic days as France collapsed, to warn London that the Caudillo and his Government were stronger than mere externals might suggest.[41] Moreover, the impressions of foreign diplomats were not, necessarily, completely authentic reflections of Spanish political realities. However, that the fragility of Franco's rule in 1940 was more than a subjective impression of foreign observers was proven by the objective weakness of its economic base.

In the midst of Hitler's coalition diplomacy of autumn 1940, when Spain appeared well on its way to being assimilated into the Nazi 'New Order' in Europe, a critical, if rather obscure voice, was raised in the very capital of the Reich. For the highly technical Berlin *Bankerarchiv* pointed out that the reluctance of the Spanish Government to enter the war was quite understandable, given their economic circumstances. Citing official Spanish speeches and statistics, it emphasised the 'extremely restricted' extent of the area under cultivation and the scarcity of basic foodstuffs, especially wheat and olive oil. Indicating that railway rolling stock had been reduced to half the pre-civil war total, that the export trade hardly existed, and that gold reserves were totally depleted, it concluded that Spain was 'economically almost annihilated'.[42]

The Spaniards did not disagree with this analysis. On 3 September 1940, officials of the Spanish Ministry of Agriculture told David Eccles that they estimated a harvest shortfall of 1,000,000 tons. The current Spanish harvest would yield no more than 2,600,000 metric tons as against a normal consumption total of 4,000,000 tons (of which 400,000 were normally reserved for seed). Even that could not be distributed throughout Spain due to the disintegrating Spanish transport system, and the fact that there was large-scale hoarding in the wheat-growing provinces. The government Wheat Board had cheated the farmers of these districts the previous year, by failing to keep its promise to replace wheat sent from these wheat-growing provinces to others, by imported wheat, and they were not going to be caught out twice. Eccles estimated that less than 33 per cent of the grain normally made available from the wheat-growing areas could be expected to be drawn therefrom. There was no wheat by early September in Malaga and Huelva, and there were supplies for only seven days in Barcelona and eleven days in Madrid. Admittedly, the Spaniards were asking for British aid when they painted such a gloomy picture, but they requested Eccles to accompany their officials on a provincial tour to prove the awful state of the people, and this with the harvest just in.[43]

In any case, there was abundant evidence to testify to the incapacity of the Spanish economy to perform even its primary function, i.e., keeping the Spanish people alive. In Cádiz and at the huge British-owned Río Tinto mines production fell drastically owing to the undernourished state of the workers. In Seville labourers refused to work overtime on account of physical weakness due to lack of food. The amount of food given to the army ranks was a good barometer of the general alimentary standard as they were, relatively speaking, pampered. By 5 November 1940, three cuts had been made in army rations in Catalonia in six weeks, and in a Dickensian scene the men at a Madrid military barracks demanded 'more' when ordered to leave the dinner-table. Reveille was not until 8.30 in the Spanish Air Force region centred on Seville, since there was no breakfast for the men.[44] Hoare told London accurately, again in November, that the staple food of the poor was chick-peas and such bread as they could get – the bread often being of a miserable quality.[45] Indeed, some of this 'bread' was smuggled out to Britain, analysed and deemed not suitable for human consumption.[46] Even then it was often unavailable. To a visiting Swedish sailor Spain

looked like 'a vast workhouse'.[47] In early November, the British
Consul in Barcelona described conditions there as 'near-famine'.[48] By
December, the German Ambassador was talking of a Spanish famine
and the Rockefeller Institute's mission visiting Europe judged
Spanish conditions to be worse than any which they had encountered
elsewhere on the continent. Hoare spoke of 'the collapse of the whole
national economy'.[49] German officers on their way to reconnoitre
Gibraltar frequently saw people fight fiercely in the streets over
crusts.[50] People were collapsing in the streets of Madrid for want of
nourishment, and soon there were armed robberies of bakeries.[51] The
head of the smelting department at the British-owned mining works
of Río Tinto, saw hundreds of men and women die from 'sheer
starvation'. He also noted how people's limbs swelled up and their
skins changed colour.[52] One of the wretched of the Andalusian earth
remembered the hard times of 1940, thus: 'We had a lot of pain in our
lives, but nothing, ever, like those hungry times after the [Civil]
war.'[53]

Hoare ascribed the main responsibility for Spain's desperate
economic plight to the economic and financial exhaustion consequent upon the Spanish Civil War. This resulted in a complete lack of
funds to build up stocks eliminated by the Civil War, which could
tide Spain over such catastrophes as the harvest shortfall of 1940.[54]
Another devastating legacy of the Civil War was the damage inflicted
upon the internal transport system, especially the railways. The
Spanish Minister of Public works declared, on 31 January 1941, the
day before the nationalisation of the Spanish railways, that 20,000
railway wagons and 1,000 engines had been destroyed in the Civil
War.[55] The severe restrictions imposed by the British on petroleum
imports excluded extensive use of road transportation as an alternative.[56] In general, the international conflict greatly impeded any
Spanish effort at reconstruction. For instance, in regard to a commodity vital to Spanish agriculture, fertiliser production in 1940 was
only 33.6 per cent of its 1929 level.[57]

However, the economic condition of Spain was actually worse by
1940 than in the Civil War period. For impelled by both economic and
ideological exigencies, the Spanish Government had established a
structure of economic control and rationing, which aspired towards
national autarky. The European war might have seemed the ideal
climate for such an attempt at internally controlled, economic
regeneration, but the Spanish Government machine was not equal to
the task. Beigbeder himself had described it to Hoare as 'la plus
detraquée du monde'.[58] But administrative incompetence had an

unfortunate propensity to turn into rampant corruption and peculation in a context of economic scarcity. Thus the Auxilio Social, the Falangist organisation with a monopoly of local relief activities, was both partial and corrupt in carrying them out. For example, when a firm manufacturing condensed milk in Barcelona was heavily fined for selling a quantity of tins at an excessive price, the firm was able to prove that it had previously donated the tins involved to the Auxilio Social, which, instead of distributing them amongst the poor, had sold them. There was often discrimination, too, against known ex-Republicans and their families by the Falange's Auxilio Social in its work.[59] Similarly, the Government's Junta d'Abastos (Supply Council) (responsible for administering such Spanish stocks as did exist) was in popular judgement singularly ill-named. One joke current in Spain in the autumn of 1940 had a perplexed Hitler, at a meeting with Franco, telling the Caudillo, that there seemed no way of beating the British since the German Army, Navy and Air Force could not force them to submit. Franco replied, in the story, 'I'll tell you how to win the war. I'll lend you my Junta d'Abastos; that will starve them out in a week.'[60] Hoare described the latter organisation as 'the best hated body in Spain'. He informed London how the Abastos organisation preyed upon, and exacerbated, the particularism which had bedevilled Spanish history. For, under existing regulations, foodstuffs could not be exported from one province to another without a licence from the Junta d'Abastos. The Junta, in fact, sold these to privileged people, or at huge prices to others. Thus the peasants could not, or did not want, to sell their produce and so was the regionalism of Spanish life increased. So, though many agricultural products were obtainable in the villages around Madrid, they could often not be purchased, or only acquired at twice the price, in the capital itself.[61] Of course, these local variations were aggravated by the prevailing transportation difficulties.

It was inevitable that such a combination of economic scarcity and official control and corruption would create a flourishing black market. Indeed, Spain's version – the *estraperlo* market – virtually superseded the domestic Spanish economy for a period. One visitor to Spain wrote home, in October 1940, as follows: 'It is not exaggerated to say that 50% of the population is starving, another 30% is underfed and the remaining 20% is enjoying life in the most wicked way, and don't care a hang for the howabout of the rest.'[62] On 5 November, Hoare was reporting that the *estraperlo* market had attained 'very large proportions' but he added that, naturally, it was only a refuge for the wealthy and middle classes; the rest of the Spanish people had only 'sullen despair'.[63] The temptation of easy and massive profits on the black market could also divert scarce resources away from productive use, with possibly significant effect on Spain's ability to sustain its people. David Eccles noted how the Spanish fishing industry which had 'supplied the want of meat quite admirably' had ground to a halt, without any fuel for its trawlers, because fishermen sold their 'exiguous [petrol] ration to private motorists at a huge profit'.[64] In October 1940, a framework of courts and special prosecutors was established to deal exclusively with crimes against the rationing laws, including hoarding by private householders. Between then and 30 June 1941, 87,888 charges were made, 1,300 estraperlistas were sentenced to hard labour, fines amounting to 5,500,000 dollars were levied, and goods worth almost a million dollars were seized, all of which gives some indication of the scale of the black market.[65] Indeed, amidst the general economic hardship of later 1940 in Spain, the Francoist authorities realised that conspicuous consumption could be as socially provocative as actual corruption. Thus, in October 1940, the organisers and guests at a banquet in Barcelona who used gold plate in honour of their foreign industrialist visitors were each ordered to pay 10,000 pesetas (c. £250) to charity. For the local authorities deemed their action to be 'incongruous, unaesthetic and unnecessarily ostentatious' and a damage to public order in the existing circumstances.[66]

Even apart from the corruption which so often permeated Spanish state economic controls, the form of some of the controls not only inhibited economic production but actually retarded it. Thus the low official price fixed for wheat was probably largely responsible for reducing the acreage sown with that crop in Spain between 1939, when the Civil War was still in progress, and 1941.[67] Abnormally bad weather compounded human error to increase suffering. The productivity of Spanish agriculture suffered further serious injury not only from the lack of imported fertilisers but also from the unusually severe winter weather of 1940–1, and the relentless drought which extended throughout those two years, and was particularly intense in Andalusia.[68]

The diplomatic significance of Spain's political and economic disarray was grasped early by some German observers. Even in the heady days of June, the Director of the Economic Policy Department in the Third Reich's Foreign Ministry informed the Madrid Embassy that, as Spain could not secure foodstuffs from France or south-eastern Europe, it would have to resign itself to acquiring grain from overseas, and that this fact would be taken account of in German economic negotiations with Spain.[69] Von Stohrer, himself, repeatedly emphasised that Spain's inherent weakness rendered its entry into the war a risky venture which might only result in adding a further burden to the German war effort. So, he continually reiterated that since Spain could not sustain hostilities for more than a few months, its entry into the war should be synchronised as far as possible with an imminent British defeat.[70] Von Stohrer summarised his argument for Berlin, on 6 September 1940, in an assessment which was remarkably similar to Hoare's appraisal at this time:

Spain is militarily and economically weak, politically disunited at home, and therefore incapable of waging a war of more than a few months' duration. All the more so because public opinion in Spain since the 3-year Civil War is averse to new warlike complications.

Spain's entry into the war ought therefore to be as late as possible . . .[71]

Von Stohrer, indeed, wanted Walter Schellenberg of the Nazi foreign espionage service to try and deflate Berlin's optimism about Spanish prospects, when the latter returned to the German capital from a mission in Madrid.[72] Admiral Canaris was also pessimistic about the value of a Spanish alliance.[73] The Spaniards, too, had qualified their June offer to Germany to enter the war, with demands for massive prior deliveries of economic necessities and military equipment.[74] Some subsequent commentators have argued that Franco early on realised the absolute limits imposed on him by the political and economic instability of his country and that, determined to avoid entry into the war, he gave verbose pledges to the Axis to join their fight, but successfully evaded doing so by making his action contingent upon a previous scale of aid from Germany which the latter could never in fact supply. In this view, Franco deliberately set too high a price on his belligerency in order to avoid ever having to sell it.[75] The certainty with which this view has often been advanced is a little surprising. Nevertheless, there is something of a consensus amongst the British expert witnesses on the influence of Spain's weakness on Franco's freedom of diplomatic manoeuvre. We have already noted how Hoare had decided, by July 1940, that if Franco was to survive in power, he had to preserve Spain's neutrality. Sir John Lomax argues in his memoirs that the failure of the 1940 harvest was the decisive factor in keeping Franco out of the war, since it made Spain dependent upon external sources of food supply, and they were controlled by Britain.[76] Sir Maurice Peterson, as has been noted, also claimed that Spain's condition was such as to preclude the possibility of belligerency.[77] Even Captain Alan Hillgarth came to feel retrospectively that there was never any real chance of Spain entering the war, as long as Britain suffered no apparently irrevocable reverse, like the loss of Egypt.[78] Lord Eccles, too, maintains that Franco's commitment to neutrality was authentic and that his dalliance with the Axis in late 1940 was a delaying tactic, employed to avoid actual engagement in their war effort.[79]

In spite of this impressive agreement amongst British observers, it has been indicated in chapter one that there is solid evidence to suggest that Franco attempted to join the Axis band for what he regarded as the kill, in June 1940. Moreover, an examination of Spain's diplomatic performance in the autumn of 1940, which is the central theme of the next chapter, will reveal another effort by Franco to link his country's fortunes with those of Germany. It will be argued that it was the niggardly German reaction to this attempt, rather than Spain's dilapidated state, which rescued it from involvement in the war. Ultimately, Hitler did find Spain's asking price too high, but its exorbitance stemmed not from deliberate Spanish intent, but from what Serrano Suñer has termed their 'great good luck' (*gran fortuna*) that 'Germany did not see how to, or would not, or could not pay [it]'.[80]

5

Strategic diplomacy: September–October, 1940

It has been noted already, in chapter two, that the German Government did not respond positively to Franco's later June offer to go to war on the Axis side. Berlin had preferred to wait upon events, to see if Spanish services could really be of use against Britain before any Nazi effort was made to purchase them. However, Britain's stubborn refusal to lay down its arms, and the formidable resistance offered by the Royal Air Force to Göring's attempts to bomb the British into submission, or to establish the Luftwaffe's mastery in their skies which would have enabled the Germans to undertake Operation 'Sea Lion', caused Nazi grand strategists to indulge in some agonising reappraisals, in the early autumn of 1940.[1] German army and navy advocates of a peripheral strategy against Britain, as an alternative to the perilous Channel crossing and frontal assault on the English mainland, emphasised the advantages of attacking British imperial outposts, particularly Gibraltar and the Suez Canal, in conjunction with the Spaniards and the Italians. Such a Mediterranean campaign could turn that sea into an Axis lake, ensure peace and quiet in the Balkans, secure the Middle East and its raw materials for Britain's enemies, and open up new offensive opportunities in the Atlantic and Central Asia.[2] This strategic conception coincided with the idea of the Nazi Foreign Minister, von Ribbentrop, for the creation of a huge continental coalition of powers, stretching from Norway to North Africa, which could act in concert to eliminate such British strongpoints as Gibraltar and generally intimidate Britain, and its non-belligerent ally, the United States of America.[3] It was apparently this latter logic which inspired von Ribbentrop to inform von Stohrer, as early as 2 August 1940, that Germany now wanted 'Spain's early entry into the war'.[4] Indeed, long before the aerial Battle of Britain reached its climax, on 15 September, and before Hitler postponed 'Sea Lion' indefinitely, on 17 September, the Führer had been persuaded to give serious consideration to strategic options other than an attempted invasion of England. The possible extension of German operations against British forces to North Africa and the Mediterranean conferred a new strategic importance upon Franco's Spain in German eyes as the avenue to Gibraltar and North Africa. Thus, in late August to early September 1940, Hitler appeared, to his army advisers, to have decided to 'rope Spain in', and to his naval advisers, to have resolved on capturing the Rock of Gibraltar from the British, an action which 'should not be considered of secondary importance, but as one of the main blows against Britain'.[5] The diplomatic prospects for such military developments also seemed promising in the early autumn of 1940, with both Spanish Foreign Minister Beigbeder and Franco impressing the Germans as anxious to enter the war alongside the Axis.[6] So, 'in order to discuss with a leading responsible Spanish statesman the question of Spain's possible entry into the war', Berlin granted Serrano Suñer's long-expressed desire to visit the Reich, and Franco's Minister of the Interior arrived in the German capital on 16 September 1940.[7]

Inevitably, the visit of the Spanish mission, under Serrano Suñer, to Berlin appeared to be an ominous development to the British. The Spanish explanation that this was a visit of a party official rather than a statesman was hardly very reassuring.[8] Certainly, the American Government was disturbed by Serrano's mission and, as will be seen in chapter six, adopted a 'go slow' policy on the large-scale economic aid which the Spanish Government had sought from Washington in early September.[9] British fears, however, were soon assuaged by a stream of information which they received from Spanish sources about the visit, information which was, in fact, remarkably accurate.

Some of this information throws light upon the motives behind the Spanish mission. Hoare was told in October by an 'A1' source, whose informant was the 'secretary' of Serrano's mission, that the real reason for the trip was that Franco and the Minister of the Interior had agreed that Britain would succumb to Germany's air attacks within a few weeks, and that Spain would have to enter the war to get its share of the spoils.[10] Franco had also told General von Richthofen, Commander of the Seventh German Air Corps, on 9 September 1940, that he thought German air attacks would break British defensive power within a few weeks. He mentioned, however, his anxiety over Spanish belligerency in a long war and stated his economic and military requirements for entry into the war.[11] According to the reports received by the British, Serrano Suñer was to offer Spain's belligerency only after he was fully certain that Britain was definitely destined for defeat, and when he had also obtained a positive German response to Spanish demands for French Morocco and Oran.[12] This indication of Spanish policy appears to be borne out by other evidence as well. Thus, the German Army Staff's report of 10 August 1940 – which seems to bear the mark of Canaris's influence – concluded that on account of Spain's weakness, its entry into the war could only be expected, if 'German–Italian successes should permit the expectation of a quick, certain and riskless attainment of Spanish aims'.[13] Again, Serrano Suñer declared, in 1945, that Spanish policy had been 'to enter the war at [the] end, at the hour of the last cartridges'.[14] The previous 19 June offer to enter the war on Germany's side seems to be explained well, too, by this interpretation: Franco was offering to fight precisely because he thought that the conflict was about to end. Again, Serrano Suñer has claimed, subsequently, that this was precisely the motivation behind Spanish foreign policy, in later June 1940:

We were convinced then that the war was over, that we must not waste time. We thought that if Spain participated in the war even though it were merely [for] a week, its rights and its credit at the Peace Conference would be very different than if it simply limited itself to applauding, which is what we were doing.[15]

Before departing for Germany Serrano Suñer gave an interview to a German newspaper in which he made some important declarations on Spanish policy, and that interview was published in full in *Arriba* while he was in Berlin. He expressed the purpose of his mission, thus: 'The Empire which we have announced as the object of our policy cannot, in our times, be an individual undertaking, but rather must be an enterprise of various concurrent wills . . .'[16] Condemning the old European order which had denied Spain 'honour, legitimate expansion, and simple independence', he asserted that Gibraltar as 'a part of the living and torn flesh of the Motherland' was owed to Spain by elementary justice. He went on to refer to the other focus of Spain's territorial ambitions, Morocco, in this manner: 'Spain's geographical position and tradition as a projection of one continent towards another possesses natural demands which only a decadent policy could abandon to the usurpation of other peoples. This is our natural expansion.'[17] Spain's imperial aspirations were also aired in an editorial of the Falange's *Arriba*, on 14 September 1940, which contrasted the alleged renaissance of the Moroccans under Spanish rule, with the economic and social degradation of those ruled by France, and spoke of the 'decomposition of authority and political effectiveness' in French Morocco. The implication was obvious:

Spaniards should replace the decadent and despotic French and 'protect' all Morocco. Serrano Suñer has also maintained that the Moroccan question was the key influence governing Franco's foreign policy in the autumn of 1940: 'In that Moroccan enterprise Franco united and identified his ideals and his country's necessities at that time.'[18] According to Serrano, if Hitler had agreed to the Spaniards' North African territorial demands, Spain would have gone to war on the Axis side.[19]

Thus, there is now extant a substantial body of evidence to suggest that Franco was seriously considering entry into the war in September. His approach was characteristically cautious and conditional. Spain was not capable of waging sustained war, and involvement in a contest of endurance would risk destruction of the Caudillo's rule. Neither ideological solidarity nor a sense of indebtedness for vital aid during the Spanish Civil War was likely to sway Franco's calculations in such dangerous circumstances. Anyway, the Germans had driven too hard a bargain for their help, and were also demanding too large a reimbursement, to have gained any lien on Franco's loyalty.[20] But abstention from the struggle of his Civil War allies might be just as risky for Franco, as premature alliance with them. It certainly would put paid to any *africanista* hopes of securing the coveted North African territories from grateful Axis hands. The satisfaction of the irredentist claim against Gibraltar also required German firepower. From this array of conflicting hopes and fears a policy emerged, designed to ensure maximum profit with minimum peril. It was surely preferable that Spain should remain aloof from the conflict until it was clear that the British cause was all but lost. Yet it might prove rather difficult to discern precisely when Britain was on the verge of collapse, as the experience of the previous June taught. As has just been noted, it seems that it was Franco's very instinct that the British were on the brink of disaster in their aerial duel with the Germans, in September 1940, that inspired his renewed zeal for a Spanish commitment to the Axis war effort then. Thus, the Caudillo wrote to Serrano Suñer, on 23 September 1940, of his belief that the German aerial 'bombardments' of Britain were 'of the greatest effectiveness' and would 'succeed in overturning the English attitude'.[21] However, Franco was also informed, by late September, that the Germans themselves had now come to doubt the imminent possibility of delivering a knock-out blow to England. He detected implicit German acknowledgement that a long war was becoming ever more likely.[22] Spain must not be too hasty. Yet, equally, to wait too long might entail missing the boat altogether. Franco hit upon this stratagem to resolve this diplomatic dilemma: Spain would hitch itself to the invincible Axis bandwagon, in secret, postponing its actual entry into the war until it had been bolstered by such prior deliveries of military and economic aid from the Axis, as would carry it safely through a short fight. Franco's Spain only needed formal recognition by its future military partners of its African territorial aspirations to ensure that brief participation in the closing stages of their struggle would yield the desired reward.

Franco expressed his diplomatic strategy to the emissary whom he had sent to Berlin, Serrano Suñer, on 21 September 1940, thus: '. . . we ought now to be involved within [the Axis], that is with recognised rights, so as to be ready within the least time to confront any situation which would oblige us to act quickly, unleashing the attack, always with the guarantee of supplies.'[23] It is interesting to note here, that even when he appears to have been moving in the direction of alliance with Germany, Franco may have wished to keep other options open. So, in early September the Spanish Government also approached the United States Government with a request for economic aid, as is noted in the next chapter.[24] The balance between the exigencies of Spain's political and economic situation, and the desire for territorial aggrandisement, was a delicate one. Indeed, these apparently conflicting interests might even be connected. Thus, Serrano Suñer told his German hosts that a foreign adventure could consolidate the Franco regime's shaky position at home.[25] Franco was above all a survivor. He avoided absolute stances and, in his determination to survive, he was both wary of, and sought active alliance with, Germany.

The British were not kept in suspense long over the Serrano Suñer mission to Berlin. They were soon informed by their 'A1' source, who based his reports on discussions with both the secretary of Serrano Suñer's mission, and the Caudillo's brother, Nicolás Franco, that the Germans had 'contemptuously' brushed aside Spain's territorial claims. Germany had, apparently, made demands for important economic concessions in any future grant of Morocco to Spain, and also demanded the right to assume ownership of major foreign concerns within Spain itself, such as the Río Tinto Company. Though not given many other details, it was clear to the British that Serrano Suñer had been disgusted by the whole experience.[26] On 8 October 1940, Beigbeder told Hoare, truthfully, that the Germans had made an effort to tempt Serrano Suñer into the continental bloc, showing him maps of Europe and expounding to him the concept of a

Eurafrican hemisphere dominated by Germany. Beigbeder described their plan, which he said included the management of all Spain's surplus products by Berlin, as 'wild megalomania'.[27]

Ribbentrop and Hitler had indeed elaborated such a grandiose scheme to Serrano Suñer in their discussions with him. But they had gone further. For they demanded – Ribbentrop had done so explicitly, Hitler implicitly – the cession by Spain of one of the Canary Islands to Germany for the defence of the strategic perimeter of this bi-continental bloc against a potential threat from the Americans.[28] Indeed, in a letter, of 18 September 1940, to Franco, Hitler not only stated the need for, and manner of, Spanish participation in the war. He also underlined the strategic significance of the Canary Islands for the German war effort:

1   The war will decide the future of Europe. There is not a country in Europe that can avoid its political and economic effects. The end of the war will also decide Spain's future, perhaps for centuries. But even today Spain is suffering, though she is still not a participant in the war. The virtual blockade imposed on Spain by England will not be loosened as long as England herself is not conquered, but will only become more severe. In the face of this, any measures for economic assistance can only be of an emergency and temporary nature. But the mere expulsion of the English from the Mediterranean will convert it into an inland sea withdrawn from English interference and again open for commerce. This alone would provide a radical solution to Spain's supply problem. And this aim can and will be attained rapidly and with certainty through Spain's entry into the war.

2   Spain's entry into the war on the side of the Axis Powers must begin with the expulsion of the English fleet from Gibraltar and immediately thereafter the seizure of the fortified rock.
      This operation must and can be successfully carried through within a few days, if high-grade, well-tried, modern means of attack and attack troops are employed. Germany is willing to provide them under Spanish command in the quantities needed.

3   Once Gibraltar is in Spanish possession the western Mediterranean is eliminated as a base of operations for the English fleet. Aside from the threat from isolated British submarines, then possible only to a limited extent, a sure connection will have been brought about between Spain and North Africa (Spanish Morocco). The Spanish Mediterranean coast itself will then no longer be endangered. . . .

6   It is . . . probable, however, that after losing Gibraltar England will try instead to seize a naval base on the Canary Islands. Therefore, the defensive power of the islands in the Canary group which might be considered for naval bases must be strengthened in so far as possible *before* the start of the war. Either before or at the latest at the same time as the beginning of the war it will in my opinion be necessary to transfer

German dive bombers or long-range fighters to Palmas. Past experience
has shown that they provide the *absolute* certainty of keeping the British
ships far away. Preparations for this should best be made before the
beginning of the war.[29]

Moreover, the German leadership had shown scant regard for
Francoist sensibilities when presented with the Caudillo's territorial
demands (for Morocco, Oran, the expansion of Río de Oro and the
favourable rectification of the Pyrenean frontier with France). The
Nazis had allowed that Morocco might fall to Spain, but only subject
to German economic claims there being met, and the granting of two
bases to Germany. Even then, German 'magnanimity' over Morocco
was qualified by the requirement that it should be balanced by Spain's
handing over its Central African colonies of Spanish Guinea and
Fernando Po to form part of the projected German-owned region
there. So, far from securing all they asked for, the Spaniards were
being asked to cede territory.[30]

The Spaniards were appalled by this German reaction to their
démarche. Serrano Suñer complained bitterly to Ciano, the Italian
Foreign Minister, in Rome, where he went on leaving Berlin, about
the 'absolute lack of tact' displayed by the Germans towards Spain.[31]
On being informed by his emissary of the German demand for a
Canary Island, Franco expressed his total aversion to the idea, declaring that it had 'justly provoked' Serrano's anger and likening the
injury which it would do to future relations with Germany, to the
damage caused to Anglo-Spanish relations by the Gibraltar question.[32] Serrano Suñer also told Ribbentrop that Franco had been
'distressed in a friendly way' by the German claim for Moroccan
bases and Franco himself, wrote to the Führer that, in the Spanish
view, such bases were unnecessary and superfluous.[33] Again, while
Franco acknowledged in his letter to Hitler that 'the presence of dive
bombers and long-range fighters, in Las Palmas' would be 'extremely
useful' to safeguard against 'the possibility of a surprise attack on the
Canary Islands by the English', he pointedly ignored the German
request for the cession of one island amongst the archipelago as a base
for their forces.[34] Serrano Suñer, in fact, specifically rejected Germany's demands for the cession of a Canary Island, Spanish Guinea
and Fernando Po, and Moroccan bases.[35]

Nor were the Spaniards happy about the neo-colonial economic
demands, articulated by the Germans, during the visit of the Serrano
Suñer mission to Berlin, to inherit French and British mining enter-

prises in Spain. Serrano Suñer had singled out the huge British owned Río Tinto mining concern from amongst those which the Germans claimed, as an 'economic Gibraltar', wrested from Spain in a period of shameful national weakness, and which it was honour-bound to regain for itself. He avoided any definite commitments to Ribbentrop over these economic demands, too.[36] He was truly implementing his chief's wishes in thus evading large-scale economic concessions to Germany. Franco was discontented enough about the German request to share in Moroccan mineral production, and he regarded Berlin's effort to establish an entrenched position in the Spanish economy proper, by acquiring control of British and French holdings and through other means, as 'unacceptable . . . in all its parts', as completely 'incompatible with the grandeur and independence of a Nation'. Franco attributed such excessive pretensions to 'German exaltation'.[37] The Caudillo, indeed, deprecated the general under-estimation of Spain's sacrifices for, and potential value to, the Nazi 'New Order' which Serrano Suñer's reports, from the Reich's capital, indicated as being prevalent in German Government circles. He even wanted his representative to remind the Germans how invaluable a testing-ground for their weapons and tactics Spain had so recently been, thus contributing 'not negligibly', according to Franco's rather brutal logic, to their victorious campaign against France.[38] Franco did derive some consolation from his own impression that Hitler's personal attitude towards Spain was more appreciative and sympathetic than that revealed by Ribbentrop and other Germans. The Caudillo was, however, deceiving himself on this point, as Serrano Suñer has pointed out.[39] A meeting with the German leader a few weeks later rapidly disabused him of such a notion.

Having been pressed during a conversation with Ribbentrop, on 24 September 1940, to declare his Government's willingness to conclude a ten-year military alliance with Germany and Italy, Serrano Suñer responded by presenting an unsigned memorandum to the Germans three days later. This document was, apparently, a Spanish draft of a secret protocol for such a military alliance between Spain and the Axis powers, and it embodied Franco's design to have his territorial ambitions formally recognised, while retaining the freedom to enter the war in his own time. The Spanish draft stipulated that, in return for its commitment to future belligerency, Spain should have its right to Gibraltar, Morocco and Oran acknowledged, and be permitted a period of Axis-aided preparation for war. Only agreement among the three powers that this preparatory phase was complete would activate the alliance. The memorandum, then, contained a draft commitment that Spain would fight, but reiterated its territorial demands as pre-conditions of its belligerency, and left Franco with the power to decide when – and therefore, if – to fight.[40] The Spanish draft protocol was filed away in the archives of the German Foreign Ministry. The Spanish mission to Berlin, of September 1940, produced no more concrete result. The basic issues in Hispano-German relations still remained to be determined and were postponed until the personal meeting between the Führer and the Caudillo which was to take place in the near future, at Hitler's request.[41]

The impact of the offhand German treatment of Franco's diplomatic advances upon the evolution of Spain's foreign policy may be assessed, it seems, as follows. Franco's disappointment, along with the growing signs that a protracted conflict was in prospect, probably did quench his apparent early September desire to go to war in the near future. But his wish to be in at the kill remained. Serrano Suñer claimed, soon after the war, that on comprehending German reluctance to satisfy the Spanish ambition for Morocco, he himself concluded that, 'thenceforward', they 'could not indulge in wishful thinking but had to shelter intransigently [behind their] claims'. He linked his alienation from the Germans on this issue with his first conversation with Ribbentrop, on 16 September, and maintained that Franco, on being informed of German recalcitrance over this vital matter, adopted an identical stance.[42] Again, when, on a guided tour of the battlefields of Belgium and France, during an interval in the Berlin talks, Serrano Suñer concluded that a long war was in prospect, he decided that the Spanish Government must 'take up a position and gain time'.[43] There is also evidence amongst the British diplomatic archives, cited below, to indicate that Franco had by early October 1940, resolved to keep Spain out of the war for the foreseeable future – that is, under this interpretation, to refrain from entering a struggle which no longer looked as if it were near its end. Yet, it is also evident that Franco pursued throughout October his project of binding Spain to the Axis in a contractual relationship: in a pact that was formal enough to enshrine recognition of Spain's North African expansion, but secret and indefinite enough to leave it the freedom of action to join, or abstain from, the fray as it chose in the developing circumstances. Franco's basic intent was to be associated with the Axis, in order to share in its apparently ineluctable triumph, but to avoid being precipitated into a perilous place in the firing-line. 'It is important for us to be within [the Axis] but not to rush,' he had advised Serrano Suñer, on 21 September.[44] As a consummate survivor, caught between the hammer of domestic crisis and the anvil of international opportunity, Franco strove to defer the stark 'either/or' choice for peace or war, which was fraught with such immediate danger. He wanted to wait upon events, but to be so situated as to be guaranteed – through belated participation in the war – a part of the spoils, at the moment of German victory. The rationale behind Franco's diplomatic manoeuvrings, subsequent to the German rebuff to his September overtures, was candidly explained by Nicolás Franco to Oliveira Salazar, on 16 October 1940. The Spanish Ambassador, recently returned from talks with his brother, spoke to the Portuguese Prime Minister, at the Caudillo's suggestion, in the following terms: '. . . war for Spain means blockade . . . entry into war should be . . . a counterbalance of concerns and necessities. Spain needs to recover; everything else must be subordinate to this, without prejudice to [its] being, at a moment of downfall, in a position to be able to give a shove which would aid its objectives.'[45]

Given the disposition on Franco's part to enter into some form of bond with the Axis, a careful diplomatic courtship by Germany might have drawn the Spaniards into the war, at Hitler's convenience, before they could pull back. What is remarkable is not that the Germans did not succeed in such a subtle enterprise, but that they never really made the attempt.

Initially, the Germans had been inclined to charm Spain into active alignment with the Axis. Thus, Halder noted on 14 September 1940, that Hitler had declared that Spain should be promised all it wanted for its war effort, even if Germany could not provide it.[46] The same cynical motivation inspired Hitler's diplomatic 'grand tour', of late October 1940, when he tried by a self-confessed 'grandiose deceit', so to reconcile competing territorial jealousies amongst Italy, Vichy France and Spain, as to constitute a great European and Mediterranean bloc against Britain.[47] In view of the rather intractable nature of this problem, Hitler had early on to define the particular priority to be attached to recruiting each of these powers into his continental coalition. Spanish belligerency had an obvious significance as part of an indirect strategy against Britain, allowing for an assault on, and the sealing of, the western end of the Mediterranean, but such a Nazi 'war on the periphery' only appealed to Hitler as a temporary expedient for the winter of 1940–1.[48] The really important contribution a belligerent Spain could make to the German war effort was a negative, preventive one. For, Hitler reasoned, the security of France's North

African colonies against British and Gaullist machinations would be guaranteed once there was 'a reliable bridge' to North Africa via a belligerent Spain.[49] However, the combined effect in September 1940, of the unsatisfactory Berlin negotiations with Serrano Suñer and the stout Vichy French resistance at Dakar led to a revaluation. Now it was necessary, Hitler told the Italians, to balance very carefully the pros and cons of collaboration with Franco. He now termed Spain 'a very dubious bridge to North Africa'.[50] It certainly did not make sense to try to secure this shaky route to North Africa by promising slices of the French possessions there to Spain. For such a promise was bound to leak out and would provoke the very anti-German movement in the French North African Empire, against which Spanish assistance was meant to provide insurance.[51]

Hitler's personal visitations of late October 1940 were an exercise in diplomatic reconnaissance to ascertain whether this conundrum could be solved. It is probably the case, as Norman Rich argues, that Hitler had not decided on the vital necessity of a Spanish entry into the war even at the time of his late October trip.[52] Meeting with Mussolini, on 12 February 1941, Franco told the Italian of the negative Nazi response to the Spanish offer of the previous September, to go to war: 'Germany did not attach much importance to Spanish intervention, and raised the question of economic concessions (mines, banking concerns, etc.) which did not make a good impression on the Spanish . . . while Serrano referred to territorial aspirations and claims, the Germans spoke more of economic concessions.'[53] This goes far to explain the crudeness of the diplomatic treatment meted out to Serrano Suñer in Berlin, which so thoroughly alienated the Spaniards. For, it was less the strategic facilities offered by Spain for the pursuit of German offensive operations against the British, than the strategic security which the Spaniards could provide against British intervention in vulnerable areas of the Axis zone of influence, which really interested Hitler. Thus, Spanish belligerency only became essential when Italy suffered its Greek disaster in November, thereby exposing Germany's vital oil supplies in Rumania to British bomber attack and creating a general military threat. Then it was absolutely necessary to close the Mediterranean, in Hitler's view, and consequently he avidly sought Franco's participation in the war.[54] By then, of course, not only had the Spaniards long been alienated by Germany's diplomacy, but the very developing strategic difficulties of the Axis were further cause for shunning Hitler's urgent pleas.

If Hispano-German relations were marked by such dramatic

exchanges in the September of 1940, Britain's relations with Spain were, late in that month, also to be characterised by drama, even melodrama. This, indeed, would concentrate British attention upon positive aspects of Anglo-Spanish relations despite the Serrano Suñer visit to Berlin. In London, Halifax prepared a paper for presentation to his Cabinet colleagues on the Spanish problem. It demonstrated the well-nigh total coincidence of his views on Spain with those of Hoare. The paper was designed as a programme to counter the advantages which Falangist proponents of Spanish belligerency claimed would accrue from active alignment with Nazi Germany. There should be a public statement about Gibraltar similar to the instructions over the Rock sent to Hoare in the previous June.[55] However, Halifax, as he told Hoare, doubted whether Churchill could be persuaded to agree to such a public declaration on Gibraltar.[56] Similarly, the Spaniards could be assured of Britain's desire to see Morocco remain peaceful and Franco-Spanish differences over their zones settled only between them. The paper emphasised, however, that Britain's primary power of persuasion was economic: Spain's Government could be certain that as long as it 'remained relatively independent of the Axis, its people could be sure of bread and a measure of economic security'.[57] Before Halifax could circulate his paper it was overtaken by events, and it was never, in fact, discussed by the War Cabinet.

On Saturday, 21 September 1940, Colonel Beigbeder invited Sir Samuel Hoare for a drive to a deserted and ruined villa on the outskirts of Madrid where he talked to the British Ambassador for almost two hours with great 'frankness and even indiscretion'. Beigbeder told Hoare that they were at a turning-point in Spanish policy. For the struggle which had been going on within the Spanish Government, between the party of the 'short war' led by Serrano Suñer and that of the 'long war' led by himself, seemed very likely to be resolved in the near future, in favour of the latter. Nevertheless, Beigbeder contended, since a long war was such a daunting prospect for Spain, and would afford the Germans the opportunity of blaming the British for the continued hostilities and even of accusing them of wanting to re-install a 'red' government, the British must attempt to consolidate the position of the 'long war' party. The Minister called for wireless propaganda about the progress of economic negotiations with Spain, and a radio statement on Anglo-Spanish political relations. The statement should aim 'to keep Spain out of the continental bloc and make it clear that she can hope for a future outside it'. Hoare affirmed that Morocco rather than Gibraltar was the real object of Beigbeder's territorial ambitions. Beigbeder thought such a statement would induce Spain to take the correct way at the crossroads before it, and might so fortify the Spanish Government that it would reject future German demands. Even if the Government's nerve did fail, a body of national resentment against German intrusion would be formed and the result would be another Peninsular War (i.e., a joint Anglo-Spanish fight against the invader). At best, it might even be possible to develop a triple alliance of Britain, Spain and Portugal.[58]

This development underlined the importance of a political and territorial understanding with Spain, which had already been raised in those September days by the unfolding Dakar operation and its possible follow-up in Morocco. Hoare did not miss the chance to urge the significance of an official British expression of sympathy with Spanish Moroccan aspirations. He told Halifax that Beigbeder's argument carried the conviction of a convert to the British cause whose own political survival was now linked with theirs. The British Ambassador articulated the three major issues at stake: the strengthening of the position of Beigbeder and his allies in Government, the consolidation of anti-German feelings, and the fact that the Iberian Peninsula, the last corner of continental Europe outside the Nazi continental bloc, could be kept from slipping into it.[59] He agreed with Beigbeder that a crucial turning-point had been reached, 'at which we must take big decisions', as he told Halifax.[60]

Halifax proved a vigorous champion of Hoare's line. Forwarding Hoare's account of the meeting with Beigbeder to Churchill, he supported the Ambassador's advice that Beigbeder's requests be met. He, also, seized the opportunity to urge upon the Prime Minister the main policy demand of the Cabinet paper which he had been preparing. This was his counsel that Hoare be given greater authority to settle minor blockade matters which caused 'so much irritation to the not so business-like Spaniards'. Halifax told Churchill that the Ministry of Economic Warfare appeared to have lost their sense of real proportion in the matter: the Spanish economy was so weak and stunted as to obviate the chance of any real leakage of goods to Germany. He continued, that to eliminate the 'major political risk' involved in the constant irritation caused by the blockade, he required a greater derogation of authority to the Madrid Embassy to 'smooth its day to day application'. Hoare's 'magnificent work in Madrid' deserved the Government's complete support, he claimed.[61]

Churchill readily agreed that Hoare should be delegated authority to settle minor blockade disputes on his own initiative, since he considered it preferable to buy the Spanish off by economic favours than by promises over Gibraltar. He, also, agreed that Hoare should stay as long as possible in Madrid since he was achieving so much. He continued, as follows:

I do not mind if the Spaniards go into French Morocco. The letters exchanged with De Gaulle do not commit us to any exact restoration of the territories of France, and the attitude of Vichy Government towards us and towards him has undoubtedly justified a harder feeling towards France than existed at the time of her collapse. I would far rather see the Spaniards in Morocco than the Germans . . . Indeed, I think, you should let them know that we shall be no obstacle to their Moroccan ambitions, provided they preserve their neutrality in the war.[62]

Under such powerful direction, it is hardly surprising, then, that the War Cabinet agreed to a public statement on Anglo-Spanish relations, including a reference to British benevolence towards Spain's Moroccan ambitions. The Cabinet also acceded to the Foreign Office request that Hoare should be empowered to settle on his own authority blockade details concerning ships and cargoes, which seemed a substantial gain for him in his running fight with Dalton. However, Halifax and Dalton had discussed blockade policy towards Spain prior to the Cabinet meeting and the agreement they reached, which was announced by the Foreign Secretary to the War Cabinet, was considered by the Minister of Economic Warfare to be 'a distinct victory over Hoare's attempted aggression against my blockade'. The real result of these discussions was to leave the effective operation of the blockade centred in London but Hoare was mollified with the assurance that, where Spain was concerned, it would be administered with as much speed and goodwill as possible.

The War Cabinet was ready also to allow Hoare to tell Beigbeder expressly, in private, that Britain was 'in principle sympathetic to the Spanish case' over Moroccan zones, which was more than Hoare had sought in the draft public statement which he had sent to London. To go so far in the public statement, Halifax thought, would alienate de Gaulle and Vichy. On the other hand, the Cabinet did baulk at including a specific reference to their readiness to discuss Gibraltar with the Spaniards after the war, in their public statement, which Hoare had suggested. Halifax did advocate Hoare's case before the Cabinet, which prompted Hugh Dalton to note that, without Cadogan, who was away on leave, the Foreign Secretary tended to have 'wild and woolly ideas'. There was unanimous opposition to Halifax in Cabinet, Churchill, adhering to his stance of the previous June, making this declaration: 'Does anyone think that if we win the war, opinion here will consent to hand over Gibraltar to the Dons? and, if we lose, we shall not be consulted.' In addition, it was felt that such a passage in the statement would provoke such parliamentary and public criticism as to destroy any impression of British goodwill for Franco, and supply damaging propaganda material to Germany. Halifax seemed to bow before this Cabinet unanimity.[63]

Undaunted, however, Halifax soon brought the question before the Cabinet again, arguing that the omission of any reference to Gibraltar would deprive the statement of most of its value. He therefore advocated a general reference to questions of 'special interest' to Spain and the consideration with which Britain was prepared to treat them. Again, Cabinet opposition to Halifax emphasised how public demands for elucidation could make the whole statement counter-productive. Nevertheless, the Cabinet eventually accepted a reworded version of such a general allusion, and was even persuaded by Halifax to accept a further addition to it suggested by Hoare.[64] The relevant passage finally read as follows:

His Majesty's Government are anxious to secure to Spain her rightful place in Europe as one of the great Mediterranean powers and it is in this spirit and in the belief that all outstanding questions can be settled amicably between the two countries that His Majesty's Government would approach any discussions which may appear desirable after the conclusion of hostilities.[65]

The approved public statement also followed the main lines suggested by Hoare, and, for the most part, even adopted his very phraseology. It noted the progress in Anglo-Spanish economic negotiations, ensuring that Spain could preserve its 'economic independence outside both the blockade and the continental bloc'. It reiterated Britain's firm adherence to non-interference in Spain's internal affairs and, apart from the generalised reference to Gibraltar cited above, recognised Spain's 'direct and legitimate' interest in North Africa, particularly Morocco, which the British Government wished to remain peaceful and prosperous. Moroccan questions, it concluded, should be decided exclusively between France and Spain.[66]

Meanwhile, in Madrid, Spanish policy did appear to be taking the direction that Beigbeder had forecast. For, in a state of great excitement, he told Hoare, on 4 October 1940, that for the first time since the latter had come to Madrid, he could give him a 'definite assurance' that Spain was not going to join the Axis Powers at war. He also said that Serrano Suñer had been completely disillusioned by his Berlin visit, and that the only danger now lay in a German ultimatum demanding a right of passage through Spain. The growing anti-German forces in Spain would have to be fostered by every means to resist such a Nazi demand.[67] The day before, Colonel Beigbeder had telegraphed the Spanish High Commission in Tetuán, Morocco, thus: 'I have got all I want.' The Commissioner phoned the Colonel of the Spanish forces at Tangier to inform him that Beigbeder had won, and Spain would not enter the war.[68]

The situation, then, appeared particularly favourable for making the statement public, and the intention in London was for Churchill to do so during his adjournment debate speech in the House of Commons, on 8 October. At Beigbeder's request, however, the publication was postponed until after the middle of the month, since German propaganda had claimed that the war would be over by then. It was re-scheduled for release, on 22 October.[69] Churchill did make a general reference to Spain in his speech, in which he expressed complete willingness to readjust the British blockade to facilitate Spain's recovery, and the intention to avoid interfering in Spanish domestic affairs. He concluded, thus: 'As in the days of the Peninsular War, British interests and policy are based on the independence and unity of Spain, and we look forward to seeing her take her rightful place both as a great Mediterranean Power and as a leading and famous member of the family of Europe and Christendom. . .'[70] The Spanish press, though reporting Churchill's speech, omitted all mention of his reference to Spain. When questioned about this omission, the Spanish Ambassador in London, the Duke of Alba, replied that such non-publication was due, in his view, to the battle in progress between the Serrano Suñer and Beigbeder camps. He added that the time would come for an agreed statement, when the ground had been prepared in Madrid by Hoare and Beigbeder.[71]

Before the British could issue their public statement, however, Beigbeder was replaced by Serrano Suñer, on 17 October 1940, as Spanish Minister for Foreign Affairs. Commenting on Serrano's appointment the German financial newspaper, *Börsen Zeitung,* gloated that if Hoare had been sent to Madrid 'to rescue for England what was still rescuable, it seems as though he has not rescued very much'.[72] Halifax told the Cabinet that, although Hoare had warned about the possibility of Beigbeder's demise, the sudden change had been unexpected.[73] Hardly a week later, Franco was conferring with Hitler at Hendaye and there might have seemed reason for pessimism in London about this turn of events.

Actually, Halifax had also told the Cabinet that the ministerial change might not signify as much as it might seem to at first.[74] Moreover, on 18 October, Hoare was told by a well-informed Spanish source that Beigbeder had been dismissed because of his growing indiscretion, which even the Spanish Generals thought was compromising them, in that it was a clear provocation to the Germans. He was also informed that Serrano Suñer, embittered by his Berlin trip, had abandoned his desire to embroil Spain in the war.[75] Serrano Suñer claims in his memoirs that Ribbentrop had complained in Berlin about a Spanish Minister in the service of the English, and Mussolini had described Beigbeder as an 'Anglophil', during his 4 October meeting with Hitler.[76] Hoare was told, too, that Hitler had virtually given Serrano Suñer an ultimatum about Beigbeder. The British Ambassador did believe that Beigbeder's conversion to the British cause might well have been too complete. He judged the ex-Minister to have been 'incredibly indiscreet', never hesitating to broadcast his anti-German views with great gusto.[77] Indeed, there was a remarkable unanimity amongst observers about the dangerously indiscreet character of Colonel Beigbeder. Hoare's very first impression of him was that he was an attractive but impulsive person.[78] An English visitor found Beigbeder inclined to be indiscreet as early as August 1939.[79] It has already been noted that he openly telegraphed news of the apparent victory of his policy-line, concerning Spain's attitude to the war, to Morocco, an action which prompted R. M. Makins, of the Foreign Office, to regret that Beigbeder should be 'celebrating his triumph so publicly and at such an early stage'.[80]

Moreover, General Franco assured the British that the ministerial changes implied no alteration in Spanish foreign policy.[81] Beigbeder had had a long and intimate meeting with Franco only two days before his dismissal and was consequently confident about his policy and position. However, he may have erred in identifying too closely his own survival with that of his policy. Hoare was disposed to accept the argument that Beigbeder's 'long war' neutralist policy had in fact triumphed, and that the leader of the former opposition to it, Serrano Suñer, would adopt it as his own, given the popular antipathy to Spanish belligerency.[82] In any case, Hoare viewed Spain's desperate economic plight as a definite bar to any Spanish adventurism.[83] He did feel, however, that Britain must, for a time, adopt a 'wait and see' policy, and he counselled against discussing the proposed public statement with Serrano Suñer. British economic negotiations with Spain were effectively suspended, too, while Serrano Suñer's views were made clear.[84] However, the British were soon assured that Franco, at his conference with Hitler at Hendaye, had evaded any definite commitment to join, or facilitate, Germany's fight against Britain.[85]

This was substantially, if not formally, correct. Franco had proved abrasive enough in personal encounter for Hitler to inform Mussolini, later, that he would rather have three or four teeth out than experience such a meeting as Hendaye again.[86] The Spaniards had been induced, eventually, to agree to sign a protocol expressing their adherence to the Italo-German Pact of Steel, of May 1939, their readiness to accede to the Tripartite Pact, concluded amongst Germany, Italy and Japan, on 27 September 1940, and their willingness to join the Axis war effort after a period of preparation.[87] Despite this formal commitment to go to war, personal contact with Hitler had not, in fact, altered Franco's basic design: to avoid immediate recruitment into the Axis front line, but to enter into a form of obligation which would secure recognition of his territorial aspirations and ensure their fulfilment, by enabling Spain to enter the contest when its allies were on the very point of victory. Franco, then, had no immediate intention of abiding by his commitment, particularly as Hitler had compounded his alienation over the offhand treatment of the Spanish leader's September initiative, by frankly admitting his strategic predicament to the Caudillo:

The purpose of this conference in Hendaye was the following: If they succeeded in effecting quite a large front against England, then the struggle would be substantially easier for all the participants and could be ended sooner. In setting up this front the Spanish desires and the French hopes were obstacles in the path.

Since France's collaboration was necessary, Spain's claims upon French colonial territory would have to be moderated. They would have to be modest enough to allow the operation of a formula according to which France might be induced to collaborate with the Axis war effort, by compensating it for any territory ceded to the German camp, out of the possessions of a defeated British Empire. This would exorcize the danger of the French African Empire defecting to the enemy.[88] Indeed, Hitler had disclosed the order of priority amongst his strategic concerns, by admitting in his conversation with Franco, that 'the great problem to be solved at the moment consisted in hindering the de Gaulle movement in French Africa from further expanding itself and thereby establishing in this way bases for England and America on the African coast'.[89] Ribbentrop, similarly, pointed out to Serrano Suñer, in his separate meeting with the new Spanish Foreign Minister at Hendaye, that it was essential to avoid the injury to 'everyone's aspirations' that would ensue from British and/or Free French control of the Vichy Empire. The German

Foreign Minister also explained that it was 'very difficult to make an exact definition of the areas that would in all circumstances be allotted to Spain', since the final reallocation of imperial territories in Africa depended on whether France assisted Germany in defeating England. French co-operation 'would facilitate and accelerate the victory'.[90]

Franco was indignant at this new revelation of Germany's lack of sympathy for Spain's territorial ambitions. He complained to Serrano Suñer (according to the latter), after the first session of his talks with Hitler, thus:

These people are intolerable; they want us to enter the war in return for nothing; we cannot trust them if they do not contract a formal and definitive commitment, in what we sign, to cede us as of now the territories which as I have explained to them are our right; otherwise we will not enter the war now . . . After the victory, contrary to what they say, if they do not commit themselves formally now, they will give us nothing.[91]

This was a shrewd judgement. Hitler had no intention of meeting Spanish demands for all Morocco and the Oran region of Algeria. He told Mussolini, on 28 October 1940, that the most Spain could expect, by way of territorial aggrandisement was 'a substantial enlargement of Spanish Morocco'.[92]

Although intimidated into signing a contractual pledge to join the Axis war effort, the Spaniards had not, in fact, obtained formal and specific recognition of their territorial aspirations in this Secret Protocol.[93] Article Five of the instrument merely promised that, when England was conquered, Spain would receive 'territories in Africa to the same extent as France can be compensated, by assigning to the latter other territories of equal value in Africa'.[94] Only three days after the Hendaye meeting, Serrano Suñer officially communicated to the Germans, 'the bitter feeling' produced in Franco and himself, by the German refusal to meet Spanish desires for greater elaboration of the promises of territorial reward.[95] However, Franco made another personal effort to get the elusive German ratification of Spain's expansionist goals. On 30 October 1940, he wrote to Hitler as follows:

In view of the necessity expressed by you of accelerating the war, including reaching an understanding with France, which would eliminate the dangers resulting from the doubtful loyalty of the French army of Africa to Marshal Pétain, [a] loyalty which would quite certainly disappear if in any way it were known that there existed a commitment or promise to cede those territories, your proposal that our territorial aspiration should not figure concretely in our pact appeared admissible to me. So, in accordance with what was agreed, I reiterate to you by this letter Spain's legitimate and natural aspirations with regard to her succession in North Africa to territories that were until now France's . . .

I reiterate, then Spain's aspiration to the *Oranesado* and the part of Morocco which is in France's hands and which connects our northern zone with the Spanish possessions, Ifni and Sahara.[96]

It is argued here that Franco was attempting less to obtain definite recompense for immediate belligerency, than to establish a relationship with the Axis that would guarantee him the fruits of victory by making a last-minute contribution to it. For, according to Article Four of the Secret Protocol, Spain would enter the war 'at a time to be set by common agreement' of Germany, Italy and itself.[97] Franco, thus, retained the right to decide if, and when, Spain should intervene in the conflict, as a resentful Hitler perceived.[98] As the State Secretary of the German Foreign Ministry, Ernst von Weizsäcker, realised when reflecting on a possible diplomatic association with Spain some days before the Hendaye meeting, 'states act according to their interests and not their treaties when it becomes really serious'.[99] The course of Hispano-German relations, in November–December 1940, described in chapters six and seven, testified to the accuracy of this assessment.

Hitler, however, was apparently encouraged by Franco's letter of 30 October to think that the Spanish leader was seriously contemplating imminent intervention in the war.[100] But he never responded to its essential purpose, which was to elicit some expression of German readiness to hand over the lands coveted by Spain in North Africa. Even the circumstances of later November 1940 – when the disastrous Italian invasion of Greece, required a German counter-stroke in the Western Mediterranean through Spanish belligerency – only moved him to promise to send Franco 'at a proper time . . . a satisfactory answer to his letter'.[101] Hitler remained too wary of provoking the desertion of the French North African Empire to de Gaulle by promising any surrender of its territories to the garrulous Spaniards, who were bound to divulge his commitment, if only to ensure that he fulfilled it.[102] The Führer's failure to meet this fundamental Spanish requirement of territorial profit entailed the frustration of his design to involve Spain in the war, as is described in chapter seven. If, contrary to the interpretation of Franco's policy outlined above, the Caudillo had still been considering immediate belligerency in exchange for the stipulated territorial gains, in late October 1940, Hitler's unwillingness to promise them would have killed this inclination. If, as has been argued, Franco had by that time been trying to reserve his share in the spoils of an Axis victory, then again, Hitler's refusal to guarantee him a return on such an insubstantial investment killed his interest in anything but the most belated participation in the war. Franco maintained his basic intent to defer Spanish belligerency until as late as possible but, henceforward, due to his failure to persuade Hitler to give a specific pledge on the dismemberment of the French North African Empire, he no longer keenly sought the opportune moment to pounce upon a stricken Britain to gain his plunder. Rather, now, was his preoccupation to postpone indefinitely the fulfilment of his duty to fight for the Axis, an obligation which now proffered no certain profit and which had only grudgingly been contracted through fear of the consequences of refusal. Had Franco been definitely assured of the imperial expansion which he wanted, he could well have been coaxed into the fight in time to play a significant part. Instead, however, by November 1940, Spanish non-belligerency was effectively stabilised and only a catastrophic and seemingly irreversible decline in Britain's military fortunes would impel Spain into active alliance with the Axis. In short, Spain would shun the conflict for as long as Britain had any real fight left in it, that is, for as long as Spanish non-belligerency was of practical value to the British war effort.

The British information on the Hendaye meeting was neither as detailed nor as accurate as that which they had managed to procure on Serrano Suñer's mission to Berlin, of the previous month. Thus, they received no inkling of the conclusion of the Secret Protocol of alliance with Germany and Italy. However, they did deduce correctly, that Franco had not sold the pass to the Germans at Hendaye. The misleading information about the encounter which some prominent Spaniards imparted to them may have aided the formation of this correct verdict. Beigbeder, despite his exclusion from the Ministry of Foreign Affairs, claimed to know that Franco had made no commitment to enter the war, but that Hitler intended to induce the Caudillo to join the struggle.[103] Franco also asserted to Hoare, on 7 November, that Hitler had not asked him to abandon his non-belligerency. Moreover, he declared that there would be no change of policy and added that 'the Spanish people would not stand a foreign invasion'.[104]

Notwithstanding Spain's alleged determination to resist this ultimate form of German pressure, its sensitivity to provoking it had frustrated Hoare's project for political concord with Franco. In sacking Beigbeder, Franco had shown his realisation that Spain could not afford to appear to be moving in the direction of Germany's enemy. British political blandishment could not allay this Spanish fear of German revenge in 1940–1, although Hoare never completely abandoned the attempt in those months. Had he been too successful in enticing Spain away from the Axis, the very strategic threat which he strove to prevent, namely, a German-occupied Spain, could have materialised. Nonetheless, as will be seen below, Hoare would, on occasion, argue that it was inevitable that the Spaniards would maintain a hostile face towards Britain, given the closeness of German forces, and the Chiefs of Staff would even conclude that this was desirable from the British point of view.[105]

However, once again the British had not been passive observers of Hispano-German exchanges. For, in his farewell interview with Hoare, on 18 October 1940, Beigbeder expressed his conviction that Germany would demand a right of passage through Spain within a few months and advised that Britain should have plans ready for such a situation, in which Franco would vacillate. The Spanish Army was, he argued, the only hope for an effective resistance and in the huge upsurge of anti-German feeling consequent upon their advance into Spain, other groups such as the Basque and Catalan separatists would join the national resistance movement. A British expedition should be prepared at once, and munitions sent to Gibraltar to strengthen the Rock and provide a stock for the regional Spanish military comman- der, General Muñoz Grandes. Beigbeder was anxious to stress, never- theless, that British troops should not enter Spain until the Spanish national movement had begun.[106] After this meeting he established clandestine contact with Hoare, though watched by both Serrano Suñer's agents and the Germans. In a series of communications in the next weeks to the British Ambassador, he again called, *inter alia*, for the building up of military supplies at Gibraltar, asked for a 'mass of aviation' to be prepared that could be sent to Portugal, advised that Dakar and Port Etienne (on the southern boundary of Spanish Sahara) should be occupied at once and requested a study of 'the intense bombardment by surprise of the Hendaye region, the entry-point of German forces'. Beigbeder stated repeatedly that he would only move himself 'in the event that foreign troops enter Spain'. In that eventu- ality he would go to Madeira, establish a Regency for the Spanish Monarchy, and declare war on Germany. He made it clear to the British that he would welcome the Republican Colonel Casado, in exile in London, into such a Regency Government. He felt that he would be supported by all Andalusia, Spanish Morocco and the Canary and Balearic Islands, as well as being able to establish a Requeté-type organisation in Catalonia. Hoare concluded that the area essentially envisaged for a joint Anglo-Spanish defence was southern Spain.[107] Whilst he admitted that he could not give any assurances about

Spanish Army resistance, Sir Samuel Hoare did request that the Chiefs of Staff examine Beigbeder's proposals and also the possibility of associated British landings in Portugal.[108] Churchill considered this development to be 'most important' and referred the matter to the Chiefs of Staff Committee for 'very careful' examination.[109] The lengthy report which the Joint Planning Staff produced emphasised the magnitude of any enterprise to aid Spanish resistance. The Joint Planning Staff were more sceptical than Beigbeder about the possibilities of Spanish resistance, and thought that, even with Spanish aid, the most that British forces could hold would be a bridgehead in southern Spain. They indicated that the main strategical importance of Spain for Britain lay in its relation to the control of the western entry to the Mediterranean, and that, therefore, the goal of any operation should be to preserve control of the Strait. The prospects of doing so were dim unless 300,000 tons of shipping were kept ready in British ports, with another 1,000,000 tons needed when the operation began, and a naval escort of eight cruisers, twenty-six destroyers and twenty-six corvettes provided. Air requirements would be six fighter and four bomber squadrons, and it would also be necessary to secure intermediate refuelling facilities in northern Spain or Portugal for the aircraft *en route* to southern Spain. The supporting equipment and personnel for the air operations would have to be sent, in advance, to the already overcrowded Rock of Gibraltar. Some form of prior staff discussions with the Spaniards were essential also. Time was 'the essence of the plan' and without the requisite preliminary preparations there would be no hope of achieving the goal of the projected operation. Landings in Portugal were ruled out due to the paucity of resources.[110]

This plan foundered on the same reef that subsequent ones would: lack of resources commensurate with the task. At the Chiefs of Staff meeting where the plan was discussed, Admiral Sir Dudley Pound declared that it was impossible to hold 300,000 tons of shipping in readiness, and that the total shipping commitment 'would be a very serious strain upon our resources'. He also thought that it would be impossible to accommodate the personnel at Gibraltar. Air Chief Marshal Sir Charles Portal, stated the basic dilemma, noting that either large amounts of shipping would have to be locked up, or British help would be too late. It was also pointed out that the operation was contingent upon the use of northern Spanish and Portuguese aerodromes, and that Germany could probably easily prevent British use of them.[111] The plan was not proceeded with. This highlighted the extent to which Britain had a vested interest in the maintenance of Spanish neutrality, for even Spain's belligerency on Britain's side would be detrimental since the British were too weak, at this stage, to make effective use of it. Spanish neutrality was the best defence for Gibraltar that Britain could have and the way that the Chiefs of Staff came to express just this view, in February 1941, is described in chapter seven.

If the British found themselves too weak ultimately to make real use of any Spanish resistance that might develop against Germany, Beigbeder, too, argued himself into a cul-de-sac of inaction. For, by November, he had decided not to approach any other Spanish Generals in advance of a German ultimatum, so that the projected national resistance movement would not look like an anti-Franco plot, and it would therefore be possible for the Caudillo to identify himself with it.[112] Indeed such convoluted logic, along with Beigbeder's characteristic flamboyance, led Cadogan, for one, to articulate his doubts about the significance of Beigbeder's communications. He commented, thus: 'I must say I find Señor B's jottings rather naive and immature.'[113] Stanley Payne does argue, too, that Beigbeder was not especially influential.[114] However, Hoare did believe that Beigbeder was on close terms with the able General Agustín Muñoz Grandes.[115] Moreover, the British Ambassador himself, had had an interesting interview with Muñoz Grandes, on 15 October 1940, in which the General had declared that he was aware that Spain had been made 'the instrument and dupe of foreign powers' during the Civil War. He was resolved to prevent this happening again. In the present conflict it seemed to the General that England was the belligerent least likely to interfere with Spain. Muñoz Grandes also noted how utterly wrong the hated Serrano Suñer had been about the length of the war, 'the ball was still in play . . . and nobody knew how it would come down'.[116]

Increasingly, Beigbeder's secret liaison with Hoare appeared to be only the most dramatic expression of a definite trend within Spanish Army circles. As early as September, Hillgarth was claiming that the Spanish Generals were making plans to resist a German invasion of their country.[117] 'Six leading Generals', according to reports received by the British, had exhorted Franco to tell Hitler at Hendaye that Spaniards would rather die fighting than submit to foreign dictation.[118] On 29 October 1940, the Duke of Alba told R. A. Butler that the Spanish Army leaders, supported by financial circles, would try to resist German pressure. He added that Spain was vacillating between the two sides in the war and would, in his view, probably come down somewhere between them.[119] The monarchist Chief of Staff of the

Spanish Army, General Martínez Campos, admitted in late November to the British Military Attaché, Brigadier Torr, that a long war was in prospect and affirmed that the Spanish Army would fight back against a German forced entry into the country. The General also pointed to the recent and pronounced swing in military and public opinion inside Spain towards adopting such a course of action. He did add, however, that the British must be very careful not to precipitate German action by word or deed, cautioning them, thus: 'We should resent it as much as we shall resent it if Germany comes in here against our will.'[120] General Antonio Aranda, the reputedly anti-Axis Director of the Superior War College, confirmed, shortly afterwards, that the Army would resist a German incursion, and quoted General Varela, the Spanish Army Minister (a Carlist) as saying that 'the people now would resist the Germans even with stones'.[121] General Varela certainly did state in November that Spain would not go to war unless attacked.[122] The possible influence of British financial 'inspiration', mentioned in chapter two in promoting certain of these attitudes among Spain's military should not be ignored.

Naturally, these declarations to British officials should be treated with some caution, particularly as the Italians were now suffering major reverses, and Britain's maritime and economic power appeared progressively more vital to Spain's survival, as its economic position deteriorated. The case of General Muñoz Grandes illustrates well the difficulty of making firm judgements about the attitudes of the Spanish military. Regarded, initially, by the British as definitely sympathetic, he was appointed by Franco in 1941 as commander of the Spanish 'Blue Division' which fought with the German Army on the Russian Front. He rapidly lost his pro-British image, and came to be regarded by London as a violent enemy. Indeed, Hitler even speculated about replacing the intractable Caudillo with him. By 1943, however, the Spanish General was reported equally appalled at the prospect of a German or a Soviet victory in the European conflict.[123]

However, other Spanish Generals seemed to display rather more consistency. Certainly, the revival in Britain's fortunes of war, in the closing months of 1940, and the increasing vulnerability of the Spanish economy were both hard facts that had to be taken into account in actual Spanish policy-making, as much as in exchanges with the British. Anyway, what is impressive is that German sources concur with the British ones, on important points. Thus, von Stohrer warned Berlin in December that a forced entry into Spain would probably provoke Spanish resistance.[124] Whatever the ultimate result of the manifestation of a Spanish will to resist a German incursion into the country, its promotion and protection rapidly became one of the main concerns of British policy towards Spain.

However, the anxiety of the Spanish Generals themselves, not to precipitate German intervention in their country apparently even exceeded their hatred of Serrano Suñer. Hillgarth believed in September that they only refrained from ousting him, because they feared such action would enable the Germans to intervene. Indeed, the Naval Attaché thought Franco would go, too, were it not for the German pressure on the Pyrenean frontier.[125] Another British Embassy official reported that popular gossip maintained that Serrano Suñer would be eliminated, but for the threatening international scene.[126] The Spanish Director of Military Operations and Intelligence asserted that Franco was quite conscious of the serious internal unrest, and was thrusting the power of effective government upon Serrano Suñer so that the latter would incur all the blame for failure in the domestic and international spheres.[127] Nevertheless, by December both Admiral Canaris and von Stohrer agreed that Franco was clearly afraid that 'the conflict of personalities and issues between S. Suñer and the military could become an acute danger for the regime if the grave misgivings of these generals toward immediate entry into the war, mainly on economic though also on military grounds, are not given heed'.[128]

As the two Germans noted, the Spanish Generals were very conscious of the extent to which economic weakness imposed severe limits upon Spain's freedom of action. The next chapter will delineate the attempts made by the Spanish Government to avert economic catastrophe in the autumn and winter of 1940, and the British and American response to those efforts. For Spain in its need could only turn to the two Atlantic democracies, and the resultant triangular exchanges constitute another definite stage in the development of British policy towards Spain. So, if the political side of Hoare's policy of attraction had been blunted by Spanish fears of German retaliation, the other positive aspect, the economic, became the dominant consideration in policy-making on Spain as the winter came on. But this time Hoare's bid to link Spain's vital interests to British support would be complicated by the need to involve the United States in the endeavour.

6

Economic diplomacy: September–December, 1940

The German newspaper, *Deutsche Allegemeine Zeitung*, had greeted Serrano Suñer's appointment as Spanish Minister for Foreign Affairs with special satisfaction, since Franco, it argued, was elevating his 'chief adviser' at precisely 'the moment when foreign policy becomes more important for Spain than home policy'.[1] Nevertheless, a striking change in the editorial line of Spain's officially-controlled newspapers, coinciding with Serrano's appointment, seemed to belie the *D.A.Z.*'s confident assertion of the primacy of foreign over domestic policy for Spain. Thus *Arriba*, the hardline Falange newspaper which, hitherto, had tried to make ideological capital out of Spain's desperate economic plight by emphasising the need for sacrifice for the common good and coining such paradoxical slogans as 'noble scarcity', and 'Spain's famine is her proud own', abruptly altered its course. Commenting on the first official speech of the new Minister of Industry and Commerce, Demetrio Carceller, (appointed the same day as Serrano Suñer), it declared that he had 'outlined very clearly the basis which sustained modern states. Just as revolution without bread and justice would be a swindle, so states do not maintain themselves, nor are their regimes effective, if they do not control the economy.'[2] 'Revolution of Bread and Justice' was the slogan of the hour, Spain's internal crisis the pressing priority. Another Spanish paper, *Pueblo*, exclaimed that 'we shall never succeed in obtaining the national amity we need for our purposes while hunger is the people's chief counsellor'.[3] Ideology was being adjusted to the practical reality of Spain's teetering economy. Of course, there was a sense in which even this terrible domestic crisis was, ultimately, a problem manageable only by foreign policy. For if Spain could not sustain its own people, it had to seek help abroad, and there were no selfless dispensers of relief around in 1940. Thus,

110

Churchill, on 3 November 1940, accepted that 'we have a very strong lever in the shape of our blockade and I believe that Spain's desire to obtain foodstuffs from the United States and this country will be the most potent factor in keeping her out of the war'.[4] The pendulum of power, in one corner of Europe, at least, was swinging back to the maritime and blockading nation, Britain, whose power to feed or starve was just as tangible to the hungry Spaniards as Germany's military might. Thus, the Germans had been unable to persuade the Franco regime by October 1940, despite applying diplomatic pressure to it from June onwards, to cease 'substantial deliveries of Spanish raw materials, particularly iron ore and iron pyrites, to England'. Director Wiehl of the Economic Policy Department of the Third Reich's Foreign Ministry accounted for this failure of Nazi diplomacy to his colleagues, thus, on 19 October 1940: 'It [the Franco administration] wants, to be sure, to curtail such deliveries as much as possible, but has pointed out that the supplies that are vital to Spain – grain and gasoline, for example – depend on the goodwill of the English, and that to this extent Spanish deliveries to England also had to be continued'.[5] Moreover, in November 1940, the Spanish Minister for the Navy, Admiral Salvador Moreno Fernández, adopted a stance of open opposition to Spanish involvement in the war or connivance at a German move on Gibraltar, across their territory. He based his opposition on reports prepared by his naval staff which demonstrated that the Royal Navy, supreme at sea, could not only cut off the flow of vital supplies to Spain but also bombard Spanish coastal cities.[6]

However, if Spain was seeking territorial concessions from Germany, then it must have seemed consistent – and prudent, given German preponderance on land – to seek its economic aid. This the Spaniards certainly did, but Germany neither had sufficient resources, nor the intention, to afford relief to Spain prior to the latter's entry into the war. It has already been noted how Wiehl informed the Madrid Embassy, in June, that Spain could not be fed by Germany or south-eastern Europe and that it would have to get grain from overseas.[7] The Reich Food Ministry indicated in September that the national grain reserves would be exhausted during the current production year, so there were no stocks to be wasted in courting Spanish belligerency.[8] Reich-Marschall Göring, in charge of Germany's 'Four-Year Plan', declared that meeting Spain's demands for grain, cotton, hemp and petroleum was 'out of the question'.[9] Hitler argued that the solution to Spain's economic problems lay in an entry into the war. He explained to Franco how the expulsion of the British from the Mediterranean would solve Spain's supply problems. Franco replied that Spain's needs were for mostly non-Mediterranean products.[10]

That Spain would only receive German economic support after joining their fight was clearly indicated by the November discussions at Obersalzberg and Berchtesgaden between Serrano Suñer, on the Spanish side, and Hitler and Ribbentrop on the German. The need to repair the damage inflicted on the Axis cause by the Italian defeats in the Eastern Mediterranean and to prevent a further deterioration there, had made Hitler conclude that 'in the present circumstances it was absolutely necessary to shut off the Mediterranean' by the conquest of Gibraltar at the sea's western outlet and by air attack upon the British naval base at Alexandria and the Suez Canal at its eastern end. Hitler saw the move against Gibraltar not only as a manoeuvre whereby the pressure on the Italians in the Eastern Mediterranean might be relieved, but also as a safeguard against a defection of French North Africa to the enemy. Anglo-Free French air bases there, he pointed out to Mussolini, 'would inevitably be disastrous for all Italy'.[11] The vulnerability of the Rumanian oil fields, whose production was vital for the German war economy, to British bomber attack, was also a major influence inclining the Führer to take vigorous counteraction in the Mediterranean area. On the same day, 18 November 1940, as Hitler strove to persuade Serrano Suñer of the desirability of Spanish belligerency, Ciano got the impression from the former that 'the most important point for the future development of the war is the Rumanian oil-bearing region'. Ciano interpreted the effort to induce Spain to become belligerent immediately on the Axis side as one of Hitler's diplomatic counter-measures to remove the threat to Ploesti.[12]

As explained in the previous chapter, Franco had almost certainly abandoned, by November 1940, any idea of going to war in the near future, but the Spanish response to a German call for Spain's belligerency had still to be guarded. Several days before his summons to the Berghof to consult with Hitler, Serrano Suñer revealed the logic guiding Spanish diplomacy then, in a conversation with the Portuguese Ambassador, Pedro Theotonio Pereira, as recorded by the latter: 'He says that he takes Germany's victory as certain, and that it was proper therefore to be wary of the position. Nevertheless, he says that England has not yet died and that one must take the greatest care on that side also.'[13] The apparent stalemate in the Anglo-German struggle made such an ambivalent attitude seem the appropriate stance to assume. The inopportune German demand that Spain join the Axis at war in the near future, voiced by Hitler in his 18 November encounter with Serrano Suñer, threatened to wreck

Spain's strategy of survival in late 1940: its policy of studied ambiguity.

According to Serrano Suñer, a meeting – prior to his departure for his interview with the Führer – with Generals Varela and Vigón, and Admiral Moreno, presided over by Franco, reaffirmed that Spain 'could not and should not' enter the conflict.[14] But Serrano Suñer could not afford to provoke Hitler by saying as much at the Berghof. Spain's real reluctance to get embroiled in the war did not, however, preclude the promotion of Franco's project of securing Axis sanction of Spain's expansion in North Africa. Serrano Suñer represented the demand for such approval of Spain's imperialist expansion to Hitler, on 18 November, as a device to boost 'public morale' in the country to the level necessary to enable it to become belligerent. So presented, it may have served a double purpose. It may have been articulated by the Spanish Minister both as the stipulated goal for which Spain might go to war, and as a diversionary tactic to underline the prohibitive cost of buying its participation in the conflict. Franco, to reiterate the argument outlined in chapter five, had no immediate intention of going to war, but a positive German reply to his imperial claims could make it worthwhile for him to do so in the future, while a negative one could only strengthen his case against belligerency based upon the absence of any assured profit which might counter the popular antipathy to war. While one can only speculate on whether such an ambivalent motivation inspired Serrano Suñer's advocacy of a clearer definition of Spain's territorial rewards in the Secret Protocol, he earnestly pleaded with Hitler for a concession on the point. Relating that Franco 'had been quite depressed and worried' about 'the vague uncertainty [with which] the Spanish aspirations in Africa had been treated in this Protocol', Serrano Suñer became so persistent in his importuning for a more specific guarantee of territorial profit for Spain that Hitler lost patience and retorted as follows: '. . . a precise statement would lead to an endless dispute and to the loss of North Africa. He would then prefer that Gibraltar remain in English hands and Africa with Pétain. The Spanish gentleman would have to believe his words, and should not insist on a precise written statement.'[15] Hitler's refusal to budge on this issue could only cement Franco's resolve to shirk his contractual obligation to fight for the Axis.

Serrano Suñer also advanced Spain's 'extraordinarily serious food situation' as an obstacle to Spanish belligerency, pointing out that the sealing of the Mediterranean, and Spain's entry into the war, would entail the cutting off of Atlantic supply-lines. He explained that, as his country was in desperate need of British-facilitated wheat imports, 'he as Foreign Minister had to tack with extraordinary cleverness' trying 'to maintain the illusion in England that [Spain] would not enter the war'. Hitler denied that Spain would receive any succour from Britain and the United States, asserting that they were set upon the economic suffocation of Franco's regime. However, Hitler and Ribbentrop also made it clear that Spain would receive no German economic assistance unless it promised to enter the war at a moment to be determined by Germany, i.e., in one to one-and-a-half months' time. Serrano Suñer appeared to bow to the Führer's will, declaring that he would endeavour to obtain economic sustenance from Britain in the interval. Indeed, he had proclaimed, during the course of his talk with Hitler, 'above supply problems . . . stood history in which Spain wanted to participate this time too'.[16]

Serrano Suñer was back in Spain hardly a week, however, before he was informing von Stohrer that the armed forces' Ministers were objecting to the limited preparatory period for Spanish belligerency, considering the economic position and the popular antipathy to war. He pointed out, therefore, that 'an early reply to the last letter of the Caudillo to the Führer [i.e. that of 30 October 1940, cited in chapter five] would be very desirable'.[17] The Spaniards certainly missed no opportunity to endeavour to persuade Hitler to give his formal assent to their African territorial aspirations, but once again evoked no reply. The conditional German offer of economic help did not ensnare Franco into surrendering his precious right to decide the moment of Spanish intervention in the war. On 29 November, the Germans were informed that Spain would consent to speeding up its preparations for war 'as much as possible', but were also advised that 'the time required for this, however, cannot today be definitely determined'.[18]

Thus, Germany would not help Spain until it became belligerent, and Spain essentially argued that it must receive massive aid before it could declare war. Hitler advocated belligerency as a solution to Spain's economic problems, whereas Franco argued that they must be solved before his country could fight. The Spanish Minister without Portfolio, the Falangist, Pedro Gamero del Castillo, articulated a few months later the main difference in the aid offered by Britain and Germany to Spain, in that the former offered Spaniards food in return for peace, whereas the Germans sought war in return for their proffered help. The Minister added that there was no-one in Spain who would not opt for the first alternative.[19] Again, this underlines the British vested interest in the maintenance of Spain's international *status quo*. The Germans urged activity and perhaps intolerable peril, the British passivity and only the present risk.

Acknowledging the huge shortfall (1,000,000 tons) in the Spanish harvest, the British Government agreed to permit 100,000 tons of cereals (except rice) to pass through their blockade each month for a period from September 1940. They adopted this interim measure since it would enable them to wait for Spain's attitude on the war to be made clear, before committing themselves to any yearly import rate.[20] However, Spain's problems were not solved simply by the British agreeing not to throttle it. Spain needed positive assistance and it was logical that it should turn to the one country with resources on the same scale as its needs, the United States of America. In early September, the Spanish Ministry of Industry and Commerce requested a $100,000,000 loan from the United States (the main expenditure being envisaged as $22,000,000 for wheat, £20,000,000 for gasoline and $20,000,000 for cotton), to be repaid through annual shipments of olive oil over a period of twenty years. Recommending that his Government accept this barter scheme, the American Ambassador, Alexander Weddell, informed Washington that the dangerous socio-economic deterioration in Spain, unless relieved, would drive the Spanish Government to fight for the Axis. He added that the British diplomats in Madrid assured him that their Government was willing to gamble on aiding Spain, and hoped to win at least the Spanish people to Britain's side. The Ambassador had told the Spaniards that any American aid would be dependent upon the continuance of Spanish neutrality and the maintenance of friendly relations with the United States.[21] The British reaction to this was to inform their Ambassador in Washington, Lord Lothian, that they would like the Americans to commence sympathetic negotiations with the Spaniards, but with Serrano Suñer in Berlin, it would be prudent to prolong such contacts until the Spanish political situation had been clarified.[22] The British need have had no worries about possible American impetuosity in the matter. Washington was extremely agitated about Serrano Suñer's trip to Berlin. Anxiety over possible public opposition within the United States to such a scheme also made for a cautious approach. Norman Davis, head of the American Red Cross, eventually suggested that relief be sent under the aegis of his organisation, thus demonstrating the American desire to help the Spaniards. Such a measure would both avoid a damaging public squabble in the United States and ensure that Spain received aid that was unlikely to contribute to any war effort. The Secretary of

State, Cordell Hull, accepted the proposal but was adamant that the Spanish Government must affirm its intention to remain outside the European conflict. He also told Weddell that the United States Government could only aid Spain if it were sure that its help would have definite and permanent economic consequences, that it was in accordance with the 'general principles of international relationships' supported by the United States, and that guarantees against the re-export of American goods were received.[23] Both Hoare and his economic officials in Madrid gave every encouragement to the Spanish Government, and the American Embassy, to secure the barter agreement, British officials actually helping the Spaniards to refashion their scheme into a more viable form.[24]

On 30 September 1940, Colonel Beigbeder, as Spanish Minister for Foreign Affairs, told Ambassador Weddell that whilst his Government could not make a public declaration of its intent to remain non-belligerent, he was fully authorised to declare that Spain would only fight if attacked, and that American economic help could only consolidate that determination. Shortly after, on 3 October 1940, Beigbeder made this dramatic announcement to the United States Ambassador: 'Your President can change the policy of Spain and of Europe by a telegram announcing that wheat will be supplied to Spain.' He repeated that declaration, adding that the first cargo arriving in an American ship 'would have a profound effect', and 'I wish to tell you that the psychological moment has arrived'. Within three days the British Ambassador, Lothian, called on Secretary of State Hull to indicate his Government's agreement with Beigbeder's view that the psychological moment for American relief to Spain had arrived. Actually President Roosevelt had, within twenty-four hours of Weddell's meeting with Beigbeder, expressed his willingness to sanction American Red Cross wheat shipments to Spain in return for guarantees against re-export and full publicity for, and participation by the American Red Cross in, the distribution of the wheat. Franco accepted this proposal, in an interview with the American Ambassador, on 8 October 1940, and gave his personal assurance that the conditions would be met, although he clearly doubted whether this Red Cross relief would be adequate for Spain's requirements. As a result the American Ambassador was instructed, on 12 October 1940, to inform General Franco that the United States would proceed with a Red Cross shipment of 6,000 to 10,000 tons of wheat, subject to the conditions articulated by Hull in September, and was prepared to begin negotiations for the extension of credits to Spain.[25]

Despite this turn of events, Cordell Hull was all the time extremely sceptical about Franco's alleged intention to remain at peace. The tone of the American press indicated how dangerous it might be for the Administration to grant credits to Spain which, after a period, might enter the war.[26] Doubtless, such considerations were acutely felt, with a presidential election only a few weeks away. Roosevelt obviously, too, moved very warily over this matter. Thus, he deleted the specific figure of 100,000 tons from the offer of Red Cross wheat made in response to Beigbeder's early October declaration.[27] The appointment of Serrano Suñer as Spanish Foreign Minister inspired even greater caution, and the Hendaye meeting aggravated American apprehension. In the absence of reassurance, American willingness to help quickly dwindled.[28] Thus, Under-Secretary of State, Sumner Welles, wrote to the President, on 29 October 1940, as follows:

As you know, there is no present plan to send wheat to Spain. The matter was under consideration upon the urgent recommendation of Ambassador Weddell prior to the recent changes in the Spanish Government. I can certainly imagine no useful purpose to be gained under present conditions by asking the Red Cross to continue the consideration of this question. I feel sure that that is your own judgment.

Roosevelt did not dissent.[29] At his first meeting with Weddell, on 31 October, Serrano Suñer expressed Spain's complete 'political solidarity' with the Axis powers, and, though the Ambassador was not disturbed by such rhetoric, Hull and Roosevelt were.[30]

So, notwithstanding the confidence of Ambassador Weddell in the continuance of Spanish non-belligerency and his earnest recommendations that the relief scheme proceed, Secretary Hull instructed him to inform the Caudillo that the American Government could only furnish him with aid if there were 'a clear cut and public declaration of policy on the part of the present Spanish Government that it not only intends to remain neutral, but that it would not undertake any kind of assistance to Germany and Italy which could aid them in their war against the British Empire'. According to the Secretary of State, the continuing execution by Franco's regime of people like Luís Companys the former President of Catalonia, also agitated American opinion to a degree likely to preclude American assistance to Spain.[31] In mid-November, Sumner Welles told the British Chargé d'Affaires in Washington, Noel Butler, that he reckoned the United States Cabinet were unanimously opposed to dispatching aid to Spain in the absence of a public declaration by the Spaniards of their determination to remain neutral.[32] The main difficulty with the American stipulation of a Spanish public declaration of intent to remain non-belligerent was, of course, that it might embroil Spain in the war, even if only as the victim, and not the perpetrator, of aggression. Thus, as two Spanish Ministers informed the American Ambassador on 19 November, with Germany on their frontier 'crouched ready to spring', such a declaration could never be published.[33]

As noted in the previous chapter, the British response to Serrano Suñer's elevation to the Foreign Ministry was initially more muted, though they also, at Hoare's recommendation, adopted a temporary 'wait-and-see' policy on economic aid negotiations. Interestingly, Ambassador Weddell had reported, on Beigbeder's dismissal, that the British Embassy in Madrid was afraid that London would react very unfavourably to this event, and towards the end of the month there were indications that Halifax was beginning to entertain some doubts about Spain.[34] Serrano Suñer's speech on assuming his new office did cause apprehension in London. In it he proudly declared that he had no respect for professional diplomacy, and he stated that he intended to make the Ministry of Foreign Affairs 'the window of Spain upon the world and the vehicle of the expression abroad of her spirit and her rights'. He concluded that his aim was to infuse the spirit of the Falange into the Ministry, and *Arriba* added, to 'falangise' the diplomatic service. A Foreign Office official noted the inauspicious similarity between Serrano Suñer's takeover at the Palacio de Santa Cruz and Ribbentrop's advent to the Wilhelmstrasse in 1937. Halifax minuted, on 31 October, 'not very encouraging'.[35] The same day he chaired a meeting at the Foreign Office, the conclusions of which were summarised in a telegram to Hoare. The British Ambassador was told that though it seemed Spain had avoided a definite commitment to the Axis, it did appear that German influence could not but become more predominant in the country. Therefore, Britain was faced with the alternatives of either continuing to be generous over supplies and credits, or of joining with the Americans to demand from the Spaniards guarantees of their resolve to stay out of the war, to resist German pressure for strategic facilities, and to lessen Nazi influence within the country. Hoare was also asked to advise whether the draft British statement on Anglo-Spanish relations should be shown to Serrano Suñer. Hoare rejected such a posing of alternative courses of action. He argued that the need for food in Spain was so desperate, and the assurances given him by Franco and Serrano Suñer about the maintenance of non-belligerency so definite, that the central issue would have to be dealt with at once. Therefore, Britain should persuade the United States to dispatch its wheat ships and start its own negotiations with the Spaniards about economic assistance. It could be made clear, though, that British help was dependent upon Spanish non-belligerency, and goodwill. Control of the rhythm of supplies would eliminate any real risks involved in such a policy, which further superfluous guarantees could not. Hoare advised against broaching the question of the British statement on Anglo-Spanish relations with Serrano Suñer until economic agreements had been made with Spain, and the Minister's views fully elucidated. Again Hoare's views were accepted with remarkable completeness as official British policy.[36]

There seemed some basis for the British Ambassador's analysis. On the day before his unfortunate interview with Weddell, Serrano Suñer manifested to Hoare his preoccupation with American wheat deliveries, asserting that to refuse such help would be 'a terrible crime against humanity and . . . an act of war against Spain'.[37] A week later, he explained away his affirmation of 'political solidarity' with the Axis, maintaining he intended no change in the policy of non-belligerency, an intention which could only be deflected by two events: an attack on, or an attempt to starve, Spain.[38] A few days later, he answered a direct question by Weddell as to Spain's reaction should it be invaded by Axis forces, by declaring that his countrymen would 'fight to the last man'.[39] Weddell kept in constant touch with Hoare who fortified the American Ambassador's efforts to coax his Government from their stance, by emphasising the identity of the British views with his own.[40] Although Hoare was inclined to blame the American Ambassador for this impasse in relations with Spain, it is evident that the former's political masters were both more suspicious of Franco's Spain, and more sensitive to domestic criticism, than their British counterparts.[41]

On 20 August 1940, Churchill, speaking in the House of Commons, had referred to the Anglo-American discussions for the lease of naval and air facilities on British imperial territory to the United States. He had commented, thus, on the significance of this trans-Atlantic deal between the 'Anglo-Saxon' powers:

Undoubtedly this process means that those two great organisations of the English-speaking democracies, the British Empire and the United States, will have to be somewhat mixed up together in some of their affairs for mutual and general advantage. For my own part, looking out upon the future, I do not view the process with any misgivings. I could not stop it if I wished; no one can stop it. Like the Mississippi, it just keeps rolling along. Let it roll. Let it roll on – full flood, inexorable, irresistible, benignant, to broader lands and better days.'[42]

However, the 'inexorable' intermingling of Anglo-American affairs threatened to undermine British policy towards Spain. For the need to march in step with the United States might force the British to abandon their chosen line of economic allurement in Spain. So, in the second week of November, the British indicated to the United States Government the implications of their intransigence over aiding Spain, for Britain's strategic position. Informing the State Department of their readiness to grant a further £2,000,000 loan to Spain, the British Government pointed out that if the United States withdrew its proffered help to the Spaniards, there was a grave danger that they would sell out to Germany and the British cause would receive a body-blow. The Americans were also told that, in the British view, the attempt to wring further guarantees of continuing non-belligerency from Franco's Spain, over and above those already supplied, could only delay the provision of vital help without affording any real additional assurance. Nevertheless, the British also expressed their wish 'to keep closely in step with the United States Government in all questions of supply and credit to Spain'.[43] The Americans were not persuaded. Sumner Welles merely replied that the United States Government could only justify the expenditure of official funds on help to Spain, before Congress and the American public, if that country were ready to 'let it be publicly known' that it had no intention of granting aid or passage to Axis forces.[44]

The Spaniards, did, in fact, urgently request a new British credit of at least £2,500,000, on 13 November, 1940.[45] A few days later, Hoare discussed the risks involved in withholding wheat from Spain with Lord Lothian in Lisbon, whence the latter was about to return (from a journey home) to the United States on the transatlantic clipper service, which operated out of the Portuguese capital. Lothian, with Halifax's approval, had his Washington Embassy communicate Hoare's earnest entreaties for American aid to Hull, despite Dalton's objections.[46] Roger Makins of the Foreign Office, on 17 November, requested his colleagues to consider, *inter alia*, whether Britain should 'keep in step' with the Americans if they refused Spain economic support. He asked them to take due account in their deliberations of the fact that Spain was on the verge of bankruptcy, possessing no pounds sterling or American dollars with which to procure vital supplies of food and raw materials from overseas. Makins also lent urgency to his request for a review of the problem of economic help for Spain by noting that Germany could 'draw on her large stores of grain' in order to induce 'an unwilling Spain to comply with German wishes, and so give the Axis at a crucial moment a major diplomatic success'. Cadogan felt the American insistence on published declarations by Spain of its intention to remain non-belligerent to be 'rather unreasonable', but doubted whether Britain could afford to part company with the United States on this issue, '*a.* owing to the political undesirability of divergence from them and *b.* owing to the doubt whether, without American participation we can outbid Germany'. Halifax thought that the 'real need' was to convince the United States Government of the 'impossibility of extracting declarations' from Franco.[47] The Foreign Office again moved to exert pressure on the American administration to soften its attitude towards Spain.

The British Chargé d'Affaires in Washington, Butler, was instructed to inform the Americans, on 19 November 1940, that 'formidable difficulties' would be created for Britain by Spain's belligerency, that reports indicated that a section of the Spanish Army was opposed to Serrano Suñer's policy but needed bolstering, and that only wheat from the United States could arrive in time to prevent the situation getting out of hand. Butler, also on instructions, again asked the Americans to drop their demand for a public declaration by the Spaniards of their pacific intent.[48] Welles once more replied rather discouragingly, confirming Butler's impression that the American Government 'regarded Spain as already sold to Germany'.[49] The next day 20 November, Lord Halifax himself spoke to Herschel Johnson, the United States Chargé d'Affaires in London, declaring that it was impossible for Franco to make such a public pronouncement of policy as the Americans demanded, and that the Spanish situation was so desperate as to require an immediate modification of the American stance. Johnson reported that he was impressed by 'the very great importance which Lord Halifax attached to an immediate alleviation of the Spanish food situation'.[50] Actually, unknown to the British, the Americans did relent to some degree on that very day, but it was a week before London was appraised of any softening of the United States line on Spain. The elaboration of British economic policy towards Spain, in the next seven days, occurred amidst continuing uncertainty on whether American economic resources would be available to amplify the programme of economic attraction. That these were depressing times for Britain's representatives in Spain is revealed by a letter David Eccles sent home to his wife, on 21 November 1940, which contained the following passage:

We are nearly sunk here, the awful process of demoralisation by corruption has begun to work in the Spanish ministries. Tired and miserable, they are ready to give in like Roumania. The U.S.A. could have rallied the position, but because of a series of unfortunate incidents – provoked by the Germans to embitter Spain's relations with America – it looks hopeless. I told you it was the last shot, but the gun is jammed and the trigger won't pull.'[51]

However, Hoare had already acted by this time to re-impress on London that Spanish neutrality was too precious a cause to be regarded as lost. So, on 19 November, he had expressed the view to his government that any change in Britain's economic policy towards Spain was too dangerous, even though the Spaniards offered constant provocation. He based his case on the strategic necessity of maintaining Iberian neutrality. For Salazar, in a recent discussion, had confirmed that a Spanish collapse into Germany's embrace would drag the Portuguese along as well. Hoare admitted that the American attitude was a 'serious complication', but urged more British pressure on Washington to alter it. He asked for the Chiefs of Staff's comments on the situation. A few days later, again requesting the Chiefs of Staff's views, Hoare emphasised the imminence of a Spanish collapse before, and absorption by, Germany and the strategic dangers which would ensue, including the depressing effect on Vichy France and the Eastern Mediterranean states. He stressed the need for urgent help, with or without Washington, and reckoned that Spain could be kept outside Germany's continental bloc for about £10,000,000 in aid, the cost of running the war for a day or two.[52] The Naval Staff in London responded to Hoare's demands for a clear-cut definition of priorities concerning Spain, with alacrity. Their chief, Admiral Sir Dudley Pound, had submitted a note on the problem by 21 November which formed the basis for the Cabinet Paper, produced by the Chiefs of Staff, on 23 November, and discussed in Cabinet two days later. The two major strategic dangers as defined by the Chiefs of Staff, were almost exactly as first delineated by Pound, and read as follows:

The retention of Gibraltar as a naval base is vital to us for the rapid prosecution of the campaign against Italy, since, without the use of this base, it would not be possible for us to maintain the blockade or to pass reinforcements through the Mediterranean.

If Sir Samuel Hoare is correct, Portugal will follow Spain. If this is so, the Germans will acquire in Lisbon a naval base, which can accommodate all classes of ships, including capital ships, and from which they can directly threaten the Western Patrol. They will thus be in a very favourable position for making a still further breach in the blockade . . .

The Paper added that the Germans could base fast raiding craft at Lisbon which could ravage Britain's sea communications from the North Atlantic to the Middle East, and with which it would be very difficult to deal since they would be active beyond the cover afforded by Britain's main fleet in home waters. Pound had concluded his note by expressing the Naval Staff's view that Britain should try, strenuously, to persuade the United States to send wheat to Spain, immediately. If they refused, Britain should itself proceed to dispatch a cargo, on condition that it would not seriously alienate the Americans. The Cabinet Paper concluded in a more general but more striking manner: 'It is clear that from the strategic point of view everything should be done to prevent Spain entering the war against us.'[53]

On the same day that the Chiefs of Staff produced their Paper on Spain, Churchill, also impressed by Hoare's argument, telegraphed Roosevelt in these terms:

Our accounts show that situation in Spain is deteriorating and that the Peninsula is not far from starvation point. An offer by you to dole out food month by month so long as they keep out of the war might be decisive. Small things do not count now, and this is a time for very plain talk to them. The occupation by Germany of both sides of the Straits would be a grievous addition to our naval strain already severe. The Germans would soon have batteries working by R[adio] D[irection] F[inding] which would close the Straits both by night and day. With a major campaign developing in the Eastern Mediterranean and the need to reinforce and supply our Armies there all round the Cape we could not contemplate any military action on the mainland at or near Straits. The Rock of Gibraltar will stand a long siege, but what is the good of that if we cannot use the harbour or pass the Straits? Once in Morocco the Germans will work south, and U-boats and aircraft will soon be operating freely from Casablanca and Dakar. I need not, Mr President, enlarge upon the trouble this will cause to us, or the approach of trouble to the Western Hemisphere. We must gain as much time as possible.[54]

Notwithstanding this concern of the leading British grand strategists, Churchill and the Chiefs of Staff, to draw the United States into a programme of economic assistance intended to uphold Spanish non-belligerency, they were simultaneously, in late November 1940, considering pre-emptive military action bound to imperil its continuance, as is described in the next chapter. The very precariousness of the British strategic position in 1940–1 and the profound repercussions which Spain's final choice for peace or war must inevitably have upon their struggle to survive, required Britain to be prepared for all eventualities there. There was, thus, a necessary ambivalence about British policy towards Spain. The British, at one and the same time, had to try and encourage Spain to remain aloof from the war, and, yet, also be prepared to strike at that country if – or even before – it joined enemy ranks. The pursuit of parallel policies of politico-economic attraction and military alertness towards Spain became so ambivalent as to border on the schizophrenic in late November and early December 1940. The evolution of strategic thought proper on Spain, during that time, is surveyed in the next chapter. It is also explained there how the Spanish takeover of the town of Tangier in north-western Morocco precipitated a crisis in Anglo-Spanish relations, and threatened to resolve the tension between Britain's twin policy-lines towards Spain by prompting London to contemplate opting for the military solution, in the second week-end of December. However, a scheme of economic support for Spain had been elaborated and communicated to the Spaniards before then.

In view of the reticence of the Americans in the matter, and the exigent needs of the Spaniards, British policy makers soon came to consider whether they ought not attempt to help Spain out of their own resources, as Hoare advised they should, if necessary.[55] Hoare had an able advocate in London for this policy review. For the Ministry of Economic Warfare official, David Eccles, who also strongly championed a programme of economic assistance to Spain, arrived there to press the case on his own, and other, Whitehall departments.[56] He managed to persuade his reluctant Minister to assent to the provision of credits for a bankrupt Spain, to enable it to purchase urgently required supplies from overseas. Dalton grudgingly acknowledged his persuasiveness:

While profoundly sceptical of the beneficial effects of the policy suggested, I am not prepared to refuse the proposals so persuasively, as always, expounded by Mr Eccles. It would be rather better to keep in step with the U.S.A. But either in accord with them, or if need be, independently, I am willing to agree [to help Spain] . . .[57]

An inter-departmental meeting of officials from the interested ministries, on 27 November, agreed not only to seek ministerial approval for the offer of a large loan to the Spaniards, but also 'that approval should be sought to give help to Spain irrespective of U.S. attitude'. Although the representatives of the Board of Trade at this meeting had wanted to starve the Spaniards 'to teach them a lesson', they were overborne by the men of the other main ministries present: the Foreign Office, the Ministry of Economic Warfare and the Treasury. It was agreed that in spite of the desirability of keeping in step with the Americans, Spanish neutrality was too valuable to be jeopardised by a slavish adherence to the United States line.[58] Halifax, however, hesitated to act independently in the matter lest it alienate the United States, so he enjoined Lord Lothian to press Washington 'hard' to help Spain and inquired whether the Ambassador thought a British decision to proceed with their aid would be 'likely to cause any serious difficulty with the United States Government'.[59]

The desperate urgency of coming to Spain's economic rescue was emphasised by an agitated Serrano Suñer in an interview with Hoare, on 28 November 1940. The excited Spanish Foreign Minister spoke to the British Ambassador in the following menacing terms:

the situation in Spain was delicate and dangerous. Spain wished to live at peace and had not finally chosen her friends and enemies. She was, however, faced with famine. Spain must eat and Spain would not be isolated. In order to prevent isolation of Spain he had made his personal contacts with Germany and Italy. Spain must be able to buy what she wanted and retain her sovereignty. His Majesty's Government was blockading Spain and starving Spain to death. . . As to wheat why should not Spain be allowed to buy what she could get in Argentine and anywhere else? There was only one way in which Spain would be driven into war and that was by British blockade. His predecessor had waited a year without getting any economic help from Great Britain and he was not prepared to let things drift in this way . . .

Hoare doubted – wrongly as is noted in chapter seven – that Serrano Suñer could purchase wheat from Argentina, but he was, in any case, left with an impression of the Foreign Minister as 'a desperate man who has failed to get wheat from Germany and sees a crisis . . . looming in the immediate future'.[60]

The Spanish situation apparently demanded precisely the swift and sympathetic response which the British had actually resolved to make, if the Americans were willing to let them go ahead on their own. However, even before the phase of pressure applied in Washington at the very end of November, the American attitude appeared to mellow. The British attempt, on 19 November, to change American minds on aid to Spain has already been mentioned. On that day, too, Weddell had reported the dangerous internal deterioration in Spain and the emphatic views of Spanish Ministers Demetrio Carceller and Gamero del Castillo, that a public declaration of Spanish resolve to refrain from any service to the Axis would be suicidal.[61] Hull was away from Washington, but President Roosevelt personally authorised Weddell to modify the American demand for such a public declaration as a pre-condition of helping Spain economically. Now 'specific and formal', but private, assurances by Franco would suffice, although any public indication of intent to remain neutral which the Spaniards cared to give would make the projected relief much more palatable to the American public.[62] On 26 November, that is after receiving Churchill's plea for aid to Spain cited above, Roosevelt told Lothian that he was willing to let food go to Spain as long as it was publicised there that it was the United States which was sending it. The President added, however, that Lothian would have to consult Hull on this topic. The Secretary of State, though alluding to the 'very strong' opposition within the United States to sending food to Spain, said that he fully appreciated British feelings about the problem.[63] Three days later, Hull assured Lothian that the United States Government had no objection to Britain sending wheat on its own initiative to Spain, and that no divergence between the policies of the two countries would be entailed. The United States position over sending help to Spain was however complicated by its connection with another contentious issue in Anglo-American relations, the dispatch of humanitarian aid by the United States to unoccupied France. Hull maintained that to send help to Spain would, given American public opinion, mean that it would have to go to France as well.[64]

Also, on 29 November 1940, Weddell had an extremely amiable two-hour interview with General Franco. Franco readily assented to the Ambassador's formula that he did not contemplate or envisage any change in Spain's foreign policy, though the Caudillo did add candidly that the future could not be foreseen. He did say, too, that Spain could not help Germany even if it wished. In Weddell's view, this constituted the 'specific formal' assurance required by the American President and he soon saw Serrano Suñer to deliver to him a note containing the conditions, cited above, which were attached by the United States Government to any Red Cross shipments of wheat to Spain. Serrano Suñer spoke seriously of Spain's terrible economic condition and contended that massive deliveries of wheat were essential. He communicated his Government's grateful acceptance of the offer and conditions the next day, 3 December. However, there the whole affair again stalled, as the State Department sanctioned no further move on the wheat proposals. For, neither Roosevelt nor Hull could bring themselves to trust Franco or their ability to induce him to stay neutral.[65]

On 29 November, the very day that Hull was giving the British a free hand to commence wheat shipments to Spain, and that Franco was assuring Weddell of his goodwill, the Political Adviser on European Affairs at the State Department, James C. Dunn, had an illuminating conversation with a member of the British Embassy in Washington. Dunn told the Counsellor of the British Embassy that Spanish aid proposals were hardly practical politics any more. He noted that the intense hostility of liberal and leftist United States Senators to Franco's regime did not give the Administration much room for manoeuvre. The United States Government, according to

Dunn, had been very close to sending aid at one time, but the Spaniards had blundered in engaging in anti-American gestures and activities such as congratulating the Chilean Government on rejecting American requests for bases for hemispheric defence, and the recent executions of Spanish Republican leaders had not helped soothe American feelings.[66] Administration sensitivity over public hostility to Spain was revealed when the Secretary of State felt it necessary to deny strongly that he had ever considered granting a £100,000,000 loan to Spain.[67] Weddell, in fact, was told, in the second week of December, that the United States could not proceed in the matter because of the 'delicate political situation'.[68] Hull had also made it clear, on 10 December, to the Ambassador that the United States Government was worried about the Hispanicism of the 'New' Spain, which contested the Monroe doctrine and American domination of South America with a vision of 'the unity of the Hispanic world'. Hull quoted Serrano Suñer's declaration of the previous September, which went as follows: 'There must not be ignored our will to project into South America a moral influence and to restore the prestige of Spanish culture in the face of the usurpation which another culture had perpetrated . . .'. The Secretary of State pointed out that a Consejo de Hispanicismo had been established in Madrid, under Serrano Suñer's control, to renew 'the glorious work of the Council of the Indies'. He also mentioned the Spanish Government's public support for Latin American Governments which refused 'to acquiesce in the imperialist designs of the United States', i.e., which had refused to grant the U.S.A. bases on their territory. Washington was also alarmed at the increasing 'falangisation' of Spain's foreign service and the extent to which the Falange's organisations in Spanish-speaking countries were being put at Germany's disposal for a propaganda campaign against the United States.[69] Welles had complained to the Spanish Ambassador in Washington, on 2 December, that official press and propaganda agencies were disseminating grossly untrue tales about the United States all over Latin America.[70] Spain's fascism, its cultural imperialism and its intimacy with the Axis all seemed to threaten vital American interests. The British decision to suspend economic assistance to the Spaniards over their action in Tangier, dealt with in the next chapter, was thus the occasion for, rather than the cause of, America's drawing-back from a programme of active economic support for Franco's Spain.

However, Weddell kept up his pleas and, alarmed at the prospect of an internal Spanish upheaval bred by economic misery, which could give the Germans an opportunity to intervene, the European Division

of the State Department won Roosevelt and Hull round to renewing
the offer to help Spain. The American Ambassador was told, on 19
December 1940, that the United States was prepared to send a few
shipments of wheat to Spain as soon as the British announced
publicly their effort to secure wheat for Spain from Canada and
Argentina. The Administration was now even willing to begin discussing the extension of credits to Spain, although Secretary Hull
told his staff that 'mountainous' conditions would be attached to any
such loans.[71] Weddell did not want the United States to wait for
Britain to move first.[72]

Yet, once more, doubts and opposition inside and outside of
Government quickly re-emerged and were fortified by press stories
about alleged differences on aid to Spain between Welles and Hull,
which further strained their already troubled personal relations. The
press articles charged that only the personal intervention of Sumner
Welles with the President had prevented Hull, influenced by the
appeasement-style, anti-Communist argument, of his intimate
adviser, Dunn, from pushing through a $100,000,000 loan for Spain.
Both the Secretary, and Under-Secretary of State publicly denied that
there had been any departmental split over Spain. They also claimed
that the idea of a $100,000,000 credit for that country had neither
been espoused nor approved at a high level in the State Department,
nor even considered there.[73] Whatever the accuracy of this general
denial, the fact that the political chiefs of the State Department were
forced to make it, tended to undermine the viability of any proposed
credits for Spain. The adverse publicity combined with the sensibilities bruised and the mutual distrust awakened inside the State
Department to render large-scale economic assistance to Spain an
overly contentious project.[74] Hull, for instance, was impressed by the
'terrific criticism' of the proposed scheme to send food to Spain, in the
absence of any intention to send milk to children in Vichy France.[75]
So the United States Government again drew back. Hull informed
Weddell, on 27 December 1940, that in view of Spain's anti-American
activities and the complication caused by the question of comp-
lementary aid to unoccupied France, the Administration could not
justify assisting Spain before the British announced their willingness
to do so.[76]

Actually, the Americans did relent, in early January 1941, and
decided to send a shipment of flour and milk products to Spain, but it
was, as Feis notes, a gesture which had by then lost significance.[77]
Roosevelt had cabled Churchill, on 31 December 1940, to urge the
necessity of combining relief to Spain with relief to Vichy France. He

argued, thus: 'I feel that it is of the utmost importance to make every practical effort to keep Spain out of the war or from aiding the Axis Powers. If the policy of affording relief is to be undertaken, I am convinced that it should be undertaken now without delay.'[78] This message secured the Prime Minister's assent to the twin schemes suggested, and the first American cargo of aid reached Spain in February, with more help to a total of 15,000 tons of food and medical supplies arriving in the spring months of 1941.[79] However, the real American priority seems to have been to aid Vichy France, which they considered essentially more susceptible to being drawn out of Germany's orbit than Spain. The British attitude was precisely the reverse, Spain being courted with offers of economic assistance whilst their blockade was applied, at least in principle, to France and was only sporadically and grudgingly relaxed, usually out of deference to American wishes.[80] Hoare, argued, with some support from Halifax, for a soft line towards France but Churchill was not consistently convinced of the wisdom of this proposed policy.[81] His instinct, as he informed the Cabinet in November, was that the Vichy French Government must be 'kept well ground between the upper and nether millstones of Germany and Britain'.[82] Churchill could flirt temporarily with an opportunistic line of collaboration with Vichy France but he never shed his disdain and distrust of that regime's intentions, just as the Americans could never bring themselves to trust Franco's Spain.[83] Anyway, Hoare's scheme of economic attraction for Spain contracted to unimpressive proportions with the unwillingness of the United States to co-operate. However, the prospects for implementing the modest British programme of economic aid seemed good.

For, given this gamble on Spain, British aid proposals had a far smoother passage than the American ones. On 26 November 1940, the Duke of Alba had inquired of R. A. Butler whether it might not be possible for Britain to continue to aid Spain unobtrusively, since a recrudescence of anarchy there would not be in Britain's interest. As Butler noted, the Ambassador now appeared less concerned with Spain's imperial ambitions and declared the aims of his Government to be to preserve internal order and secure food for its people. He had also sought British help with the Americans.[84] As mentioned above, the British, at this very time, were agreeing to afford further economic help to Spain, but far from hoping to persuade the Americans to forge ahead with assistance for the Spaniards, they had been afraid that Washington's recalcitrance in the matter would frustrate their own scheme of assistance. However, again as mentioned above, the British got the 'green light' from Washington to proceed with their own plan of economic support for Spain on 29 November 1940. The British then acted quickly to convey their offer to the Spaniards. On 3 December, Hoare, acting on his Government's instructions, told the Spanish Government that, on account of Spain's grave economic plight, Britain was prepared to give a loan of £2,000,000 immediately, and 'if the political situation developed favourably', the amount would reach £4,000,000 by June 1941. Britain would also grant navicerts for 1,000,000 tons of wheat for the next year, and do its best to arrange the supplies of that cereal to Spain. The Spaniards were informed that Britain was making this 'most exceptional offer' notwithstanding the overt hostility shown to it by Spain, and it would be withdrawn if the Spanish Government gave aid to Britain's enemies. But if Spanish behaviour proved that Britain's trust had been well placed, for instance by exercising restraint at Tangier and consulting with the British over the unilateral authority Spain had assumed there, then more economic help might well be forthcoming. The British offer of help was subject only to the proviso of full publicity in the Spanish media for the supplies which they would obtain.[85] Cadogan explained the rationale behind the British offer, and their hopes for it, to the Military Attaché at the United States Embassy in London, General Raymond E. Lee, on 3 December, as the American recorded:

British believe that they will be able to keep them out by rationing them just enough to keep them going. Suñer was unable to arrange for any food from Germany and so must depend on Britain and western hemisphere. Cadogan believes British plan will be more successful than American, which was to give Spain nothing at all.[86]

The immediate Spanish reaction seemed to justify British confidence. Serrano Suñer had responded effusively when told by Hoare of the British offer of aid. He expressed his gratitude for the offer and his willingness to meet the British condition of publicity for their aid with 'full amplitude'. Serrano Suñer's fixation with the speedy arrival of grain to rescue Spain from starvation remained:

Spain was in a desperate position. They could not wait weeks or even days whilst negotiations were going on. Was it not possible therefore to do something at once? If His Majesty's Government let Spain have 100,000 tons of wheat at once an imminent crisis would be avoided and the whole situation would change.[87]

Von Stohrer reported to Berlin, on 9 December 1940, in equally striking terms, on Serrano Suñer's obsession with saving Spain from famine:

All the thinking and endeavour of the Spanish Government and especially the new Foreign Minister (Serrano Suñer) revolve round the provision of bread. The Minister spoke very gravely to me several times lately about the evermore rapidly deteriorating situation, which greatly impaired the Government's freedom of action; Herr Serrano Suñer emphasised as a result, that for the time being *all* other questions including that of war or peace would have to wait upon those measures which might cause an alleviation or at least a non-aggravation of the famine in the situation.[88]

It was the British, however, who heeded Serrano Suñer's pleas and respected his apparent foreign policy priorities. For, only a few days after Hoare's interview of 3 December with the Spanish Foreign Minister, they made an offer of immediate wheat supplies, as is noted below. This move appeared to portend a real *rapprochement* between Britain and Spain. The signs of such a development indeed began to multiply in late November to early December 1940. An Anglo-Spanish–Moroccan agreement, enabling Spain to buy some manganese, phosphates and wheat from French Morocco, had been concluded on 29 November. This agreement demonstrated the intention of the new anti-autarkist Spanish Minister of Commerce and Industry, Demetrio Carceller, to continue trade with the sterling area, despite German pressure.[89] The Anglo-Spanish financial agreement, signed on 2 December, which extended the control established by the Clearing Agreement of 18 March and required the Spaniards to yield the remainder of their free sterling, indicated a similar will to maintain trading relations with the British currency area.[90] Carceller had been appointed to his office the same day as Serrano Suñer and, indeed, had accompanied the latter to Berlin. However, hard-headed businessman that he was, the new Minister soon proved solicitous of British and American help. Hoare soon believed him to be a new ally within the Spanish Cabinet.[91] Carceller spoke to motor industry representatives, on 5 December 1940, and told them that Spain had been saved by British aid from enforced military and economic alliance with Germany. British help, according to Carceller, was also responsible for an improvement in Hispano-American relations.[92] Hoare thought that at last there was 'a real chance of starting a new chapter in Spain'. Alba told R. A. Butler, on 11 December, that he was very hopeful about the new turn in Anglo-American–Spanish relations resulting from the democracies' proposals for wheat supplies to Spain.[93] On 7 December 1940, the Spanish Government had received Britain's own specific wheat proposals: Britain offered to supply

10,000 tons at once from its stocks in Argentina, and 40,000 tons after 15 December; 25,000 tons of Britain's Canadian wheat stocks were also immediately available, and it was hoped to arrange for Spain to purchase 200,000 tons in Argentina in the future. If shipping difficulties could be solved, 'very large stocks' in Australia might be tapped. The only condition attached was that Spain should formally reassure Britain about its actions in, and intentions over, Tangier.[94] However, this latter condition proved unexpectedly troublesome, and the Tangier problem swiftly escalated into the first major crisis in Anglo-Spanish relations during the war.

7

The Tangier crisis

Serrano Suñer's trip to Obersalzberg in November 1940, and the way in which he drew the Germans' attention, then, to the economic obstacles in the way of immediate Spanish entry into the war, have been noted in the previous chapter. However, on 28–9 November, Franco's willingness to initiate and accelerate preparations for his war effort on the Axis side was communicated to Berlin.[1] This news was welcome to Berlin as Hitler had by then decided upon the absolute necessity of an early Spanish entry into the war.[2] For only by capturing Gibraltar and sealing off the Mediterranean could he eliminate the threat of the French colonies in North Africa defecting to the British, and relieve the dangerous situation in the Eastern Mediterranean and Balkans, all stemming from the Italian *debâcle* in Greece.[3] Operation 'Felix' to capture Gibraltar and close the Straits, whilst securing the Iberian Peninsula against British retaliation, had been long in gestation. All that was required for its implementation was Franco's formal assent to German forces crossing the Spanish frontier, on 10 January 1941, with the attack on Gibraltar to commence around 4 February.[4] Hitler sent Admiral Wilhelm Canaris, Chief of the Abwehr, and an expert on Spanish affairs, to obtain the Caudillo's agreement to this German timetable for an offensive against the Rock. However, Canaris knew enough about the economic and political realities of Francoist Spain, and its Caudillo's strategic priorities, to discount, in advance, any chance of success for his mission to Madrid.[5] Indeed, if the post-war testimony of Captain Wilhelm Leissner, wartime head of Abwehr operations in Spain is to be credited, the Admiral assured the Spanish General Vigón that Spain could safely refuse Hitler's demand that it join the fight. It is tempting to speculate that it was for such a dramatic service that the Spanish Government awarded Canaris's widow a pension on his murder by the Nazis, late in the war.[6] However, Franco did have other

133

reasons to be grateful to Canaris, not least for the valuable help which the German had rendered the insurgent cause during the Spanish Civil War, as an advocate of, and assistant to, Francoist interests within the Nazi regime.[7]

Anyway, Franco required little prompting to inform the Führer's representative, on 7 December 1940, that it would be impossible for Spain to enter the war at the required moment. He pointed out that apart from its military unpreparedness and the vulnerability of its islands and colonies to British naval action, Spain's chronic economic position, especially the food shortages which it was experiencing, and its deficient transport system precluded any immediate entry into the war. Indeed, Franco was emphatic in his refusal to accept Hitler's proposed schedule for an attack on Gibraltar: '. . . Spain could not enter the war within the immediate future. She could also not carry on a lengthy war without exacting unbearable sacrifices from the Spanish people.' Moreover, when requested by Canaris to suggest an alternative date to the 10 January 1941 for the entry of German troops into Spain and their race towards the Rock, Franco 'replied that since the removal of these difficulties did not depend alone upon the wishes of Spain, he also could not fix any definite date, such as might be subject to change because of circumstances'. Once more, Franco promised that 'his attention and his efforts would be directed toward hastening and completing the preparations' for Spanish belligerency, but Berlin was not deceived.[8] On 11 December, Hitler ordered the termination of all preparations for Operation 'Felix' because the necessary political precondition, an acquiescent Franco regime had not been realised.[9] Hitler did not consider forcing his way through Spain.[10] This disinclination is probably best explained by adhering to the view that Hitler had decided, soon after the fall of France, to attack the Soviet Union and was, therefore, determined to avoid any open-ended military commitment, like an invasion of Spain, which could deflect or postpone the Nazi thrust eastwards. This was the retrospective guess of Major-General Mason-Macfarlane, then Deputy-Governor and G.O.C., Gibraltar, who thought that Hitler must have made up his mind to attack Russia soon after the defeat of France.[11] 'Mason-Mac's' guess is borne out by one modern historian's detailed research into this complex problem.[12]

Ribbentrop attributed Franco's aversion to immediate involvement, in late 1940, to the Italian reverses in the Balkans which, he alleged, had caused the Spaniards to assume 'an attitude of obvious waiting'.[13] Indeed, Canaris had reported home to Berlin, of his 7

December meeting with the Caudillo, in these terms: 'General Franco made it clear that Spain could enter the war only when England was about ready to collapse.'[14] Both Franco and Serrano Suñer subsequently denied that the Caudillo had said anything of the sort but the latter's open assertion to the Germans, that Spain could only endure a very short war, was simply another way of saying the same thing.[15] Moreover, as State Secretary von Weizsäcker noted, the Spaniards could hardly own up to the fact that they wanted 'solely to play the part of the vulture'. Indeed, von Weizsäcker drew consolation from the fact that Franco's intention to enter the war 'only at the last moment before the victory of the Axis' had been disclosed, since the Spaniards' confession revealed them to be useless strategic associates for the Third Reich.[16] However, the strategic stance adopted by Franco, by December 1940, was of considerable value to Germany's enemy, Britain. For the British, had they but known it, had got all that they wanted from Spain by that time. Spain would remain non-belligerent as long as Britain seemed to suffer no apparently irrevocable disaster, like the loss of Suez. That is, Spain would probably remain neutral for as long as Britain really required its neutrality. In such circumstances, then, only a direct attack on Spanish or Iberian-owned territory, or an attempt to starve Spain, would provoke Franco's belligerency. Ironically, the escalating Tangier crisis would tempt some influential British minds to toy with just such action. The Tangier affair also provided critics and opponents of Hoare's policy-line with solid grounds for their complaints and scepticism. It seemed both a justification of their past hostility and an opportunity to press their attack home. But the most serious threat to the established policy came from a previous supporter who now felt compelled to question whether it should not be abandoned: Churchill, himself. Although the consistent critics would also contribute to the atmosphere of crisis, and complicate its resolution.

On 3 November 1940, the Spanish military commander in Tangier, Colonel Yuste, issued a proclamation abolishing the main institutions of the International Administration, the Committee of Control, the Legislative Assembly and the Mixed Bureau of Information, appointing himself Governor of Tangier and delegate of the High Commissioner of Spanish Morocco. The city, thirty-five miles southwest of Gibraltar, and its surrounding zone were an enclave within Spanish Morocco, and had been established an international zone by the Anglo-Franco-Spanish Convention of 1923 and confirmed as such by the Agreement of 1928, to which Italy also adhered. Tangier had been demilitarised and defined as a permanently neutral and internationally administered city under the sovereignty of the Sultan of Morocco. As was mentioned in chapter two, Tangier had been occupied on 14 June 1940, by Spanish Khalifian troops, with the alleged 'object of guaranteeing the neutrality of the Zone and the City', and the Spanish Foreign Minstry had announced, at that time, that the International Administration and the interests of other powers would be respected.[17] The British Government were not very disturbed by Spain's November action. They did, through Hoare, record a formal protest against the Spanish action, but they also evinced their willingness to discuss the issue with the Spaniards and made clear their readiness to recognise the latter's special interests there.[18] *The Times* editorialised that Tangier was but 'a small piece in a large problem, and the final settlement of the problem must necessarily await the conclusion of the war'.[19]

However, there were others who were not willing to take either so restrained or so long-term an attitude. On 13 November, the Labour M.P., Cocks, and the Liberal, Mander, questioned the Spanish action in the House of Commons. They, thus, commenced a parliamentary onslaught on their Government's response to the Tangier problem which was to continue through every remaining week of the session. Cocks argued that it was vital to Britain's interest, that Tangier remain neutral and unfortified, and Mander condemned 'this high-handed unilateral act of aggression'.[20] The irritation caused by the Spanish takeover in Tangier, was compounded by the arrival in that port, on 3 and 4 November, of two Italian submarines taking refuge from British pursuit. The Spanish claimed that the two vessels were damaged, and therefore allowed them to stay beyond the twenty-four hour period permitted to sea-worthy warships under international law. Another Labour M.P., Noel-Baker, had hoped that it would be made known to the Spanish Government that Britain could hardly justify the continued supply of oil to a country so negligent of Britain's rights, and so helpful to its enemies.[21] This parliamentary sniping went on into December when more events seriously embarrassed Government policy. The critical trend within the Commons was strengthened by the 'leak' of the news concerning the British Government's attempt to eject Negrín from Britain in response to Francoist complaints, a matter already mentioned in chapter three.

When Hoare repeated the British protest and their reservation of the commercial, legal and political rights, which they enjoyed under the agreements of 1923 and 1928, to Serrano Suñer, on 30 November 1940, the Minister claimed that Spanish action had been necessitated by the clear French intention to reassert their predominance in Tangier, and the dangers caused by an International Administration which included opposed belligerents (i.e., Britain and Italy). He also stressed that Tangier was now an ordinary part of the Spanish Protectorate. However, he assured Hoare that the economic rights of foreigners would not be interfered with, that he was willing to discuss such matters, and that there was no reason why Tangier should be fortified.[22] Nevertheless, the very next day a law was promulgated in Madrid establishing a new juridical regime for Tangier, emphasising its incorporation into the Spanish Protectorate in Morocco.[23] As noted already in the previous chapter, the British had intended to indicate to the Spaniards that their cessation of unilateral action over Tangier would constitute the kind of behaviour likely to evoke even greater British economic assistance. However, they were too late to forestall the 1 December decree, since their loan offer was not conveyed to the Spaniards until two days later. Roger Makins of the Foreign Office was perturbed by the latest Spanish unilateral act not for its own sake, but because it might jeopardise the political feasibility of economic aid to Spain. He commented, thus: 'It is a major interest that we should keep Spain out of the war, it is a very minor interest that the Spaniards should have control of Tangier. But in the public mind we shall be assisting a government which has deliberately flouted us.' R. A. Butler, who as Under-Secretary of State for Foreign Affairs had to bear the brunt of the Commons' attacks on the Government's Spanish policy, as the Foreign Secretary was a peer, was anxious too, that parliamentary susceptibilities be allowed for in any dealings with Spain.[24]

However, worse was to come. For, on 3 December, in a minor riot a crowd of Italians inflicted some damage on the British Post Office and a British-owned store in Tangier, and the attack received widespread publicity in Britain.[25] Halifax was in fact, at this stage very anxious to furnish economic assistance to Spain, particularly wheat, as rapidly as possible. He recognised, however, that such action would be open to the objection that Britain was supporting a country which was acting contrary to its international agreements and British interests.[26] Accordingly, he instructed Hoare, on 4 December, to impress upon Serrano Suñer that Spanish action was jeopardising British aid to Spain. He wished the Spaniards to suspend their Tangier decree, pending conversations with the British, and to concede that Tangier's International Administration should not 'in principle' be eliminated. He admitted to the Ambassador that he by no means wanted to sacrifice the policy of aiding Spain for the relatively insignificant

Tangier issue, but pointed out that the latter had a negative influence on parliamentary and public opinion which, ignorant of Britain's strategic requirements, tended still to be very much against helping Spain. Spanish behaviour over Tangier also indicated a rather unpromising attitude on their Government's part.[27] Hoare bridled at raising the general issue of Tangier's international status again, since its abolition had met with such widespread and enthusiastic approval in Spain, even from Britain's friends, such as the generals. He advised that rather than get enmeshed in tricky negotiations, Britain should maintain its protest and reserve its rights. It would then be possible to discuss detailed issues, like the rights of British businesses in Tangier.[28]

However, the political temperature in Britain went on rising. R. A. Butler was questioned in the House of Commons, on 4 December, about the status of Tangier, the anti-British riot and the continued presence of the Italian submarines there. Noel-Baker again offered advice: Spain should be told that any attempt to retain the Italian ships beyond the permitted time would result in British action to root them out. Butler could only reply that the Government had made their views plain to the Spanish Administration.[29] No wonder that the harassed Under-Secretary of State commented, thus: 'The Negrín incident has shown how much Parl'y animus on Spain remains. There is an impression that it is we who do the giving and they the misbehaving . . . Are Parl'y considerations strongly enough pressed on Sir S. Hoare?'[30] Halifax certainly directly urged them, and many other considerations, upon Hoare. Again, the Foreign Secretary informed his Ambassador, on 7 December, that he would find it very difficult to push through a scheme of aid for Spain unless the Spanish Government relented somewhat over Tangier. The intense parliamentary and public reaction to the attack on British property in Tangier and the continued presence of Italian submarines there, meant that Britain must retain liberty of action concerning the economic help which it had offered Spain. The Spanish Government should suspend the operation of its decrees on Tangier, where they impinged upon Britain's interests, and also consult with the British Government before embarking upon any further action injurious to their interests. The Spanish Government was certainly responsible for the satisfactory settlement of the Tangier riot and the disposal of the submarine question. If the Spanish Government did not agree to the immediate internment or departure of the submarines, Britain would act as it thought fit towards these warships and also over the question of wheat supplies. In addition, until the juridical situation could be ultimately defined, the 1,700 Britons in Tangier should be assured of their commercial, political and personal rights. According to Halifax's definition, 'political rights' included the continued employment of the British officials working in the International Administration.[31]

On 11 December, R. A. Butler again had to run the gauntlet of critical Commons' questioning on Tangier.[32] However, on that day too, the Spaniards at least seemed to respond to Britain's protests and pleadings. Hoare gave Serrano Suñer an *aide mémoire* elaborating Halifax's viewpoint, and the Minister, in reply, conveyed definite assurances as to non-fortification and the safeguarding of British rights and interests. Serrano Suñer also promised circumspection in and, if possible, consultation with, Hoare before any further change and stated that the Italian submarines would be interned after the end of the month.[33] Halifax accepted these assurances and was about to sanction wheat deliveries when the Spaniards suddenly replaced the officials of the International Administration (including several Britons), on 13 December 1940, with Spanish personnel.[34] The two Italian submarines also slipped out of Tangier, on 13 December, much to the dismay of the British, as Serrano Suñer had managed to give them the strong impression that the vessels were in such a state of disrepair, as to prevent their departure before their internment fell due at the end of the month. Halifax concluded that they must have been permitted an illegal sojourn in Tangier. In what Cadogan described as a 'snorter' of a telegram, Halifax informed Hoare that the latest Spanish move in Tangier, in complete defiance of British representations, was bound to generate such parliamentary ill-will towards Spain that any economic support for that country would hardly be politically possible.[35] Although Hoare reported to London that the departure of the Italian submarines, allegedly 'without complete repairs, with no torpedoes and in an unseaworthy condition' was due to his protests in Madrid, this latest evidence of apparent Francoist bad faith provoked doubts and fears in one of the most devoted Parliamentarians.[36] For Churchill suddenly emerged as the leading sceptic of Spain's good faith.

Amidst Adolf Hitler's ominous diplomatic 'grand tour', of late October 1940, George Orwell was moved to a despondent conclusion: 'the same feeling of despair over impending events in France, Africa, Syria, Spain – the sense of foreseeing what must happen and being powerless to prevent it, and feeling with absolute certainty that a British government *cannot* act in such a way as to get its blow in first.'[37] However, just such increasing unease that the Germans might try to pre-empt the British once again by seizing certain strategic locations, and a growing concern to anticipate them, did come to dominate the thinking of Britain's grand strategists towards one region, in late 1940. On 25 September 1940, General George V. Strong of the United States Army reported to his Government, on his return from London, that the British assumed that the Axis would enter the Iberian Peninsula, at some stage.[38] It has already been noted in chapter three, that the British plan was to meet – or even anticipate – such a contingency by seizing naval bases amongst the Portuguese Atlantic Islands which would provide some substitute for Gibraltar, at least for Atlantic warfare. It was also deemed necessary to deny these islands to the enemy. However, recognising that the Germans might well attempt to seize the islands – particularly the Azores – in advance of an actual move into Spain, the directors of Britain's war effort were forced to consider a preventive action, themselves, in the autumn and winter months of 1940.

It was the British worry that they might not be able to discern an enemy move, before it was too late, which first caused them disquiet. The British were unable, due to shortage of warships, to maintain a permanent naval patrol off the Azores, which alone could guarantee sufficient advance warning of a German action to ensure its frustration.[39] At the end of October 1940, conscious of their inability to keep a continuous naval vigil over the Azores and anxious about a German *coup de main* against them 'as a preliminary to an advance into Spain', the Chiefs of Staff inquired of the Foreign Office whether a British preventive occupation of those islands would embroil them with the Spaniards. The Foreign Office's reply was that such British anticipatory aggression would be 'almost certain to bring Spain into the war'.[40] But even before that letter was received, the Chiefs of Staff again returned to the issue, in considering a report on 7 November 1940, from the Joint Planning Staff which counselled that if the Germans did secure a hold on the Azores archipelago, during the winter of 1940–1, then there should be no British attempt to wrest the islands back until the following summer. The Chief of the Imperial General Staff, Sir John Dill, felt it was so important to avoid the danger of the Azores being lost to the Germans that 'there was much to be said on military grounds for establishing ourselves there forthwith'. The Chairman of the Chiefs of Staff Committee, the First Sea Lord, Dudley Pound, retorted that the Azores would be no substitute for Gibraltar.[41] Nevertheless, two days later, when Air Chief Marshal Portal again fretted over the possibility of Germany grabbing the Azores first, and the daunting prospect of attempting to retaliate in winter conditions, there was no dissent voiced. The Committee unanimously resolved (Dudley Pound, of course, included) that Operation 'Brisk' (against the Azores) should be executed 'as soon as possible', because of military considerations, and that Operation 'Shrapnel' (against the Cape Verde Islands) should be carried out simultaneously.[42]

The British wariness of Germany's designs on the Atlantic Islands, which had led the Chiefs of Staff to decide to snatch at them, was, in fact, only too well-grounded. Britain's grand strategists were, at last, guessing German intentions reasonably accurately. On 26 September 1940, in conversation with the Commander-in-Chief of the German Navy, Grand Admiral Raeder, Hitler declared that if it was decided to recruit Spain into the Axis war effort, then the Canary Islands 'and possibly also the Azores and Cape Verde Islands would have to be seized beforehand by the Air Force'.[43] Hitler maintained his interest in a prior occupation of the Atlantic Islands, as a prelude to a move into Spain in the succeeding weeks. In a major conference with his staff officers on 4 November 1940, Hitler announced his determination to capture Gibraltar 'as soon as possible' and ordered the preparation of occupation forces for the Canary and Cape Verde Islands.[44] The Chief of the Operations Division of the German Naval Staff, Rear-Admiral Fricke, was against occupation of the Cape Verdes on the grounds that they could only be taken and held with difficulty, that they were of little use to Britain and that a move against them might also provoke very grave 'political disadvantages', with possible Anglo-American retaliation against the Azores and other Portuguese territory.[45] However, Hitler was set upon action against the Atlantic Islands. His fixation with them, indeed, had earned him the sobriquet of 'the Island Jumper' in staff-officer circles.[46] 'Führer Directive' number 18, of 12 November 1940, exemplified this preoccupation. It was concerned, *inter alia*, with the preparation of Operation 'Felix' to 'drive the English from the Western Mediterranean', by conquering Gibraltar, closing the Strait and preventing them from alighting anywhere in the Iberian Peninsula or the Atlantic Islands. The Spanish defence of the Canaries was to be bolstered, the Cape Verdes occupied by the Germans and the occupation of the Azores and Madeira was also to be considered.[47] Grand Admiral Raeder attempted, in a conversation, on 14 November, to dampen Hitler's enthusiasm for the Atlantic Island projects. Raeder accepted that it was vital to deny the Canaries to the British, but he asserted that an assault on the Azores was 'a very risky operation', that it was 'unlikely' that German occupation forces could hold out against

British counter-attack and that, in any case, naval defence of the shipment of supplies to the islands would be too onerous. Raeder also argued that the Cape Verdes and Madeira could be safely ignored since they were useless as naval bases both to Germany and its enemy. Nevertheless, Hitler stubbornly required further study of the Azores operation. He expressed his perspicacious belief that 'the British would occupy the Azores immediately upon our entry into Spain' to his very sceptical naval chief and pointed out that these islands also afforded Germany 'the only facility for attacking America if she should enter the war with a modern plane of the Messerschmidt type, which has a range of 12,600 km'.[48] However, on the following 5 December, Hitler finally abandoned all plans for offensive action against the Atlantic Islands, realising that they were beyond his military means.[49]

The very acuteness of the British Chiefs of Staff's estimation of the imminence of the German menace to the Portuguese Atlantic Islands could have produced a disastrously counter-productive result. If they had maintained their 9 November resolution to strike at the Azores and Cape Verdes, they would have pressed their political leaders for the execution of a diplomatically dangerous enterprise, whose preventive purpose was to be rendered irrelevant by Hitler's self-denying ordinance of only a few weeks later. However, the Chiefs of Staff did soon have second thoughts on the wisdom of immediate occupation of the Islands. Dudley Pound re-emerged as the champion of caution at their meeting, on 11 November, calling for an appraisal of 'all possible German re-actions [*sic*] to Operations "Brisk" and "Shrapnel" ', before the Committee recommended their immediate implementation. The Chiefs of Staff Committee accepted this advice, asking the Joint Planning Staff to assess whether the Germans would respond to British execution of the Atlantic Islands' projects by entering Spain.[50]

The Joint Planners report considering this question, as adopted by the Chiefs of Staff, was ready by 21 November 1940, and it surveyed the premises and prudence of a preventive British move against the Portuguese Islands. Noting the War Cabinet had resolved, the previous summer, to seize the Azores and Cape Verde Islands 'in the event of Spanish or Portuguese hostility' or 'when it became clear beyond reasonable doubt that either of these Powers intended to intervene against us', the Chiefs of Staff now argued that this strategic policy required 'urgent reconsideration' for these reasons:

a The Germans will have appreciated, as we have, the vital importance to us of the Azores, if Gibraltar becomes unusable as a base, and they will have laid their plans accordingly. We cannot afford to take the chance of being forestalled.

b In view of other urgent commitments for the fleet we cannot maintain a constant and effective naval patrol off the Azores.

c The Germans can sail an expedition from French or Scandanavian ports with a fair chance of reaching the Azores without our knowledge.

d Once ashore the Germans will organise the defences rapidly and it will require a major expedition to dislodge them employing our available resources in landing craft carriers (i.e., Glen ships). Even then during the winter months weather conditions at the Azores are normally unfavourable for an opposed landing.

e It is uneconomical to keep the two Marine Brigades (one at home for the Azores and one at Freetown for the Cape Verde) and the Commandos (Azores), together with their shipping, waiting for a German move which we cannot count on forestalling.

Taking these considerations into account, the Chiefs of Staff decided that the only reliable 'method of safeguarding the bases in these islands is for us to take the initiative and occupy the Azores and Cape Verde Islands now'. However, the possible strategic disadvantages that might ensue from such a pre-emptive strike were not ignored in the report:

On the other hand supposing we seize the Azores now we might be worse off than before, particularly from the naval point of view, if the Germans either

a Advance into Spain and threaten Gibraltar as a result of our action – although this would be largely neutralised if the Spaniards resisted the Axis and allowed us to use the Canaries, or

b Obtained by threats the use of the Canaries as a base for surface ships and U-boats, possibly without advancing into Spain.

Admitting that the ultimate British decision for or against seizure of the Atlantic Islands would be a 'very grave' one, 'either way', the Chiefs of Staff formally requested a meeting of the Cabinet's Defence Committee in order to allow them to present their views on this important issue to the politicians.[51]

The latter report on policy towards the Atlantic Islands was indeed considered by Britain's primary grand strategic committee, the Defence Committee (Operations), chaired by Churchill, on 25 November 1940. It provided the occasion for a full-scale debate amongst Britain's grand strategists on the expediency of striking first, and soon, against the Portuguese Islands. That Churchill was worried about the German threat to those islands is revealed by his minute to First Lord of the Admiralty, Alexander, of 23 November, re Royal Navy dispositions and the whereabouts of the German pocket-battleship, *Admiral Scheer*: *Renown* [battlecruiser] and *Ark Royal* [Aircraft-carrier] are particularly well-placed at Gibraltar to deal with *Scheer* should she by any chance, as is not to be excluded, attempt some enterprise in the Azores. You may have a crisis there any day.'[52] any day.'[52]

Dudley Pound opened the Defence Committee meeting of 25 November, by recalling the 'anxious consideration' which the Chiefs of Staff had been giving to a pre-emptive seizure of the Azores and Cape Verdes. He declared that the arguments for and against such action were 'very evenly balanced', with the manifest importance of obtaining the Azores as a replacement for Gibraltar counterpoised by the realisation that a preventive occupation 'might precipitate a German advance into Spain and Portugal, and thus bring about the loss of Gibraltar earlier than might otherwise happen'. For the First Sea Lord the crux of the matter lay in whether the Spaniards and Portuguese would welcome the action as 'a sign of activity on our own part' or whether they would be sufficiently antagonised to fail to oppose a German move into the Peninsula. The notion that a British seizure of the Portuguese Atlantic Islands might actually be welcomed in Lisbon or Madrid was bizarre. Lord Halifax intervened to debunk it:

an occupation of the Azores by us would cause a very unfavourable reaction in Portugal, and would bring into play the mutual treaty of defence existing between Spain and Portugal. This might well precipitate the crisis which we were anxious to avoid. We might therefore, lose Spain and Portugal for the sake of securing a very small recompense.

'Considerable' discussion ensued.

It was argued that 'much would be gained' if even a token resistance to a German advance could be stimulated in Spain and Portugal. Even though this would probably require the dispatch of a substantial expeditionary force to the Peninsula, a British strongpoint in Lisbon or Ceuta (the town on the Spanish Moroccan coast opposite Gibraltar) would be a much greater strategic asset than the Azores. It would be counter productive, therefore, to kill the Iberian will to resist a German incursion by prematurely grabbing at the islands. The fragile bloom of Spanish resistance to a German entry into their country, which had only recently made a tangible appearance, was already receiving close attention in London; its nourishment would become an increasing preoccupation of British policy-makers towards Spain in succeeding months.

Sir John Dill, however, contended that the Germans would invade the Iberian Peninsula when they judged the moment was right and could easily brush aside any Spanish opposition. Britain could not send forces large enough to hold Lisbon or Ceuta, but 'by seizing the Azores now, we should save something from the wreck'. Churchill, however, felt that an occupation of Ceuta might be extremely advantageous and not necessarily beyond British means. On his suggestion, the Chiefs of Staff were invited to examine the feasibility of a British capture of Ceuta 'in the event of a German advance into Spain'.

The opinion was also expressed that the Germans might be refraining from an incursion into Spain only through reluctance at acquiring 'yet another hostile population which was already in a state of semi-starvation' to hold down. A British seizure of the Azores would not necessarily overcome this reluctance and provoke them to invade Spain. Lord Beaverbrook thought that Hitler had already decided to turn eastwards and supported 'the immediate seizing of the Azores as a measure to strengthen our naval position, on which in the long run everything would depend'.

Dudley Pound, however, explained that a German occupation of the Iberian Peninsula and the Canaries would necessitate a re-routing of Britain's South Atlantic convoys westward via Trinidad and Nova Scotia. The Azores would not really compensate for enemy occupation of the Canaries, but if the Royal Navy could secure use of the latter islands, through Spanish resistance to advancing Germans, Britain would be well-placed to control European overseas trade. There was ready agreement amongst those attending the meeting that 'if by any means inducement could be offered to General Franco to resist the Germans, and in the event of a German attack in the Peninsula to give us facilities in the Canaries and on the Spanish mainland, our own position would be much improved'. Further debate led to a consensus that the case for executing Operations 'Brisk' and 'Shrapnel' at once was 'not overwhelming', and that 'it would consequently be better to wait and see whether a suitable moment would not arise before long'. The operations were to be held ready at forty-eight hours' notice to ensure that any opportunity for their implementation could be seized, whilst 'the general situation should be watched, and . . . the matter should be reconsidered after the lapse of ten days or a fortnight'.[53]

The danger that Britain would incite Spain's active hostility by moving against the Portuguese Atlantic Islands was thus deferred, but that postponement, of course, resulted in the issue coming up for review precisely when the Spaniards chose to take their final unilateral steps to absorb Tangier into their Moroccan zone. Then, the worry over the vulnerability of the Atlantic Islands to a pre-emptive German move fused with the apprehension generated by the high-handed Spanish actions at Tangier. Moreover, matters became even more complicated in the interval, with additional influences developing to push British grand strategists and Churchill, in particular, towards considering striking first at Spanish territory and the Portuguese Islands.

The result of the investigation into the practicability of the Ceuta project, however, did not give any encouragement to aggressive action against Spain. Churchill told the Chiefs of Staff in early December that the decision about the execution of such an expedition could be made later; the important thing was to have the plans ready.[54] The Prime Minister was clearly keeping his options open. Actually, as the Joint Planning Staff pointed out, Operation 'Challenger' (the projected move against Ceuta), was only feasible as a spontaneous action by the British. It could not effectively occur in response to a German initiative, since Britain was simply too weak to hold the necessary shipping and forces in readiness. Therefore, the expedition would probably arrive too late to be of any use. In addition, circumstances prevented the necessary prior discussion with the Spaniards. Even a direct British assault on Ceuta, however, naturally provoking Spanish resistance, would hardly achieve the goal of such an expedition: the securing of an alternative site to Gibraltar, from which to maintain Britain's control of the Strait. For Ceuta and the surrounding region were too vulnerable to attack from the Spanish mainland to provide a substitute base for the Rock.[55] This report's negative conclusion demonstrated that the continuance of Spanish neutrality really provided the sole means by which Britain could retain control of the Strait of Gibraltar. Discussion of the Ceuta project, however, was subsumed under the general review of British strategy towards Spain occasioned by the Spaniards' 13 December action at Tangier.

However, the problem of the Portuguese Islands kept the pot boiling in the first fortnight in December. For British anxiety over the Atlantic Islands was not suspended pending the reconsideration of the question of proceeding against them immediately. Churchill disclosed his continuing disquiet by adding an extra condition to those already approved by the War Cabinet, the previous 22 July, as justifying the seizure of the islands. He personally amended a telegram to Hoare, on 28 November 1940, to inform the Ambassador that the Azores and Cape Verdes would be seized not only in the event of actual Spanish or Portuguese hostility, or when it became 'clear beyond reasonable doubt' that either country's belligerency was imminent but, also, if either state was 'found or deemed to be incapable of protecting its neutrality'. This last criterion was so subjective that it would leave Churchill complete freedom of action to jump on the islands, if and when he decided to, which is probably what he wanted. The telegram to Hoare was actually sent to secure his assessment of the effect of a 'sudden occupation' by British forces of the Azores and Cape Verde Islands on Spain, 'of the likelihood and effectiveness of Spanish resistance' to a demand by Germany to pass troops through their country, and of the possibility that either the Spanish Government or 'important sections of [the] Spanish army' would accept Britain's assistance and grant it base facilities in the Canaries in the latter circumstances.[56] Hoare's reply of 3 December, to the effect that the Spanish Government would regard Britain's occupation of the Portuguese Atlantic Islands as an attack upon the Peninsula has already been mentioned in chapter three. He also believed that such arbitrary British action would kill the nascent Spanish will to resist German incursion, destroy any hope of receiving a Spanish request for Britain's aid for a resistance movement, and probably result in a Spanish invitation to the Germans to come into the Canaries. Only the 'over-riding claim of military necessity' would justify a British seizure of the islands in Hoare's view. Sir Walford Selby, British Ambassador to Portugal, agreed with Hoare's appraisal.[57] The case for caution, then, was powerfully advocated by Britain's representatives in the Iberian Peninsula.

Judging by a conversation Cadogan had with Halifax, Butler and two other Foreign Office men on 13 December, opinion in London was hardening against precipitate action towards the Atlantic Islands. Cadogan, himself, was sure that the British 'shouldn't initiate anything'. He got the impression that Halifax shared his view, and that even Churchill was coming round to it.[58] But on that very day, with the onset of the crisis in Anglo-Spanish relations caused by the Tangier affair, there apparently emerged just such an imperative strategic need as Hoare had postulated as necessary before Britain should abandon restraint and go for the islands.

For there was an additional dimension to the genesis of the Tangier crisis and it lay precisely at the point where the Spanish problem merged with Britain's wider strategic concerns, in late November –December 1940. Churchill's febrile mind strove to discern not only strategic dangers, but opportunities as well. With the British military revival about to find tangible expression, at last, on land with an offensive against the Italians in Egypt, the Prime Minister was alert to the political capital which Britain might derive from the North African thrust. He intended to get the Cabinet to sanction the execution of Operations 'Brisk' and 'Shrapnel' should the desert offensive achieve any substantial results.[59] However, the very scale of the British success in their Western Desert assault, soon led Churchill away from concentrating upon its positive political side-effects, to dwell upon its negative consequences. For, as the British attack, on 7 December onwards, turned into a massive rout of the Italian forces, Churchill saw that Hitler was bound to respond, but where and when? Hugh Dalton recorded Churchill's musings at a mid December meeting:

The P.M. says that he is quite sure that Hitler cannot lie down under this. Perhaps within three weeks and certainly within three months, he must make some violent counter-stroke. What will it be? An attempt, at long last, to invade us? Perhaps a gas attack on an immense scale . . . Perhaps a blow through Spain, perhaps through France, perhaps through Bulgaria to Salonika. Any of these might be awkward and troublesome, and we must be prepared to face difficult hours . . .[60]

Although concrete evidence of German intentions was slim, the fact that Britain was so strongly entrenched in the Eastern Mediterranean could not but prompt worry in London that Hitler might retaliate at the western end of the sea. Thus, though Churchill had an amiable luncheon at the Spanish Embassy, on 5 December 1940, his fears were barely concealed. So, while willing to assure the Duke of Alba of his readiness to keep Spain supplied, and of the tight rein being kept on Negrín, he made an anxious inquiry: 'Will Spain be able to resist German pressure?' Even a declaration of friendship, on the Prime Minister's part, was tinged with apprehension: 'As far as we are concerned, we wish to have the best and most friendly relations with you and if these change, you may be sure that it will not be our fault. I detest communism as much as you could detest it.'[61] The Spanish threat began to weigh heavily upon Britain's grand strategists. The Joint Intelligence Sub-Committee of the Chiefs of Staff (J.I.C.) agreed, on 13 December, that such a German move into Spain would be strategically sound, and was in accord with the slight evidence available, like the recent military preparations in the Gironde region of south-west France. The Committee noted that a German presence in the Iberian Peninsula could extend their blockade and submarine effort against Britain, seal off the western end of the Mediterranean, render Dakar and the West African coast liable to rapid German occupation and substantially repair the injury of the Italian *débâcles*.

They thought that even a German occupation limited to the western half of the Peninsula was possible.[62] However, the J.I.C. did dismiss the possibility of any imminent German move against the Atlantic Islands since aerial photo-reconnaissance missions over the ports in the Bay of Biscay had detected no signs of the build-up of the naval forces required for such an operation.[63] Menzies, Head of Britain's S.I.S., thought that the Germans would 'do a Norway' on the west coast of the Iberian Peninsula.[64]

It was the way that the Spanish action at Tangier united in Churchill's mind with his speculations about Hitler's possible riposte to Britain's Eastern Mediterranean success, which led him to contemplate drastic action towards Spain. The Spanish dismissal of the British officials of the International Administration, on 13 December, despite Britain's previously conciliatory attitude over Tangier, and its offer of economic help, seemed explicable only in one way: Spain had gone over to Britain's enemies. Thus, Cadogan recorded a meeting with the Foreign Secretary on the following morning (Saturday, 14 December), in these terms:

H. called at F.O. at 10. He had been worried all night by P.M. about Spain. True, the Spaniards have behaved v. badly about Tangier ... But I do *not* think it means they are in with the Germans, and I do *not* think that, on that assumption, we should jump into the [Atlantic] islands.[65]

Churchill had been bothering others as well. Dudley Pound, doubt-less prodded by Churchill, had ordered naval Force 'H', in the early hours of Saturday morning, to proceed towards the Azores from Gibraltar to safeguard them against a German *coup de main*, and had arranged British submarine dispositions to 'deal with a German descent upon the Atlantic Islands, or on Spanish ports'.[66] Clearly, the Prime Minister was not as willing as the J.I.C. to place absolute trust in the negative results of photo-reconnaissance over the Bay of Biscay. Moreover, Churchill requested the Chiefs of Staff to be ready to advise him at an 11 a.m. meeting, that same day, at Chequers, about 'the launching of Brisk and Shrapnel Operations forthwith' and the dispatch of an expeditionary force to Spanish Morocco.[67] The Chiefs of Staff gathered in the Cabinet War Room, at 8.30 a.m. on the Saturday morning, to prepare their brief. They agreed among them-selves that, if Spain were really hostile, Britain had neither the forces nor resources to do anything about it. If Spain actually asked for assistance, then a small force might be spared. Although they also agreed that Operations 'Brisk' and 'Shrapnel' could be launched within about forty-eight hours.[68]

At Chequers, later that morning, Churchill expressed his fears and doubts to Admiral Pound, Air Chief Marshal Portal, Lieutenant-General Haining, Vice-Admiral Phillips, and Major-General Ismay:

now ... we had established ourselves more firmly in the Eastern Mediterranean it seemed more and more likely that Hitler would take some action in the Western end. All he had got to do was to square or push aside the Spaniards; and it seemed very likely that he was preparing a coup of some kind in that direction; the Spanish move at Tangier looked suspiciously as though Franco had sold himself.

Churchill explained that he had summoned his top service advisers to review the current disposition of convoys and reinforcements. For, given the dangerous situation brewing in Spain, it would be prudent to concentrate resources so as to be able to respond appropriately to developments there. He declared that if the Germans went into Spain, Britain would retaliate by occupying the Atlantic Islands and landing a force in Spanish Morocco. He also suggested that British forces might land at Tangier the moment the Germans entered Spain, with the good excuse to hand that they were protecting the international status of the city.[69]

The comments of the service chiefs at the morning session of the Chequers meeting were confined to the technical aspects of the problems raised. They pointed out the cost of taking Ceuta, and its strategic worthlessness, owing to its vulnerability to air and artillery bombardment from Spain. Tangier, too, with 'very bad harbour facilities' and only one aerodrome, was hardly worth the effort of taking it. But the Chiefs of Staff did not inform Churchill of their early-morning unanimity on the general impracticability of any action against a hostile Spain. Nor was there any discussion, before the meeting broke up for lunch, of the premises of the proposed military policy, i.e., whether Britain should strike pre-emptively at Iberian territory, or not.[70]

However, Halifax appeared for the luncheon at Chequers, concerned to debate just that fundamental issue. The Foreign Secretary was well primed for the defence of the existing policy-line on Spain by Messrs Cadogan, Strang and Roberts of the Foreign Office.[71] He conducted a comprehensive defence of the Foreign Office's view, early in the meeting's second session, arguing thus:

the danger of a Spanish move into Tangier depended on the degree to which it was an Axis plot ... it was more probably the outcome of Spanish nationalism; since if it was part of a German scheme to get hold of Gibraltar, would not they have preferred facilities in Ceuta or Southern Spain? And there were other factors. In the first place Spain was desperately anxious for wheat; secondly it was reported that the Generals were preparing a coup d'etat against Suñer; thirdly Franco himself and the Army were very much against getting involved in the war. In addition, it was thought . . . that Hitler would be more likely to move into Italy than into Spain . . . [therefore] . . . the Spanish move into Tangier was not an Axis plot, and any intervention on our part would put Spain definitely into the Axis camp.[72]

Churchill replied that there should definitely be no British move until Serrano Suñer's response to their 'very outspoken' message on the Spanish 13 December action at Tangier had been received.[73] Both Halifax's argument and Churchill's answer clearly show, again, that the Prime Minister had contemplated attacking first. However, Halifax's argument was sufficient, for the moment, to coax Churchill away from immediately embarking upon such a drastic course of action. But Churchill was still convinced that the danger of Spain's defection to the Axis was real enough to require serious precautionary measures, on Britain's part. He got the Chiefs of Staff to agree to strategic redispositions and to sanction plans which would ensure that the British would be 'crouched not sprawled'. 'Thus', Churchill persuaded the meeting, 'if the Germans were to make any move into Spain or Spanish Morocco, or alternatively if we had absolutely certain information that they intended to do so, we should be in a position to undertake BRISK and SHRAPNEL, and also to establish a bridge head at Tangier' or in Spanish Morocco.[74] This formula still maintained the British option of a preventive strike against Spain. The British Government would be the judge of whether Germany was about to move into the Iberian Peninsula. Churchill's continuing preoccupation with the threatening situation in Spain, which prompted him to keep alternative courses of action available, was revealed on the day after the Chequers meeting. When news came in, then, that all communications had been severed with Switzerland, the Prime Minister was disposed to regard this development as 'the preliminaries of an operation against Spain'.[75]

Still, the inherent ambivalence in the British attitude towards Spain, a mixture of hope and fear, was evident in the directive issued to carry out the sense of the 14 December Chequers meeting. Britain's military planners were required to consider not only the appropriate British response to a German move to gain control of the Western Mediterranean with Spanish acquiescence, but also to assess what assistance Britain could give to the Spaniards, if they resisted Germany.[76] However, the Chiefs of Staff only confirmed their previous pessimism, concluding that all that could be done was to assist a friendly Spain to deny Spanish Morocco to the Germans.[77] Churchill was unhappy with this result, observing that Britain would have to take 'some action' to contest German action in the Western Mediterranean, and that if the Spaniards did resist, they would surely expect British support on the Spanish mainland. So, the Defence Committee, on 16 December 1940, instructed the Chiefs of Staff to reconsider all possible British operations in Spain and North-West Africa.[78] Although the Joint Planning Staff (who prepared the actual plans for consideration by the Chiefs of Staff) naturally complied, they agreed again, on 19 December that there was probably little that could be done, whether Spain was friendly or hostile.[79]

It is interesting to note the German assessment of the Spaniards' assimilation of Tangier, given the extent to which Churchill had interpreted it as indicative of a pro-Axis commitment on their part. Von Stohrer informed the Reich Foreign Ministry that the incorporation of the Tangier Zone into Spanish Morocco was explained by the Spaniards' disapointment at Germany's failure to satisfy their territorial ambitions: therefore, Franco's Spain had decided to take 'Tangier at least' for itself.[80] Similarly, the German Consul in Tetuán, Spanish Morocco, summarised for Berlin in late December the consistently anti-German activities of the Spanish authorities there. He mentioned the Spaniards' 'morbid jealousy' of the German influence in Morocco and, referring to the continuing Spanish designs on French Morocco, he concluded, thus:

The Spanish policy here in this country is a bad sign for the future, if Spain should really succeed in gaining possession of the French Zone entirely or even in part. Spain would have only one aim: she would never rest until the last German had left the country – the heart's desire, openly expressed, of the Secretary-General of the Alta Comisaría here . . .[81]

The Spanish absorption of Tangier was, in fact, a clear example of imperialist expansion, as the Spaniards themselves, indeed, openly declared. The Falangist paper, *Arriba*, stated that 'an exact sense of opportunity', a necessary characteristic for the execution of foreign policy, then, had made possible the assimilation of Tangier.[82] Serrano Suñer denounced, early in January 1941, the 'international greed' which had produced the 'great artifice of the internationalisation of Tangier' which 'was a constant aggression against Spain'. He also explained the specifically indigenous inspiration of the Tangier takeover: 'the case of Tangier enters fully into the ambit of our geography, our history and our natural right'.[83] The Spaniards' absorption of Tangier may have been precipitated by their anxiety over a possible French attempt to re-establish their pre-eminence there. Serrano Suñer, anyway, told both Hoare and Ribbentrop that this was so.[84] Judging from the way he mentioned the point in conversation with both Hitler and Ribbentrop, Serrano Suñer was also well aware of the fact that a foreign adventure might relieve the heavy domestic pressure on the Franco regime.[85] As already mentioned, Hoare did note the widespread approval in Spain, even amongst Serrano's enemies like the Generals, of the Tangier takeover.[86]

Moreover, although the Spaniards may have underestimated the British reaction to their move at Tangier, their progressive absorption of the city, despite mounting British protest, was a definite sign of the intensity of their will to empire. Thus, even in their desperate economic circumstances, they risked jeopardising British economic aid for the sake of Tangier. Indeed, the effects of ideological inspiration and material need may have coincided in promoting a forward Francoist policy at Tangier, as David Eccles noted, on 4 November 1940:

The Spaniards have seized the Tangier zone. Why? Not at the Germans' request in order to prepare a base for an attack on Gibraltar, but because they must do something to justify to themselves their Civil War. When bread is lacking men desire, more than ever, to prove to themselves that they do not live by bread alone. A little glory, and they can put up with hunger.[87]

However, the very life and death struggle in which Britain and Germany were engaged tended to foster a reductionist habit in interpreting the behaviour of neutrals: those who were acting against one's interests must be acting in favour of the enemy. Churchill, initially, seems to have fallen into this form of facile analysis over Tangier. He chose to view what was essentially an autonomous Spanish action as inspired and/or controlled by Germany. Churchill had rightly perceived that Hitler would try to offset Britain's Eastern Mediterranean advantage by action at the other end of the sea. But he was erroneously inclined to regard the Tangier affair as evidence of Spanish acquiescence in a German counter-stroke. However, he remained intellectually open enough to let his Foreign Secretary disabuse him of such a notion. Churchill's susceptibility to the opposing point of view on strategic policy towards Franco's Spain was a crucial factor in preventing British anticipatory attacks against that country. This quality was complemented by the concomitant faculty which he displayed for moderating second thoughts concerning offensive action against Spain. Indeed, with the departure of Halifax from the Foreign Office, in late December 1940, Churchill's own wary reconsiderations progressively became the decisive influence in inhibiting rash British moves over Spain.

If the immediate danger of a violent British response to Spain's unilateral actions had passed, the Cabinet were in no mood to tolerate such behaviour without some effective reply. Even the Foreign Office indeed had come round to the view that some display of British firmness was necessary to correct the apparent Spanish conviction that Britain could be squeezed indefinitely. A member of the Joint Planning Staff told a Foreign Office official, on 15 December, that they were worried that the Anglo-Spanish dispute at Tangier might jeopardise the Spanish co-operation which was 'absolutely essential' if Britain was to counter a German entry into Spain successfully. Such Spanish collaboration afforded the only hope for holding on to the Strait in the Joint Planners' view, and they wished the Foreign Office to know also that Tangier was 'absolutely unimportant' strategically. It was pointed out in reply that strategic considerations had always been, and remained, the determinant of Britain's Spanish policy. A firm attitude on Tangier was necessary, however, since otherwise the Spaniards might think that they could get away with more or less anything, and that impression could entail the realisation of those very strategic dangers which British policy sought to avoid.[88]

This stiffening of the official British attitude towards the Franco regime was also evident at the War Cabinet on Monday 16 December. Churchill stated, at this gathering, that a German move into Spain would cause Britain 'great embarrassment'. Halifax contended that whilst the Spaniards had clearly behaved very badly in Tangier, the point at issue was whether it seemed that they had sold themselves to the Axis to such a degree as to require breaking off relations and withdrawing Britain's offer of economic aid. In the resulting discussion, the disturbing similarity of Spain's behaviour to that of Italy before Mussolini declared war was stressed. Nevertheless, it was also pointed out that almost all the Spanish people, and the generals, wanted to stay out of the war. Again, Spain's takeover in Tangier, which it had coveted for some time, could hardly be of much help to Germany. The Cabinet eventually approved the course of action advocated by Halifax: namely, that the Spaniards should be requested to submit in writing their proposals to cover Britain's demands over Tangier, that Britain's wheat and credit proposals be suspended, but that Spain be allowed to import as much as 1,000,000 tons of wheat for the coming year, as well as other food-stuffs, through the British blockade 'from wherever [else] she could obtain supplies'. Halifax had warned the members of the Cabinet that in approving this policy-line they might have to make a choice between breaking with Spain or climbing down over Tangier. However, the Cabinet not only approved of Halifax's newly tough line, but also asked that Serrano Suñer be told that Britain was not afraid of adding Spain to its enemies, since it could then be meted out the same treatment as Italy was receiving.[89]

Halifax relayed these instructions to Hoare, elucidating the rationale behind them most clearly in a letter of 21 December:

... I am awaiting with considerable anxiety at this end to hear how you may be able to handle this lot of difficulties about Tangier. No one at this end wants to break the general policy that you have been pursuing with such success: nor is Tangier intrinsically worth it. But I think as a symbol we must insist on some measure of co-operation or as much of it as you can get. In the last resort, for your information, I think the Cabinet would put first in the order of priority the not coming to a rupture with Spain but they are very much concerned to try and get their action presented in as favourable a light as possible, and this not only in view of Parliamentary difficulties here but having regard to reactions at your end.[90]

As the Foreign Secretary informed his Ambassador, a statement by Serrano Suñer giving Britain concrete assurances over Tangier would eliminate both British governmental doubt and political criticism. Thus, the British Government would have to be convinced of Spain's goodwill before economic assistance would be renewed, in spite of their anxiety to avoid a breakdown in relations with Spain.[91] So, although Halifax had deflected the threat of offensive action, military or economic, against Spain, the positive, supportive side of Hoare's policy was, yet again, getting bogged down.

Indeed, the British Government was forced to remain constantly aware of the domestic political susceptibilities involved in policy concerning Spain. For the parliamentary dissent over the official British handling of the Tangier affair continued right up to the Adjournment Debate of 19 December. F. S. Cocks, the Labour M.P., who was one of the most persistent critics of the Government's reaction to the problem and who was, in fact, in regular communication with Admiral Gaunt, a leading light of the British community in Tangier, delivered a major speech on the issue.[92] Citing the Negrín episode as an example of the way that 'the discredited policy of appeasement' was still being applied to Spain, he called for drastic measures, including military operations, if necessary, to maintain the neutral and unfortified character of Tangier. Rather than 'fawn on a Fascist dictator and submit to blackmail', Britain should hint to Franco that it held a hostage for his good behaviour in the person of an alternative leader, Negrín, who would attract the support of Spain's people. Noel-Baker was equally critical of appeasing Franco, and hoped the Government would realise that using the means available to put pressure on the Spanish Government could well be the safest course to adopt. The M.P.s of course, did not know of the suspension of the British offer of economic support to Spain. Nor did R. A. Butler inform them of it in his reply, but he did deliberately take note of the advice given by Cocks and state that the Spanish action in Tangier was bound to influence British public opinion. He also declared that whilst co-operation between Britain and Spain was clearly desirable, both parties would have to be willing to contribute towards achieving it.[93]

Hoare was instructed to secure Spanish written guarantees on non-fortification, the political and economic rights of British subjects, adequate compensation for the dismissed British officials of the International Administration, currency questions, the maintenance of existing British institutions such as the post office, and the definite reservation of British and other countries' rights under the Convention of 1923 and the supplementary Agreement of 1928. Satisfaction for the attack on the British post office was also sought.[94] The Ambassador, however, was, predictably, unhappy with the suspension of Britain's economic help to Spain. He wrote to Halifax that with the Germans on the Pyrenees, the Spanish Government, like the Vichy French one, was a captive administration. He doubted whether the implications of this situation were realised in London, for the standard of conduct demanded from a free government could not be expected of them. It was indeed necessary for the Spaniards to maintain a smoke-screen of hostility to Britain for their own safety. He also pointed out that Britain's Spanish policy was purely self-interested and not designed to secure bouquets from the Spaniards. Halifax circulated the Ambassador's views as a War Cabinet Paper.[95] More specifically, Hoare was anxious to start the British wheat deliveries, even before the conclusion of a settlement over Tangier, and he requested authority to proceed with some deliveries at his own discretion. He was afraid that the Germans would initiate a propaganda campaign accusing Britain of attempting to starve Spain. Halifax grudgingly conceded this authority, but only if the Ambassador felt that the Spaniards were giving substantial satisfaction in return.[96] He explained the Foreign Office's position to Hoare, thus: 'We have . . . hitherto stood pat on the line that we won't starve Spain by interfering with food shipments but as long as the Spanish Government remain, to put it mildly, unhelpful we don't see why we should give them active assistance to obtain foodstuffs . . .'[97]

On 20 December, Hoare reminded Halifax that what he termed 'our joint policy' had come a long and successful way since the dismal days of June 1940.[98] However, the Ambassador quite suddenly lost his powerful ally. On 23 December Churchill replaced Halifax with Anthony Eden as Foreign Secretary. When Eden had resigned his Foreign Secretaryship in 1938 over the Italian problem, his Under-Secretary, Lord Cranborne, had followed suit. At the start of December 1940, Lord Cranborne, then Colonial Secretary, had written to Halifax expressing grave doubts about the wisdom of Britain's attempt to send wheat to Spain. To Cranborne, Serrano Suñer was just one more totalitarian, to whom conciliation was only a sign of weakness and a temptation to disregard British interests, as Tangier demonstrated. He requested that Britain demand definite proof of Spain's goodwill before sending wheat.[99] Halifax had politely rejected Cranborne's criticism, emphasising the Chiefs of Staff's view that it was vital that Spain be kept out of the war.[100] But he described Cranborne's outburst as 'an echo of old controversies', in a letter to Hoare.[101] The problem for Hoare, now, was that with Eden back at the Foreign Office, the old controversies about appeasement might revive with Britain's Spanish policy as their primary focus. He, therefore, acted with speed to impress upon the new Foreign Secretary the necessity for his policy-line, particularly when hostile propaganda in Spain was suggesting that Eden's return to the Foreign Office meant a new British commitment to the 'Reds'.[102] He sent the Foreign Secretary an exposition of his views, on 24 December 1940, arguing that a policy of economic aid to Spain, far from being appeasement once again, was 'entirely a strategic policy for the purpose of winning the war'. If Spain was to be kept out of the war it had to be allowed to ensure its economic survival, otherwise the Germans could intervene. Spanish and British interests coincided, in Hoare's view, since both the British Government and the Spanish people wanted to keep Spain from entering the war, economic help being both a means available to Britain to induce Spain to remain outside the conflict, and a good reason to the Spaniards for doing so.[103]

Hoare was correct to be apprehensive about his new political master. For not only did Eden dislike him personally, but the new Foreign Secretary was also very sceptical of the wisdom of the Hoare–Halifax line on Spain which he defined, a short time later, as 'doling out help at intervals to a Government which treated us with blunt discourtesy, while its principal Minister (i.e. Serrano Suñer) openly sided with our enemies'. His instinct was to refuse any further help until the Spaniards behaved like true neutrals.[104] Eden was even more reluctant than Halifax to consider facilitating Spanish wheat shipments, unless tangible evidence of Spain's goodwill was forth-coming. He minuted, 'we should surely *not* send the wheat until we have some satisfaction over Tangier?' Thus, though Hoare wanted to start sending cargoes of wheat to Spain if the negotiations over Tangier looked like dragging on, he was instructed that he should secure concessions on some points, at least, before granting facilities for the purchase of a cargo of wheat. Further Spanish concessions could be met by further shipments of wheat.[105]

There was other evidence of Eden's doubts about the existing policy towards Spain. Referring to the great change in the Spanish situation with the growth of a will to resist Germany, and the concurrent economic deterioration, Hoare reminded the Foreign Secretary, at the end of 1940, that the only yardstick applicable to Britain's Spanish policy was whether or not it contributed to a British victory in the war. He accepted his Government's decision that it was essential that the Iberian and North African ports be kept from falling to Germany. It was vital, therefore, that Spain be kept at peace, even if this involved putting up with Spanish provocation and political criticism in Britain. For the great possibilities of a new Anglo-Spanish Peninsular War coalition, and the integration of Spain into the Atlantic orbit of the United States and Britain, were at stake. Hoare's analysis was well received by the officials of the Foreign Office, one of them, William Strang, even having the temerity to defend appease-ment as 'a legitimate diplomatic operation when conducted from strength and not as a means of shirking an issue'. He did add, though, that Britain's Spanish policy was not, in his view, really appease-ment.[106] However, impressing his private secretary (in mid-1941), as having 'always hated this appeasement policy' of Franco's Spain, Eden was not enthusiastic about Hoare's turn of year argument. For, although the Foreign Secretary did admit the necessity of maintain-ing Spanish non-belligerency, he also commented, as follows:

There is no dispute, I should hope anywhere that it must be an object of our strategy to keep Spain out of the war in present conditions. Every day that we have the use of Gibraltar is a day gained – But there may well be, there should be, intelligent discussion and examination of the best means of achieving that most desirable result.[107]

In an interview with the Duke of Alba, on 27 December 1940, Eden insisted that any improvement in Anglo-Spanish relations depended upon the Spanish Government meeting the British requirements over Tangier. British goodwill would have to be reciprocated if any progress were to be made.[108] Again, when he became aware of an impending American Red Cross shipment of foodstuffs to Spain in early January 1941, Eden was concerned lest there be 'too many such ships' sent there.[109]

Thus, although Serrano Suñer agreed to negotiations between British and Spanish officials for a provisional settlement over Tangier, and to Hoare's relieved surprise conceded rapidly most of the points at issue, the Foreign Secretary remained somewhat suspicious. Certainly Serrano Suñer's role in these exchanges was not such as to inspire confidence. He was often either (probably genuinely) ill, or absent, in January when needed to sign letters or elaborate his oral and written assurance to the British Government. He baulked at giving more than verbal assurance to consult with the British before effecting any further change in Tangier. This was accepted eventually but Eden and, indeed, his officials were somewhat less happy about the untidy form of the nascent agreement. This consisted of a memorandum drawn up in a rather haphazard fashion by the Spaniards to meet the British demands; a note from Hoare accepting the memorandum; a reply from Serrano Suñer accepting Hoare's covering note, but not in terms confirming the Ambassador's understanding of the memorandum as expressed in his note; and another letter from Serrano Suñer giving an explicit assurance that Spain would not fortify Tangier. Eden was reluctant to let Hoare sign the agreement with Spain before he had seen its text, and he regarded the documents as 'so "ragged" as to be almost unintelligible'. He was also unfavourably impressed when the legal proceedings against the alleged ringleader of the Italian attack on the British premises in Tangier in early December merely resulted in derisory fines. He pressed his Ambassador to secure amendments in the memorandum, particularly with regard to the assurance of non-fortification and concerning the legal system to apply to British subjects should the Mixed Tribunal (the International Administration's Court) be abolished. The British wished it specified that, should the Mixed Tribunal 'cease to function', then a Consular Court would come into operation under the capitulatory system of justice, based on the General Treaty of 1853 with the Sultan of Morocco. The economic regime in Tangier, and the rights of British subjects under it, still remained to be defined. The Foreign Office was particularly anxious to secure a definite reassurance about the re-introduction of the capitulations, i.e., a guarantee that British subjects should be under British legal jurisdiction. However, in a stormy interview with Hoare on 28 January, Serrano Suñer refused to change one word in the memorandum, alleging that Franco thought that he had already given away too much.[110]

Hoare's attitude to these negotiations was that, while Britain was at war, facts must be accepted as they were and London should 'not think too much about juridical questions'. This meant, he felt, provisional acceptance of the Spanish incorporation of Tangier and collaboration with the Spaniards, to convince them that Britain was their friend and Germany their foe.[111] He reiterated, in a letter to Brendan Bracken of 6 January, that he was neither trying to prop up Franco nor engaged in appeasing Spain. Rather, was he attempting to preclude the possibility of Spanish belligerency, and to engender Spanish resistance against a German invasion. 'Some of the great' in London, he thought, might over-react to Spanish inefficiency and provocation and neglect the absolute necessity of 'winning the final Spanish coup'.[112] Certainly, one of 'the great' remained wary of the Spanish manoeuvrings over Tangier. Eden minuted on 4 January 1941, thus, about the Anglo-Spanish Tangier negotiations: 'I hope that all will in fact turn out as well as Madrid appears to believe. We are not so entirely without cards; for we have the food.'[113] However, the Foreign Secretary did listen to Hoare's pleadings that Britain relent to some degree on its total suspension of economic assistance to Spain. He explicitly granted Hoare authority, on 5 January 1941, to facilitate some wheat shipments to Spain during, and depending on, the course of the Tangier negotiations.[114] However, given Eden's doubts about Spain's good faith and Serrano Suñer's corresponding prickly elusiveness, the negotiations dragged on into February.

Although Eden remained unhappy about the state of Anglo-Spanish relations, the New Year witnessed a radical reappraisal by Britain's grand strategists of the imminence of the danger emanating from the Iberian Peninsula. There was some hard evidence to support this revised judgement. For, in late December 1940, the Yugoslav double agent, Dusko Popov, who acted in the Allied interest, arrived in London with vital information, which he had acquired within Abwehr circles in Lisbon, where he was being trained for his ostensible espionage activities in Britain. Popov had learned of the early December visit by Canaris to Madrid, and of the Admiral's failure to persuade Franco to agree to admit German troops into Spain in January 1941 for an attack on Gibraltar. Amongst the de-briefings which Popov experienced in London was one by William Cavendish-Bentinck, the Foreign Office representative on, and chairman of, the J.I.C., whose particular interest was Popov's 'story of Admiral Canaris's venture in Spain'.[115] The information provided by Popov, possibly complemented by other sources, led the J.I.C. to report, with conviction, that Franco would not agree to an entry of German soldiers into his country and that Hitler would not attempt to move into Spain without the Caudillo's agreement.[116]

There were other encouraging signs emanating from Spain also attracting official British attention at the year's turn. Thus, right at the start of 1941, the Chiefs of Staff accepted a recommendation from the Joint Planning Staff that the occupation of the Azores should be postponed because of the 'friendlier feeling . . . evident in Spanish official circles, especially in the Army' towards Britain, and the fact that 'in spite of the Tangier episode, opposition to Germany appears to be hardening and the likelihood of military resistance to a German invasion is becoming greater'. This meant that Britain should have 'reasonable prospects' of securing bases in Spanish Morocco and the Canaries, which would be strategically much more advantageous than only getting the Azores as an alternative to Gibraltar.[117] The Future Operations (Enemy) Planning Section of the Joint Planning Staff also reckoned that Hitler would not force his way into Spain.[118] Attlee perceptively pointed out to the Prime Minister, too, that Hitler's limited oil stocks were likely to induce him to choose a Balkan campaign from the options open to him, for by so doing he would be going where there was oil readily available. Spain, on the other hand, Attlee emphasised, would make the most severe demands on Hitler's limited resources.[119]

In addition to these reassessments of Hitler's intentions concerning Spain, promoting a renewed restraint amongst British strategists, Hoare's Naval Attaché, Captain Hillgarth, came to see the Prime Minister in London to counsel strategic caution. Churchill himself, in a cable to Hoare, testified to the impact of Hillgarth's visit, stating that he 'greatly impressed us with the work you are doing'. Churchill also brought him before the Defence Commitee on 8 January, where again, the Attaché spoke to 'great effect'.[120] Churchill further relayed to his Chiefs of Staff, on 7 January 1941, Hillgarth's view that it was increasingly unlikely that Franco would either permit a German entry into Spain or join the Axis war effort. The Prime Minister now also thought it highly improbable that the Germans would invade Spain before the following April. Therefore, he exhorted the Chiefs of Staff to avoid at all costs provoking the Spaniards or precipitating the Germans into taking violent action against them. 'Brisk' and 'Shrapnel' were now only to be implemented if the Germans were invited, or forced their way, into Spain. Whilst there could be no absolute certainty that Hitler would avoid a Spanish commitment until next spring, Churchill thought it 'a reasonable working assumption' that he would do so.[121] He repeated his changed evaluation of the Spanish situation a few days later, at a meeting of the Defence Committee: 'A German advance through Spain at this season, however, would be a most dubious enterprise; it did not look as if

Spain would either give permission or yield to force, and therefore prospects of a German advance had receded.'[122]

Actually, even before Hillgarth's visit, Churchill had been contemplating again, in late December, the idea, which he had first raised the previous July, that France might resume the struggle against Germany from its North African colonies. So, on 31 December, a message was sent to Marshal Pétain stating that Britain could dispatch a force of up to six divisions to aid a new French war effort in North Africa. Although Pétain's reaction was unfavourable, Churchill continued to hope, for much of January, that General Weygand, Delegate-General for French North Africa, to whom the message had also been communicated, would rejoin the fight.[123] Hoare had been informed of the original British *démarche* to Pétain, and he quickly indicated to Churchill its implications for Spanish affairs. He maintained that Franco–Spanish co-operation was essential for any such venture because of the vulnerability of the only line of communication between French Morocco and Algeria, the railway, to attack from the Spanish Moroccan Zone. Consequently, Hoare believed, the French must be persuaded to view the Spaniards as necessary allies rather than as potential enemies.[124] Churchill responded favourably to Hoare's argument, drafting a telegram in reply, on 13 January, which went as follows:

My hope is that the Germans will not go through Spain by favour ever, or by force at least until the Spring; and that in this interval the Pétain Government will be so maltreated by Germany that they will allow Weygand to re-open the war in Africa.

This would be strategically and politically more important to us than anything that could happen in Spain. If, however we send troops to help Weygand via Casablanca or other West Atlantic ports, we will insist that the French make good offers to the Spaniards in Morocco and Tangier, which we would endorse, contingent on the Spaniards playing straight. It ought therefore to be possible to reconcile the conflicting interests to which you have drawn attention.

Due to Foreign Office objections the telegram actually sent to Hoare, instead of declaring Britain's intent to insist on good French offers on Tangier and Morocco, stated less strongly that Britain would 'be in a position to press the French authorities to give some satisfaction to the Spanish claims in Morocco'. For Eden and Cadogan had disliked the emphatic language of the Prime Minister's draft, were hesitant to judge what might be a 'good offer', and pointed out that Britain could not insist on France surrendering its rights in Tangier without doing the same itself. Churchill approved these amendments, but the earlier draft is valuable as an indication of the direction of his own thoughts, and the extent to which by January 1941, he had come to dwell upon the advantages of diplomatic co-operation with Franco's Spain rather than of the likelihood of imminent hostilities with that country.[125]

On several occasions, in January and early February 1941, when the hope of a French re-entry into the war was still entertained in the Foreign Office, Hoare and his Military Attaché, Torr, incurred official disapproval when they encouraged Spanish designs on Morocco. Hoare was told that he should maintain an attitude of reserve in the matter.[126] So, just as with the Dakar expedition, Britain's strategic hopes for French North Africa could conflict with its desire to take account of Spain's Moroccan susceptibilities and ambitions. Similarly, as we have seen, Hitler's fears over the French North African colonies had fatally complicated his autumn attempts to attract Spain into his anti-British coalition. The hope and the fear, then, of a renewed French belligerency greatly reduced the willingness of both Britain and Germany to court Franco's Spain by offering to support territorial claims against French North Africa. In any case, by 12 February, grumbling that Weygand had made no reply to Britain's 'great offers', Churchill had decided that the General would only act in response to drastic German pressure on the Vichy Government.[127] Churchill's diagnosis was correct and Weygand never led his forces back into the fight. Churchill, indeed, had been counselled by Halifax early on, that to try to coax the 'fundamentally anti-British' Weygand, or any of the Vichy leaders back into the war, would be a fruitless exercise.[128]

However, the prospects for active Spanish opposition to the Nazis seemed better. Indeed, Captain Hillgarth had come from Spain not merely to persuade the Prime Minister of Franco's aversion to becoming engaged in the war. He also elaborated a large-scale scheme of support for Spanish resistance to a German invasion. The Chiefs of Staff accepted his proposals for the formation of a British group to act as a nucleus for guerrilla warfare against the invading Germans and for the dispatch of a British liaison delegation to Gibraltar, which could establish contact with Spanish headquarters directly the Germans entered Spain. They rejected his more daring requests for the delivery of oil and war materials to Spain, on the grounds that its future intentions concerning the war were not so clear as to warrant such an expression of British trust.[129] Moreover, when the Joint Planners reviewed their conclusions on possible British military support for Spanish resistance to German aggression, they decided, once more, that Britain could only help the Spaniards consolidate the defence of their Moroccan territory.[130]

Although the Foreign Office tended to feel that Hoare was a little over optimistic about the prospects of Spanish resistance to a German invasion emerging, the signs that such a movement might indeed develop began to multiply in the first months of 1941.[131] General Aranda was as explicit as ever about the Spanish Army's determination to resist a forcible German entry into the country. He even claimed, during the last German attempt to drag Spain into the war in late January and early February, that Franco had nominated him as his successor should anything happen to the Caudillo.[132] Even more impressively, General Vigón, who had for a long time been adamant that Britain was bound to lose the war, turned up in Portugal making discreet enquiries as to whether Britain would support a Spanish resistance against a German invasion, and if the British could be trusted not to overthrow the Franco regime. In late February, General Muñoz Grandes told Hillgarth that he would resist a German entry under any circumstances.[133] By March the Spanish Chief of Staff, General Martínez Campos, was both soliciting a promise of British aid in the event of an invasion and suggesting that the problem of sending supporting British forces in sufficient time to be of use, yet not so early as actually to anticipate and, therefore, precipitate a German move, could be solved by stationing British forces in Portugal, ready to come to Spain's help, if need be.[134] The Germans also complained to Franco, on 21 January, about 'certain military elements' in Spain that 'unwittingly played England's game'.[135] These alleged intentions of the Spanish Army to resist a German invasion were, of course, never put to a test, which Portuguese Ambassador Pereira believed, at the time, they would not pass.[136] But the Spanish Government certainly did stoutly resist the severest diplomatic pressure from Germany, in late January and early February 1941.

Hitler's inclination, in the immediate aftermath of the rejection by Franco of his early December effort to involve Spain in the war, was to consider abrogating the Secret Protocol concluded with the Caudillo the previous October.[137] This document, already mentioned in chapter five, had effected Spain's accession to the Pact of Steel and embodied its readiness to join the Tripartite Pact and the Axis powers at war. Hitler was feeling no more forgiving when he met with the Italian Ambassador in Berlin, Dino Alfieri, on 19 December 1940, and denounced Franco's attitude, in these terms: 'Spain had taken a very cool and negative attitude . . . Italy and Germany might have expected more gratitude from Franco after what the Duce and the Führer had done for the Caudillo, who in the last analysis owed his whole existence to them. They would have to remember that attitude.'[138] The German leader was still resentful at Franco's ingratitude when he wrote to Mussolini, at the end of December 1940, but by that time he was also beginning to contemplate a further effort to recruit Franco into the ranks of the Axis:

Spain, under the impression of what Franco considers to be the changed situation, has for the time being refused to co-operate with the two Axis Powers. I fear that Franco is committing here the greatest mistake of his life. His idea that he can obtain grain and other raw materials from the democracies in thanks for his aloofness, is in my opinion unrealistic näiveté. They will put him off with promises until the last kilogram of grain in the country has been used up, and then the fight of the democratic powers against him personally will start. I regret this, for we had made all the preparations for crossing the Spanish border on January 10 and attacking Gibraltar at the beginning of February. In my opinion the attack would have led to success in a relatively short time. The troops for this were excellently selected and trained, and the weapons were especially designated and readied for the purpose. From the moment in which the Strait of Gibraltar was in our hands the danger of any kind of untoward behaviour on the part of French North and West Africa would have been eliminated. For this reason I am very sad about this decision of Franco which does not take account of the help which we – you Duce, and I – once gave him in his hour of need. I have only a faint hope left that possibly at the last minute he will become aware of the catastrophic nature of his own actions and he will after all – even though late – find his way to the camp of the front whose victory will also decide his own fate.[139]

It was Hitler's continuing concern over the possibility that the French North African colonies might desert to the British camp, mentioned in this letter to Mussolini, which prompted him to make one last attempt to induce Spain to enter the conflict, even though the prospects for success were 'scarcely promising'.[140] Ribbentrop told Ciano, on 19 January 1941, that he regarded 'Spanish intervention to be of decisive importance, since it would allow the occupation of Gibraltar and the control of North Africa which is intended to paralyse any possible attempt at sedition by the French'.[141] Hitler explained his concern to Mussolini, on the same day, in these terms:

The Fuehrer speaks at length on the French situation and does not conceal his scepticism as to the stability of that situation. He stresses that there are profound dissensions between Pétain, Weygand and de Gaulle, but there is also a common hatred – that towards the Axis Powers. One cannot, therefore, rule out a surprise in the French attitude, and the Fuehrer is following the situation in North Africa with the most careful attention. In this connection, he considers closer Spanish adhesion to the policy of the Axis and her intervention in the war to be a factor of fundamental importance.

Hitler attributed Spain's 'hesitant and faithless attitude' to the 'personal activity' of Serrano Suñer and the influence of the Catholic Church on the Spanish Government, and not to Franco himself. He urgently requested Mussolini to try and persuade the Spanish leader to bring his country into the war alongside the Axis. With Italian forces retreating before the Greeks in the Balkans and the British in North Africa, Mussolini was in no position to refuse what Ciano described as 'the hard task of bringing back home the Spanish Prodigal Son'.[142] The Germans themselves, endeavoured in the interim to bend Franco to their will. Von Stohrer was even ordered by Ribbentrop, on 21 January 1941, to threaten Franco bluntly that 'unless [he] decides immediately to join the war of the Axis Powers, the Reich Government cannot but foresee the end of Nationalist Spain'.[143] But Franco was neither intimidated by German menaces nor convinced by Mussolini's very tepid presentation of the case for Spanish belligerency, at their meeting at Bordighera, on 12 February 1941.[144] Serrano Suñer, who was also present at this encounter, emphasised the basic Spanish pre-condition for entry into the conflict, assured territorial gain: 'The Spanish intend to enter the war but wish guarantees. At Hendaye they were given nothing concrete. The Vienna Protocol is extremely vague. That Protocol should therefore be modified.' The Spaniards also stressed that their exigent economic needs – particularly for grain – would have to be satisfied before they could fight.[145] Mussolini reported the Spanish requirements to Hitler, but the Führer was no more willing, in February 1941, than he had been, in October–November 1940, to grant these Spanish demands. The Germans realised that further pressure would be futile. On 22 February 1941, Ribbentrop informed von Stohrer that it was 'unequivocally clear' that Spain was not going to enter the war on Germany's side. He therefore instructed his Ambassador to maintain, thenceforward, an attitude of cool aloofness with regard to the question of Spanish non-belligerency.[146]

A letter sent by Franco to Hitler, on 26 February, confirmed the German assessment that little more could be done with the intractable Caudillo for the immediate future. As part of the pre-Bordighera phase of German pressure on Franco, Hitler had written to him on 6 February. The Führer had tried to imbue the Spaniard with a sense of ideological community with the Axis against 'Jewish international democracy' which would never forgive Franco his Spanish Civil War victory, and would snatch back Tangier at the first chance. Only an Axis victory, Hitler had asserted, would maintain Franco in power. Dismissing the notion that Britain would really help the Spaniards economically, he had reminded the Spanish leader that Germany stood ready to assist 'on the greatest possible scale as soon as the date for Spain's entry into the war was definitely settled'. He had reiterated his intention of guaranteeing some territorial reward to Spain, but had also contrasted its 'large territorial demands' with the 'very modest' claims raised by Germany and Italy who had borne the burden of the war until then. Hitler had concluded with a rhetorical flourish citing 'the most implacable force of history' which bound Franco, Mussolini and himself to one another, and advised that in such 'grave times' nations could 'be saved by stout hearts rather than by seemingly prudent caution'.[147]

Franco, however, did not care to cast caution aside. He did accept Hitler's view in his reply that the three dictators were 'indissolubly linked in a historic mission' and protested his complete solidarity with Hitler's cause and his confidence in its victory. This did not prevent him from pleading Spain's economic weakness as a bar to early entry into the war. Since the Spanish people were 'suffering from extensive starvation' and were 'experiencing all possible privations and sacrifices', he could hardly demand more of them, he explained to the Führer, without securing some prior improvement in their condition. Accepting that the closure of the Strait of Gibraltar was 'not only indispensable for the immediate relief of Italy but probably also a prerequisite for the end of the war', he contended, however, that it was also essential 'that the Suez Canal be closed at the same time'. He continued, thus: 'Should this latter event not take place, we who would like to offer to you the effective commitment of our military strength, have to state in all sincerity that Spain's position in a prolonged war would become extremely difficult.' Franco also challenged Hitler's interpretation of his claim for territorial profit and, in doing so, repudiated even the imprecise obligation which he had contracted to fight on Germany's side several months before:

You speak of our demands and you compare them with yours and those of Italy. I do not believe that one could criticize the Spanish demands as excessive. The less so if one considers the tremendous sacrifices of the Spanish people in a struggle which was a glorious precursor of the present war. An appropriate statement concerning this point is still lacking in our agreements. The Protocol of Hendaye – permit me to say this – is, in this respect, rather vague and you undoubtedly remember the motives, which do not exist today, for leaving matters vague and open. The facts in their logical development have today left far behind the circumstances which in October brought about this Protocol, so that it can be considered obsolete at the present time.[148]

Hitler perceived that, 'under a flood of assurances and fine phrases', Franco 'had practically denounced the Hendaye agreement', but a punitive expedition against Spain did not fit into his schedule for the foreseeable future, with the campaigns against Greece and the Soviet Union in the offing. The Führer had to accept his rebuff, as he told Ciano, on 25 March 1941: 'One could not draw any conclusions from [Franco's] attitude; one simply had to accept it, since there was an interest in at least maintaining the appearance of good relations.'[149]

However, the Germans were not the only ones coming to terms with Franco's continuing neutrality as the best that could be expected from Spain for the foreseeable future. Thus, the British Joint Planning Staff's rather negative reconsideration of their plans to aid the Spaniards in the event of a German invasion, which had resulted from Captain Hillgarth's far-reaching proposals for supporting Spanish resistance to German aggression, have been noted above. But the Joint Planners also came to an illuminating incidental conclusion: they refused to plan for the contingency that Spain might actually allow British troops to enter its territory before any German move. Such a development, they pointed out, would not be in Britain's interest since the inevitably consequent German invasion would destroy any hold over the Strait of Gibraltar maintained by an Anglo-Spanish force. Alluding to the degree of control of the Strait then enjoyed by Britain, on account of Spanish neutrality, they reached this conclusion: 'It is therefore greatly to our advantage to maintain Spanish neutrality. We consider that . . . until the Germans are reduced in strength and mobility we should endeavour to keep Spain outwardly friendly to the Axis and avoid any action that may force the enemy to invade the Peninsula in order to forestall ourselves.' Spanish neutrality, then, was the best defence of Gibraltar that a beleaguered Britain could have. If Hoare could argue that it was inevitable that Franco's Spain should remain overtly hostile to Britain, the Chiefs of Staff accepted the conclusion that it was actually in Britain's interest that it do so.[150] This emphasises the British vested interest in Spanish non-belligerency: i.e., in the preservation of the international *status quo* in the Iberian Peninsula. Along with Franco's new-found resolve to uphold that *status quo*, even if only to consolidate his regime internally, this produced a community of strategic interest between Britain and Spain. Only a British judgement that Spain was about to move against them, or a Spanish calculation that Britain's downfall was imminent, might induce either side to ignore, temporarily, such considerations of mutual strategic vulnerability, since both the previous contingencies would render them irrelevant.

Understandably, then, the importance of Spanish neutrality had reasserted itself in Churchill's scale of strategic priorities by early February 1941. It has already been seen that, by early January, he had ceased to regard Spain as offering any immediate danger to Britain. Indeed, the emphasis in British strategic thinking on Spain shifted back, after Hillgarth's visit, towards considering ways of supporting a Spanish resistance movement, rather than retaliating against a likely Spanish enemy. The lingering Tangier dispute now seemed irrelevant and, possibly, damaging. So Churchill minuted to Eden, on 6 February 1941, in this vein: 'I really cannot take interest in the Tangier quarrel, considering where we stand in other matters and the proportion of events. Do you not think you could let Ambassador Hoare [*sic*] round it all up and get it out of the way?'[151]

Eden had maintained his scepticism about Spain's good faith until early February, although he approved Hoare's action, of 17 January, in sanctioning two shipments to Spain of Canadian wheat amounting to 15,000 tons. Another contract for the supply of 50,000 tons of wheat from British Government stocks in the Argentine had also been signed.[152] Such concessions, however limited, were timely. For Serrano Suñer had delivered a menacing discourse to the female section of the Falange in Barcelona, on 11 January 1941, in which he expressed 'a conditional threat of war', as he later described it himself, in response to what he saw as British economic strangulation. He declaimed, as follows:

we must say that the problem [the procurement of food for the Spanish people] must be resolved now, for this winter, and quickly!, without dilatory procedures. We need bread so that the people may eat; we need bread so that the people may work, not one day, not two days, but all the days. And if faced with this, which is a simple demand of our right to life, the nations were insensitive to our demands and denied us bread or made the work of the Spanish people impossible, or demanded [our] honour as the price, then . . . there is no danger, no pain and no death which could stop us![153]

Serrano Suñer's hectoring *per se* did not intimidate the British Government into liberalising their economic policy towards Spain. Thus, Eden was still inclined to adopt a stiff line towards Spain: 'No credits until we see some results', was one of his primary preoccupations in conducting British policy towards Spain, in the last week of January.[154] But the fear that a propaganda campaign spearheaded by Serrano Suñer would affix blame for Spain's economic plight upon the

British, was prominent in the case which Hoare presented for relaxing the blockade of Spain.[155] Serrano Suñer threatened to embark on just such a course of action, when he denounced British policy, in a conversation with the Portuguese Pereira, on 29 January 1941:

Serrano then proceeded to attack the policy of the English towards Spain. He believed that their lack of vision was only comparable to their ferocious selfishness. While people were dying of hunger and despair all over Spain, England doled out grain by grain a pittance of wheat ... Until the new harvest, 800,000 tonnes of wheat were needed. Without that amount, half Spain would starve. And in the face of this monstrous dilemma the English were envenoming and embroiling the negotiations and made no more than hypocritical promises. Their behaviour was so vile that when the limits of patience were exceeded, he, Serrano, would denounce to the country the hidden designs of England, responsible for Spain's famine and misery.[156]

Franco, himself, informed Pereira during an audience with the Portuguese Ambassador, the same day, that he was 'very disgusted' with British methods of work in applying the blockade to, and conducting economic negotiations with, Spain. Accusing the British of impeding their negotiations with the Spaniards by raising difficulties of their own making, Franco voiced much the same complaints as Serrano Suñer, but without the latter's 'exaggerations or rancour'.[157] The British Government's response to Hoare's pleas for a return to a more generous economic attitude towards Spain, is described in the next chapter.

However, before Anglo-Spanish economic *rapprochement* could develop any momentum, the obstacles placed in its progress by the unresolved Tangier dispute would have to be removed. On 18 January 1941, a report had been received in London that General Weygand would lead French North Africa back into the fight against Germany.[158] This naturally generated some discussion within the Foreign Office about the need to reconcile conflicting Franco-Spanish interests in North Africa. William Strang pointed out that in fact Britain might deem it desirable to reverse its policy towards Spain, and indicated that it had an excuse to hand in the unsettled Tangier affair. He added, though, that the Central Department of the Foreign Office did not recommend such a course of action. The rapid disappointment of the hopes about Weygand's return to the fight, already mentioned, cut short such speculation. However, this French complication only exacerbated Eden's exasperation and, indeed, bewilderment over Britain's Spanish policy. He revealed his frustration to his Foreign Office colleagues, on 26 January 1941: 'I do not pretend that I am happy with that policy as it is at present conducted; indeed my difficulty is to find the policy beneath the multiplication of concerns[?] and devices which seems to take its place.'[159] He told Hugh Dalton two days later, that he was baffled as to what Hoare was doing in Madrid and that he intended to tell him to implement his instructions.[160]

Nonetheless, the very next day, Eden apparently decided that enough was enough and he accepted William Strang's advice that Britain should not risk losing what it had already gained in Tangier by holding out for full satisfaction of its demands.[161] He now determined to conclude the affair as quickly as possible, even if the Spaniards refused to improve on their existing assurances over Tangier. He was now even ultimately prepared, he told the War Cabinet, to waive the demand for an explicit Spanish declaration of intent to re-introduce the capitulatory system of justice, should they abolish the Mixed Court of Tangier. Remarking to his Cabinet colleagues that such additional guarantees would probably be worth no more in reality than those already received, he argued that the practical reasons for accepting the existing arrangements over Tangier were convincing. With the prospect of French re-entry into the war clearly in mind, he stressed that should the war, as seemed possible, extend to North (?–West) Africa, Spain's general attitude could be of the utmost importance.[162] (The Foreign Secretary had, thus, clearly aligned himself with his Central Department in declining to overthrow the established Spanish policy for the will-o'-the-wisp of renewed French belligerency.) The War Cabinet approved, on 5 February, Eden's proposal to make a further attempt to secure the amendments desired by Britain in the Tangier documents, but also, in the last resort, to accept them as they were, should the Spaniards refuse to budge.[163] Churchill's 6 February minute, urging the Foreign Secretary to wind up the Tangier quarrel as quickly as possible, shows that the former felt that even this procedure was too dilatory. However, Hoare had already on his own initiative again tried, unsuccessfully, to change Serrano's mind, so Eden told him on 6 February 1941, to go ahead and conclude the agreement.[164] He was able to reply to Churchill's minute by telling him that Hoare had been instructed, that very day, to sign the existing documents.[165]

Much to the Foreign Office's annoyance the Spaniards proved elusive for the next few weeks. However, the agreement was finally signed on 22 February 1941, and the British did actually manage to secure some minor alterations to it. The British recognised provisionally, the *de facto* Spanish occupation of Tangier, but they maintained their original protest, reserved their rights under the 1923 and 1928 instruments and obtained guarantees for British political, economic and legal rights in Tangier. They were also given an assurance that the Zone would not be fortified. The dismissed British officials were to be compensated. The Spaniards, in their turn, reminded Great Britain of the nature of their action at Tangier, which was 'absolutely, the incorporation of the said Zone in that of the Spanish Protectorate in Morocco', and they received British recognition of their special interest in the Tangier Zone.[166]

The way that the relatively minor Tangier dispute rapidly produced a serious challenge to the continuance of the existing policy-line on Spain is explained by two factors: first, there was the general anti-Francoist opposition in Britain which condemned the futility of this new version of appeasement, and which found justification in the Spanish action at Tangier; second, the wide perspective of British strategic interests came to focus on Tangier, too, as events seemed to suggest that the most likely source of new danger was Spain. Together, these concerns produced the crisis which Halifax and Hoare managed to defuse, though, once again, only at the price of delaying and enervating the positive effort to attract Spain into Britain's orbit, which they advocated.

8

The limits of attraction

The frustration of the British scheme for a joint programme of Anglo-American aid to Spain in late 1940, and the Tangier imbroglio, as a whole, illustrate clearly the combination of influences tending to thwart Hoare's effort to attract Spain into a close political relationship with, and economic dependency upon, Britain. The Spaniards' own wariness of the dangers inherent in too public an intimacy with Germany's enemies was an evident factor. They were already defying that mighty military power by declining to fight on its side. To flaunt political and economic accord with the Reich's foes, in addition to a refusal to enter the lists against the British, could be suicidally provocative. The Spaniards' own truncated will to empire, as expressed in their takeover of Tangier, also made for a conflict of interest with the British. The Americans' sullen suspicion of Spain's future intentions greatly diminished the attractiveness of the economic temptation which Britain might present to the Spaniards. The British, for all their willingness to risk a try at courting Spain with the bait of economic aid were, simultaneously, forced by the very desperate nature of their struggle with Germany, to maintain an alert vigil over the developing strategic situation in the Iberian Peninsula and elsewhere. This constant scanning of the strategic horizon for new signs of menace meant that the entire effort to woo Spain could be hastily interrupted or abandoned, if the apparently threatening circumstances seemed to require preventive British military action. One of the main purposes of this book, of course, is to explain how such pre-emptive action was forestalled. However, the effect of the abrupt breaks in the process of economic courtship, associated with such occasional reinterpretations of Spain's strategic intentions, was to weaken its momentum and to lessen its impact. Moreover, as indicated in the previous chapter, the British could conclude that overt Spanish antipathy to Britain was inevitable and might even be

173

desirable, since a non-belligerent, publicly pro-German Spain, was the best defensive rampart for Gibraltar that Britain had. This paradoxical conclusion – i.e., that it was actually in Britain's interest for Spain to seem to be Germany's friend – was based upon the mutual Anglo-Spanish interest in keeping the Iberian Peninsula out of the war for as long as possible. Yet, for all the logic of this view, there remained the British fear that Spain might retrace Italy's route to war, especially if the war appeared to be taking such a decisive turn as had drawn the Italians into the ring in June 1940. It could still happen, then, that non-belligerency might turn out in practice to be not an insurance against, but rather the prelude to, Spanish belligerency on the Axis side. It was, perhaps, this worry which prompted the continuing British effort to attract Spain into its economic and political sphere of influence in 1941. Whatever the motivation, the British effort to draw Spain into their orbit persisted throughout much of that year.

Although Eden, as mentioned in the last chapter, had resigned himself, by the end of January 1941, to coming to terms with the Spaniards over Tangier, he did not share Hoare's satisfaction when the latter reported on the 29th of that month, that the Argentinian Government had just arranged to sell 400,000 tons of their wheat to Spain.[1] This, clearly, would serve to relieve the immediate Spanish food crisis, but also carried the implication that Spain might be less susceptible to British economic pressure.

Nevertheless, Britain's naval power remained the determinant of Spain's economic survival, for the British could still refuse to let the Argentinian wheat through their blockade. Hoare was quick to request that his Government enlarge the quotas of imported wheat allowed to Spain to 200,000 tons each for February and March, though he doubted whether the small Spanish merchant fleet would, in fact, be able to carry that much.[2] Hoare, also, at this time urged upon his Government, and the Foreign Secretary in particular, the need to take a comprehensive view on Spanish policy, ignoring minor provocations and hostility. He argued that a broad military and economic policy covering both the Iberian Peninsula and the Atlantic coast of Africa should be formulated, based upon Anglo-American co-operation. He felt that in view of the strategic importance of that Atlantic littoral to the security of the United States, Washington might be prevailed upon to articulate a new Monroe doctrine defining the vital interest of the United States in the integrity of the area. A vigorous policy of Anglo-American political and economic help, Hoare thought, might well coax even the disagreeable Spanish Government into their orbit, given the way Spanish public opinion had turned in Britain's favour. He called for a joint study of the issue by Britain and the United States.[3] One Foreign Office official was quick to point out that such an ambitious scheme might well wreck Britain's carefully developed Spanish policy by provoking a German invasion before Britain could really fortify Spain's powers of resistance. He argued that Spanish fear of just such a German move effectively ruled out any real improvement in Anglo-Spanish relations, and added that Britain's existing attempt to strengthen the Spanish will to resist, was much more likely to create real opposition to a German move than any attempt at political co-operation with the Franco Government.[4] So Hoare might succeed only too well in his policy methods, in drawing Spain away from Germany, and thereby ruin his chances of achieving his policy goal, the perpetuation of Spanish non-belligerency. Moreover, Eden informed Hoare that it would be premature to 'give some general assurance to the Spanish and Portuguese Governments' which Britain might have neither the power nor the American support to honour in practice.[5]

However, an individual in a more exalted position in the British Government hierarchy was willing to countenance the economic aspects, at least, of the programme advocated by Hoare. Thus, Churchill instructed the Foreign Office, on 12 February 1941, as follows:

In Spain we must not worry too much about Tangier and tiresome claims and legalities. We do not know what will come of the Franco–Musso talks; but assuming Ambassador Hoare and Attaché Hillgarth are right about their Generals and Spain refuses to give Hitler passage or join Axis immediately, it becomes of the utmost importance to crash in food, i.e. wheat, as much as we can, and persuade the President of the U.S.A. to act similarly. The few weeks remaining before the snows melt in the Pyrenees are of extreme importance. The more food we can bring in the better. This will give the best chance of a favourable reaction when the German invasion comes on Spain. Don't boggle, but feed.
  Pray take this as a general directive.

Churchill reiterated his argument to R. A. Butler over lunch the next day.[6] Eden replied to the Premier's directive, on 14 February, just before beginning his air journey to the Middle East, to coordinate military and political action to help Greece meet the expected German assault upon it. The Foreign Secretary was not willing to be as generous, or as trusting, as Hoare and Churchill:

I do not think that Spanish politics can be so simplified and I much hope that you will allow *the general line* I have laid down after much thought to stand; i.e., turn tap on but *regulate it* and be ready to turn it off. Ambassador Hoare has agreed to this. (N.B. Spain is sending food to Germany as it is and Suñer would send more if he could, Generals or no Generals. M.E.W. should, I think, be given a chance of their say on the American aspect.

I have no doubt that if Spain had had food and petrol she would long since have been more tempting to Hitler.[7]

Hugh Dalton agreed that Britain should be ready to 'turn the tap off' at any moment. But he felt, too, that economic policy was 'generally' in conformity with what Churchill desired.[8] Certainly Hoare was told, on 15 February 1941, that the Ministry of Economic Warfare was now prepared to permit Spain to import 200,000 tons of bread grains in both February and March. Though the extra 100,000 tons a month for February and March (i.e., in addition to the 100,000 tons a month rate agreed to the previous September) were to be regarded as advances upon the following quota period. In addition, it was felt that the Spanish administrative restrictions upon the movement of cereals amongst the provinces were the real reason for the severe local dearths, and it was hoped that these would be removed before Britain was asked to let further wheat through its blockade after 31 March.[9] Yet Hoare was also informed the same day that the British Government was anxious to implement the policy of economic assistance to Spain as rapidly as possible, and the sooner the better, so Churchill's message had clearly got through.[10]

Moreover, a chance occurrence served to boost the momentum behind this renewed British policy of economic assistance to Franco's Spain. Bad weather delayed Eden at Gibraltar, while *en route* to Cairo, and gave Hoare the opportunity to plead his case, in person, on 17 February. The Chief of the Imperial General Staff, General Dill, who was accompanying Eden to Egypt, was also present at this discussion on Spain, as was Major General Mason-Macfarlane, now also head of the British Liaison Delegation to Spanish Headquarters in the event of a German attack. Hoare found Eden very friendly, and their talk resulted in an apparently comprehensive conversion.[11] In an almost confessional telegram after this meeting, Eden apparently renounced his doubts about Britain's Spanish policy:

Enforced wait here has given me an opportunity to consider fully our Spanish policy. As you know I have never been happy with this policy . . . My instinct . . . was to refuse any further help to Franco, Suñer and company until they behaved to us as a true neutral should.

But matter is not quite so simple. We have been now for long enmeshed in policy of help for Spain. It is by no means certain that Suñer would be sorry if we now took a tough line. He would then certainly seek to lay blame for Spain's starvation on us and this would facilitate his efforts to bring Spain in on side Axis. Nor would Salazar agree with a change in our policy now. On all these counts I accept that we are tied to a policy of help to Spain despite conduct of its Government so long as Spain is not at war with us.[12]

He went on to argue that such an analysis entailed a joint Anglo–American programme of aid for Spain through food supplies, which ought to be implemented as soon as possible. Although he still thought that such deliveries ought to be very carefully regulated, an opinion reinforced by the warning of the British Military Attaché in Spain, that Spain must not be allowed to build up such stocks as to present a pretext or temptation to the Germans for intervention. So, Eden counselled, 'we must help them, we must give them power to resist but we must not give them too much'.[13]

Eden also personally cabled to Churchill the unanimous view of the Gibraltar meeting that Operation 'Blackthorn' (the project to help the Spaniards deny their Moroccan territory to the Germans) would not secure Spanish support, since it would be viewed, at best, as an attempt to consolidate the British hold over the Strait, and at worst, as an effort by Britain to expand into Morocco. He emphasised that the unanimous conclusion was that Britain must furnish help on the Spanish mainland, in the event of a German invasion, where it could 'appeal to national pride and form [a] nucleus for national resistance'. He called for military and air support based on Cádiz comprising two divisions, one army tank brigade, and four fighter and four bomber squadrons. He hoped that, in tangibly strengthening the resolve of the Spanish generals to resist a German invasion, such a scheme would have a desirably deterrent effect on the Germans. He also told the Prime Minister that Britain should be more generous about supplying the Spaniards with essentials, especially wheat, and trusted that it would be feasible to involve the United States in the scheme.[14]

Apparently unaware of the depth of the Foreign Secretary's previous doubts about his Spanish policy, and his own possibly decisively persuasive role at Gibraltar, Hoare informed R. A. Butler that he had found Eden 'a hundred per cent behind our Spanish policy' and that 'he could not have spoken more definitely to this effect'.[15] Perhaps the most significant aspect of Eden's conversion was his admission that the policy laid down by Halifax and Hoare had really been in operation for too long to permit any radical change of course, and his consequent acceptance of the absolute priority they had always assigned to preserving Spanish non-belligerency, however provocative and unfriendly Spanish behaviour might seem. As Eden told the Prime Minister, there was unanimity at the Gibraltar meeting that British interests would be best served by keeping the war out of the Iberian Peninsula.[16] Eden also clearly accepted the method advocated by Halifax and Hoare for securing the agreed goal of Spanish non-belligerency: namely, the policy of aid, economic and maybe, also, political and military. Thus, Eden not only ended up accepting the Hoare–Halifax line on Spain, his very acceptance of it was in large part due to their persistence in maintaining that policy for the last months of 1940. Halifax and Hoare had actually articulated a Spanish policy from which not only Eden, but the entire British Government did not deviate for the really crucial period of the war, despite occasional and temporary crises. So, the results of that six month policy-making partnership between Halifax and Hoare were indeed lasting.

Hoare, naturally, fully endorsed the Foreign Secretary's request for large-scale economic and, if necessary, military aid to Spain. He agreed with Eden that a more ambitious British programme of military support for Spanish resistance to invading German forces, would stiffen the generals' attitude to the Germans and thereby possibly deter them. At worst, Britain would have the Spanish Army and people on its side. However, Hoare felt such military aid presupposed a more comprehensive scheme of economic help. He thought that the hitherto rigid blockade should now be used 'as a flexible instrument in support of high policy'. This meant not only involving the United States in a massive scheme to buy Spain off, but also, deliberately tolerating and even encouraging by pre-arrangement with the Spaniards, leakages of goods through the blockade via Spain to Germany. This stratagem, in Hoare's view, would effectively help the Spaniards appease the Germans, and probably diminish the latter's irritation at continued Spanish neutrality.[17] The Ambassador, then, could be just as conscious as the Foreign Office of the risks involved in appearing to be too successful in attracting Spain into Britain's orbit. However, his solution was not to abridge the effort, let alone abandon it, but rather to conceal it.

Neither the Foreign Office nor the Ministry of Economic Warfare, however, considered it sound policy to condone breaches of the British blockade system by the Spaniards. They felt that such minor concessions would hardly placate the Germans and that it would be 'a tactical mistake' to try to bolster the position of Britain's apparent friends inside the Spanish Government, like Carceller, by such violations of the blockade, which could only be a gain for the Germans. Rather should Britain try to help pro-British Spaniards by 'concrete and constructive' means, that is, a programme of Anglo-American economic aid to Spain 'on a much larger scale than hitherto'.[18]

Hoare had followed up his late February plans for help to Spain with an agitated cry, on 2 March, for further British assistance to Spain before Serrano Suñer seized the chance to drag an exhausted country into the war.[19] The Foreign Office was concerned at this stage, that Serrano Suñer might be consciously refusing to receive just such additional economic aid as Hoare called for, since he seemed to be avoiding formal acceptance of a further British loan of £2,500,000. Hoare was not sure, at first, whether Serrano Suñer was deliberately set upon sabotaging closer Anglo-Spanish economic relations.[20] He thought, subsequently, that Serrano Suñer's dogmatic belief in Spanish autarky did find expression in his reluctance to ratify the loan agreement.[21] According to British information, the Minister of Commerce and Industry, Carceller, had to carry a threat of resignation to the limit before Serrano Suñer changed his mind and agreed to approve the loan arrangement.[22] Again, however, fear of offending the Germans, who were, apparently, pressing the Spaniards to abstain from such economic collaboration with Britain, also played its part.[23] Eden regarded the signing of the Supplementary Loan Agreement, on 7 April 1941 (six months after negotiations for it had begun), as a 'diplomatic victory over the Germans and Suñer, who did their very level best to stop it'.[24] Makins, of the Central Department of the Foreign Office, who agreed that the signing of the agreement represented a victory for the British over Serrano Suñer and the Germans, expressed the British reasons for concluding it, thus:

The real reason for the Loan Agreement is that we are endeavouring to keep Spain from joining the Axis, that we have to do so without the prospect of using military force, and that the only weapons at our disposal are those of economic assistance (or pressure) and propaganda. The Loan Agreement was a practical demonstration of the advantage to Spain of remaining neutral and of becoming dependent for supplies on the sterling area. It also stemmed the rising tide of German and Falangist propaganda that Britain was starving Spain.[25]

Serrano Suñer had denounced the 'very arbitrary' British blockade system which was hindering the relief of a 'desperate' shortage of food in Spain, in an interview published in the American magazine, *Life*, on 31 March 1941.[26] The negotiations for the Loan Agreement also produced a solid economic gain for Britain by inducing Carceller – who had withdrawn his ministerial resignation when the loan deal went ahead – to assent to the supply of a large quantity of mercury to Britain in return for wheat and rubber bought with sterling. The strong opposition of Serrano Suñer and the Germans was responsible, or so the British thought, for the removal of the mercury deal from an annex of the Loan Agreement, but 'a secret gentleman's agreement' sealed the bargain all the same.[27]

Even before the Loan Agreement was signed, however, it was

realised in the Foreign Office that it embodied as much as Britain was able to do for Spain, at that time. 'Additional assistance must come from the United States', Makins remarked, on 12 March 1941.[28] On 13 March, with Churchill's directions to help Spain in mind, and believing that the ongoing 'struggle in Spanish politics' made it vital to strengthen Britain's friends and to 'isolate the Minister for Foreign Affairs by every possible means and with the shortest possible delay', the Foreign Office dispatched a request for the provision of large-scale economic assistance to Spain, to the British Embassy in Washington, for forwarding to the American Government. The British suggested, *inter alia*, that the United States should offer a $20,000,000 credit to Carceller (not to Serrano Suñer) to fund Spanish purchases of American goods.[29]

The initial American response to this British suggestion was distinctly chilly. In conversation with Ambassador Weddell and Colonel William Donovan (personal representative of the United States Secretary of the Navy, Knox, 'on special mission' in Europe), on 28 February 1941, Serrano Suñer had announced what he claimed was his Government's attitude towards the warring Powers: 'We hope for and believe in the victory of Germany in the present conflict.'[30] Such rhetoric was hardly likely to convince Washington to react more sympathetically to suggestions to aid Spain. Weddell thought that Serrano Suñer's declaration was not 'startlingly new' and advised his Government to send food to Spain for as long as the Spaniards remained non-belligerent.[31] Hull agreed that one could set little store by Serrano Suñer's pronouncements, but he remained very sceptical of the feasibility of maintaining Spanish non-belligerency by economic hand-outs.[32] Atherton, Chief of the European Division at the State Department, reiterated to British officials that an United States dollar credit for Spain was 'politically impossible' on account of the antagonism aroused in the United States Government and nation by the Spaniards' pro-Axis and anti-American stance.[33] Halifax, now British Ambassador in Washington, also observed that the officials in charge of American foreign trade were using the export licensing system 'deliberately to penalise Spain' by denying it sulphate of ammonia urgently needed for its rice crop, and other commodities.[34]

However, the vigorous pressing of the British case – particularly, by David Eccles of the Ministry of Economic Warfare who arrived in Washington in early April 1941 – for economic help to Franco's Spain, on the grounds of the vital strategic necessity of keeping that country out of the Axis war effort, seemed to change the official American mind.[35] So, by 22 April 1941, Eccles was able to report that the ice was thawing in Washington, with an apparent American disposition to cease discrimination against Spain in the issue of export licences, and to engage in a barter scheme with the Spaniards whereby their olive oil could be exchanged for ground-nut oil and wheat supplied by the United States.[36] Eccles was informed, by 29 April 1941, that Hull and Welles had agreed 'in principle to a forward policy' in the matter of economic assistance to Spain. The American Ambassador in Madrid was being instructed to see Franco to tell him that the United States was 'ready to feed Spain'.[37] But Franco unexpectedly avoided receiving Weddell, and against this seemingly small obstacle the whole project of large-scale Anglo-American aid to Spain was wrecked.

Franco's reluctance to receive Weddell derived, apparently, from a heated encounter between the American Ambassador and Serrano Suñer, on 19 April 1941, when Weddell, as instructed by his Government, gave 'forceful' expression to the 'absolute determination' of the United States to play a part in the successful defeat of 'the forces of aggression', and the scale of the American effort to that end.[38] It was Weddell's other remarks on that occasion which incensed the Spaniard. The American Ambassador went as far as to voice the hope that Spain had not 'renounced its sovereignty' since he was able to produce two air-mail envelopes addressed to Americans in Spain bearing a German postal censor's stamp. Moreover, Serrano Suñer claimed, afterwards, that when he asked for one of the envelopes so as to conduct an investigation, Weddell tore it in two, only handing one half to him. Weddell also commented on the fact that a recent reading of the Spanish press had given him the impression that many pieces 'had been originally drafted in some foreign language perhaps German'. Serrano Suñer was so outraged that he told the American that his attitude was 'most offensive', and declared next day, to the German Ambassador, that he would have thrown Weddell out 'or, better still, slapped his face if he had not been the representative of a foreign power'.[39]

Reflecting, the day after, on his interview with Serrano Suñer Weddell decided that it would be better to communicate his Government's declaration of their resolve to stick with Britain until the final destruction of the Axis, to Franco directly. Serrano Suñer, he thought, might not relay the message to the Caudillo, or report it only in a 'diluted or garbled form'.[40] However, he also felt, as he told the State Department, that an interview with Franco would only yield 'practical results' if he were also authorised to inform the Spanish leader of the United States' readiness to give 'sympathetic consideration' to

Spain's economic requirements.[41] It was this appeal by Weddell, not, as the British thought, the able advocacy of David Eccles which moved the State Department to adopt an apparently more generous economic attitude towards Spain. As Feis notes, the British appeal had only been met in Washington by 'a half-hearted search for some type of offer that would supplement Britain's appeal to the Spanish people'. 'Nothing would have come of it', but for the Ambassador's intervention.[42] Weddell was authorised, on 30 April 1941, to tell Franco of his Government's willingness 'to give immediate and careful consideration' to the means by which Spain could secure the surplus American commodities which it needed, such as wheat, corn and cotton. The idea of granting a loan to Spain was still unpalatable to the Roosevelt Administration. However, as Eccles had discerned, Washington was now seemingly prepared to deal with Franco's Spain 'through an exchange of commodities without resort to credit transactions'. A barter arrangement, in which 25,000 tons of Spanish olive oil was exchanged for 'an equal quantity of peanut oil from the United States, plus the large quantity of wheat (c. 200,000 tons) representing the difference in the market price of olive oil and peanut oils', could realise an immediate United States intention to help and, also, provide a basis for future Hispano-American trade.[43] The essential condition which the United States attached to even the commencement of discussions with Spain upon such economic collaboration was unchanged from the previous December: a public statement by Madrid to the effect 'that Spain intends to remain outside of the present war and does not contemplate extension of aid to the Axis powers'.[44]

However, as already mentioned, Weddell's request for an interview with Franco was not granted. For Serrano Suñer informed the American, by letter on 27 May 1941, that the Caudillo was too busy to see the Ambassador for the time being, and that any special communication could be channelled through the Spanish Foreign Minister.[45] When Weddell, at Washington's direction, protested at being denied access to the Chief of State, Serrano Suñer retorted with a note which resulted in a suspension of top-level diplomatic contacts between the United States and Spain in Madrid until the following autumn.[46] In his reply of 13 June, the Spanish Foreign Minister accused Weddell of making a 'scene' during their 19 April interview and of acting with an 'habitual want of moderation'. He also complained of the 'crude language' of the Ambassador's recent protest. He considered Weddell's declarations to be 'offensive to the dignity of the Spanish state', and declared that it was his duty to ensure that such 'inadmissible' language as the Ambassador had used of late in visits to the Ministry of Foreign Affairs should not be heard by the Spanish Chief of State. Serrano Suñer argued that the 'scene' caused by the American Ambassador 'on the occasion of an incident involving possible censorship' was the 'only reason' for the current strain in relations between Weddell and himself, a personal dispute which should not involve the United States Government 'whose suggestions or desires' Franco and the Foreign Ministry would 'consider with all correctness'.[47] However, the personal quarrel provided the occasion for a full-scale Hispano-American diplomatic confrontation, which killed the prospect of a programme of United States economic assistance to Spain for the duration of the Second World War. On 16 June, Atherton made it plain to Eccles that the State Department had definitely given up any idea of affording economic succour to Spain.[48]

The British were naturally disappointed and frustrated that such a trivial affair should have intervened to quench the seemingly reawakened American desire for closer economic relations with Spain. Once again, they were inclined to lay some blame on Weddell for this fresh setback to their efforts to coax the United States into economic co-operation with Spain.[49] However, the State Department directed Weddell to inform Serrano Suñer in response to his note that he had been acting 'with the full knowledge and approval' of the United States Government in his efforts to secure an interview with Franco.[50] Charles Halstead points out that Weddell had subsequently exacerbated his clash with Serrano Suñer, on 19 April, over German influence in Spain, by forwarding to him (on 15 May) a post-card which the Ambassador's wife had received in Madrid on that day. The card had been posted within the city, but had taken thirty-two days to arrive and, in the interval, had passed through the hands of a German military censor, who had affixed his stamp to it. Weddell was moved to inquire 'as to whether the German government . . . was maintaining a censorship of official and private correspondence within the boundaries of Spain'. Halstead argues that this additional challenge could only have rekindled Serrano Suñer's resentment.[51] Still, as Halstead also notes, Washington had requested Weddell, in March 1941, to find out whether there was German censorship of American mail in Spain.[52] Nevertheless, Halstead does assign much of the responsibility for the beginning and prolongation of the dispute to the Ambassador's 'unreasonably offensive' tone and 'intransigence'.[53]

Whoever was to blame for the outbreak of the quarrel, it must be questioned whether the affair can be explained solely by concentrating upon the personal stances of Weddell and Serrano Suñer, in view of the fact that the row developed into a sustained diplomatic deadlock between the United States and Spain. Did the American and Spanish political chiefs back their agents in the dispute because it suited their own political purposes? It may be instructive to note that the onset of the squabble coincided with the close of a round of dazzling German victories in the Eastern Mediterranean and North Africa. The fate of Yugoslavia, indeed, destroyed by German assault in less than two weeks between 6 and 17 April, underlined the appalling risks involved in seeming to deviate from Germany's political line. It was hardly the season for open intimacy between Spain and Britain's non-belligerent ally, the United States.

The Spanish Minister of Commerce and Industry, Carceller, told Hoare, on 17 June 1941, that Franco felt it was too 'dangerous' for him to see Weddell at that time. As Carceller truthfully explained, Mussolini had been putting pressure recently on the Caudillo to side with the Axis.[54] This latest Axis attempt to influence Spain stemmed from the meeting between Hitler and Mussolini at the Brenner, on 2 June 1941. There the Führer bemoaned the fact that he had been prevented by Franco's veto from taking Gibraltar the previous February, since with two German armoured divisions passing thence to North Africa he could have put an end to Vichy French 'blackmail'. As Ribbentrop interjected, 'no kind of pressure could be applied to France, because of the danger of the defection of North Africa and . . . the French were perfectly aware of this'. Commenting on the 'general situation', Hitler declared the following: 'The only danger that still existed was the defection of French North Africa. One must try to prevent that by skilful diplomacy. Besides, one could perhaps still succeed in pulling Spain entirely over to the side of the Axis.' He added that the situation in the Western Mediterranean required an effort 'to bring the Spaniards to the adoption of at least a friendly attitude towards the Axis'.[55] Mussolini exerted himself to make it. He requested Ciano to write a letter the next day to Serrano Suñer 'emphasizing the advisability of Spain's adhering to the Tripartite Pact'.[56] Mentioning the recent Axis triumphs in the Eastern Mediterranean and the imminent expulsion of the Royal Navy from that sea, Ciano asked this rhetorical question: 'Can Nationalist and Falangist Spain remain indifferent and absent in the face of events of such great import for our life and our future as Mediterranean Powers?' What the Italians wanted was not, necessarily, immediate Spanish belligerency, but public Spanish alignment with the Axis, as Ciano explained: 'Spain, even without throwing herself into the conflict, should publicly show that the banner of Falangism is side by side with that of the Fascist and Nazi revolution at this decisive moment of history.' The Italian Foreign Minister acknowledged that there were 'already secret agreements' (namely Spain's promise, *inter alia*, in the Secret Protocol of Hendaye to join the Tripartite Pact of Germany, Italy and Japan in its own good time), but what mattered was the actual 'responsibility' that was assumed, which alone would confer entitlement to a place in 'the world of tomorrow'. Mussolini added a personal note to Ciano's letter to drive the point home: 'Spain must *at least* adhere to the Tripartite Pact . . . By subscribing to the Tripartite Pact, Spain comes once more into line as far as tomorrow's European settlement is concerned.'[57] The Spanish reply, of 11 June, to this Italian *démarche* did not deliver a firm refusal to consider the suggested action, and it even accepted that some political advantages would accrue to the Axis and Spain from such a step. However, it also listed the disadvantages, prominent amongst them being that 'the shipping space of 300,000 tons (of grain, maize, gasoline, etc.) . . . *en route* would be lost and a total blockade would be immediately imposed on Spain'. Serrano Suñer stated that his country was 'resolved to take and fill her place at the side of the Axis Powers' and therefore 'wanted to perform really useful service to the common cause and not exhaust her contribution in gestures'. He also inevitably requested that Spanish territorial aspirations 'be taken into account' by Hitler and Mussolini.[58]

So, Carceller's assurance to Hoare of 17 June that Franco had resisted the Duce's urgent counsel was true. However, the Spanish Minister added that it was evident to him that Franco was 'very nervous' of engaging in any public action at that moment, such as an interview with Weddell, which could be regarded as 'a move in the anti-Axis direction'.[59] It is possible that the relentless rise of the German military star throughout the summer of 1941 convinced Franco of the prudence of not settling the diplomatic quarrel with Britain's friend, the United States, even with the main body of German forces committed to the eastern campaign. It must be admitted, though, that Franco did receive Hoare on 28 June 1941, apparently undeterred by fear of offending German sensibilities. Moreover, he emphasised his opinion to the British Ambassador, on that occasion, that the 'strained relations' with the United States were 'not political but purely personal'. Hoare replied that he thought it 'tragic that great issues should be held up upon a personal dispute'.[60] Indeed, it does seem incredible that personal pique should have so paralysed Hispano-American relations, without any decisive impetus from reasons of state. Still, the 'New' Spain may just have been sensitive enough to have over-reacted to Weddell's affront to its *amour propre.*

Nevertheless, the conversation between Carceller and Wiehl, the Director of the Economic Policy Department of the German Foreign Ministry, in early September 1941 (the month in which the Spaniards finally took the initiative to heal their breach with the United States) should also be noted, in this regard. For it seems to reveal a sensitivity in at least some Spanish official quarters to Germany's reaction to a re-establishment of Hispano-American commercial relations, and the political reconciliation which must precede it. Carceller protested Spain's unswerving loyalty to the German cause, on that occasion, in spite of the 'increasingly critical weakening' of his country's economy resulting from the Anglo-American response to this Spanish attitude. Observing that, if Germany wanted Spain to be fighting fit, its lifeline to overseas sources of supply must be restored, the Spanish Minister pointed out that the activities of the German Embassy's press section in Madrid, which ensured that the Spanish press adopted a stridently anti-British tone, would certainly sever that life-giving link.[61] Carceller declared himself convinced that 'a certain moderation could bring about a resumption of imports'. The German recorded him arguing thus:

Naturally the Spanish press would be bound to continue supporting the German side as before, only there would have to be a halt to sharp attacks, insults and vituperation against Germany's enemies. It would also be highly effective (and Carceller mentioned this point several times) if the Americn Ambassador in Madrid would finally be granted his wish for a personal audience with the Caudillo, something which had been denied him for months. If Franco would see the Ambassador for only fifteen minutes, it could be assumed that the American Government would, for instance, issue export clearance for six Spanish tankers which are lying in American ports ready to sail, loaded with paid-for gasoline . . . all Franco would have to tell the Ambassador was that the Spanish Government intended to continue in its present policy. Each party could then interpret this in its own way, the Americans as a continuation of Spanish neutrality, the Spaniards as a continued policy of unlimited support of Germany.[62]

Whether this declaration may be viewed as demonstrating a concern to warn the Germans in advance of the impending Spanish attempt to reopen contact with Washington and Weddell lest Berlin take offence is, perhaps, debatable. What is clear, though, is that the American reaction to the Spanish position did persuade the Spaniards that they must compose their dispute with the United States. For, the United States Government had expressed its displeasure over the

Spanish situation by applying increasingly severe economic pressure to Spain. This took the form of delaying, and denying export licences for shipments of urgently-required goods, especially oil, to Spain, even though these cargoes of commodities fell within the quotas agreed by the British as necessary to meet that country's genuine needs. However, it would be incorrect to account for such economic pressure by tracing it simply to American annoyance over the Serrano Suñer–Weddell quarrel. Irritated the United States Administration certainly was, but the row merely aggravated pre-existing American suspicion of, and ill will towards, Franco's Spain. Feis explains that the offer of a barter deal which Weddell had been authorised in April to convey to Franco when he saw him, was not, in fact, a serious one. It was a 'test rather than a business bid' and was meant 'to enable Weddell to stay in the game rather than to play the hand'.[63] Moreover, when Atherton informed Eccles of the abandonment of this plan, because of the breakdown of diplomatic relations in Madrid, the American did not conceal his pleasure at this turn of events.[64] It seems, indeed, that many people within the American Government relished the opportunity supplied by the row, to start squeezing Spain economically. According to Feis, the officially-inspired delays in the clearance of oil shipments to Spain began spontaneously. These were produced by an 'unarranged click of attitude' amongst the governmental departments concerned and the absence of intervention by the State Department to expedite the shipments. Its officials were too conscious of the 'rude treatment' Weddell had received in Madrid to exert themselves for the sake of helping Spain.[65]

However, Franco delivered a speech, on 17 July 1941, which prompted the Americans to apply their economic pressure in a more systematic fashion. Having accused the United States of preventing the Spaniards from shipping 100,000 tons of wheat from a 'friendly' North American state (presumably Canada), during 'the moments of greatest crisis' in 1940, he denounced American efforts to attach conditions of good behaviour to their proffered economic assistance, in these terms: 'when it appeared that Spain was offered the prospect of help and economic collaboration for her re-construction, behind the generous appearance . . . there always appeared the attempt at political interference incompatible with our sovereignty and with our dignity as a free people.'[66] Franco also warned the United States of the 'criminal madness' of active intervention in the conflict, which could only result in 'universal war'.[67] This discourse, and the British reaction to it, are analysed in chapter nine. But its immediate consequence in Washington was to crystallise the uncoordinated economic squeeze on Spain into a deliberately directed 'strategy of gradual pressure'.[68]

On 1 August, the American export licensing system for petroleum products was applied to Spain. Two days later, on the suggestion of Secretary of the Interior, Ickes (who was antipathetic to Franco's regime), United States tankers were withdrawn from the trade carrying oil to Spain. The State Department had agreed to this measure 'to cause the Spanish Government to behave more decently, not to force a collapse'.[69] Spanish mismanagement of the sailings of their tankers compounded their difficulties.[70] There was vociferous political protest inside the United States against even this restricted flow of oil to Spain.[71] Weddell, despite his feud with Serrano Suñer, was unhappy about this American coercion of Spain, believing United States economic policy to be 'unnecessarily restrictive and retaliatory'. Although accepting that the American Government's power to supply, or deny, oil to Spain constituted 'trump cards' in their 'political and economic relations with Spain', he communicated to Washington, on 16 September 1941, his opinion that the 'psychological moment' to play those cards had not yet arrived.[72]

However, even the resolution of the dispute between Weddell and Serrano Suñer in Madrid at the end of September, did not induce the Americans to restore the flow of oil to its previous rhythm or scale. The Spanish Ambassador in Washington, Juan de Cárdenas, who mediated between Weddell and Serrano Suñer in Madrid to settle their quarrel, had returned from the United States to do so. Prior to leaving Washington, he had had an uncomfortable encounter with Secretary of State, Hull, which dramatically demonstrated the profound animosity towards Spain that the Franco Government's actions had managed to provoke in the American Government. Hull recorded his own bitter denunciation of Spanish behaviour, in their meeting on 13 September, thus:

I . . . proceeded to say that while it was most disagreeable even to recall our experiences in dealing with the Spanish Government, I must state that in all of the relations of this Government with the most backward and ignorant governments in the world, this Government has not experienced such a lack of ordinary courtesy or consideration, which customarily prevails between friendly nations, as it has at the hands of the Spanish Government. Its course has been one of aggravated discourtesy and contempt in the very face of our offers to be of aid. I said, of course, we could not think of embarrassing, not to say humiliating ourselves by further approaches of this nature, bearing in mind the coarse and extremely offensive methods and conduct of Suñer in particular and in some instances of General Franco. I said that when I thought back about the details of the conduct of the Spanish Government towards this Government what had happened was really inconceivable.[73]

But the more tangible expression of American vexation embodied in their steady curtailment of oil supplies to Spain was the most effective influence in persuading the Spaniards to mend their bridges with Washington. Thus when Weddell proved resistant to the suggestions of Cárdenas that he make a move to end the deadlock, Serrano Suñer took the initiative, extending an invitation to the Ambassador to call on him.[74] In their conversation, on 30 September, Serrano Suñer and Weddell agreed 'to sponge over the past' and the Ambassador raised the prospect of increased Hispano–American economic co-operation. Serrano Suñer commented that Spain's economic requirements were of two main kinds, those of a 'pressing nature' and those which might await discussion. Serrano Suñer singled out gasoline from the former category since it was 'not alone a need but a vital political matter' and because 'delays in receiving this commodity had provoked disappointment and bad feeling not alone in Government but among the people'. He added that 'if Spain's nonbelligerency meant anything to the British cause Spain must not be "strangled" in respect to motor fuel'. At a later stage in their talk, Serrano reminded Weddell that the gasoline problem was of 'pressing and vital importance for Spain'.[75] Weddell was easily able to discern the reason for Serrano Suñer's access of reasonableness, as he informed Washington: 'It is therefore obvious to me that it is only increasing economic pressure that has brought about the present attempt through the instrumentality of Cárdenas to normalise relations.'[76] Cárdenas himself, had described the Spanish need for American help, 'especially gasoline', as 'desperate' in conversation with Weddell a couple of days before the latter's talk with Serrano Suñer. He told the American Ambassador on that occasion too, that 'certain official circles' in Spain were under the impression that there were intentional delays in the dispatch of oil from the United States in order to exert pressure upon the Spanish Government.[77] Franco also revealed Spanish anxiety over their economic plight in his interview – at last granted – with Weddell, on 6 October 1941. The Caudillo referred to wheat, cotton and gasoline 'as absolutely necessary for his country'. Serrano Suñer, who was also present, reiterated that the Spanish situation 'resulting from the gasoline lack was extremely bad and was not alone provoking hostility but crippling transportation'. Franco readily answered the Ambassador's inquiry, as to whether the Spaniards were interested in improving commercial relations with the United States, in the affirmative.[78] The bout of American pressure had produced the desired result which, the State Department admitted to the British, was 'to bring home to the Spaniards the possible consequences of their failure to mend their ways *vis-à-vis* the Americans'.[79]

Still, even though the Americans had pushed the Spaniards into a more tractable mood, they neither hastened to reward Madrid with closer economic relations, nor even restored the oil supplies to Spain to their former volume. The constriction of the delivery of oil to Spain increasingly reached asphyxiating proportions. By this time, many of the governmental departments represented on the United States 'Economic Defense Board' (the Departments of State, the Treasury, War, the Navy, Agriculture, Commerce) had become resolute in their opposition to any resumption of a steady and substantial flow of oil to Spain.[80] Their resolution was fortified by reports that the Spaniards were transferring some of their American-supplied oil to Britain's enemies, either at sea by trans-shipment or through re-export upon its arrival in Spain.[81] The British were quick to reassure the Americans that these stories were unfounded.[82] They gave this assurance notwithstanding their knowledge that U-boats had been clandestinely refuelled and resupplied from a German ship at anchor in the harbour of Las Palmas, in the Canary Islands, and the recent success of their diplomatic pressure in inducing the Spanish authorities to withdraw the two suspect German vessels into the inner harbour there, where they could not carry on such activities.[83] With official Spanish connivance, the Germans did, in fact, arrange the replenishment, at Spanish ports, of the fuel and other stocks of sixteen of their U-boats, on as many separate occasions between March and December 1941. These operations were, however, terminated – apart from two emergencies caused by mechanical failure in 1942 – in December 1941, when the British secured positive evidence about them, on interrogating the captured survivors of U434 and U574, both of which had recently received fresh supplies at Vigo. The resultant British protest was sufficiently strong to frighten the Spaniards into putting a stop to this German operation, 'Moro'.[84]

There was, therefore, some solid ground for the American suspicions. Indeed, one of the main problems the Germans encountered in mounting these resupply operations from Spain was the dearth of fuel there, suitable for powering the U-boats.[85] So the various British and American restrictions upon Spain's imports of oil did create a definite obstacle to the German resupply of their submarines assuming large-scale dimensions there. Yet it also seems clear that the

Spanish Government would not have sanctioned any sizable scheme which would have excessively antagonised the Americans and the British. In early December 1940, when Serrano Suñer communicated to the Germans his Government's agreement to their stationing tankers at remote points on the Spanish coast to refuel German destroyers, he 'strongly urged that the utmost discretion be observed in carrying out these operations'.[86] Again, when in the wake of the British discovery of the Las Palmas supply operations, in July 1941, the Germans tried to involve the Spaniards in a cover exercise by getting them to acquire ownership of a German vessel in Tenerife, they failed. The Spaniards were, evidently, too worried about the menace inherent in reduced oil supplies from the United States to risk provoking it or Britain.[87] Moreover, it should be noted that the two particular American concerns were unfounded. There was no transfer of oil from Spanish tankers to German vessels on the high seas, nor was there any systematic re-export of American-supplied oil from Spain to the Axis countries. The Germans did procure fuel inside Spain which was used to refill the tanks of some U-boats, and that oil, therefore, did aid the German submarine campaign in the Atlantic, but not greatly. The British seem to have estimated the true proportion of these matters. Weddell relayed to Washington, on 7 October 1941, the considered judgement of a petroleum expert from the British Ministry of Economic Warfare: 'he and the British Embassy recognise that there are probably isolated quantities of petroleum products disposed of clandestinely but they consider that the aggregate amounts involved would be insignificant'.[88]

Hull was satisfied enough with this British assurance to recommend to Roosevelt that oil shipments to Spain should continue, a recommendation accepted by the President.[89] However, Herbert Feis, Adviser on International Economic Affairs to the State Department, was less happy about having to depend upon British guarantees that their surveillance proved that Spain had not re-exported oil to Axis destinations. He consequently proposed, on 1 October 1941, an independent American examination of the problem and, indeed, called for a whole new approach on oil supplies to Spain. He believed that the manipulation of petroleum deliveries as a 'diplomatic instrument' could secure both economic benefit, in the form of Spanish commodities which the Americans wanted, and political advantage, in the form of guaranteed good behaviour from the Spaniards. Under-Secretary of State Welles transmitted these ideas to Roosevelt at the end of the month. While his verdict was awaited, the flow of oil to Spain was almost completely cut off.[90]

This policy review coincided with the outbreak of further public controversy in the United States over economic relations with Spain. Published statistics of the United States Treasury erroneously gave the impression that there had been considerable quantities of high grade aviation gasoline and lubricant shipped recently to Spain. The redoubtable journalist, I. F. Stone, attacked the oil trade with Spain as a whole, and these apparent former deliveries in particular, in his newspaper, *P.M.* He even charged that this oil was being passed on to the Germans.[91] The Treasury corrected its mistake, supported by the British Embassy in Washington, but the uproar demonstrated once again to an Administration already acutely sensitive to public opinion, the level of domestic opposition that might be expected if the oil trade with Spain was resumed on anything like its former scale.[92] The State Department had responded to Stone's attack by declaring that it was elaborating a new system to control the use of oil by Spain.[93] It had, in fact, consulted with the British and obtained their approval for such a scheme, as early as 11 November 1941.[94] After much reflection the State Department presented its proposals, in the shape of an *aide-mémoire* to Cárdenas, in Washington on 29 November. The American offer was, as Feis subsequently described it, 'given without warmth, given because the American government did not think it could afford disorder in Spain', since, as the British argued, such a situation could provoke Spanish belligerency, directly or indirectly.[95]

The American *aide-mémoire* expressed their readiness 'to continue the supply of petroleum products . . . in quantities sufficient to meet Spain's requirements for transportation and other essentials'. Apart from an understanding that American-supplied commodities must not be 'employed in any manner useful to the interests of Germany or Italy', the *aide-mémoire* stated the fundamental precondition for a renewal of regular oil shipments to Spain: the establishment of a supervisory control by United States agents over the distribution and use of oil inside Spanish territory. The presence of such agents, who must be afforded 'free access to all Spanish facilities for receiving, shipping, storing and refining petroleum products', would provide Washington with accurate information about the uses to which their oil deliveries were being put, and safeguard against any violation of the conditions on which they were being made. Washington was also prepared to permit the Spaniards to purchase such goods as they could on the open market in the United States, and to help them obtain their minimum needs of scarce American commodities, but required Spain's guarantee that it would facilitate the export of certain Spanish products, such as wolfram, mercury and olive oil to the United States.[96]

Cárdenas was unhappy about the rough language of the American proposals. An official of the British Embassy in Washington found him to be in 'marked distress' over some of its phrasing, especially the repeated references to the word 'control' in the proposed American supervision of the Spaniards' distribution and employment of oil imports from the United States. However, although pressing for changes in the wording of the *aide-mémoire*, he accepted – after a few days – the idea that the Americans should mount a watch over the use which the Spaniards made of the oil which they received from the United States. He also told the State Department that his Government would be prepared to supply official statistics and information relating to Spanish transportation, distribution and consumption of petroleum products, which the Americans were also demanding. The State Department, however, appeared to be unsure as to the next move. The *aide-mémoire* had been given to Cárdenas, seemingly, only for his comments. It was then decided to present it to the Spanish Government through Weddell in Madrid. But, though the Spanish Ambassador was told by the Americans to take no further action, neither was Weddell instructed to act in Madrid. The year ended with no further effort to initiate Hispano-American economic negotiations.[97]

In fact, the Japanese attack on Pearl Harbor on 7 December, and the Axis Powers' declarations of war on the United States four days later, had interrupted these tentative steps towards the resumption of normal Hispano-American commercial relations. The enthusiastic accounts in the Spanish press of early Japanese victories in the Pacific and Hull's anxiety over a German move into the Iberian Peninsula led the American Government to suspend, in practice, all oil shipments to Spain.[98] This action was the culmination of a process of slow strangulation of Spain in regard to oil supplies which had reduced its stocks to 39,071 tons of petroleum products by the end of the year. The inadequacy of these reserves is demonstrated by the fact that SPain had consumed 114,252 tons of oil during the last three months of 1941 (having been able to import 82,936 tons in that same period).[99] With Spain's emergency restrictions upon consumption already having damaged its internal economy, and complete collapse of the Spanish transportation system threatening with the imminent exhaustion of national oil reserves, the British attempted to persuade the Americans that it was not in the Allied interest that Spain should founder economically.

On 19 December 1941, the British case for economic support of Spain was telegraphed to Washington. As previously, the primary justification for such action was strategic necessity, which was as urgent, according to the British military advisers, now that the United States and Britain were co-belligerents, as before when the latter fought alone:

it is most important on strategic grounds to maintain the neutrality of the Peninsula as long as possible. The severest strain would be imposed on Allied resources if Spanish and Portuguese bases on the mainland, in North Africa and the Atlantic Islands were to fall into enemy hands, if Gibraltar became unusable as a naval base, if our increasingly important supplies, particularly of iron ore, mercury and wolfram from the Peninsula were cut off, and if we were to lose the use of Lisbon and Gibraltar as staging points for the passage of personnel and aircraft to the United Kingdom, the United States and the Middle East and Far East.

This message, which was, apparently, communicated to the Americans on 29 December, also recalled Britain's attempts to consolidate Spanish non-belligerency by limited economic assistance which would prove to the Spanish Government 'or at least influential elements in Spain' the desirability of continued association with the sterling area and the American continent. Reiterating that Britain could only then meet a 'very limited quantity' of Spain's economic needs, the British hoped that the 'paramount strategic importance of keeping the Iberian Peninsula out of the war' would persuade the Americans to continue as far as possible supplying Spain, and to desist from being 'too exigent' in their negotiations with the Spaniards. The policy was pressed upon the Americans as the one best calculated to prevent or postpone Spanish belligerency by influencing Spain's Government, and to encourage anti-German groups within the country who might actively resist Axis forces entering it, if the worst came to the worst.[100] Eden was worried when the United States Government seemingly failed to understand the 'urgency and importance' of keeping the Iberian Peninsula out of the war by adopting a less unyielding attitude in economic policy towards Spain. On 1 January 1942, he requested that Churchill, who was in Washington, should intervene with President Roosevelt. Halifax endorsed Eden's suggestion. Churchill did put in a word with Roosevelt, on 5 January, for the wisdom of rationed economic assistance to Spain for strategic reasons.[101] There was some give within the United States Administration when the diplomatic officers of the State Department asserted themselves, despite Hull's reluctance, to relax the embargo on oil exports to Spain, to avoid what they saw as the strategic blunder of driving Spain into Germany's arms. They made a serious – and successful – effort to get their economic talks with Spain under way. Cárdenas's representations over the wording of the *aide-mémoire* had had some influence. The version which was sent to Weddell on 8 January 1942, for presentation to the Spanish Government, and which was handed to Cárdenas on 13 January, was modified to substitute a regulatory system of American supervision over the Spanish oil trade for the 'control' system which had been originally proposed. The regulatory system was to be set up and administered by the American, British and Spanish Governments in consultation.[102] Hoare considered the United States *aide-mémoire* to be still 'harsh and schoolmasterly in tone', but the Americans were not disposed to be generous towards Spain.[103] Weddell was informed, on 12 January 1942, that it was the insistence of the British Government that Spain be sent some oil to keep its economy functioning to the extent of being able to produce commodities required by the Western Allies, that had persuaded the United States Administration to relax its virtual economic boycott of Spain. The American Ambassador was further told that his Government did not 'regard as a major consideration the possible effect, if any, of [their] proposal on the Spanish Government's general policy, and ... would consequently base [their] decisions regarding exports to Spain on whether a valuable and tangible *quid pro quo* could be obtained from Spain'.[104]

A reluctant Spanish Government did accept the American proposals 'in principle', on 28 January 1942, but the combined suspicion and animosity with which the United States Government regarded Spain and the Spaniards' resentment at American dictation, along with their fear of provoking the Germans, ensured that the attainment of agreement over renewed American oil shipments to Spain and other commercial relations would be a troubled and protracted procedure. Eventually, at the end of July 1942, the United States agreed to permit Spain to import 492,000 tons of oil a year, which was the equivalent of the carrying-capacity of the Spanish tanker fleet and represented about sixty per cent of previous Spanish consumption.[105] An Anglo-American economic agreement with Spain in the form of a joint supply–purchase programme also went into effect in July 1942. This agreement enabled the Allies both to buy the Spanish commodities which they wanted and to engage in pre-emptive purchases of materials such as wolfram, woollen goods and mercury, valuable to the German war economy. The Spaniards were also able to secure many of the supplies they required from the Allies, at least in some measure. Actually, in 1942 the Spaniards filled their part of the

bargain rather more effectively than the Americans, with the promised quantities of United States goods only arriving in Spain in
reduced amounts or not at all. Hoare reported, on 22 October 1942,
that having amassed a balance of ten million dollars from this uneven
trade with the United States, the Spanish Government 'could not
disguise their suspicion of and resentment over the American
attitude'.[106] Nevertheless, the basic framework of Allied–Spanish
commercial relations for the remainder of the Second World War had
been set. The economic exchanges were essentially on a *quid pro quo*
basis, as the Americans had desired. The British did not abandon their
primary motive in trade with Spain, which was to entice the
Spaniards into economic collaboration with the Allies.[107] However,
the Americans remained more hard-headed and hard-hearted. Feis
describes their feelings towards Spain in 1943, thus:

The State Department wished to send as little to Spain as might be needed to
avoid internal trouble, and to win the battle against Germany, for strategic
supplies. It wanted to drive a hard bargain and was not wholly averse to
coercion. The B.E.W. (Board of Economic Warfare) favoured a policy of
sending even less and did not seem to worry over what might happen in
Spain.[108]

This American inclination to use economic force to coerce the
Spaniards into following courses of action desired by Washington,
actually produced a total embargo on oil exports to Spain between
January and April 1944. This coercive campaign was primarily
intended to force the Spaniards into stopping all supplies of wolfram
(the ore which yields the alloy tungsten, an element much used in
modern munitions manufacture) to Nazi Germany. It required considerable pressure from London to persuade Washington to settle, in
early May 1944, for a significant reduction in the volume of Spanish
wolfram exports to Germany, and the resumption of Allied oil
deliveries to Franco's Spain, this time under British auspices and
from their sources of supply.[109] For the Roosevelt Administration
was faced with a presidential election again, in November 1944, and
was politicaly sensitive to charges of supplying pro-Axis 'neutrals'
with vital commodities. Indeed, Secretary Hull told Lord Halifax, on
17 April 1944 in Washington, that the renewal of American oil
supplies to Franco's Spain, in the absence of a complete Spanish
embargo on exports of wolfram to Germany, for a period, would be
the most 'terrific dynamite' at a time when all the 'polecat' groups
were doing their utmost to damage the President's re-election
chances.[110] However, British representations to the United States
Government, throughout the war, worked against a complete breach

in Hispano-American economic relations with only a limited but very significant success.

That was a defensive action, however: an effort to prevent economic suffocation of Franco's Spain by the United States. The British hope of involving the United States in a joint and substantial scheme of economic aid to Spain withered away during the second half of 1941 in the bleak atmosphere generated by hostility, fear and distrust on both the American and the Spanish sides. Far from the prospect of American economic aid sustaining the Spanish will to remain outside the war during the crucial eighteen months, June 1940 to December 1941, as the British hoped, they came to fear, by the last weeks of 1941, that the degree of United States economic pressure upon Franco's Spain was such as to risk the realisation of its belligerency on the Axis side. Of course, it may be argued that it was this very American pressure which impressed upon the Spanish Government the economic disaster which awaited them if they dared to deviate from their non-belligerent stance, although it was a procedure that clearly could be followed to a counter-productive conclusion, which was precisely the British concern. However, the unwillingness of the United States Government to support and amplify the programme of economic attraction which the British wished to establish to bring Spain into politico-economic association with them, undermined the entire project. The British simply had not got the resources to do the job. That they knew this has already been pointed out (pp. 179–80).

When Hoare realised, in the first weeks of July 1941, that American economic assistance for Spain might not be forthcoming, he contended that Britain should still be able to offer an 'attractive programme' to Madrid by enabling the Spanish Government to acquire raw materials which it desired from within the sterling area and in South America. Makins of the Central Department of the Foreign Office had no such illusions. He minuted, on 13 July, as follows:

we alone are not in a position to give increased economic assistance to Spain. This has in fact been the position for some time now. The Spaniards have plenty of sterling, but cannot easily obtain or ship the full amount of the quotas which the M.E.W. are prepared to allow them.

... the only effective method at the moment of using the economic weapon in Spain is for the United States to give a direct or indirect dollar credit combined with export licences for certain commodities.

If the United States Government refuse to play over direct assistance, or if their policy is stultified by the stupidity of the United States Ambassador in Madrid, then it is clear that we can only tinker with the problem ...[111]

Moreover, not only was Britain increasingly unable to guarantee

Spain the supplies it needed, but the Spanish market, itself, was becoming an ever more convenient source from the British point of view, for certain commodities they required. The relative propinquity of Spain to Britain entailed a shorter sea journey to fetch these goods, and also permitted the use of vessels not suitable for employment on oceanic routes. This meant a substantial saving of precious merchant shipping space.[112] This was all the more vital in that the German onslaught on the convoys and craft which sustained the British war economy was taking a heavy toll. Exploitation of the untapped Spanish sources also relieved other overstrained foreign markets. The British Government, increasingly, sought to purchase iron ore, pyrites, potash and mercury, amongst other Spanish goods.[113] Thus, in the second half of 1942, Spain exported 312,000 tons of iron ore to Britain, an amount which accounted for a very significant proportion of British armament steel production.[114] With British imports from Spain escalating, and the difficulty of supplying its wants from the sterling area increasing, the Spanish Government began to accumulate sterling balances. Indeed, they did not need to draw on more than £1,000,000 of the loan they concluded, on 7 April 1941, with Britain. Ironically, Britain was to some extent becoming economically dependent upon Spain rather than the other way round. As Medlicott notes, for the rest of the war 'the problem was to find enough goods to send to Spain in order to obtain the pesetas necessary for Allied purchases'.[115] This development also tended to subvert the politically preferred British policy of 'controlled assistance' supported by sterling loans to Spain. For, from the second half of 1941 onwards, the British always had to be sure that, when supplying Spain with scarce goods, they acquired some correspondingly valuable commodity in return.[116] The increasingly commercial trend of Anglo-Spanish economic transactions coincided with the American desire that such reciprocal exchange constitute the basis for economic relations with Spain. It is, thus, hardly surprising that those relations did come to be founded on the respective economic self-interest of the Anglo-Americans on the one side, and the Spaniards, on the other.

Another influence fostering these tendencies, was the fact that Spain became again, from the latter part of 1941 onwards, an important context in which to wage active economic warfare against Germany by way of a pre-emptive or preclusive purchasing campaign. With the German invasion of the Soviet Union extending into the winter of 1941, it became desirable to try to prevent Germany clothing its troops for the Russian winter with Spanish wool and skins. After December 1941, when Far Eastern sources of supply were closed to Germany, Spain became a potential alternative supplier to the Nazi Reich of such significant commodities as wolfram, lead, zinc, mercury, olive oil, wool and skins.[117] Wolfram, in particular, was the object of an intensive but only indirectly and partially successful Anglo-American pre-emptive campaign to deny the important Spanish – and Portuguese – supplies to the Germans.[118]

Yet, the fact that the vagaries of global wartime economics did bestow some abnormal bonuses upon Spain, did not compensate for the general weakness of the Spanish economic system. In any case, throughout the period, 1940–1, which is the concern of this study, the situation remained basically unchanged, characterised by a rachitic economic infrastructure and popular privation. Argentina continued to help Spain with food, promising another 380,000 tons of wheat and 2,000 tons of meat in April 1941, for example.[119] Portugal, prompted by the British, also extended a credit of 50,000,000 escudos to Spain by an agreement, of 2 July 1941, for the acquisition of Portuguese colonial products.[120] The economic facts of everyday life, however, remained grim for the average Spaniard. In February 1941, Hoare reported that there were numerous deaths from hunger in the Seville district of southern Spain. The crowds begging food from British merchant vessels docked there had grown so large that the police broke them up, but the local customs officers also asked the British sailors for food.[121] In March, the Asturian miners were reported to be fainting from hunger in their scores at work every day.[122] In April, the British Consul in Barcelona reckoned that the wages of employees in the local woollen and cotton industries were thirty per cent higher than in 1935, but that food and clothing cost two to three hundred per cent more than then. Railway communications in and around Barcelona were still 'chaotic', and the port virtually deserted.[123] The British Consul in Málaga reported, on 23 July 1941, that the already 'most difficult' food situation there was actually deteriorating.[124] The same consulate observed in September that the 'black market' had become 'an integral part of the whole system of food distribution' and that the official organisations which controlled all reserves of supplies were the 'real offenders'. The embittered local citizenry recognised that the occasional severe fines imposed on 'black marketeers' were 'shameless attempts on the part of the officials concerned to eliminate outside competition'. The consular report closed by recording a popular consensus on one point: 'People of all shades of opinion agree that never in living memory has Spain had to suffer the consequences of a more corrupt and inefficient administration'. Strang, head of the Central Department of the Foreign Office, noted that this report was in line with all the others reaching London from Spain.[125] The typhus epidemic raging in Spain caused another Foreign Office man to comment, in August 1941, that but for the European conflict the Spanish domestic situation would have attracted front-page publicity in, and large scale organised relief from, the outside world.[126] The British Consul in Barcelona highlighted the significance of the food question in his report home, on 10 November 1941. He noted that the local 'educated and politically-minded' Spaniards had abandoned their interest in talking about the war, the likelihood of a German entry into Spain and the Franco regime, to concentrate solely on the topic of whether each individual would get enough to eat in the oncoming winter. Remarking that a large employer admitted his workers were frequently fainting through hunger, over their machines, the Consul concluded, thus: 'it is perhaps no exaggeration to say that the future of the present regime hangs not so much on its political ideology as on its ability to feed the population'.[127] The internal economic situation in Spain remained, throughout 1941, as insuperable a barrier as before to risky international adventurism by the Spanish Government. The economic squeeze applied to Spain by the United States cut in oil deliveries, in later 1941, weakened the Franco regime's ability to engage in, and raised still further the cost of, such perilous international entrprises. Although there was the concomitant danger inherent in such severe pressure that it would drive the Spaniards into a desperate and defiant act of belligerency. But the Caudillo was not, it seems, prone to such suicidal gestures.

The British plan to bind Spain to them by a programme of economic support died a lingering death in the second half of 1941, as described above. Britain's economic appeal was limited without the massive resources of the United States to back it up and the Spaniards' vulnerability to German intimidation and retaliation probably set a definite limit on the economic aid which they could afford to accept from the Reich's enemies. Franco's Spain did not become Britain's loyal client, but remained, in view of the German refusal to dole out economic help without a return by way of Spanish belligerency, dependent upon the British and Americans for its economic survival. This outcome was consonant with Britain's national interest, even though the British had hoped that greater Anglo-Spanish political affinity might develop, if the Spaniards were provided with a more tolerable level of economic subsistence. Greater intimacy between

Spain and Britain might have provoked the Germans into violating Spanish non-belligerency, and it was the preservation of the Iberian Peninsula from involvement in the war which constituted the supreme goal of British policy towards Spain.

For the same reason it may also have been fortunate that the policy of political blandishment practised by Britain towards Spain, by way of some expression of sympathy and support for the latter's territorial designs on French Morocco, came to nothing. The Foreign Office's directive to Hoare in February 1941, to abstain from giving encouragement to such Spanish ambitions, lest it might jeopardise prospects of renewed belligerency by French North African forces on the anti-Axis side, has been mentioned in the previous chapter. The same fear that they might frustrate such an important development as the re-entry of a large French army into the fight against the Axis or, at least, subvert the French will to resist German penetration of North Africa, ultimately obstructed any resumption of the British effort to court Spain by a policy of political attraction based on the advancement of Franco's *africanista* ambitions.

In the second week of May 1941, the British Consul in Tangier, Alvary Gascoigne, reported that his Spanish opposite number had counselled that Britain should 'give the Spanish Government a free hand in the French Zone, in view of the German threat to French Morocco'.[128] The receipt of this report coincided with Britain's bombing of airfields in Vichy French-ruled Syria, via which the Germans had begun sending aircraft and supplies to the anti-British Iraqi Government of Rashid Ali, then in conflict with British forces.[129] Official French connivance at this German operation provided an occasion for a clean break with Vichy France, if the British were so inclined. This breach in Anglo-French relations, in turn, would free the British of any concern that pledges of political support for Spain's North African territorial aspirations would antagonise Vichy France. Strang of the Foreign Office, however, thought in the early days of the spring 1941 crisis in Anglo-French relations caused by Middle Eastern affairs, that the time was 'not ripe for any drastic departure of policy'. He conceded that a British promise to back Spanish claims on French Morocco in the post-war peace settlement might serve 'to keep Spain out of the war and . . . strengthen the will of the Spanish Government to resist German demands'. But he was still sure that the inevitable disclosure of such an Anglo-Spanish deal would kill any hope of French resistance to German penetration of North Africa.[130]

Even the full-scale fighting in Syria, in June 1941, between Anglo-

Free French and Vichy French forces (leading to the defeat of the latter in July) did not alter the prevailing attitude in the Foreign Office on this issue. On 6 June 1941, two days before the British move into Syria, Hoare called London's attention to the fact that there was a need for the British 'to define more clearly [their] attitude towards Spanish aspirations in Morocco', in view of the impending rupture in Anglo-French relations and the importance of making a gesture towards the Spanish Army whose 'chief . . . interest' was Morocco. With the Anglo-French hostilities in Syria localised, the Foreign Office did not feel that the moment was propitious for relaxing their ban on proffering political support for Spanish claims on Morocco. Hoare was told, on 14 June, that until the British had abandoned hope of possible French resistance to German infiltration or invasion of North Africa, they would have to continue to abstain from affording any official encouragement to the Spanish ambitions. However, Eden noted, on 16 June, that the time would very soon come when Hoare could be given 'a little more latitude'.[131] When that occasion did arrive, somewhat belatedly, in the following October, the Foreign Secretary actually upheld the veto on extending official British approval to Spanish expansion into French North Africa.

Indeed, there was post-war controversy between the British and Spanish Governments over 'unkept promises' allegedly made by London, in October 1941, to back Spanish designs on French North Africa. Franco charged in a speech, on 18 May 1949, that these pledges were given at a meeting attended by Churchill, Eden, Hoare and the British Chiefs of Staff. Hoare denied, on 21 May 1949, that he had ever attended 'a meeting of this kind' or heard of its taking place.[132] Crozier records that the Spaniards were able to point to a contemporary British press item to the effect that Churchill, Eden, Butler and Hoare had been guests at the Spanish Embassy in London on 2 October 1941.[133] Eden denied in the House of Commons, on 22 June 1949, that Churchill and he had ever entered into any commitment to support Spanish claims on French territory, and the then Foreign Secretary, Ernest Bevin, also declared that Franco's assertion was 'unfounded', without any evidence available in the archives of the Foreign Office to support it.[134] Nevertheless, Serrano Suñer quoted the Duke of Alba's contemporary report to Madrid of the gathering of 2 October 1941, in his *Entre Hendaya y Gibraltar*, first published in 1947, i.e., before the public Anglo-Spanish dispute over the episode in 1949. According to Alba's telegram, as published in Serrano Suñer's book, Churchill spoke in the following way in a 'general conversation': 'if England wins the war . . . France will owe it much and it

[owe] France nothing, so that England will be in a position to exert strong and definite pressure for France to satisfy Spain's just claim in North Africa'. Churchill also underlined, according to Alba, the opportunity presented by post-war French and Italian weakness, for Spain to become the 'strongest power in the Mediterranean' – a point also mentioned by Franco in his May 1949 speech. The Prime Minister, apparently, offered Britain's 'determined aid' to the Spaniards to achieve that status. Churchill only allegedly asked, in return, that Spain should not let the Germans pass through its territory.[135]

Alba's apparently contemporary account of Churchill's utterances seems credible, particularly if it is remembered that the Spanish Ambassador recorded the remarks as made in 'general conversation' and not enunciated in a formal meeting, as Franco maintained in his post-war speech. Churchill's contribution to a meeting of the Defence Committee, on 15 October 1941, just under two weeks after the lunch at the Spanish Embassy, certainly reveals a concern on his part, at that time, to define British policy towards Spain's territorial ambitions. Replying to a charge made by Beaverbrook that Britain was guilty of culpable 'procrastination and idleness' in failing to strike at Germany while it hammered the Russians, Churchill declared, *inter alia*, the following:

If General Auchinleck won a victory and cleared Cyrenaica, he might then be able to push on to Tripoli. This, in turn, might lead Germany to press the French to give them the use of Bizerta, a request which Weygand might decide to refuse. We might find ourselves invited to send forces to Casablanca. If this contingency arose, it would be necessary for us to be prepared immediately to put forward proposals on the following lines. We would undertake to restore France to her former greatness but in return the French would have to promise forthwith concessions in Morocco to the Spaniards, and thus fortify the latter in their resistance to a German advance through their country. In order to put forward such proposals, however, we required to know exactly what these concessions should be and the Foreign Office should work out concrete proposals.

Eden felt it would be 'unwise' to overestimate 'the effect of concessions on the Spaniards', since Portuguese sources affirmed that Franco's Government would not resist a German entry into Spain. He accepted, however, that Britain should have its terms ready for a more favourable turn of events in Spain. Thus, he accepted the meeting's request that he draw up proposals on possible French concessions to Spain's North African aspirations. They could be presented to Weygand if he appealed to the British for their help against Germany, as their 'condition for giving full support to the rehabilitation of the

French nation'.[136] The novel aspect of Churchill's suggestion lay in its stipulation that the French would have to pledge themselves 'forthwith' to territorial concessions to Spain. He was, therefore, contemplating having something more concrete to offer Franco than promises of British support in the post-war settlement.

Although the hypothetical situation which the Prime Minister envisaged as appropriate for the implementation of these proposals did not come about, the policy review within the Foreign Office is illuminating. For, it revealed the continued reluctance of that British Ministry to risk alienating the French for the dubious advantages of a deal with Spain. Strang observed, on 18 October, that the Germans were apparently making known their disinclination to back Italian and Spanish claims on French territory. The British, he therefore advised, should take care that their view of the desirability of French concessions to Spain in Morocco should only be divulged if, and when, Weygand appealed for British assistance. He concluded thus: 'Otherwise, knowledge of this attitude on our part might well predispose the Vichy Government and General Weygand still further against resistance to Germany.'[137] Cadogan thought that the Spanish claim to territorial expansion in Morocco did not rest on 'very firm' legal or historical foundations, but felt it would be 'justifiable' if Britain found it expedient to support it.[138] Eden informed his officials, on 19 October, that he was 'not enthusiastic for this plan' but agreed, as he had at the Defence Committee meeting, that it might be prudent to have it in reserve.[139] Eden circulated, under his name, a note containing the results of the policy review, to the members of the Defence Committee, on 28 October 1941. This document did acknowledge that there were 'reasonable military and economic grounds from the Spanish viewpoint' for some adjustment of the frontiers of the French and Spanish Moroccan Zones in the latter's favour, but its conclusion was decidedly negative. Emphasising the difficulty of inducing the French to yield Moroccan ground to the Spaniards, it counselled against trying to persuade them to do so, in any case:

It seems unlikely that our offer to endorse the extreme Spanish claim [which the British defined as an extension of the Spanish Moroccan Zone's boundary to north of Rabat along a line which would include the length of railway between that city and Tasa] would have a decisive influence on Spanish policy; and it is a claim that would be hard to justify. The endorsement of any claim against French Morocco would seriously indispose General Weygand and indeed all French military authorities. It might be held to conflict with our promise to restore the 'greatness' of France. We should have to consult President Roosevelt before making this 'commitment'.

For all these reasons, I should not recommend that we pursue the idea of attempting to extract a cession of French Moroccan territory in favour of Spain.[140]

Churchill did not challenge this conclusion. The Foreign Office's judgement that Spain was unlikely to be tempted by relatively minor frontier rectifications in Morocco was surely correct, but it is also instructive that they shied away from pressing even such modest concessions on the French. The inconvenience, and even danger, of antagonising the Vichy French came to outweigh, decisively, the possible advantages of political collaboration with Spain in 1941 for the British, as it had for the Germans, in 1940–1.

Even had the Foreign Office survey of the problem produced approval for Churchill's suggestion that British terms should be ready for presentation to Weygand, the idea would have been quickly overtaken by events. For, General Weygand was dismissed from his position as Vichy French Delegate-General to North Africa, in November 1941, due to German pressure.[141] Notwithstanding this development, which naturally generated pessimism in London about the possibility of any real French resistance to Germany emerging in North Africa, the Foreign Office did not remove the prohibition on official encouragement of Spanish expansion there. Thus, Hoare was gently reprimanded, on 14 December 1941, for a declaration he had made, a few days earlier, in a conversation with General Orgaz, High Commissioner of Spanish Morocco. Hoare had dangled the bait of British support for Spain's imperial aspirations, in speaking to Orgaz in the following terms: 'More than once I had, on instructions from His Majesty's Government, stated that we were not unsympathetic to Spanish aspirations in Africa. If Spain was to take advantage of our goodwill we must proceed by frank discussion and not by a sudden coup.' Some Foreign Office men thought that recent French developments rendered it unnecessary to shun an understanding with Spain over Morocco any longer, but Strang thought that it would be premature 'to upset the apple-cart' until the Vichy Government had finally assumed an overtly pro- or anti-German stance. Deputy Under-Secretary of State, Orme Sargent, approved this view. So, right at the close of the main period covered by this book, Hoare was again directed to desist from nourishing Spanish designs on Morocco with assurances of British sympathy.[142]

Thus, for the greater part of the period of Britain's struggle for survival in 1940–1, there was no serious British effort to attract Franco's Spain into political co-operation with them by promises of present or future support for its desired territorial aggrandisement in

North Africa. In 1941, the British attempt to court Spain over this issue was confined to Hoare's unauthorised declarations in Madrid, and to the vague and informal protestation of Britain's readiness to champion Spain's case after the war, which Churchill seems to have made to Alba in October. The Foreign Office blocked any more formal attempt to reach accord with Spain over Morocco. The possible repercussions of such a manoeuvre on Anglo-French relations made it too potentially costly to countenance. The actual influence of the occasional British expressions of goodwill towards Spain's African aspirations on Franco and his Government must have been slight. One need only recall the Caudillo's refusal to accept Hitler's promise of future bounty to realise how unimpressed he must have been by such British assertions of political sympathy and pledges of post-war support. Again, Franco's persistent efforts to persuade Hitler to specify the territorial gains which Spain would receive, in return for its belligerency on the Axis side, demonstrate clearly which of the two sides in the war the Caudillo reckoned would be able to deliver the goods to him. He retained his belief in the inevitability of German victory throughout 1940–1, and well beyond, according to Serrano Suñer.[143] This conviction also entailed the maintenance of a discreet political distance between Spain and the power apparently destined for ineluctable defeat. A victorious and vengeful Hitler could make Franco pay dearly for any foolish attempt to guarantee Spain's territorial aggrandisement by political concord with Britain. If the British programme of political attraction addressed to Franco did not assume impressive dimensions, then, in 1940–1, neither was the Spanish leader willing or able to respond to it.

There was another area where British policy might have assumed a positive, supportive aspect towards Spain. This was in the possible extension of British military assistance to Spanish forces resisting German invasion. It will be recalled that Eden had transmitted to Churchill the unanimous recommendation of the Gibraltar meeting, of 17 February 1941, that Britain should be ready to lend sizable military help on the Spanish mainland to those Spaniards resisting German entry into their country. Although the Chiefs of Staff still felt that they would only be able to help the Spaniards hold their Moroccan Zone, they instructed the Joint Planning Staff to study the implications of the proposals emanating from the Gibraltar gathering.[144] The Joint Planning Staff did not change their minds either. They reported back, on 21 February 1941, that even the suggested force 'could do no more than stiffen Spanish resistance and in the event of a Spanish collapse would be inadequate to hold the Cape Tarifa Peninsula and Gibraltar or even to defend itself'. Moreover, since the British force would have to come by sea after the German move, and the Spaniards could not be expected to resist effectively, Britain's aid would be too late, as well as too little. Spanish Morocco was deemed, again, to be the only feasible focus of a British attempt to retain control of the Strait. When a Foreign Office official, present at the Joint Planning Staff's deliberations, indicated that if British operations on the mainland were precluded, then the attempt to hold Spanish Morocco could not be made (given the inevitable Spanish opposition to such a self-interested British manoeuvre) the Joint Planners agreed, but had no solution.[145]

However, the review of strategic policy towards Spain was not completed before Hoare on 9 March 1941, again presented the case for British military support to bolster Spanish resistance on their mainland territory.[146] Hoare argued that, even if the Spaniards collapsed and the British expeditionary force was withdrawn or destroyed, the British would secure definite gains from their investment. They should acquire not only Spain's naval and merchant fleets, but also the right to use the Spanish islands – the Canaries and the Balearics – and Spanish Morocco, quite apart from having enkindled continuing guerrilla resistance to the Germans inside the Iberian Peninsula. Successful Spanish resistance would be of 'inestimable advantage' to the British cause by 'dislocating the German programme, saving the Straits, keeping Germans out of North West Africa and retaining . . . a bridgehead into Western Europe and for United States a *point d'appui* if they [came] in'.[147] Churchill directed the Chiefs of Staff to comment on Hoare's advice.[148] With Britain by this time committed to the dispatch of an expeditionary force to Greece to help meet the expected German onslaught, the Chiefs of Staff 'reluctantly' concluded that Britain could not 'for the time being, contemplate operations, even on a limited scale, in Spain or in Spanish Morocco'.[149] Churchill agreed to this line 'in general principle', although maintaining that it remained 'very important' to encourage Spanish resistance to German entry into their country, because it would enable Britain 'to take their islands as allies, and perhaps to get a footing on the African shore'.[150] The inexorable logic of Britain's military weakness imposed itself on its grand strategists, however, yet again. Churchill approved a telegram, drafted by the Chiefs of Staff, and sent to Hoare on 19 March, in the Prime Minister's name. It underlined the gap between what was strategically desirable and Britain's already strained strategic resources:

We fully agree with you as to what we should like to do, if we could, to encourage Spanish resistance. You know full well that for the moment we have a pretty heavy overdraft and it is difficult to draw further on our capital.

Nevertheless we cannot tell yet how the ebb and flow of the war in the Atlantic and at our own front door, and further afield in the Balkans and the Middle East, will affect what we may find ourselves able, either to earmark, or to send to Spain.[151]

In fact, the 'ebb and flow of the war' ensured that there was no resurrection of the projects to send British military assistance to Spain for the remainder of the period while Britain fought without direct American participation in the war. The run of British defeats in North Africa, Greece and Crete, and the subjugation of Yugoslavia, in April–May 1941, greatly reduced the possibility of substantial Spanish military resistance to a German Iberian incursion emerging in the immediately succeeding months.[152] The German assault on the Soviet Union shifted the main theatre of operations decisively eastwards, for the immediate future. This meant that Germany was unlikely to intervene in Spain until it had, at least, stabilised the eastern front, and the need for Britain to be ready to come to the aid of resisting Spaniards, should such appear was, therefore, less urgent. Paradoxically, however, the spring and summer months of 1941 during which this diversion of the German war-machine eastwards took place, also witnessed acute anxiety in London over the risk that Spain might be drawn into war on the Axis side. As is explained in the next chapter, the immediate response of some British strategic planners to Hitler's Eastern Mediterranean victories in the spring, was to assume that Spain was lost. The public Spanish manifestations of solidarity with Germany's anti-Bolshevik crusade in the summer, eventually turned this assumption into the virtually unanimous view of Britain's grand strategists, for a time. Once more, the scales of British strategic planning towards Spain tilted to the negative side, where Britain concentrated upon preventive strikes to anticipate the serious menace which Spanish involvement in the Axis war effort would present.

However, before analysing this final aspect of British policy towards Spain in 1941, there remains an undercurrent in Anglo-Spanish relations which should be briefly assessed here, because it involved the possibility that Britain might lend encouragement to certain political developments within Spain. This clandestine dimension, as it were, to Anglo-Spanish contacts lay in the communication which British representatives in Spain managed to maintain with certain prominent Spaniards, who were disaffected with Franco's rule, in spite of being partisans of the Nationalist cause in the Spanish Civil War. These were Spanish Army generals, for the most part, and Hoare and his staff spent much time in 1941 recording, for transmission to London, their perpetual plans and plots to unseat their detested foe, Serrano Suñer, and even to depose Franco himself.

Beigbeder had, of course, been one of the first leading Spanish officers to enter into secret liaison with the British, and he kept the channel open in 1941. Thus, for instance, in conversation with the British Military Attaché, Torr, on 28 May 1941, he requested financial and other assistance from the British for his scheme of organising a Moroccan nationalist rising in the French Zone, if the Germans entered it, or Spain. He announced his readiness to try and stir up resistance on the Spanish mainland, but thought the more immediate danger was a German occupation, with the connivance of the Vichy French authorities, of Casablanca and Dakar. He condemned Serrano Suñer as 'the fanatic . . . leading Spain to her ruin', since the latter was anxious that Spain win its place in the Nazi 'New World Order' by immediate belligerency alongside the Axis. He admitted that Franco had kept a rein on Serrano Suñer until then, but also maintained that they shared a conviction that the British Empire was 'already as good as dead'. Beigbeder also incisively assessed the Caudillo's attitude to the war, on this occasion:

Franco does not want war, nor does he want the Germans to come into Spain. His innermost wish is that the war may be brought to an end by the blockade of England and that the English will give in as soon as possible, whilst at the moment of the armistice he will declare himself belligerent, *but with the Germans not in Spain.*[153]

The Foreign Office, however, remained doubtful about the significance of Beigbeder's contact with them. Makins noted that the ex-Minister was 'not a very reliable informant'.[154] The Foreign Office did become inclined, however, to see some sense in Beigbeder's appraisal of the political prospects of the other Spanish Generals who expended so much energy in 1941 intriguing against Serrano Suñer, and even Franco.

Discussing the schemes which he intended to set in motion after a German entry into Spain, with the British Assistant Military Attaché, Lubbock, Beigbeder reiterated his resolve 'never to play the "Mexican general" '. He repeated, too, his view that a military Government which overthrew Franco's regime 'was bound in the end to fail, owing to mutual jealousies, inexperience and competition for places among the generals concerned'. Moreover, Beigbeder added that, with the exception of General Aranda, the generals did not discern the seriousness of the menace involved in German dominance, so that they would be even more likely 'to fall under German influence' after seizing power, than Serrano Suñer himself.

Although aware that Beigbeder's view might be coloured by the fact that the disaffected generals had excluded him from their circle, the Foreign Office men, including Eden, were by November 1941, ready to accept that Spain's continuing vulnerability to German pressure meant that any Spanish Government would be greatly subject to German influence.[155]

However, Hoare and other British representatives in Spain had been disposed to view the anti-Serrano Suñer movement within the generals' ranks as potentially pro-British. Thus, reporting on 5 August 1941, that 'most' of the generals had concluded that Franco and Serrano Suñer would have to be 'eliminated', Hoare observed that these officers 'would become definitely pro-British in the event of any German disaster in Russia' and were, anyway, 'anxious to insure against a German defeat'. He thought that the military opposition movement might assume the form of either a 'Monarchist parliament' or a 'Regency Government acting in close contact with King Juan' (the exiled claimant to the Spanish throne). Hoare added his opinion that the development of such a movement would 'be most beneficial to the British interest'.[156] On 12 August, Hillgarth reported that Serrano Suñer and Franco could not last much longer, and held out the prospect of an alternative government to replace the Caudillo's, if he proved obstinate, or the Germans invaded Spain. This new executive was to include Generals Aranda and Orgaz and the right-wing civilian politicians, José María Gil Robles and Pedro Sainz Rodríguez. Hillgarth asserted that this 'so far unofficial government' was intent on establishing a constitutional monarchy in Spain, but had as their first priority 'an understanding with Great Britain'. Noting that the embryonic government intended to present its list of ministers to the British Government for their prior approval, Hillgarth predicted that London would 'soon have a genuinely friendly government' in Spain.[157]

The British were informed, in late October 1941, that if the alternative Government assumed power because of, or was faced with, a German invasion, it would fight back, with the military members of the new régime based in Spanish Morocco and the civilians on the Canary Islands. Such a movement of national resistance would clearly be allied to Britain and, indeed, London was also told that the conspirators had already arranged to invite the British into the Canary Islands in such an eventuality.[158] However, it was not so evident that a change of regime produced by exclusively internal pressures would lead to a pro-British Government. When the 'chief civilian leader' of the alternative Administration (Pedro Sainz

Rodríguez) produced a document on such a change of regime, in November 1941, it stipulated that there should be an 'immediate explanation' offered to each belligerent power, after the *coup* which, along with 'no change in [Spain's] international attitude would rapidly establish the new situation from the external point of view'. Continuity in foreign policy, rather than a move in the British direction seemed to be the likely result of the restoration of the 'Traditional Representative Monarchy of Spain'.[159]

Indeed, in April 1941, the German Ambassador to Spain, von Stohrer, was ready to view a new Spanish Government based on the disgruntled generals with equanimity, since he believed them all (with the exception of the Carlist War Minister, Varela) to be friendly to Germany. He told Berlin that the military party was in continuous contact with the German Embassy.[160] However, Serrano Suñer did denounce General Aranda to von Stohrer, on 10 October 1941, for having 'taken up contact with the British Ambassador' and having been 'close to organising a military plot to give a new direction to Spanish foreign policy'. Serrano Suñer extended his condemnation to 'all of these political intriguers, generals and so-called politicians who . . . were suing for England's friendship in expectation of an English victory'.[161] Serrano also singles out Aranda in his *Memorias* as an 'intelligent and calm man' who early on began to doubt that the Germans would win the war, and so established contact with the English and the Americans.[162] Strang of the Foreign Office was willing to acknowledge, at the end of October, that the pro-British character of the generals and their friends must be 'notorious' in Spain, but he was worried about the venality of many of this group who, of course, were receiving clandestine payments from Britain. It was possible that they would betray the British cause for greater financial reward from the enemy. Moreover, Strang was moved to query whether it should be British policy to work actively for the overthrow of Franco's regime or for the emergence of an alternative military government.[163]

Although the question of the ultimate international loyalty of a generals' Government was clearly connected with the problem of promoting its establishment, it was also important to determine whether it was in Britain's interest to interfere in domestic Spanish politics in such a manner. When Hoare posed this question to London, at the end of May 1941, in the form of an inquiry from Britain's 'very best source' (probably Juan March) in Spain as to whether the British Government wanted an internal Spanish upheaval to unseat Serrano Suñer, the ambivalent Foreign Office response demonstrated their awareness of the risks and ambiguities inherent in such an exercise. The Foreign Office reply (drafted by Cadogan and approved by Eden) asked Hoare whether he was sure that the 'very best source' would not double-cross the British if they committed themselves. It also pointed out that, as they derived 'certain advantages' from the existing Spanish situation, there should be 'reasonable hope' of a *coup* succeeding, before they backed it. Yet, in spite of dubbing the venture 'a tremendous gamble', the Foreign Office decided that 'internal trouble would be preferable to unopposed German entry into Spain'. Hoare was, therefore, directed to state that the British Government would like to see the elimination of Serrano Suñer by an anti-Falangist *coup*, but that it was for Spaniards to decide whether such a change was possible.[164] However, this promised show-down with Serrano Suñer did not materialise, like the many others which were bruited about in 1941.

There was concern, however, in the Foreign Office during the following autumn, over the position taken by the British Military Attaché in Spain, Torr, on instructions from Hoare, in conversations with Generals Kindelán and Aranda, in later September and early October, respectively. Torr vigorously disputed the generals' contentions that it was inopportune or unncessary to force Serrano Suñer out of power. So, 'great caution' was urged upon the Embassy in Madrid, on 8 October, in making any suggestions in relation to Spanish politics, 'even to friendly generals', since there seemed 'little likelihood' of their actually moving against Serrano Suñer.[165] It was reported in the last days of October, that the generals were yet again, on the brink of a *coup* to oust Serrano Suñer and 'if necessary' Franco, but were worried whether the British and Americans would guarantee 'adequate supplies' of foodstuffs and oil to Spain. Sainz Rodríguez, reportedly, emphasised that the Army leaders were 'relying on an immediately more generous policy' after the *coup*, since otherwise the new regime would be as detested as its predecessor. The Foreign Office's response was, again, guarded. Cadogan reminded his colleagues, on 31 October, that it would be 'fatal' for Britain to be 'caught meddling in internal politics in Spain'. Again, the message went out, on 5 November, to Britain's representatives in Madrid that they must eschew giving the impression that they were interfering in Spain's domestic affairs. The Spanish conspirators should be told that Britain would do its best to help, but in fact there was probably little it could do to expand the flow of supplies to Spain 'very appreciably'. It was felt in London that it was internal Spanish maladministration and corruption which were responsible for popular privation there, so it was up to any new Government to put its own house in order. Moreover, the British diplomats were specifically enjoined to avoid any definite economic promises lest they be seized upon by the Franco regime as an excuse for charging Britain with attempting to bring about political change in Spain by economic pressure.[166]

Indeed, it was at this time too, that the Foreign Office endorsed Beigbeder's assessment that a generals' Government would be likely to fall under German domination. Eden had circulated the dispatch containing Beigbeder's appraisal as a War Cabinet Paper, on 10 November, with a memorandum under his own name, which pointed out that it might well be to Britain's advantage that the Franco regime continue in power, hated as it was for its pro-German stance, until strategic circumstances changed to the extent of permitting any alternative Spanish Government to follow 'a truly independent policy'.[167] The ambivalent British attitude towards a possible change of regime in Spain was revealed, a few weeks later, when Eden challenged his officials' advocacy of an absolute 'hands off' policy towards internal Spanish politics and, on being reminded of the War Cabinet Paper which he had sanctioned, declared that he should not have approved it. This revealing episode was sparked off by Hoare's telegram home of 28 November, which reported yet again, that Spanish opinion was incensed against Serrano Suñer and that the suggestion had been made that an Anglo-American economic blockade should be imposed upon Spain to give the Foreign Minister the *coup de grâce*. Hoare advised against such direct dictation to the Spaniards, but did feel it would be useful to point out to those who wanted to listen that Serrano Suñer was continually obstructing the development of relations with Britain, which could only improve in his absence. The Foreign Office men concerned with policy towards Spain proceeded to draft a telegram in accordance with the Cabinet Paper of 10 November, informing the Ambassador that a change of regime in Spain would 'not necessarily' be to Britain's advantage, because such a new administration would probably have to bow to German pressure, and could not be given increased British economic help. There was also a counsel of caution against intervention in internal Spanish politics. Eden, when he saw the draft telegram, damned its argument as 'false from start to finish'. He stated his reasons for disagreeing with its line, on 1 December, thus: 'We may be unable to remove Suñer, it may be unwise to try (tho' our Embassy has been anticipating triumph daily for a year) the generals may be broken reeds, but I would dearly love to see Suñer go and maybe Franco too, and I am certainly not prepared to pretend otherwise.' In the ensuing, internal Foreign Office debate, although regretting having sanctioned the War Cabinet Paper of 10 November, Eden readily accepted that 'a premature attempt to change the [Spanish] regime would be disastrous'. He approved a redrafted telegram which changed the emphasis, but not the sense, of the instructions to Hoare. It was sent, on 3 December, and read, as follows:

I agree that we should stand aside and not appear as taking any steps to secure removal of present Minister for Foreign Affairs much though I should like to see him go.

A change of regime might not moreover be an unmixed advantage for us until German influence lessens and our own capacity for supporting a more friendly regime in Spain is increased. Attitude of non-intervention in Spanish domestic political scene would at present in any case be best.[168]

Thus, did the British refrain from lending any real aid or encouragement to the opposition to the Franco regime which had formed within the ranks of the Nationalist victors of the Civil War. It is interesting to note that the Germans also instructed their Ambassador in Spain not to become involved in the internal political struggle there, at one stage in 1941. State Secretary, von Weizsäcker, had argued in a message to his Minister, Ribbentrop, on 11 May 1941, that Germany should avoid entanglement in domestic Spanish political squabbles, unless it was ready to back its words with active intervention, in case of necessity. Since almost all the Spanish generals were reported to be pro-German, the injury to Germany's interest would 'perhaps not be too great if Suñer should not be able to deal effectively with his military opposition'. An order from Ribbentrop was sent to Ambassador von Stohrer, on 13 May, commanding him to maintain 'the strictest reserve' towards the internal political crisis in Spain.[169] So the Germans also realised that they derived advantages from the status quo in Spain, which it would be foolish to upset until the general strategic situation made it convenient to do so. The British had reached the same judgement by late 1941. Neither power afterwards really altered its basic view that Francoism was the least unacceptable and most reliable force to preside over Spain for the duration of the European hostilities. The British Embassy in Madrid continued its dalliance with anti-Franco monarchists and military men into 1942.[170] Hitler, too, was tempted, particularly in 1942, to support a radical Nazi–Falangist conspiracy to unseat Franco.[171] Ultimately, however, the risks involved in deliberately destabilising the Franco regime were too great for Britain and Germany. Already heavily engaged in the immense complications of a world war, they settled for the strategic stability which Franco's rule ensured in one corner of Europe.

Left to their own devices, the military-based opposition grouping succeeded neither in forcing a change of regime in Spain, nor even in ousting Serrano Suñer from power in 1941. Indeed, the London observers of the Spanish scene had soon come to doubt the likelihood of any political *coup* engineered by the Spanish generals, in spite – in part, because of – the frequent predictions by Hoare and his staff that such an event was imminent.[172] Eden had misgivings, as early as 27 April 1941, that the British Embassy in Madrid was 'being fooled' and remained sceptical when, for example, Hoare reported, on 22 November, that Spain was 'nearer to a *coup d'état* than at any moment in the last year'. The Foreign Secretary remarked that this report was likely to prove 'as valuable as scores of others from our ever hopeful and ever mistaken Embassy'.[173] The inaction of the generals justified Eden's scepticism on this latter occasion, as on previous ones. The failure of the Spanish generals to achieve even their minimum goal, i.e., the political demise of Serrano Suñer, can be traced to several sources. Notwithstanding the difficult and fluid circumstances in which they had to operate, personal irresoluteness should not be ignored in explaining the lack of political decisiveness displayed by the generals. Von Stohrer characterised Aranda as 'the most energetic representative of the military party', and he certainly seemed to be a central figure in the military's conspiratorial cabal.[174] However, the British, who probably got to know Aranda rather better than the Germans, considered him to be 'unreliable and illogical' and to be veering about 'like a weathercock'.[175] The disaffected generals were, also, lacking any firm unity of purpose. Most of them espoused the restoration of Spain's monarchy and were anti-Falangist, but the real unifying force amongst them was a negative one: resentment at Serrano Suñer's political pre-eminence.[176]

However, Serrano Suñer's place in the Francoist hierarchy, in fact, received a setback in May 1941, when the Caudillo engaged in a characteristic reshuffling and rebalancing of the diverse forces gathered in his right-wing regime. This affair is briefly described, in the next chapter, where its influence upon the attitude of Britain's grand strategists towards Spain, at an important moment in their policy deliberations, is explained. Its impact upon Spain's internal political scene was probably to strengthen Franco's personal position, whatever the subsequent ups and downs in his political fortunes in 1941. One commentator even interprets the political realignment, of May 1941, as the 'true configuration of Francoism' which would remain 'essentially immutable during the following three and a half decades'.[177] According to Serrano Suñer, himself, 'from that moment the "F.E.T. de las J.O.N.S." was above all Franco's party'.[178] By a series of appointments to key positions in party and state, Franco appears to have entrenched his personal dictatorship to a degree which would have required a more organised and vigorous challenge to dislodge it than the generals were able to mount. Serrano Suñer's political reverse may also have defused the disaffected military's resentment with Franco, for a period, thereby enervating their stamina and resolution as potential conspirators against the Caudillo. Finally, the concern that domestic political disturbance in Spain might also provide foreign powers with the opportunity to intervene there, or give the defeated Republican Spaniards the chance for a second round of the Civil War, probably also deterred the military dissidents from open rebellion.

Thus, just as it had endured strong diplomatic pressure in late 1940 and early 1941 from Germany, Franco's regime weathered internal political unrest and American economic boycott during the latter year. It was, however, the power which had earnestly striven to provide some support for Franco's Spain, and had seriously reflected on extending more, that also came to constitute the greatest threat to the Spaniards' non-belligerent status in 1941. The need to be ready to discern, and to confront, strategic dangers emanating from Spain always underlay the British attempts to court that country. The development of the war drew this concern to the forefront of British policy-making towards Spain, in the spring and summer of 1941. During the middle months of that year, the British anxiety to anticipate active Spanish hostility and a German move into Spain prevailed over more positive efforts to promote Anglo-Spanish solidarity.

9

The exhaustion of diplomacy

In a dispatch which he sent to London, on 1 May 1941, Sir Samuel Hoare admitted that Spain was 'shaking under the shocks' of the recent British defeats in the Eastern Mediterranean. Nevertheless, he refused to subscribe to 'the doctrine of Calvinist inevitability' which deemed Spanish belligerency on the Axis side to be ineluctable. He therefore repeated his oft-expressed call for extensive Anglo-American aid to Spain, for a United States propaganda campaign there to publicise the scale of their support for Britain's fight, and for some effort to mobilise Latin American influence against Spanish adherence to the Axis.[1] Makins of the Foreign Office, however, did not see that there was much more Britain could do to consolidate Spanish non-belligerency. He minuted, on 9 May 1941, in reaction to Hoare's advice, thus:

This despatch clearly reveals the extent to which the resources of our diplomacy in Spain are being used up. Sir S. Hoare, like a squirrel in a cage, returns again and again to the same points, which are already being dealt with as far as we can deal with them. His further proposals depend on action . . . by the U.S. Government, and the Ambassador is disposed to think that the Americans will readily dance to this tune. I am afraid he is somewhat over-optimistic about this.[2]

The course of Hispano-American relations in the second half of 1941, described in the previous chapter, fully justified such pessimism about the prospects of boosting Britain's diplomatic appeal to Spain with United States backing. However, the depletion of Britain's powers of diplomatic influence in Spain, in the spring of 1941, was not merely due to its own meagre means, or the reaffirmed American reluctance to supplement them. For, the British ability to carry diplomatic weight was badly hurt by the run of military defeats which they suffered in North Africa, Greece and Crete, between late March and late May 1941.

The great hopes generated in London by the revival of Britain's military fortunes in later 1940, were cruelly dashed by the British Eastern Mediterranean reverses of the following spring. The reaction to these defeats in the British Government was not only one of despondency. There was also some agitated debate inside the Foreign Office about ways and means of rescuing Britain's failing cause. Cadogan sought to dissuade Eden from action for its own sake, on 28 April 1941, since it would lead to the waste of precious military resources, however 'disappointing and humiliating' it was 'to look forward to another year of the defensive'. Cadogan summarised his impressions of his talk with Eden, thus: 'He professed to agree. I begged him to believe that diplomacy could only be prepared in our munition factories. But will o'the wisps have a fatal attraction for him and Winston.'[3] Eden, indeed, was still threshing about in search of some means of salvation, on 9 May. Cadogan recorded his encounters with the Foreign Secretary on that day, in these words: 'Meeting at 4 on Spain with A.[nthony Eden]. He is always jumping about the room, itching to "do something". He has to be humoured, but the best one can do is to restrain him . . . Meeting on Persia – to see what we can "*do*". I've told him 100 times – make more *tanks*!!'[4] Four days later Cadogan found Eden to be 'like a cat on hot bricks' and, right at the end of May, the Foreign Secretary returned to the quest for some suitable way to revive Britain's flagging fortunes. Cadogan had another meeting with him on this subject, on 30 May:

5.15. talk with A. about Turkey and Russia. He keeps on feeling that there's something to be *done* – diplomatically . . . Fact is that with our military weakness and the sensational ineptitude of our commanders, diplomacy is completely hamstrung . . . You can't do anything nowadays with any country unless you can (a) threaten (b) bribe it.[5]

However, even amidst the serious military defeats which it had suffered in the Eastern Mediterranean in the spring of 1941, Britain did retain some power with which to hurt a hostile Spain by way of economic blockade and other naval action. The Spaniards remained aware of this, and despite the disasters of the spring, reports from Spain assured London that Franco would not join Britain's enemies until the Germans had conquered Egypt and the Suez Canal, thereby closing the Mediterranean's eastern gateway.[6] The Duke of Alba, declared in conversation with Eden, on 8 May, that he was 'fairly confident' that Franco would decline to allow German troops pass through Spain, as long as Britain held the Suez Canal.[7] The British, in fact, were not really concerned that Franco's Spain might wage war against them, of its own volition. But they were worried that, after the recent Balkan and Eastern Mediterranean events, Franco would bow to German demands for entry into Spain, and that no Spanish resistance would be mounted to the arrival of German troops.[8] Even Hoare, for instance, had to admit, on 30 May, that 'after Yugoslavia and Greece the will to resist that was growing so well at the end of the year, has for the time being faded out'.[9] The British Joint Planning Staff's Future Operations Section presented a comprehensive review of 'Future Strategy', on 14 June 1941, which was largely accepted by the Joint Planners and the Chiefs of Staff. Churchill was inclined to regard such long-term plans as necessarily speculative and, therefore, not to be accepted as official policy. He felt that this review, in any case, had been quickly overtaken by events, notably the German attack on the Soviet Union.[10] But the paper did express, in regard to Spain, a strategic assessment which found only wider and more emphatic acceptance amongst Britain's grand strategists after the German thrust eastwards. When outlining Britain's 'Defensive Strategy Overseas' it stated the following:

We do not believe that Spain, though she may procrastinate until Germany's hands are freed elsewhere, will offer any organized resistance once she is faced with an ultimatum of immediate enforcement. Even if she did resist, we are unable to give effective military assistance, and, within three to four weeks, Germany would be in a position if not to capture Gibraltar at least to deny us the use of the naval base. In the more probable event of Germany acting with the passive or the active assistance of Spain she should reach her objective in a matter of days.

At any time that Germany chooses and whatever line Spain may take the naval base at Gibraltar can, therefore, be denied to us. We believe that sooner or later Germany will take this action.[11]

Germany's triumphs in the Eastern Mediterranean had swiftly reawakened the Spaniards' sense of vulnerability to German military incursion. The British strategic planners' assessment of the likely Spanish reaction to a German invasion of their country was, in fact, borne out by the contacts between Spaniards and the German Embassy in Madrid, during May 1941. The Spanish attitude, as revealed in these messages, showed their concern that a German march into Spain might be imminent. An 'absolutely reliable inform-ant' told von Stohrer, in early May, that Serrano Suñer had expressed the hope that Germany would not 'resort to military measures in Spain without the consent of Spain' since 'the reaction of the Spanish people would be very vigorous'. The Spanish Foreign Minister report-edly added the following, however: 'We could not and would not resist . . . since the Germans are very much stronger. Moreover, we want to and shall enter the war.'[12] Further warnings from Serrano Suñer against unilateral intrusion into Spain by Germany because it would antagonise all its Spanish friends, were relayed to Berlin on 9 May.[13] Von Stohrer reported home, on 30 May, that he and other German diplomats in Spain, had recently been 'repeatedly' counselled by 'official and unofficial' friends that a forced entry by Germany into the country would alienate all pro-German Spaniards and provoke costly sabotage against the unwelcome Nazi forces. The Ambassador observed that he no longer thought there would be 'an official opposition, particularly after the events in Yugoslavia', but also felt that an incident could easily cause bloodshed.[14]

Apparently recognising the futility of forcibly resisting a German move into Spain, the Spaniards tried to postpone the fatal day with cautions that might give the Germans pause, without giving them cause for keen resentment. The German attack on Russia relieved their immediate anxiety but did not modify the hardening British belief that Spain was bound to fall under Germany's occupation, sooner or later. One important factor hindering a pre-emptive British military action likely to provoke Spanish belligerency, in the previous months, had been their reluctance to destroy the Spanish will to resist German pressure. In the spring and summer of 1941, however, the British – as already mentioned – came to feel that no such Spanish resistance to Germany would manifest itself. If Britain still wielded enough power to deter Spain from immediate aggression against it, London strategists were uncomfortably aware that there was little chance, at that time, of fostering the Spanish spirit of opposition to foreign dictation. As Cadogan strove to point out to Eden, diplomatic power, all too clearly, in the spring and summer of 1941, came out of the barrel of a gun, and the inferiority of Britain's fire-power to Germany's had been dramatically demonstrated by the Eastern Mediterranean battles. Britain, without United States backing, had little enough with which to bribe Spain, but the general European strategic situation in the middle months of 1941 rendered such a diplomatic exercise rather pointless, anyway. In such circumstances, the conviction that Germany would sweep, unopposed, into Spain in its own good time suggested the prudence of anticipating the inevitable loss of Gibraltar by seizing a substitute base. Indeed, the temptation to do something about this impending injury before it was too late, eventually became almost irresistible.

The first danger, in 1941, that British preventive action might precipitate Spanish belligerency actually arose before Britain's reverses in the Eastern Mediterranean, and resembled the first such episode in 1940. As in July of the previous year, it was Churchill's spontaneous instinct, in March 1941, that the British should strike pre-emptively at Portuguese territory which first threatened to embroil Britain and Spain. He informed the Chiefs of Staff, Cadogan and R. A. Butler, on 22 March, that he was 'coming to the conclusion' that Britain should seize the Cape Verde Islands. He was particularly worried over recent losses at sea which seemed to suggest that U-boats were operating from these islands, and was also impatient at the immobilisation of valuable forces and shipping involved in holding an expedition to the Atlantic Islands in readiness. Once again, he was inclined to dismiss the possibility that a British occupation of the Cape Verdes would provoke, by itself, a German entry into the Iberian Peninsula, or dispose the Portuguese and Spaniards to let the Germans in.[15]

The Chiefs of Staff quickly reported back to the Prime Minister that there was no evidence to suggest that German submarines were working from the Cape Verdes, but they also advised that there were now 'grounds for considering the seizure of the Atlantic Islands in order to forestall the Germans'.[16] Cadogan had attended the Chiefs of Staff Committee meeting which had discussed the Prime Minister's minute and had informed those present of the current alarm in the Foreign Office about German activities in, and their menace to, the Iberian Peninsula, with Britain's 'available means' for counter-balancing Germany's pressure 'virtually exhausted'. There was agreement that the Germans might be about to launch a sea and air-borne campaign against Portugal, with simultaneous occupations of the Azores and Cape Verdes.[17] These were the grounds which the Chiefs of Staff had considered before, as possibly justifying a British pre-emptive action. They informed the Prime Minister that the apparently deteriorating Spanish political situation made it less necessary for the British to avoid stifling the Spanish will to resist German invasion, and less likely that Britain would be invited into the Canaries. But they were concerned about giving the Germans an opportunity to operate from the Canaries, with their 'excellent facilities as a base for surface forces, submarines and long distance aircraft'. Bases in the Azores and Cape Verdes could not really help the British protect their very important South Atlantic convoys via Freetown from murderous German assault, from the Canary Islands, and all maritime traffic would probably have to be re-routed via the western Atlantic. The Chiefs of Staff, therefore, concluded thus:

we consider the determining factor is whether the Germans would get the use of the Canaries as a result of our action. So long as there is a chance that, if we do not disturb the situation, the Spaniards will continue to resist German pressure, we think that we should refrain from seizing the Atlantic Islands. As soon as it appears reasonably certain that Spain is joining the Axis camp or that an invasion of Portugal is imminent, we should act.[18]

Churchill responded by declaring that neither Cabinet nor Parliament would accept abandonment of the South Atlantic convoys via Sierra Leone since 'it would entail a fatal paralysis of [Britain's] food supply and war effort'.[19] Moreover, he maintained, at a Chiefs of Staff meeting on 24 March, that Britin 'could not remain inactive in perpetual apprehension of Spanish and Portuguese susceptibilities'.[20] The meeting agreed to review the position again in two days' time.[21] Nevertheless, the Prime Minister, apparently, decided to stay his hand once more, and another month was to elapse before British grand strategists considered launching preventive strikes against the Atlantic Islands again. In spite of Churchill's reputed talent for going 'off at a tangent' in strategic matters, he retained the capacity for second thoughts about precipitate action which might provoke Spanish belligerency.[22] Hoare's persistent counsels of caution had had their effect. Even in his minute of 22 March, suggesting that the moment might have come to seize the Cape Verdes, Churchill expressed his awareness – on the basis of Hoare's 'able telegrams' – of how seriously the latter would object to such a venture.[23] However, one result of the March episode was to focus attention on the Canaries as the most valuable alternative base to Gibraltar, and it was these Spanish Islands which became the primary target of Britain's Atlantic Islands' project, in the spring and summer of 1941.[24]

By 22 April, the day afer it was resolved that British forces should evacuate Greece, there was widespread fear in London that Spain would soon have German forces on its soil. At a Chiefs of Staff meeting on that day, Major-General Davidson, the Director of Military Intelligence, reckoned that 'an early German advance south-westwards seemed almost a certainty'. Cavendish-Bentinck, of the J.I.C., 'agreed that Spain might sign a Tripartite Pact at any time now and that a German advance towards Gibraltar might well take place within the next month or so'.[25] Cadogan thought that Spain was 'gone' unless British forces had a Libyan success, which he did not expect.[26]

Hoare was worried in Madrid too. He reported home, on 22 April 1941, to the effect that 'most secret French sources' maintained that Franco had agreed to adhere to the Tripartite Pact but had deferred his signature as Spain was still unprepared for war, and the Canary Islands remained vulnerable to British attack. These French sources also, according to Hoare, stated that the 'Spanish General Officer

Commanding Cadiz' had declared that staff plans 'to render Gibraltar untenable' were now fully complete and that the general expected an arrival of German troops in Spain, 'in the near future'. Hoare still counselled that 'at this critical moment' it was 'important to extend rather than restrict Anglo-American help', but added the following proposal: 'I suggest that you should urgently consider the question of immediate occupation of the Canary Islands as soon as the German forces cross the Spanish frontier'.[27]

On 23 April, Churchill did place an expeditionary force, aimed at Portuguese Islands, at forty-eight hours' notice to sail.[28] The Chiefs of Staff were 'gravely concerned', on the same day, to learn that little had been done to assemble the forces and shipping necessary for a substantial expedition against the Atlantic Islands. They agreed that, 'in view of the situation in South-West Europe', immediate priority should be given to the organisation of such a force and to the plans for its use.[29] The Joint Planning Staff produced a report on the Atlantic Islands projects, that very day. It advised that the moment suggested by the Chiefs of Staff in their minute of 23 March to Churchill, as opportune for the seizure of the islands – namely, when it seemed 'reasonably certain' that Spain was 'joining the Axis camp' or an invasion of Portugal was imminent – had arrived. It declared the following:

Although Spain has not yet thrown in her lot with the Axis, events in the Balkans and Cyrenaica have strenghened Germany's hand and Axis pressure on Spain is now increasing. It has, in fact reached a point where we are doubtful whether our diplomacy alone is still able to influence Franco in keeping Germany out of Spain . . .
. . . there seems little doubt that within a few weeks Gibraltar will become unusable as a naval base, either due to German action with Spanish acquiescence or due to Spanish action, egged on by Germany.[30]

The Joint Planners also counselled that Britain should concentrate upon capturing the Spanish Grand Canary Island, to forestall this imminent danger, since it now had the resources, in terms of assault shipping, landing craft and fighter aircraft to occupy these islands, which offered much superior strategic advantages to the other Atlantic archipelagos. Therefore, they recommended that a large expeditionary force (over 11,000 troops with naval escort) be formed, and that the War Cabinet be asked to authorise its launching to seize the Canaries as soon as it could be made ready – in about three weeks' time.[31] The Chiefs of Staff agreed that 'recent developments in Spain' required that the preliminary preparations, advised by the Joint Planners, be made, and asked Churchill, on 24 April, to allow them 'to plan and prepare an expedition to seize the Canaries as soon as possible'.[32] He agreed 'wholeheartedly' to all preparations being undertaken to execute Operation 'Puma' against the Canaries. However, he implied that he was not yet certain that the moment for irrevocable action against Spain had come, by adding that the 'final decision' about launching the expedition 'could be taken nearer the time when the forces were ready'.[33] Eden approved the project 'in principle'.[34] This was a far cry from Halifax's time at the Foreign Office, when the Foreign Secretary had always vigorously championed the case against aggressive action towards Spain. This problem was 'likely to come to the fore very prominently during the coming weeks' and the above view taken by the Chiefs of Staff was 'for a short term only'.[35]

Before the meeting on 24 April in which he authorised the formation of a force for 'Puma', Churchill had decided to inform President Roosevelt of the 'increasing anxiety' shared by the British Naval Staff and himself over Iberian vulnerability to German pressure, and the possibility that Gibraltar would be 'rendered unusable'. He told Roosevelt that Britain had been holding two expeditions in readiness to seize the Azores and Cape Verdes once Spain was attacked, or 'gave way'. Observing, however, that Britain could not maintain a continuous naval patrol off the islands, Churchill requested that the President send an American naval squadron on a cruise to their vicinity, a maritime manoeuvre which might deter, as well as provide forewarning of, a German move against them.[36] In a further message to Roosevelt, on 29 April, Churchill declared that he regarded 'the Spanish situation as most critical'.[37] However, the Prime Minister was disappointed by Roosevelt's reply of 1 May which, although stating that the new United States naval patrol system in the Atlantic would extend to the western sides of the Azores and Cape Verdes, emphasised the 'utmost importance' of refraining from attacking the Portuguese Islands, until a German assault upon them was imminent, or an attack on Portugal had occurred. Moreover, Roosevelt added that in the event of a British seizure of the Azores it would have to be made 'very clear' to the American people that it was a defensive action and not meant to establish any permanent British occupation of these islands.[38] Clearly, the President was concerned about the baleful influence, which an apparent exercise in British imperialist expansion at Portugal's expense, would have on American public opinion. Churchill was dissuaded from sending a sharp response to Roosevelt's message, other points in which had also worried him, but he did retort that Britain might feel it necessary to strike pre-emptively at the islands in circumstances other than those specified as legitimate by the President.[39] Roosevelt did not challenge Churchill on this point, in his conciliatory reply to the Prime Minister of 3 May.[40] Churchill responded in kind, on 14 May, candidly pointing out that it would be 'very difficult' for the British 'to avoid being either too soon or too late' in attempting to anticipate a German move against the islands.[41]

This slight breach in the Churchill–Roosevelt entente was thus soon healed and the episode, anyway, appears to have helped influence the American President towards considering a United States occupation of the Azores to forestall German action – but not without Portugal's consent.[42] On 22 May, Roosevelt ordered that a United States force should be ready to seize the Azores within a month and in one of his famous fireside chats, on 27 May, mentioning the Azores and Cape Verdes, *inter alia*, he underlined the 'old-fashioned' common sense of preventive action to forestall 'a probable enemy' from securing a strategic advantage.[43] But Roosevelt only wanted to act if invited into the Portuguese Islands by Salazar, after a German entry into the Iberian Peninsula.[44] Portuguese protests about the reference to their Islands in Roosevelt's 27 May speech only strengthened his belief in the necessity of such a prior invitation.[45] However, the British were still ready to move against the Portuguese Islands and the Grand Canary – as Churchill informed Roosevelt, on 29 May 1941 – once Gibraltar was rendered unusable, or they were 'sure' that this was going to happen.[46]

Notwithstanding their growing concern in late April that Spain was lost, Britain's grand strategists had not launched Operation 'Puma' when it was ready in May. For, a fortuitous political development in Spain had caused them to change their minds about the imminence of the danger to Gibraltar. On 2 May, Hoare correctly predicted that Franco would be making some new ministerial and army command appointments, including that of Colonel Valentín Galarza Morante to the Ministry of the Interior, a portfolio over which Serrano Suñer had retained *de facto* control, despite becoming Foreign Minister in October 1940.[47] Hoare reported, apparently accurately, that Galarza was pro-ally and anti-Serrano Suñer.[48] This ministerial promotion did occur, on 5 May 1941, and was followed by a series of changes in the personnel occupying important posts in the administration and army, which apparently weakened the radical Falangists' position. Hoare advised London that this 'revolution' had not been 'a movement inspired by any change of foreign policy' but was 'essentially the expression of Franco's personal determination to stick to power and manage his own affairs'.[49] Indeed, the anti-Falangist Galarza who had been serving as Franco's political secretary, was clearly appointed as a loyal *franquista* to the key Ministry of Gobernación, to consolidate the Caudillo's personal hold on power in Spain. At his first official meeting with Hoare, on 13 May, the new Minister described himself as 'Franco's man to the death'.[50] However, there was a natural temptation for the British to interpret these political changes inside Spain, which undermined Serrano Suñer's and the radical Falange's power-base, as in Britain's interest. Thus, Eden told the War Cabinet, on 12 May, that the governmental changes in Spain appeared to be to Britain's advantage.[51] He complimented Hoare, on 17 May, on his 'share in these most beneficial changes', and the British also indulged in some self-congratulation, assuming that their 'consistently helpful' policy had contributed to this apparent political reverse for the radical Spanish Falangists.[52] Hoare, himself, actually attributed the changes in Francoist administrative and army personnel to the financial bribes which Britain had been doling out to prominent Spaniards, particularly Spanish generals, as mentioned in chapter two. He telegraphed to Eden, thus, on 10 May 1941: 'No doubt you have realised that the political changes here are directly due to secret plan of which you and the Prime Minister are aware', and added a personal admission, five days later in a letter to the Foreign Secretary: 'I never believed that our plan could have worked so well.'[53] Hugh Dalton although not always easily swayed by Hoare's arguments or claims from Madrid, was inclined to accept the Ambassador's advocacy, on this occasion as his cryptic diary entry, for 16 May 1941, shows: 'In Spain the Cavalry of St George have been charging; hence some of the recent changes; hence also Attaché H's concern for J.M.'s tinplate.'[54] The 'Cavalry of St George' was a traditional description of the coins which had been Britain's main contribution to the continental coalitions in which it had fought against any power seeking domination over Europe. 'Attaché H' was Hillgarth, 'J.M.', Juan March and the 'tinplate' clearly the money used to bribe Spanish generals.

However, as Hoare rightly discerned, Franco had been primarily motivated by his own will to hold on to power in his political manoeuvrings of early May. When open opposition to Galarza's appointment emerged – many of the new appointments were made to fill the vacancies caused by Falangist resignations in protest at Galarza's promotion – Franco was ready to draw its teeth by absorbing it into his administration in a further realignment. The Falange even secured an unprecedented two places on the Council of Ministers, and wrested control of the press and propaganda services from the Ministry of the Interior.[55] The British were unhappy with this Falangist come-back. Eden minuted, on 23 May, thus: 'I am not convinced that Suñer has lost on the general outcome of these exchanges; nor in consequence that we have gained.'[56] In fact, Serrano Suñer's political influence had suffered irreversible injury.[57] He had even tendered his resignation in the earlier stages of the affair, but Franco had refused to accept it.[58] The Germanophil radical Falange had been tamed by Franco, notwithstanding their subsequent unsuccessful attempts to conspire with German Nazis against him. The Caudillo was more firmly in the saddle than ever.

Moreover, Franco's political reshuffle had also safeguarded his position in a way which he could not have envisaged. For, the initially favourable impression which Galarza's appointment caused in London, convinced Churchill that it would be inopportune to invade the Grand Canary and drag Spain into the war. At the Defence Committee, on 9 May, he declared that it would be unwise to launch 'Puma' in advance of 'adverse developments in Spain' since 'such a course was undesirable and would have an unfortunate political effect'. Although agreeing to the final preparations for the operation being made, Churchill was clearly deciding against pre-emptive action at this stage.[59] He came down firmly against a preventive move five days later. Eden told another meeting of the Defence Committee, on 14 May, that 'the situation in Spain was a little easier', and Churchill declared that 'in view of the present situation he could not allow the Expedition to sail now'.[60] The Committee accepted that 'the recent favourable political developments in Spain made it inadvisable to take a decision now to sail Expedition "Puma"', but also agreed that the force should be held ready to sail.[61] The British would still be prepared to retaliate swiftly against, or even anticipate, a German move into Spain. A compound of accident and Churchill's ability to ponder the wisdom of a pre-emptive strike against the Canaries had rescued Britain from provoking war with Spain. It was Churchill's reassessment, alone, which stopped such action a few months later.

The Defence Committee reaffirmed their opinion, on 10 June, that 'Puma' should not be executed 'in the near future as the political situation was unfavourable for it'. As the Chiefs of Staff had accepted that the expedition could only attack the Grand Canary in the ten moonless days of each month, so as to be obscured from the coastal batteries there, this 10 June decision meant that 'Puma' could not be undertaken before July, when the next 'dark period' occurred.[62]

Circumstances were such then as to persuade British strategists that the time had definitely come to seize the Grand Canary.

Several factors produced this renewed concern to anticipate the loss of Gibraltar. Firstly, there was the urgency of being prepared to meet the latter contingency. In their general review of 'Future Strategy' of 14 June, the Future Operations Section of the Joint Planning Staff stated that so 'vital' was it to ensure possession of an alternative base to Gibraltar that they would have proposed 'immediate action to secure . . . the Canaries' but for the fact that it was necessary to reinforce the Middle East speedily via the Rock, in those critical days. However, Britain 'must at all times be prepared to act instantly' if there were signs 'of Germany's attention turning to the Western Mediterranean' since German occupation of the Iberian Peninsula was 'inevitable'.[63]

Moreover, the most momentous strategic development, of June 1941, also gave British strategists reason to feel that they should anticipate the resurgent threat from Spain. Eden informed Hoare that Churchill and he felt that the German invasion of the Soviet Union, of 22 June, should give the Ambassador 'a respite' in his labours to keep Spain outside the war.[64]

The Spanish reaction to this event, however, emphasised the apparently temporary nature of this reprieve. An official spokesman of the Spanish Foreign Office spoke of the 'satisfaction' with which his Government regarded the German assault on Soviet Russia, while the Spanish press hailed it as a crusade against Communism.[65] According to Hoare, 'the whole of Spain' now viewed Hitler 'as a providential deliverer of the world from the Red Anti-Christ'.[66] On 24 June, Serrano Suñer harangued a large crowd in Madrid, declaring Russia to be 'guilty' of the Spanish Civil War and announcing that its 'extermination' was 'a demand of the history and the future of Europe'.[67] A group of around 400 Falangist demonstrators proceeded, after Serrano's speech to attack the British Embassy, breaking its windows.[68] Hoare was extremely indignant over this incident and uncharacteristically wanted to suspend economic collaboration with the Spaniards, for a few days at least. The Foreign Office thought this would be 'shortsighted'. However, a swift official Spanish apology soothed Hoare's 'easily wounded' feelings – to use Eden's description.[69] Eden, however, was soon irritated by further manifestations of Hispano-German solidarity. He commented on a report of Serrano Suñer's early July declaration of Spain's 'moral belligerency' alongside Germany in its 'crusade against Asiatic barbarity', thus: 'I hardly think that we need fuss ourselves to hurry food to these people'.[70] In mid-July, he saw the dispatch of units of Spain's 'Blue Division', which had been organised to fight on the Russian front, as 'further reason for toughening our attitude to Spain'.[71]

Actually, Franco's decision to dispatch a division to participate in Hitler's war with the Soviet Union was a gesture of more limited significance and a move more consistent with the foreign policy pursued by the Caudillo up to that time, than the British initially realised. Far from betokening an imminent Spanish intention to attack Britain, the commitment of the Blue Division to the Nazi struggle with Soviet Communism was meant to involve Spain in hostilities only to an extent limited enough for it to tolerate, but sufficient enough to secure it some of the spoils of Germany's victory and a place in a German-dominated Europe. The Falangist poet-politician, Dionisio Ridruejo, who fought in the Blue Division, had been prompted by precisely these considerations to work for the mounting of a Spanish expeditionary force to be sent to the eastern front. According to his diary entry for 4 July 1941, Ridruejo noted that he did not intend the formation of the Blue Division to be an 'anti-communist action'. Rather was it meant to constitute a 'minimal and possible intervention by Spain in the war (in the whole war)'. This carefully calculated Spanish engagement in a geographically remote theatre of the war in Europe would also satisfy the requirement of 'being present with some title at the decisive moment' because no country which remained aloof from that definitive struggle could expect any real future in the post-war continental order.[72] Serrano Suñer, subsequently, defined the significance of the contribution made by the soldiers of the Blue Division to Franco's foreign policy, thus: 'Their sacrifice would give us a title of legitimacy to participate one day in the dreamed-of victory and exempted us from the general and terrible sacrifices of the war.'[73] That the Spanish decision to organise the Division was not the prelude to, but rather a substitute for, their full-scale engagement in the war alongside Germany, was made clear to Berlin, as early as late June 1941. For, when von Ribbentrop, in accepting the Spanish offer of a volunteer legion to use against the Russians, suggested, on 24 June, that 'a public declaration that Spain was in a state of war with the Soviet Union would be appropriate and desirable', Serrano Suñer effectively demurred. Full of apparent solicitude for the Axis, the Spanish Foreign Minister pointed out the disadvantages inherent in such a course of action for both Madrid and Berlin:

Personally he [Serrano Suñer] was inclined to believe that England and possibly America would react to such an announcement if not by a declaration of war on Spain, then undoubtedly by the imposition of a blockade, which would entail cutting off all supplies now in transit as well as seizure of the Spanish ships now held in the United States under the order blocking Spanish assets . . . Complications for Spain would also be detrimental to Germany during the Russian campaign.[74]

Von Ribbentrop received the Spaniards' message loud and clear. He again instructed von Stohrer, on 28 June, that he should not broach the topic of possible Spanish belligerency with the Foreign Minister, thenceforward, as it was clear that 'Suñer's repeatedly proclaimed desires for war, after all, were not really to be taken seriously'.[75]

However, to the attentive British the brave words and bold gestures of Francoists, in the days following the German invasion of the Soviet Union, appeared to be all too genuine portents of an impending Spanish intervention in the war on the Axis side. Britain's grand strategists were increasingly in the mood to believe that Spain was irrevocably wedded to Germany's cause. A speech delivered by Franco, on 17 July 1941, seemed both to confirm the worst British fears about his strategic designs and to suggest the prudence of anticipating them by prior military action. Addressed to the National Council of the Falange, on the anniversary of the military rising against the Spanish Republic, Franco's speech stressed the need for 'iron discipline', unity and effort to rebuild Spain's greatness and economic prosperity. However, in addition to the disparaging remarks which he directed at the United States, on this occasion (already mentioned in chapter eight), Franco made some barbed references to Britain. He sneered at its 'destroyers-for-bases' deal with the United States, of 2 September 1940, as 'the exchange of fifty old destroyers for the shreds of an empire', and denounced the 'inhuman blockade of a continent'. Britain was clearly also included in the category of those 'age-long enemies' of Spain who continued to practise 'intrigues and treachery' against that country, because they 'never forgave [it] for having been great'. Asserting that the war had been 'badly planned' and that the Allies had lost it, he concluded with a rhetorical appeal:

At this moment, when the German armies lead the battle for which Europe and Christianity have for so many years longed, and in which the blood of our youth is to mingle with that of our comrades of the Axis as an expression of firm solidarity, let us renew our faith in the destinies of our country under the watchful protection of our closely united Army and the Falange.[76]

Anthony Eden was certainly offended enough by Franco's outspokenness to want to take a much tougher line with the 'badly' behaved Caudillo.[77] He was reinforced in his inclination 'to stiffen up to Franco' by a conversation which he had on 18 July, with Sir Auckland Geddes, who was a regional commissioner for civil defence, Chairman of the Río Tinto company, and a former Conservative M.P. and Cabinet Minister. During their meeting Geddes dismissed Franco as being 'completely under the thumb of Serrano Suñer' and condemned British policy for 'backing the wrong horse in Spain', since its rulers were 'a small clique of men who looked solely to a German victory and whose policy it was to call in the Germans and to make Gibraltar untenable'. Geddes also claimed that the defeated Spanish Republicans were the natural material from which to form an anti-Falangist movement in Spain and expressed his conviction that Britain's war aim 'must be to exterminate every Fascist government'.[78] At a meeting with his advisers in the Foreign Office, on 19 July, Eden revealed his concern to abandon the appeasement of Franco's Spain and considered the implications of alternative courses of action, as his Private Secretary, Oliver Harvey, recorded:

It was recognised that the Germans can come in whenever they want and Franco will welcome them. At present the Germans aren't ready. What was the good of our present policy? We get certain fruits and iron ore from Spain – so long as Spain is at peace we have unmolested use of Gibraltar as harbour and staging airplane base – these could be interrupted if we upset Franco. A.E. wondered if we could incite the Spanish Reds to revolution. Dept. thought they were broken reeds – Negrín discredited. Question of 'PUMA' not possible after September. If it is important if not vital, to have done this, if Germans came into Spain – then decision should clearly be taken now. A.E. is going to raise it at Defence Committee next week.[79]

However, feeling that Franco's speech compelled a fundamental review of British policy towards Spain, Eden also presented the basic problem to the War Cabinet, in a memorandum of 20 July 1940: 'the question is whether we wish at this moment to pick a quarrel with the Spanish Government'.[80] At the Cabinet itself, in the early evening of 21 July, the Foreign Secretary observed that 'General Franco's recent speech seemed to show that he had ranged himself with Serrano Suñer and that there was no question of his taking the lead in the defence of Spain against German invasion or penetration'. Remarking that the Russo-German conflict had probably 'greatly reduced any chance of Spain resisting German pressure', he reformulated the central quesion: 'we should have to decide whether we were ready to leave matters to develop until it suited Germany to bring Spain into the war'. The War Cabinet accepted Eden's advice that this matter should be referred to the Defence Committee for further consideration in its meeting, later that night. The Cabinet also approved the Foreign Secretary's suggestion that Britain should desist from trying to push the Americans into continuing to provide, 'against their will', economic facilities for Spain. Eden also intended to respond to Franco's abuse with some form of British economic retaliation.[81] However, the resultant review of economic policy towards Spain merely produced a directive, in August 1941, that in every economic deal with that country the governing consideration must be 'whether or not it would be of definite advantage to British interests'.[82] This rubric seems to have had little practical effect. It could only have reinforced the developing tendency for Anglo-Spanish economic relations to be founded upon a basis of self-interested exchange.

However, the review of Britain's strategic policy towards Franco's Spain yielded more serious results. After a marathon meeting, on the night of 21 July, the Defence Committee agreed 'in principle' that operation 'Puma' should be launched against the Canaries at Britain's 'own chosen time and that all preparations for carrying it out in August should proceed'.[83] For all the apparent final decisiveness of this gathering, its proceedings had exasperated the Foreign Office representatives, Eden and Cadogan, who had been present at its deliberations. Not only was it prolonged by endless harangues from Churchill but the service chiefs present also revealed a remarkable ignorance of, and seeming indifference to, the likely impact of German aerial attack, from the relatively nearby African coast, on British army and naval forces operating on and around the Canary Islands. Cadogan recorded in his diary how the military experts were embarrassed:

9.45 Defence Committee. An appalling ramble. Decided to do 'Puma' in August. I then put up A. [Eden] to ask how far the objective was from the mainland. None of the C's of S. could answer! (Ye Heavens! After Namsos and Crete!) Alexander said 500 miles (I had said 120). Pound measured it roughly on a Mercator's projection of the world hanging up on the wall. Said he made it about 150! This is really shattering.[84]

Indeed, in an internal Foreign Office memorandum on operation 'Puma' of 9 July 1941, Makins had noted that the Spanish colony of Río de Oro, on the African coastline south of the Canaries' archipelago, was 'a natural aerodrome' whose flat terrain only needed 'maintenance and development' to act as *point d'appui* for air force action against the islands. He had also pointed out that the Canaries lay about the same distance from Río de Oro, as did Crete from mainland Greece, the scene only weeks before of a decisive victory by German aircraft and airborne troops over the British troops garrisoning that island and the royal naval ships protecting it. Cadogan had expressed his worry, in a comment on the Makins' memorandum on 10 July, that Britain's strategic experts seemed to have neglected 'the question of whether, even if we seize one of the islands, we can hold it against an attack from Río de Oro', and concluded, thus: 'We really must not again ignore the lessons we have had.'[85]

However, undeterred by these omissions in the strategic planning for 'Puma', Churchill reconfirmed his faith in the need for, and urgency of, undertaking the operation at a meeting of the Chiefs of Staff, which he chaired, two days later. The Prime Minister clearly expressed his own thoughts, during this gathering:

> The Prime Minister said that the political position in Spain had hardened. He thought that at any moment Spain might go over to the German camp. For these reasons he was in favour of carrying out Operation 'Puma' at the earliest opportunity. It might be of course that before the forces could sail the position might have radically altered, if so, it would be necessary for His Majesty's Government to cancel the sailing of the expedition. He stressed the vital imporatnce of the success of the operation.

Churchill directed that 'Puma' be executed during the favourable moon period in August, that its organisation should be given 'priority over all else', and that the Grand Canary was 'to be captured at any cost', while operations against the other Atlantic islands could be subsequently carried out 'as convenient'. However, he emphasised his intention of keeping an open mind on 'Puma' by declaring that the decision to execute it 'would be subject to . . . veto . . . at the last moment if some insuperable objection . . . arose'.[86] Next day, in the War Cabinet, Churchill took a similar line, informing that body of the 'provisional decision' to execute 'Puma' in the light of the 'hostility' to Britain evident in Franco's recent speech. The Prime Minister advised his Cabinet colleagues that Britain would be wise 'to make certain of securing the Canary Islands' lest the Germans anticipate them with their own occupation of the Spanish Atlantic archipelago. Churchill did admit, too, however, that the substantial Spanish forces on the islands would be likely to mount a strong defence against invasion and that the expected British victory would only come after 'hard fighting'.[87]

One major step was taken, however, to improve the expedition's chances of success. For, forces that had been organised previously to occupy the Azores and Madeira were incorporated into those destined for the Canary Islands.[88] The Canaries' expeditionary force quickly reached a size of 24,000 troops, to be escorted by one battleship, three aircraft carriers, three cruisers and nineteen destroyers. The Operation, given a new code-name, 'Pilgrim', also required almost the entire existing British fleet of assault-shipping and landing-craft.[89] Still, the strain that 'Pilgrim' would impose upon Britain's overstretched force of destroyers influenced the Chiefs of Staff to recommend that the operation should be postponed until September when the destroyer situation would have eased considerably.[90] There were some other factors which helped to induce the Chiefs of Staff to counsel postponement, on 29 July, and these seem to show that reservations were resurfacing in some quarters about the wisdom of precipitating Spanish belligerency. Thus, the Chiefs of Staff pointed out to Churchill that a month's delay meant an equivalent extra period in which to pass ships through the Mediterranean, via Gibraltar, and would also furnish the British with an additional month's supply of Iberian products. They also relayed Eden's view which revealed evidence of second-thoughts: 'although perfectly prepared to "jump the fence" in August, if this were necessary on military grounds, he would much prefer a postponement'.[91] Oliver Harvey had had reservations, soon after the 21st of July decision to launch the operation against the Canaries, on the grounds that such a British move would necessarily provoke Spanish belligerency before a German incursion into Spain had made retaliation by Britain absolutely essential. He expressed his doubts to the Foreign Secretary and they may have had some effect.[92] Indeed, even Churchill, although concerned about a possible German assault on Gibraltar in the interval, agreed, on 1 August, to defer 'Pilgrim' until September.[93] The period in September during which 'Pilgrim' could be executed was extended, too. The Chiefs of Staff were informed, on 2 August, that the commanders of the expedition had decided that it was feasible to launch it in conditions of partial moonlight, which reduced the number of unsuitable days for its implementation to only five per month.[94]

On the other hand, Churchill's meeting with President Roosevelt at Argentia, Newfoundland, from 9 to 12 August, lent encouragement to the idea of executing 'Pilgrim' in September. Roosevelt told Churchill, on 11 August, that his information indicated that Germany might move into the Iberian Peninsula, on 15 September, and stated his readiness to dispatch an American expedition which was being prepared, to occupy the Azores on that date, if he received 'a direct request' from Salazar for help. Churchill, in his turn, informed the President of the British decision to launch 'Pilgrim' in September. The American leader was not deterred from repeating his intention of occupying the Azores subject to the condition he had stipulated, when the Prime Minister pointed out that the British operation might provoke a German entry into the Iberian Peninsula.[95] Churchill regarded the projected American occupation of the Azores as 'eminently satisfactory' since it would draw American soldiers and ships nearer the war zone. He declared to a Chiefs of Staff meeting on the battleship *Prince of Wales*, on 11 August, that 'in view of the President's favourable reaction to the information that we intended to carry out operation "PILGRIM" it seemed more than ever important that we should launch the expedition in September'.[96] But, Cadogan, who was also present, was not sure that the American position on the Atlantic Islands did, in fact, justify a pre-emptive strike by the British. He argued that 'the situation as now ... disclosed was advantageous ... if Germany violated the Iberian Peninsula', but thought things would be 'rather different' if Britain made the first move: either the Portuguese would claim the British had wantonly brought Germany's wrath upon them (thus precluding any possibility that they might seek American aid to defend the Azores, a precondition which Roosevelt had specified as 'essential' for the dispatch of American troops there) or the Germans would not retaliate, and Britain would find it difficult to justify its action. However, Churchill felt that the decision to launch 'Pilgrim' at the 'first favourable opportunity' should be maintained, but remarked that 'there was still plenty of time to take the final decision'.[97]

Yet, notwithstanding the seeming advantages of an anticipatory assault on the Canaries, Churchill drew back, once more, from provoking hostilities with Spain. Just as the initial interpretation in London of Franco's speech had produced the decision to attack Spanish territory, a reassessment of its import assuaged apprehension sufficiently to help cause the suspension of 'Pilgrim' in September. In late July, Hoare had reported the claim by the Spanish Minister of Industry and Commerce, Carceller, that Franco's speech was meant to reassert the Caudillo's pre-eminence over Serrano Suñer, both in domestic politics, and in relations with the Axis – perhaps, as a prelude to demoting him.[98] The initial British judgement that Franco's oration had ranged him alongside Serrano Suñer was mistaken. Serrano Suñer, himself, viewed Franco's discourse as 'premature', as he explained to von Stohrer, on 26 July 1941. He told the German Ambassador that he considered the Caudillo's speech to be inopportune because 'it suddenly opened the eyes of the English and the Americans about the true position of Spain'. He continued, thus:

Previously the English Government especially kept on believing that only he ... was pushing for war, while the 'wise and thoughtful' Caudillo would preserve neutrality unconditionally. That illusion has now been taken from them. They had come to realize that Spain, in understanding with the German Government, would enter the war at a suitable moment.

These assertions of Serrano Suñer might seem to justify the British suspicions, but the key point relating to possible Spanish belligerency in his talk with von Stohrer was that Spain would enter the war 'at a suitable moment'. In July–August 1941, as before, Britain would have to be mortally wounded, before that 'suitable moment' came for Spain.[99] Serrano Suñer asserted, later, that Franco had refused his help in preparing his July 1941 speech and that he had been 'amazed' by its contents.[100] Nicolás Franco also admitted to David Eccles in Lisbon, on 6 August, that his brother 'had gone too far' in his speech but maintained that the Caudillo's 'remarks were for internal consumption'.[101]

During 1940–1, Hoare was neither directly involved in the grand strategic debates over, nor it seems fully informed about, possible military preventive action against Iberian-ruled territory. However, he was apparently more aware of British offensive intentions in August 1941 than previously. He detected, from 'official and unofficial' hints that 'some' people in London had come to regard Spain as 'inevitably' Britain's enemy. He felt that this was 'premature' but was ready for Anglo-Spanish hostilities if Britain were militarily strong enough 'to challenge Franco and to resist a German occupation of the Peninsula and the Straits'.[102] In the absence of such an assurance from his Government, Hoare prompted his Service Attachés to discourage rash action. Hillgarth advised Churchill, on 12 August, that a British seizure of the Canaries would earn Britain the enmity of the entire Spanish people.[103] Torr, the Military Attaché, visited London, where he told the Chiefs of Staff, on 20 August, that 'the disadvantages of a premature occupation of the Canary Islands would far outweigh any advantages'. Dudley Pound now accepted that a premature move would be most 'undesirable'. He secured approval for a search for measures which would permit the launching of the expedition in adverse winter weather conditions, thus relieving Britain of any absolute necessity of executing 'Pilgrim' in September.[104] Dill, the C.I.G.S., informed Hoare that Torr had 'greatly influenced the opinions of the Chiefs of Staff' and, he imagined, 'a good many others'.[105]

Dudley Pound informed Churchill and Eden, on 28 August, that because circumstances then 'did not appear to warrant the launching of . . . "Pilgrim" in September', the Chiefs of Staff proposed to send the more unseaworthy vessels of the expedition to Freetown, whence they could join an assault on the Canaries during the winter.[106] He was preaching to the converted. For, Churchill, independently, had come to doubt the wisdom of executing 'Pilgrim' in September.

As a precautionary move, Churchill had asked on 25 July for 'the fullest possible text of the translation of Franco's recent speech'.[107] He did not have time to read it 'thoroughly' until August but, on doing so, he changed his perception of Spanish intentions. He wrote to Eden, of his altered interpretation of Franco's speech, on 16 August, as follows:

It does not make so hostile an impression upon me as I have derived from the summaries and extract. I do not think it would be a sound deduction from this speech that Franco had given himself over to the Axis. There is much to be said for the suggestion of Ambassador Hoare that Franco was trying:
(a) to put himself at the head of his own movement and
(b) to reconcile Germany in advance to some arrangement by which Suñer would be restrained or excluded.
I do not think that this speech by itself, in the absence of further development [sic], could be taken as a basis for . . . PILGRIM . . . such action would have to be justified on other grounds . . .[108]

Churchill was, thus, glad that 'Pilgrim' could be held ready during the winter months since otherwise Britain would 'have been forced to take a very difficult decision and might well have made a false move'. Eden was 'very relieved', too, because 'it would be an enormous advantage if [Britain] could avoid taking the first step'.[109]

No other grounds for launching 'Pilgrim' emerged, and the expedition was disbanded in February 1942. Britain had, after all, refrained from shutting, in its own face, the most accessible door to the Eurafrican war through which Anglo-American forces would pour, in November 1942. Hoare's constant counsels of prudence had clearly promoted this result, but Churchill's readiness to listen to such cautionary advice, and his capacity for reassessing pre-emptive projects, were decisive in preventing Britain from precipitating Anglo-Spanish hostilities. Churchill's role in the evolution of British strategic policy towards Spain during 1940–1 merited Pownall's grudging, contemporary tribute, at least: 'His judgement in matters strategical is bad and hasty, nevertheless in some things he has a flair for foreseeing the future.'[110]

Indeed, Churchill's strategic perspicacity concerning Franco's attitudes towards the war did not desert him as the conflict developed into a global struggle in 1942. Thus, the commander-in-chief of the projected Allied landings in North Africa, General Eisenhower, reported, on 27 August 1942, the British Prime Minister's discerning assessment of the likely Francoist reaction to Operation 'Torch', 'Spain: will do nothing . . .'[111] However, there were British views opposed to the Prime Minister's estimation of the probable Spanish response to 'Torch'. Although the J.I.C. eventually decided that the possibility of a Spanish military move to interrupt the preparations for, or execution of, Operation 'Torch' was 'highly unreal', its chairman, Cavendish-Bentinck did warn his Foreign Office colleagues, on 21 August, that to funnel the entire Anglo-American expeditionary force through the Strait of Gibraltar for landings in Algeria, in part to occupy Tunisia as quickly as possible, would be 'rather a gamble'.[112] For, Cavendish-Bentinck pointed out, a landing confined to the Mediterranean coast of North Africa would place Allied 'necks in a noose with the rope end in Franco's hands'.[113] Presented with such an obvious opportunity to do grave damage to the Anglo-American war effort, and inevitably subject to severe German pressure to act, even the cautious Caudillo might not be able to refrain from pounding the Allied men and *matériel* crowded onto the Rock and the troop transports filing through the Strait of Gibraltar. Indeed, Sir Samuel Hoare returned from Madrid to London to warn his government of precisely this danger, in these urgent terms, on 29 August 1942:

The temptation to cut our lines of communication will be very great. We shall appear to have put our neck between two Spanish knives and Spanish knives are traditionally treacherous. The Germans will be on General Franco's back, dinning into his ears: 'Now is your time. You can cut the Allied throat, destroy the naval and air bases at Gibraltar and win a dazzling reward for your country in North Africa.' Let no one underrate the power of this temptation, or think that because nine Spaniards out of ten do not want war, General Franco might not risk it for the big stakes that in these circumstances it might offer him. He and his brother-in-law have made no secret of their wish to see Germany win the war. What better chance than this could they have of expediting a German victory? Spanish help might take one of two forms. Spanish guns, manned by Spanish troops, might fire on the harbour and aerodrome of Gibraltar and immobilize them in a few hours, or German bombers be permitted to operate from Spanish territory. In both cases action might be swift and very damaging.[114]

Concern at possible Spanish interference with, or acquiescence in a German move against, the Allied occupation of North Africa was also troubling the mind of the United States Army Chief of Staff, General Marshall, in August 1942. It was prominent amongst the influences which prompted the American Joint Chiefs of Staff and President Roosevelt to insist, successfully, in late August, that the 'Torch' landings take place on a wider front, to include the seizure of Casablanca, on the Atlantic coast of Morocco.[115] The forces bound for the latter destination would not have to make the possibly risky passage through the Strait of Gibraltar, under the shadow of guns situated on both Spain's mainland and its Moroccan coastline. However, even this strategic adjustment to avoid a dangerous concentration of Anglo-American forces in and around the Rock entailed further cause for possible friction with Franco's Spain. For, the American soldiers stepping ashore at Casablanca would be burying, once and for all, Franco's hopes of assuming control over French Morocco. Indeed, clearly aware of the imminent Anglo-American move into North Africa, both the new Spanish Foreign Minister, General Jordana, and the new War Minister, General Asensio, warned British representatives in Madrid, on 5 November, that the Allies should steer clear of French Morocco.[116]

However, the Allied powers took political precautions, in addition to their military redeployments, to ensure Spanish complaisance towards Operation 'Torch'. Thus, early in the morning of 8 November 1942, as the Allied troops disembarked in North Africa, United States Ambassador, Carlton Hayes, delivered a personal communication from President Roosevelt to General Franco, which contained the following passages:

It is because your nation and mine are friends in the best sense of the word and because you and I are sincerely desirous of the continuation of that friendship for our mutual good that I want very simply to tell you of the compelling reasons that have forced me to send a powerful American military force to the assistance of the French possessions in North Africa.
We have accurate information to the effect that Germany and Italy intend at an early date to occupy with military force French North Africa.

. . .

I hope you will accept my full assurance that these moves are in no shape, manner or form directed against the Government or people of Spain or Spanish Morocco or Spanish territories – metropolitan or overseas. I believe the Spanish Government and the Spanish people wish to maintain neutrality and to remain outside the war. Spain has nothing to fear from the United Nations.[117]

Hoare presented a similar British message of explanation and reassurance to Jordana, later that same day.[118] In assuring Franco that they meant him and his regime no harm, the Allied statesmen were satisfying the Caudillo's primary diplomatic requirement. For, as Spain's first socialist Minister for Foreign Affairs since the Civil War, Fernando Morán, has noted, the 'essential goal' of Francoist foreign policy throughout the Caudillo's long period in power never varied. It always remained 'the maintenance of the regime and its incumbent, General Franco'.[119] Doubtless, it was Churchill's comprehension of

Franco's unwillingness to risk his own political future in an assault upon the Allies as they landed in North Africa, however vulnerable at that precise moment they might appear, which caused the Prime Minister to divine correctly the actual Spanish reaction to 'Torch' – although even Churchill had expressed some concern, in the middle of September, about the Spaniards' attitude towards the large-scale preparations being made at Gibraltar for the operation.[120]

So, despite the definitive frustration of Franco's designs on Morocco consequent upon the Allied landing there, Jordana informed Alba, on 27 November 1942, that not only had this Anglo-American move been foreseen by the Spaniards but they actually regarded it 'with serenity'.[121] Certainly, some *africanista* and Falangist elements appear to have urged military intervention, against the Allies, on Franco in the immediate wake of Operation 'Torch'.[122] However, the Caudillo saw not military but political opportunity in the Anglo-American move into his vicinity, as Jordana again informed Alba:

Another important matter to which I want to refer is the improvement of our relations with the Anglo-Saxon countries. Previously, there has been, if not tension, then a strained atmosphere in our relations with England and with the United States and he, who so unerringly directs our policy, wishes to eliminate it as far as possible, with all due prudence and circumspection.[123]

In adhering to the principle of only cautious and careful *rapprochement* with the Atlantic democracies, Franco could go to considerable lengths to assure Hitler's Germany, while it still remained strong, that he had not defected to the enemies of Nazidom. Thus, Franco's Spain concluded, at Germany's instigation, another Secret Protocol with the Third Reich, on 10 February 1943, according to which the Spaniards promised to defend their territory against Anglo-American invasion, as soon as they were provided with Nazi war *matériel*.[124] However, this declaration of intent to defend Spain against Allied attack did not prevent Franco from making gradual and grudging steps towards diplomatic accommodation with the British and Americans. The Caudillo, who had dared to flirt with belligerency in the Axis interest only when Britain had been beaten to its knees in later 1940, was not the person to throw in his lot with the Axis, in early 1943, as the Germans reeled back under the combined blows of El Alamein, 'Torch' and Stalingrad.

Indeed, with the Anglo-Americans moving across North Africa from west and east and with the Wehrmacht locked in ever more mortal combat with the Red Army, the tide of battle was moving from the borders and shores of Franco's Spain. The British had already won the battle for the maintenance of Spanish non-belligerency in 1940–1 (indeed, by late 1940), but by late 1942 to early 1943 that battle was seen to be won. However, it remained to be seen whether Franco's rule in Spain could survive the collapse of the other dictator powers in Europe.

Conclusion

> Politics are the conduct and the course of the historical struggle of nations for life. The aim of these struggles is survival.[1]

In view of its strategic plight in 1940–1, Britain had a vital interest in the continuance of Spanish neutrality. Franco's shaky regime, too, clung to its non-belligerency as a lifeline in the context of its grave domestic crisis. Spain's political, economic and military weakness forced it to abstain from any decisive intervention in international affairs. Britain, in its unequal contest with Germany, clutched at Spain's very debility as at least one barrier against the further deterioration of its own perilous strategic position. This common vulnerability drove Britain and Spain together, despite mutual suspicion and ideological antipathy and, ultimately, tended to defuse the recurring tensions in their relations, in 1940–1. The British Government contemplated offensive military action against Spanish territory several times in that period, but drew back from the brink each time. The Spaniards, too, after the autumn of 1940, restricted themselves to propaganda attacks on Great Britain. This basic identity of interest between the British Government and the Franco regime concerning Spain's international position determined the essential pattern of their relations. This is not to ignore the fact that each side, occasionally, seriously considered moving against the other: Spain being prevented from doing so by the chilly German response to its initiatives, in June and September 1940, and Britain being saved from precipitate action, principally, by Halifax's intervention, in December 1940, and Churchill's second thoughts, in August 1941. However, it is important to notice that each country only sought to disregard the primary strategic exigencies when it temporarily thought that the position of the other rendered them irrelevant, i.e., when British defeat seemed imminent, or Spanish involvement in the war appeared inevitable.

There was an additional influence making for adherence to non-belligerency in Spain. In spite of its inferiority to Germany in terms of absolute force, Britain did possess, through its naval strength and global economic resources, a combination of powers very tangible to a country deep in an alimentary and general economic crisis. If in the end Britain was not able to dispense really substantial economic favours to Spain, it did permit, and facilitate, a sufficient flow of basic supplies to prevent economic collapse there. Britain did not, at least, employ its economic muscle and naval power to strangle Spain.

It was the negative aspect of Britain's Spanish policy, indeed, that came to predominate. Britain refrained from action that was bound to drive Spain into Germany's arms. In spite of Hoare's strenuous efforts to fashion British policy into a coherent endeavour to wean Spain from the Axis and to consolidate the Spanish will to resist, even forcibly, German pressure, the negative aspect repeatedly came to the surface. So, as has been described, Hoare and Halifax had to exert themselves to restrain and moderate British behaviour, lest it provoke Spanish belligerency. When Britain did embark upon definite attempts to attract Spain into its orbit, the enterprises were subverted by American distrust of Franco and Spanish fear of the Germans. As Hoare noted, the Spaniards had to preserve a veneer of hostility towards Britain, for their own safety and, the Chiefs of Staff were ready to add, such public Spanish hostility towards Britain was the most secure safeguard of the British position in the Strait of Gibraltar available during 1940–1.

If the goal of British policy towards Spain in 1940–1 – the continuance of Spanish non-belligerency – was attained, then it was achieved by both the conscious efforts of British policy-makers and by good luck. Franco's regime, too, survived the war, but it seems that that feat also depended on a deal of good fortune. Serrano Suñer subsequently defined the wartime stance of Franco's Spain in these terms: 'We put ourselves in a condition to avoid being overwhelmed by a German thrust and, in case of their victory, to be situated in a tolerable position.'[2] In fact, it seems that the position of Franco's regime would have been far from 'tolerable', if the Nazi Reich had emerged victorious after a long, hard war. Hitler never forgave Franco for refusing to enter the fray when he needed his services, in late 1940 and early 1941. If one can credit his off-the-cuff remarks, the Führer was contemplating using Republican Spaniards working in German labour camps, 'old shirt' Falangists and the Spanish Blue Division against Franco's Government when 'the hour for the overthrow of this parson-ridden regime' came.[3] Albert Speer remembered Hitler as angrily denouncing the 'fat little sergeant' whom he had encountered at Hendaye, who could not grasp the Führer's 'far-reaching plans'.

Speer also recalled Hitler's threat to get even with the Spanish leader by employing Red Spaniards against him: '. . . one of these days we'll be able to make use of them. When we call it quits with Franco. Then we'll let them go home. And you'll see what happens then! But with us on the opposite side. I don't give a damn about that. Let him find out what I can be like!'[4] It is not the least of historical ironies that the Soviet Red Army saved Franco from Hitler's retribution.

Writing his own account of his long Spanish mission, Hoare put to himself the question once posed to the abbé Siéyès: *'Qu'est ce que vous avez fait pendant la révolution?'* Citing the abbé's answer, *'J'ai existé'*, Hoare replied, 'I too had existed'.[5] Existence, national existence, was the central Anglo-Spanish concern in 1940–1. There is, of course, a sense in which, as Martin Wight pointed out, survival is the stuff of all foreign policy-making, since it involves 'the ultimate experience of life and death, national existence and national extinction'.[6] Yet, both Britain and Spain, in their respective situations, lived very near the margin of international existence and extinction in the period 1940–1. The need to survive was the pressing exigency, and the will to survive, the constant and immediate inspiration of their foreign policies. They conducted diplomacies and strategies of survival. The very fragility of their international positions tended to repress recklessness at crucial moments in their relations. In short, Spain found it could not afford to gamble with its non-belligerency, whereas Britain decided it could not but afford to gamble upon it. In doing so, Britain survived the agonising period when it stood alone against the power of Nazi Germany without losing Gibraltar, or seeing the Iberian Atlantic ports fall into Germany's hands, while Franco bought precious time to consolidate his rule.

Both Britain and Spain, indeed, were in the market to beg, borrow or steal as much time as they could, in 1940–1. Franco, for one, hardly needed Hitler's reminder in early February 1941, that 'time is one of the most important factors in a war'. The Führer was complaining then that Franco's refusal to sanction the attack on Gibraltar for early January, had meant the loss of a precious two months 'which might otherwise have helped decide world history'.[7] Hoare was no less aware of how valuable a strategic asset additional time was for his country. Reflecting on the first year of his mission in Spain, he summarised its purpose, and its record, thus, on 11 July 1941:

I had come on what was really a purchasing mission for the purpose of buying time – local time for the fortification of Gibraltar and world time for British recovery after the French collapse. Thirteen months ago it looked very much as if there was no time to buy. But somehow or other the months have passed and the raw material that we were so anxious to purchase has been found.[8]

Britain bid for time in Spain as elsewhere, in its struggle to survive. As it turned out the breathing-space which Britain fought to secure in 1940–1 was not only vital to its own survival. It proved to be of material assistance to the anti-Nazi cause as a whole. Josef Stalin, in his hard-headed way, assessed the contributions of the major Allied powers to the destruction of Nazism, thus: 'Great Britain provided time; the United States provided money and Soviet Russia provided blood.'[9] The successful British effort to buy time in Spain was a not insignificant part of its role in the defeat of Nazi Germany.

However, the time to entrench his rule inside Spain, which Franco had purchased by abstaining from active involvement in the Axis war effort, might have seemed to be running out by later 1944, as German Nazism succumbed to the combined forces of Anglo-American democracy and Soviet Communism, equally antagonistic, in principle, to the fascist origins and institutions of the Spanish regime. Certainly, Viscount Templewood (the title which Hoare had adopted on being elevated to the peerage, on 3 July 1944) drew the attention of his Government, on 16 October 1944, to 'the Spanish anomaly' which was becoming 'more and more conspicuous' as the 'other totalitarian governments in Europe' were destroyed.[10] The Central Department of the Foreign Office took the Ambassador's point and advised Eden, on 30 November 1944, that 'the survival of a totalitarian regime in Spain, which at one time openly favoured and supported the Axis would be an anachronism after the defeat of Germany'.[11] Franco might be expected to have shared this belief in the incompatibility between a post-war democratic order in Western Europe and the survival of his authoritarian regime, so tainted by its previous associations with the Axis. Indeed, in conversation with Ciano before the outbreak of the Second World War, the Caudillo had professed to believe that 'the survival of the Franco regime after the defeat of the other and older totalitarian regimes is out of the question'.[12]

However, much to the dismay of Templewood who wanted to see a restored constitutional monarchy replace Franco's corporatist dictatorship as Spain's political system, the Caudillo appeared 'complacent and unruffled' in the face of British criticism of the continuing fascist tendencies within, and repressive policies of, his regime.[13] Templewood could only conclude that Franco remained 'convinced that he can successfully maintain the double policy of totalitarianism within Spain and friendly relations with the Allies outside'.[14]

However, Franco's complacency was not so absolute as to ignore the need to make some overt moves to mend his relations with Britain, in particular, and the democracies in general. Thus, he assured an American press correspondent, in late 1944, that far from favouring fascism in policy and principle, his regime was, in fact, an 'organic democracy' which had pursued a course of honourable neutrality throughout the Second World War.[15]

Again, the then Francoist Foreign Minister, José Félix de Lequerica (Jordana had died in office in August 1944), asked of Templewood, on 3 October 1944, before the latter's departure for England, that he 'put the Spanish position in a friendly light in London and a specific assurance to [Eden] and the Prime Minister on behalf of the Spanish Government that Spain was anxious not only to break away from Nazi and Fascist influences but to follow the direction of Great Britain in the field of future politics in Western Europe'.[16]

However, the most serious Francoist effort at reconciliation with Britain, took the form of a letter written by the Caudillo, on 18 October 1944, to the Duke of Alba to express the Spanish leader's ideas 'in frank, explicit and straightforward terms', so that they could be reported 'faithfully and with the utmost frankness to our good friend, the British Prime Minister'. Observing that Spain was willing to play its part 'in the future concert of Westen Europe', Franco explained that only Spain had the resources and resolve to join Britain in defending 'a devastated Continent' against 'the insidious might of Bolshevism'. Still Franco's access of concern for Europe did not distract him from mentioning one more parochial matter, which he wanted Alba to elucidate for Churchill:

To conclude – I think you must make one thing quite clear, in view of the activities of bad Spaniards who from outside the country speculate on the possibility of internal changes, and who, relying only on the strength of their passions, might fancy they could effect a *rapprochement* by giving Britain a better bargain – the very idea is so fantastic that we ought not even to discuss such a possibility – you must emphasise that any such hypothetical change of regime, I say this with all due emphasis, would serve the interests of Russia alone. In foreign affairs all of us responsible Spaniards think alike, and history shows that it is not so difficult to win Spain's friendship and her heart.[17]

The fervently pro-monarchist Duke of Alba, who would resign his ambassadorship a year later as part of the post-war pressure on Franco to step down in favour of the Bourbon pretender to the Spanish throne, tried to impress on the British 'what a wonderful opportunity' Franco's *démarche* had given them to disabuse him of the illusion that his regime would find a safe and significant position in the post-war European scene: 'Franco had "asked for it", and with complete freedom and privacy we could "let him have it".'[18]

Churchill, certainly, had no hesitation in dashing Franco's hopes of an early post-war Anglo-Spanish alliance directed against Soviet Russia, correcting the Caudillo's 'misconception that His Majesty's Government are prepared to consider any grouping of powers in Western Europe or elsewhere on a basis of hostility towards or of the alleged necessity of defence against our Russian allies'.[19] However, in a revealing criticism of the first Foreign Office draft of the prime ministerial reply to Franco's letter, Churchill had complained of the omission of any mention of 'the supreme services' rendered by Spain to the British war effort by its 'not intervening in 1940 or interfering with the use of the airfield and Algeciras Bay in the months before TORCH in 1942'.[20] An amendment to the effect desired by the Prime Minister was made in the reply to Franco, but this episode was not an insignificant incident in terms of Churchill's general attitude towards the problem of the future of the Franco regime. For, there was a comprehensive debate within the British Government in November 1944, upon the appropriate attitude to adopt towards Franco's Spain as the war in Europe drew to a close. A series of proposals from the unlikely combination of Templewood, Attlee and Eden all suggested that the British Government apply political, and if necessary economic, pressure to Franco's Spain to effect a change in, or maybe even of, the Falangist regime there.[21] Eden even suggested that if Franco ignored a warning to liberalise the Spanish political system then the Allies might retaliate with such economic sanctions, as the suspension of oil exports to Spain. This particular proposal provoked serious opposition from Churchill who criticised it, thus:

This is a very serious proposal ... definitely to interfere in the internal Government of a country with whom one has not been at war and who has done us much more good than harm in the war is a serious step. I am no more in agreement with the internal Government of Russia than I am with that of Spain, but I certainly would rather live in Spain than Russia.

. . .

You need not, I think, suppose that Franco's position will be weakened by our warnings. He and all those associated with him will never consent to be butchered by the Republicans, which is what would happen. It is a life and death matter in Spain and I do not think we should, without more careful consideration, make ourselves responsible for starting another blood-bath. What you are proposing to do is little less than stirring up a revolution in Spain. You begin with oil: you will quickly end in blood.

... Already we are accused in many responsible quarters of handing over the Balkans and Central Europe to the Russians, and if we now lay hands on Spain I am of opinion that we shall be making needless trouble for ourselves and very definitely taking sides in ideological matters. Should the Communists become masters of Spain we must expect the infection to spread very fast both through Italy and France . . .

At this time every country that is liberated or converted by our victories is seething with Communism. All are linked together and only our influence with Russia prevents their actively stimulating this movement, deadly as I conceive it to peace and also to the freedom of mankind.

. . . I should of course be very glad to see a Monarchical and Democratic restoration, but once we have identified ourselves with the Communist side in Spain which, whatever you say, would be the effect of your policy, all our influence will be gone for a middle course.[22]

The British War Cabinet, on 27 November 1944, effectively endorsed the prime ministerial line, approving Churchill's intention of sending 'a rough reply' to Franco's letter but not dissenting from his view that the 'wise course' to adopt towards the Caudillo and his regime was to leave them to ' "stew in their own juice", while refraining from any active steps to encourage [their] overthrow'. Indeed, one of the Labour ministers, Ernest Bevin, was even concerned to moderate the tone of the Prime Minister's reply to Franco's communication, lest (as was noted in the introduction) the Spanish Left should be incited to undertake 'unwise and precipitate action'.[23] As during the Spanish Civil War, ideology and national interest seemed to coincide in determining, if not British support for, at least tolerance of, the continuance of the Franco regime in Spain.

Apparently appreciating that British and Allied disapproval of his political system would not be expressed in direct and dangerous action against him, Franco was not overly dismayed by the subsequent diplomatic quarantine imposed upon his state by the victorious Allied community of nations, in the post-war period. The Potsdam Declaration, of 2 August 1945, did exclude 'the present Spanish Government' from membership of the new United Nations Organisation, 'in view of its origins, its nature, its record and its close association with the aggressor States'.[24] Britain, France and the United States did issue a formal Tripartite Declaration, on 4 March 1946, asserting that until the 'peaceful withdrawal of Franco . . . and the establishment of an interim . . . government under which the Spanish people may have an opportunity freely to determine the type of government they wish to have and to choose their leaders', Spain could not expect to enjoy 'full and and cordial association' with the western powers.[25] Spain encountered serious difficulties and Spaniards endured severe shortages in the later 1940s as a hostile world denied credits to, and even restricted trade with, the Franco regime.[26] However, throughout this period of international isolation,

Franco clung to power, convinced that there were better days ahead. This conviction was grounded in the instinct that ideological conflict was bound to rend the wartime 'Grand Alliance' once its common enemy, Nazi Germany, had been defeated, and was also based on the view that Spain was uniquely placed to exploit to its own advantage such a deterioration in relations between the Soviet Union and the Western democracies.

Franco had actually mentioned the very matter which he believed would guarantee his long-term survival, as Spain's ruler, in his letter, of October 1944, to Churchill, cited above. Therein, the Caudillo had asserted 'Spain is a country of strategic importance', while Foreign Minister de Lequerica told the retiring American Ambassador, Carlton Hayes, on 5 December 1944, that Spain was 'a natural bridgehead between the American continents and Europe' and that 'if the United States, now obviously the greatest military nation in the world, was to play its proper role in the post-war period, it should realistically utilise Spain as a special bulwark in Europe'.[27] It was precisely this belief that Spain had a diplomatic bargaining counter of great value in its natural geopolitical endowments that steeled the will of the Franco regime to endure post-war international ostracism. Assuring Spain's Ambassador in London, in December 1945, that the Francoist state need not yield to 'the current situation of virulent attacks since it is fundamentally false and illogical and . . . undoubtedly transient', the then Spanish Minister for Foreign Affairs, Alberto Martín Artajo, explained why their country could expect a satisfactory end to its international isolation: 'it possesses a geographical position which in the development of modern arms and especially of aviation makes of our friendship an element all the more desirable and valuable'.[28]

Essentially, Franco's strategy of survival, in the years immediately after 1945, consisted in sitting out the international siege, until the 'natural' antagonism between the communist and capitalist blocs crystallised permitting him to gain admittance to the Western alliance by rendering it valuable strategic service.[29] Western military advisers did not doubt the importance of Spain's geopolitical situation for their collective defence, as the counsel of the British Chiefs of Staff to their government, on 10 May 1951, shows:

Spain occupies an important geographical position particularly in relation to Allied sea communications in the Western Mediterranean and Eastern Atlantic areas. The availability of Spanish ports and airfields would be of assistance in the control of sea communications in these areas. If the French Atlantic coast fell into enemy hands, use of Spanish bases would be of considerable value in meeting the increased submarine and air threat to Allied convoys.

If Russia were to occupy Spain she would gain valuable naval and air bases from which to intensify her operations against Allied sea communications in the Atlantic; and by closing the straits of Gibraltar, she could deny the Western Mediterranean to Allied shipping, which, coupled with an occupation of Italy, would place her in a favourable position to invade North Africa. Furthermore, once Spain is occupied the defence of Portugal becomes impossible and additional Atlantic ports would fall into enemy hands.

In the event of the collapse of the Allied position in Western Europe, by far the best natural defence barrier is the Pyrenees. This position is very strong defensively, but owing to the narrow exits at both ends of the mountain barrier it has disadvantages as a base from which to launch a major land offensive into France. However, if the line of the Pyrenees could be held, it would have the greatest strategic advantage in the short term of enabling us to maintain a front in Europe, to keep a foothold on the European mainland, and to keep open the entrance to the Western Mediterranean.[30]

Grand strategic opinion in the United States did not dissent from this assessment. Indeed, in April 1950, the head of the United States Joint Chiefs of Staff, General Omar Bradley, communicated to his political superiors the Pentagon's view that Spain's 'geographical position' made it the ultimate defensive redoubt against Soviet invasion in Western Europe. Its capacity to resist Soviet aggression should be fortified by American military aid, otherwise the United States would retain no European springboard from which to re-conquer the continent.[31]

If transatlantic military opinion on the desirability of incorporating Spain in the western system was united, Anglo-American political views on this issue diverged somewhat. Thus, Britain's Labour cabinet resolved, on 5 July 1951, 'to inform the United States Government of our strong opposition to the closer association of Spain in the defence of Western Europe and to urge them to abandon their policy of promoting the association of Spain with the Western democracies'.[32] But this advice ran against the tide of opinion in Washington. Certainy, America's Democratic President, Harry Truman, was no friend of Franco's Spain, being particularly offended by its denial of religious liberties to his Baptist co-religionists.[33] His initial reaction to the Pentagon's advice, of April 1950, cited above, was to dub it 'decidedly militaristic' and 'unrealistic'. However, some judicious playing of the Catholic and anti-Communist cards by Spanish lobbyists in a United States increasingly dominated by a cold war consensus overcame even presidential opposition.[34] In July 1951, Admiral Forrest Sherman conferred with General Franco on the terms of 'an agreement of collaboration between Spain and the United States for the defence of the West against the danger of aggression from Communist Russia'.[35]

The way was clear for the negotiations which eventually produced the Pacts of Madrid, the United States–Spanish Defence, Economic Aid and Mutual Defence Assistance Agreements, of 26 September 1953. These executive agreements consisted of a package whereby Spain granted strategic facilities to the United States in return for military and economic aid.[36]

The Franco regime, which had been born in civil war and had survived world war, was now finally and firmly established in a secure position by its integration into the alliance system of one side in the global confrontation known as the cold war. By biding his time Franco had endured to become a champion of the 'Free World' in its diplomatic and strategic competition with the Soviet bloc. But there had been a time, in 1940–1 when only the skill of Britain's diplomacy and the restraint of its strategy, along with the crassness of Nazi statecraft and Franco's own good luck, had spared him from fatal involvement in the Axis war effort.

Notes

Introduction

1 Winston S. Churchill, *The river war* (London, 1899), 1973 edn. (London), p.134.

2 David Stafford, 'The detonator concept: British strategy, S.O.E. and European resistance after the fall of France', *Journal of Contemporary History*, 10 (1975), 185–217; Lawrence R. Pratt, *East of Malta, west of Suez: Britain's Mediterranean crisis, 1936–1939* (Cambridge, 1975), p. 192.

3 The two major reviews of future and general strategy conducted by the British Chiefs of Staff, during the period after the French collapse and before the American entry into the war, were those of 4 September 1940 (CAB 66/11, W.P. (40)362) and 31 July 1941 (CAB 80/59, C.O.S. (41)144(o)). This latter paper, with one paragraph deleted, was handed to the United States Joint Chiefs of Staff on 10 August 1941, during the Churchill–Roosevelt meeting at Argentia, Newfoundland. The amended text, C.O.S. (R)14, is in CAB 80/30. The paper was a digest with minor modifications of a Joint Planning Staff review of future strategy of 14 June 1941 (J.P. (41)444 in CAB 79/12).

4 CAB 69/1, D.O. (40) 34th Mtg., Min. 1; CAB 80/30, C.O.S. (41)505.

5 Brian Bond (ed.), *Chief of Staff: The diaries of Lieutenant-General Sir Henry Pownall* (2 vols., London, 1972–4), II (1974), *1940–1944*, p. 8. The official account of this meeting is D.O. (40) 39th Mtg., Min. 1 in CAB 69/ 1, which records Churchill as making this point in an only slightly less emphatic manner.

6 Charles B. Burdick, *Germany's military strategy and Spain in World War II* (Syracuse, 1968), p. 28; *Documents on German foreign policy* (D.G.F.P.), Series D, XI (London, 1961), 94–6, 99, 106, 154; CAB 79/5, C.O.S. (40) 195th Mtg., Min. 6; C.O.S. (40) 223rd Mtg., Min. 1.

7 'Führer Conferences on Naval Affairs', (F.C.N.A.), H. G. Thursfield (ed.), *Brassey's Naval Annual* (London, 1948), p. 141.

8 Winston S. Churchill, *The Second World War* (6 vols., London, 1948–54), II, *Their finest hour* (American edn, Boston, 1949), 519.

9 Charles B. Burdick, ' "Moro": the resupply of German submarines in Spain, 1939–1942', *Central European History*, 3 (1970), 282.

10 B. H. Liddell Hart, *The defence of Britain* (London, 1939), p. 68.

11 CAB 79/9, J.P. (41), 154.
12 CAB 79/55, C.O.S. (41) 21st Mtg. (o); Hoare to Churchill, 30 July 1941, Templewood Papers, XIII, 16; Hoare to Churchill, 22 January 1942, ibid.
13 Churchill, *Their finest hour*, p. 518.
14 The historian is Henry Pelling in his *Britain and the Second World War* (London, 1970), pp. 91–2.
15 PREM 3/361/1.
16 Dalton Papers, diary 24, 2 March 1941.
17 Sir Desmond Morton to R. W. Thompson, 8 September 1961, R. W. Thompson, *Churchill and Morton* (London, 1976), p. 179.

1. Britain and the birth of Franco's Spain

1 Dalton Papers, diary 22.
2 Jill Edwards, *The British government and the Spanish Civil War, 1936–1939* (London, 1979), pp. 1, 24, 102, 111; Glyn Stone, 'Britain, non-intervention and the Spanish Civil War', *European Studies Review*, 9 (1979), 136–8, 144; B. Liddell Hart, *The memoirs of Captain Liddell Hart* (2 vols., London, 1965), II, 129–30, 134–5.

  Anthony Eden, Foreign Secretary from December 1935 until February 1938, did not adopt an attitude contrary to the ministerial majority view in support of Franco until 1937. (Earl of Avon, *The Eden memoirs* (3 vols., London, 1960–5), I, *Facing the dictators* (1962), 441; John Harvey (ed.), *The diplomatic diaries of Oliver Harvey, 1937–1940* (London, 1970), p. 34).

  Even then, as Republican Spain's Ambassador in London noted, Eden's conversion to a preference for a government victory in the Civil War was not expressed in a 'favourable, frank and resolute inclination', on the Foreign Secretary's part, towards the Republic. (Pablo de Azcárate, *Mi embajada en Londres durante la guerra civil española* (Barcelona, 1976), pp. 39–40).

  Indeed, Eden told an M.P. in July 1937 of his hope that the Spanish civil conflict would end in stalemate, with 'some middle Government' emerging from this deadlock. (Nigel Nicolson (ed.), *Harold Nicolson: diaries and letters* (3 vols., London, 1966–8), I, *1930–39* (1969 edn., 303).)
3 W. N. Medlicott, Douglas Dakin and Gillian Bennett (eds.), *Documents on British Foreign Policy, 1919–1939* (hereinafter cited as D.B.F.P.), 2nd Series, XVII. *Western pact negotiations: outbreak of Spanish Civil War, 23 June 1936–2 January 1937* (London, 1979), 209.
4 Edwards, *British government*, p. 215.
5 Ibid., pp. 18–19.
6 Ibid., pp. 40–3; D.B.F.P., 2nd Series, XVII, 101–2.
7 Ministère des affaires étrangères, Commission de publication des documents relatifs aux origines de la guerre, 1939–1945, *Documents diplomatiques français, 1932–39* (hereinafter cited as D.D.F.), 2ᵉ Série (1936–39), III, *19 juillet–19 novembre 1936* (Paris, 1966), 173–4; Dante A. Puzzo, *Spain and the great powers*, reprint (New York, 1972), pp. 78–82; Raymond Carr, *The Spanish tragedy: the civil war in perspective* (London, 1977), p. 147. See also, Mijail Koltsov, *Diario de la guerra española* (Madrid, 1978), p. 45.

8 Manuel Azaña, *Obras completas* (4 vols., Mexico, 1966–8), IV (1968), p. 609.

9 James Cable, *The Royal Navy and the siege of Bilbao* (Cambridge, 1979), pp. 55–76, 95–8, 177, 179–80, 188; Edwards, *British government*, pp. 101–2, 108–10, 112–17, 129–31; Keith Feiling, *The life of Neville Chamberlain* (London, 1946), pp. 351–2; Hugh Thomas, *The Spanish Civil War*, 3rd edn. (Harmondsworth, 1977), pp. 827–9, 856.

10 FO 371/24115, W 973/5/41. Vansittart did also state, however, in this Foreign Office memo, of 16 January 1939, that he did not believe that it was British Government policy 'to wish Franco to win'.

11 'Normas para tener en cuenta en las gestiones del Duque de Alba con el Gobierno Británico', 25 April 1938 (Ministerio de asuntos exteriores), Alba Papers, Caja 1^A, No. 1.

12 FO 371/22644, W 5504/83/41.

13 Alba arrived in London from Spain on the night of 27 April 1938. It is possible that he conveyed, immediately and informally, his administration's anxiety concerning the reopening of France's frontier with Republican Spain, to senior British politicians by activating some of his many contacts inside conservative and establishment circles. Alternatively, British ministers may have received some other, or earlier, expression of Spanish nationalist alarm at this development. In any case, by one means or another, sooner or later, the message did get through.

Indeed, the British Government hardly needed much prompting. For, on 15 March 1938, the Cabinet had accepted the suggestion of the then Home Secretary, Sir Samuel Hoare, which was fully supported by Prime Minister Chamberlain, that 'heavy pressure' be applied to 'the French Government to bring their policy in regard to Spain into line' with Britain's. It was agreed that the appropriate occasion on which to raise this matter, *inter alia*, with French ministers would be during an official visit by them to London 'as soon as circumstances' permitted. The latter condition is explained by British reluctance to meet members of Léon Blum's second Popular Front Government which had assumed office on 13 March 1938. Its radical inclinations in the international sphere, which included the relaxation of border restrictions on the trans-Pyrenean delivery of arms and munitions to Republican Spain, antagonised British policy-makers, intent as they were on appeasement of the fascist powers. Only when the Blum Government fell, on 8 April, was the way clear for the London inter-ministerial encounter of 28–29 of that month, at which the new French Premier, Daladier, and the new foreign Minister, Bonnet, could be subjected to British pressure to reseal the Pyrenean frontier. D.B.F.P., 2nd Series, XIX, *European affairs, July 1937–August 1938* (London, 1982), 1047, 1049, 1051–2; Anthony Adamthwaite, *France and the coming of the Second World War, 1936–1939* (London, 1977), p. 84; Joel Colton, *Léon Blum: humanist in politics* (New York, 1966), 1974 edn., pp. 259, 297–9.

14 FO 371/21591, C 3687/13/17; D.D.F., 2e Série, IX, *21 mars–9 juin 1938* (Paris, 1974), 565–9, 597–9.

15 United States Department of State, *Foreign relations of the United States* (hereinafter cited as F.R.U.S.), *1938*, I (Washington, 1955), 92.

16 Edwards, *British Government*, p. 174; David Dilks (ed.), *The diaries of Sir Alexander Cadogan, 1938–1945* (London, 1971), pp. 77–8, 82; D.D.F., 2ᵉ Série, IX, 760, 1023–5.

17 D.G.F.P., Series D, III, *Germany and the Spanish Civil War, 1936–1939* (London, 1951), 664–5, 653.

Hans-Henning Abendroth contends, in his valuable study of Nazi Germany's policy towards the Spanish Civil War, that Jordana's instancing of Alba's report on British efforts to obtain the closure of the Spanish–French border, in a conversation with German Ambassador von Stohrer on 19 May 1938, was a diversionary tactic on the Foreign Minister's part. For, Abendroth maintains, Jordana was concerned to ward off Germany's attempt to conclude a formal treaty of friendship with Nationalist Spain that would greatly reduce Franco's future freedom of diplomatic manoeuvre. Such a motive may have partly inspired the Spanish Foreign Minister's view (which, he claimed, was shared by Franco) that his regime could not afford to alienate Britain at such a delicate juncture in diplomatic and military developments, by public alignment with Germany. However, Abendroth's dismissal of Jordana's citation of Alba's report as 'nothing more than a difficult to refute (*schwer widerlegbare*) lie' seems contrary to the other extant evidence mentioned above and below. (Hans-Henning Abendroth, *Hitler in der spanischen Arena: die deutsch–spanischen Beziehungen im Spannungsfeld der europäischen Interessenpolitik vom Ausbruch des Bürgerkrieges bis zum Ausbruch des Weltkrieges, 1936–1939* (Paderborn, 1973), pp. 211–13.)

18 Harvey (ed.), *Diplomatic diaries of Oliver Harvey*, pp. 148–9.

19 Alexander Werth, *France and Munich: before and after the surrender* (London, 1939) (New York, 1969), p. 177; Adamthwaite, *France*, p. 188; Edwards, *British Government*, p. 174.

20 FO 371/22627, W 8723/29/41.

21 D.D.F., 2nd Série, IX, 1023–5. See also, D.D.F., 2ᵉ Série, X, *10 juin–2 septembre 1938* (Paris, 1976), 55–6.

22 D.B.F.P., 2nd series, XIX, 1127–33; Malcolm Muggeridge (ed.) *Ciano's diplomatic papers* (London, 1948), pp. 216–18, 220–1; Malcolm Muggeridge (introd.), *Ciano's diary, 1937–1938* (London, 1952), pp. 129, 133; Dilks (ed.), *Cadogan diaries*, pp. 83, 85.

23 Adamthwaite, *France*, pp. 105, 188; Geoffrey Warner, *Pierre Laval and the eclipse of France* (London, 1968), p. 145.

24 Sir Eric Phipps to Halifax, 23 June 1938, Phipps Papers, 1/20. Similar interaction between British policy-makers and elements within the French Government who were against, or afraid of, active support of the Spanish republic had produced the scheme for international non-intervention in the Spanish Civil War in August 1936. (Edwards, *British government*, pp. 15–30; Stone, 'Non-intervention', 138–45.)

25 FO 371/24116, W 1855/5/41. See also, FO 371/22627, W 8723/29/41 and FO 371/24115, W 973, W 1405/5/41.

26 Thomas, *Spanish Civil War*, p. 847; John F. Coverdale, *Italian intervention in the Spanish Civil War* (Princeton, 1975), p. 360.

27 De Azcárate, *Mi embajada*, p. 389.

28 Ibid., pp. 383–4; F.R.U.S., *1938*, I, 236.

29 F.R.U.S., *1938*, I, 212.

30 De Azcárate, *Mi embajada*, pp. 385–6.

31 Quoted by Coverdale, *Italian intervention*, p. 362.

32 Ibid., pp. 374–8; Edwards, *British government*, pp. 206–7.

33 Teniente general Francisco Gómez Jordana y Sousa to the Duke of Alba, 2 October 1938, Alba papers, Caja, 1ᴬ, No. 1; Sir Robert Hodgson, *Spain resurgent* (London, 1953), pp. 84–5; Edwards, *British government*, pp. 107, 188, 203.

Britain also extended important commercial facilities to Nationalist Spain, from December 1936 onwards. (Edwards, *British government*, pp. 72–6; Angel Viñas, J. Viñuela, F. Eguidazu, C. F. Pulgar and S. Florensa, *Política comercial exterior en España (1931–1975)* (2 vols., Madrid, 1979), I, 154–6.)

34 D.B.F.P., 2nd Series, XVII, 152. At this time the C.O.S. were a sub-committee of the (Cabinet) Committee of Imperial Defence. On the outbreak of war in 1939, however, the C.I.D. was dissolved and the C.O.S. were elevated into a War Cabinet Committee. They became subject, as well, to the daily 'supervision and direction' of Churchill, as Prime Minister and Minister of Defence, on the latter's assumption of the leadership of the British Government in May 1940. (Sir James Butler (ed.), *History of the Second World War, United Kingdom military series: Grand strategy* (6 vols. London, H.M.S.O., 1956–76), II, by J. R. M. Butler, *September 1939–June 1941* (London, 1957), 5–6, 180.)

35 Quoted by Pratt, *East of Malta*, p. 41. See, also, CAB 65/6, W.M. 105(40) 7.

36 Elizabeth Monroe, *The Mediterranean in politics* (London, 1938), p. 43; Churchill, *Their finest hour*, American edn., p. 519. See also, CAB 79/5, C.O.S. (40) 223rd Mtg., Min. 1.

37 Martin Blinkhorn, 'Spain: "the Spanish problem" and the imperial myth', J. C. H., 15 (1980), 16–21. See also, D.G.F.P., Series D, III, 762.

38 J. W. D. Trythall, *Franco: a biography* (London, 1970), p. 149.

39 Hugh Thomas (ed.), *José Antonio Primo de Rivera: selected writings* (London, 1972), p. 83.

40 Ibid., p. 132.

41 Ibid., pp. 74, 82–3; Blinkhorn, 'Spain', 18–19.

42 Ian Gibson, *En busca de José Antonio* (Barcelona, 1980), p. 32.

43 Herbert Rutledge Southworth, 'The Falange: an analysis of Spain's fascist heritage', in Paul Preston (ed.), *Spain in crisis: the evolution and decline of the Franco regime* (Hassocks, Sussex, 1976), p. 5.

44 Ramón Serrano Suñer, *Entre Hendaya y Gibraltar*, 2nd edn. (Barcelona, 1973), p. 236. See also, D.G.F.P., Series D, III, 762.

45 José María de Areilza and Fernando María Castiella, *Reivindicaciones de España*, 2nd edn. (Madrid, 1941), p. 46.

46 7 August 1940.

47 Alba's dispatch no. 807, 5 August 1940, Ministerio de Asuntos Exteriores (hereinafter cited as M.A.E.), legajo R. 985, Expediente 12.

48 Herbert R. Southworth, *Antifalange: estudio crítico de 'Falange en la guerra de España: la unificación y Hedilla' de Maximiano García Venero* (Paris, 1967), p. 40.

49 De Arielza and Castiella, *Reivindicaciones*, p. 98.

50 Southworth, 'Falange', p. 15.
51 Teniente general Francisco Franco Salgado-Araujo *Mis conversaciones privadas con Franco* (Barcelona, 1976), pp. 156, 179. See also, Southworth, *Antifalange*, p. 38.
52 Southworth, 'Falange', pp. 12–14.
53 'Documents of the New Spain – 1', *Bulletin of Spanish studies*, 16, No. 63 (1939), 144.
54 Charles R. Halstead, 'Spain, the powers and the Second World War', unpublished Ph.D. (University of Virginia, 1962), p. 75; idem, 'Spanish foreign policy, 1936–1978', in James W. Cortada (ed.), *Spain in the twentieth-century world: essays on Spanish diplomacy, 1898–1978* (London, 1980), pp. 45, 85 (note 12).
55 Angel Viñas, 'La administración de la política económica exterior en España, 1936–1979'. *Cuadernos económicos de información comercial Española* No. 13 (1980), 179.
56 D.G.F.P., Series D, III, 124, 236, 274–5, 286–7, 408–9, 533, 553, 576–77, 581.
57 Trythall, *Franco*, p. 155.
58 Coverdale, *Italian intervention*, pp. 153–6, 413–14.
59 Muggeridge (ed.), *Ciano's diplomatic papers*, p. 291.
60 D.G.F.P., Series D, III, 880–1, 884–6.
61 Ibid., 885.
62 D.B.F.P., 2nd Series, XVII, 156.
63 Ibid., 2nd Series, XVI, *The Rhineland crisis and the ending of sanctions, March–July, 1936* (London, 1977), 638–9.
64 Ibid., 2nd Series, XVII, 120.
65 Ibid., 49–50.
66 Edwards, *British government*, pp. 22–39; Stone, 'Non-intervention', 138–45.
67 Quoted by Coverdale, *Italian intervention*, p. 97.
68 330 H.C. DEB. 5s., cols. 1807–8. Eden had been equally explicit in his analysis of the aim of non-intervention in the House, on 1 November 1937: 'We may have our own sentiments as to what we want to happen in this matter, but the main object has been to neutralise and localise this war and to prevent it spreading to Europe as a whole.' (Quoted in F.R.U.S., I, 191.)
69 Edwards, *British government*, pp. 60–1.
70 Ibid., pp. 164–9; Coverdale, *Italian intervention*, pp. 351–2; Harvey (ed.), *Diplomatic diaries of Oliver Harvey*, pp. 83–4, 92–7. Pratt maintains that Eden's disagreement with Chamberlain's policy-line towards Mussolini ultimately sprang not from principled anti-fascism but from 'resentment against [an] upstart have-not' imperialist, whose challenge to Britain's Mediterranean position, the Foreign Secretary felt, should be confronted rather than appeased. (Pratt, *East of Malta*, pp. 86–7.)
71 Harvey (ed.), *Diplomatic diaries of Oliver Harvey*, pp. 51, 57; Pratt, *East of Malta*, pp. 92–3.
72 Hickleton Papers, A4. 410.11.1: 'Record of events connected with Anthony Eden's resignation, February 19th–20th, 1938'.
73 Maurice Cowling, *The impact of Hitler: British politics and British policy, 1933–1940* (Cambridge, 1975), pp. 143–76.

74 Edwards, *British government*, pp. 196, 199; D.G.F.P., Series D, III, 142.
75 K. W. Watkins, *Britain divided: the effect of the Spanish Civil War on British political opinion* (London, 1963), 1976 reprint (Westport, Connecticut) pp. 142, 144–5, 158–63, 178, 181–95; Bernard Donoughue and G. W. Jones, *Herbert Morrison: portrait of a politician* (London, 1973), pp. 225–32, 262–3; Michael Foot, *Aneurin Bevan* (2 vols., London, 1962, 1973), I, *1897–45*, 1975 edn., 225–38, 253–6, 263–9, 277–81, 286–93, 296; Alan Bullock, *The life and times of Ernest Bevin* (3 vols., London, 1960–83), I, *Trade union leader, 1881–1940* (1960), 591–6. See also, Ben Pimlott, *Labour and the left in the 1930s* (Cambridge, 1977), e.g., pp. 4–5, 202.
76 Donoughue and Jones, *Morrison*, pp. 608–9, note 104.
77 Ibid., pp. 226–32, 235, 258–9, 262–4.
78 Quoted by Watkins, *Britain divided*, p. 189.
79 Foot, *Bevan*, I, 275; Watkins, *Britain divided*, p. 189; CAB 66/57, W.P. (44) 622.
80 CAB 65/48, WM 157(44) confidential annex (C.A.).
81 Watkins, *Britain divided*, pp. 166–7, 180–1.
82 One exception to the non-interventionist consensus among Labour's leaders was Herbert Morrison but, as already noted, he was too much of a party loyalist to break ranks on the issue (Donoughue and Jones, *Morrison*, pp. 258–9).
83 Thomas Jones, *A diary with letters, 1931–1950* (London, 1954), p. 231.
84 D.B.F.P., 2nd Series, XVII, 62–3.
85 Quoted by Cowling, *Impact of Hitler*, p. 166.
86 Azaña, *Obras completas*, IV, 805.
87 De Azcárate, *Mi embajada*, p. 40.
88 FO 371/20530, W 8628/62/41; Angel Viñas, *El oro de Moscú: alfa y omega de un mito franquista* (Barcelona, 1979), pp. 149–50, 183–4 (Note 10); Herbert Rutledge Southworth, 'Conspiración contra la república', *Historia 16*, June, 1978.
89 Coverdale, *Italian intervention*, pp. 78–9; Liddell Hart, *Memoirs*, II, 134–5.
90 Stephen Spender, *The thirties and after: poetry, politics, people (1932–75)* (London, 1978), Fontana edn., p. 82.
91 Foot, *Bevan*, I, 285.
92 Pratt, *East of Malta*, pp. 88–92; D.B.F.P., 2nd Series, XIX, 254, 340–1. Coverdale does not even credit Nyon with being directly responsible for the suspension of the Italian submarine campaign (Coverdale, *Italian intervention*, pp. 315–16).
93 Donald Lammers, 'Fascism, communism and the foreign office, 1937–39', J.C.H., 6 (1971), 67, 84–6; Gottfried Niedhart, 'British attitudes and policies towards the Soviet Union and international communism 1933–9', in Wolfgang J. Mommsen and Lothar Kettenacker (eds.), *The fascist challenge and the policy of appeasement* (London, 1983), p. 288.
94 Edwards, *British government*, pp. 64, 85, 99.
95 FO 371/24115, W 1752/5/41.
96 Feiling, *Chamberlain*, p. 394. See also, e.g., Brian Bond (ed.), *Chief of Staff*, I, *1933–1940* (London, 1972), p. 188.
97 Jordana to Alba, 26 June 1939, Alba papers, Caja 1^A, No. 1.

98 Ivan Maisky, *Spanish notebooks* (London, 1966), p. 146.
99 Edwards, *British government*, pp. 80–98; Charles E. Harvey, 'Politics and pyrites during the Spanish Civil War', *Economic History Review*, 31 (1978), 89–104; Wolfgang Schieder, 'Spanischer Bürgerkrieg und Vierjahresplan. Zur Struktur nationalsozialistischer Aussenpolitik' in Wolfgang Schieder and Christof Dipper (eds.), *Der Spanische Bürgerkrieg in der internationalen Politik (1936–1939)* (Munich, 1976), pp. 172–84; Hans-Erich Volkmann, 'Die NS-Wirtschaft in Vorbereitung des Krieges' in Hans-Erich Volkmann, Wilhelm Deist, Manfred Messerschmidt, and Wolfram Wette (eds.), *Das Deutsche Reich und der Zweite Weltkrieg*, I, *Ursachen und Voraussetzungen der deutschen Kriegspolitik* (Stuttgart, 1979), pp. 317–23.
100 Edwards, *British government*, p. 64; D.G.F.P., Series D, III, 400.
101 Abendroth, *Hitler in der Spanischen Arena*, pp. 310–11.
102 Ibid., pp. 307–11, 390–1.
103 W. N. Medlicott, *The economic blockade*, I (London, 1952), 510; David Eccles (ed.), *By safe hand: letters of Sybil and David Eccles, 1939–42* (London, 1983), pp. 19–20, 25–6, 29–31, 34–5, 43, 50–1, 55–7, 61–2, 67, 72–81, 83–92; 'Annual (Foreign Office) report: Spain', 1940–1, copy in Templewood Papers, XIII, 20.
104 Medlicott, *Economic blockade*, I, 510; 'Annual report: Spain' 1940–1, annex A, copy in Templewood Papers, XIII, 20
105 Klaus-Jörg Ruhl, 'L'alliance à distance: les relations économiques germano–espagnoles de 1936 à 1945', *Revue d'Histoire de la Deuxième Guerre Mondiale*, 118 (1980), 86–7.

2. Defining a policy

1 Watkins, *Britain divided*, pp. 84, 88, 95–6, 98, 102–3, 104–5, 107–8, 137, 139; Morton to Thompson, 11 July 1961, Thompson, *Churchill and Morton*, pp. 159–60; Martin Gilbert, *Winston S. Churchill*, V, *1922–1939* (London, 1976) pp. 785, 1035.
2 Quoted by the Spanish newspaper, *Arriba*, in its editorial, 'Si Churchill fuera Español', 8 August 1941; Thomas, *Spanish Civil War*, pp. 822–3, note 3.
3 PREM 4/21/2A.
4 This phrase is Hoare's description of the purpose of his mission, in a letter written a few days after conferring with Churchill about it: Hoare to Sir Andrew Duncan, 26 May 1940, Templewood Papers, XIII, 1b.
5 Kenneth Young (ed.), *The diaries of Sir Robert Bruce Lockhart* (2 vols., London, 1973–80), II, *1939–1965*, 56–7.
6 CAB 65/7, WM 123(40)12; Dilks (ed.), *Cadogan diaries*, pp. 282, 286.
7 J. A. Cross, *Sir Samuel Hoare: a political biography* (London, 1977) pp. 172–3, 325–6; Churchill's 'Prime Minister's personal minute' to Eden of 6 August 1943, PREM 4/21/2A; Avon, *Eden memoirs*, II, *The reckoning* (London, 1965), 95–6. So annoyed was Churchill at Hoare's reforming stance when Secretary of State for India, that the champion of the 'diehard' Tory opposition on the issue declared in 1934, 'I will break this bloody rat Hoare's neck if I risk my own.' (Quoted by Cross, p. 172.)
8 D.G.F.P., Series D, XII (London, 1962), 944. Hoare was also viewed by

another German observer, in September 1940, as a possible instrument for establishing peace between Britain and Germany. See D.G.F.P., Series D, XI, 80, where Hoare is described as 'half-shelved and half on the watch in Madrid'.

9 Hickleton Papers, A7.8.4: Halifax diary, 12 May 1940; Dilks (ed.), *Cadogan diaries*, p. 282; Cross, *Hoare*, pp. 321–4; Lord Chatfield to Halifax, 24 May 1940, FO 794/19; Eccles (ed.), *By safe hand*, p. 101.

J. A. Cross (p. 323), is inclined to doubt Cadogan's contemporary record of Sir Samuel's initial refusal to accept the Madrid Ambassadorship, but the confirmatory evidence which he seeks is contained in the Halifax diary entry cited above.

Hoare's hopes of becoming Viceroy of India were dashed the following October, when Churchill told him that he 'must in no wise be considered as committed to any particular solution of the personal and political issues involved in the selection of a new Viceroy' (Churchill to Hoare, 23 October 1940, Templewood Papers, XIII, 16).

10 Dilks (ed.), *Cadogan diaries*, pp. 286–8; Hoare to Halifax, 27 May 1940, FO 794/19.

11 Dilks (ed.), *Cadogan diaries*, p. 287.

12 Hickleton Papers, A7.8.4: Halifax diary, 17 May 1940. The 'special' character of Hoare's mission, originally, derived from the idea of sending him on a brief visit to Madrid but, when it was decided to appoint him as Ambassador instead, the term was retained as part of his Ambassadorial designation for constitutional reasons. For, Hoare wanted to keep his seat in the House of Commons, and only his description as Ambassador Extraordinary 'on Special Mission' was judged by the Attorney General to exclude him from holding 'an office of profit under the Crown' incompatible with his remaining M.P. for Chelsea. Hoare was also precluded from receiving any salary for his Ambassadorial role, though he did receive increased 'expenses' (F.O. 794/19).

13 Dilks (ed.), *Cadogan diaries*, p. 288.

14 Memorandum of 21 May 1940, PREM 4/21/2A.

15 FO 371/24511, C 6521/75/41.

16 F.O. memorandum, 21 May 1940, PREM 4/21/2A.

17 Churchill's handwritten comment on Hillgarth to Churchill, 27 July 1940, PREM 4/21/2A; Churchill, *Their finest hour*, p. 519. See also, the 'Prime Minister's personal minute' to Eden, 6 August 1943 and Hoare to Churchill, 12 June 1940, PREM 4/21/1; copy in Templewood Papers, XIII, 16: 'I have got . . . a really excellent Naval Attaché in your friend Hillgarth. I am finding Hillgarth a great prop.'

18 Personal interview with Captain Hillgarth, 27 January 1977; Hillgarth's memorandum for Hoare, 2 June 1940, Templewood Papers, XIII, 2.

19 Pereira *Memórias* (2 vols., Lisbon, 1973), II, 205.

20 FO 794/19; FO 371/24527, C 7049/6013/41.

21 Templewood, *Ambassador*, pp. 22–3.

22 Ibid., p. 31.

23 Hoare to Bracken, 6 June 1940, Templewood Papers, XIII, 17.

24 Eccles (ed.), *By safe hand*, pp. 101–2, 104, 115, 157–8.

25 Hillgarth's memorandum for Hoare, 2 June 1940, Templewood Papers, XIII, 2.

26 Ibid.
27 Templewood, *Ambassador*, pp. 22, 32–3.
28 Ibid., p. 28.
29 Hoare to Halifax, 11 October 1940, Templewood Papers, XIII, 20.
30 Hoare to Halifax, 3 June 1940, Halifax Papers, FO 800/323.
31 Halifax to Hoare, 19 June 1940, Halifax Papers, FO 800/323.
32 Ibid.
33 FO 371/24515, C7200/113/41. See also, the inter-departmental meeting of 20 June 1940, on economic policy towards Spain which approved Hoare's recommendation: FO 371/25178, W9 109/5114/49.
34 D.G.F.P., Series D, IX (London, 1956), 620–1.
35 Heleno Saña, *El Franquismo sin mitos: conversaciones con Serrano Suñer* (Barcelona, 1982), pp. 164, 170–1.
36 D.G.F.P., Series D, X, 16; ibid., IX, 585–7; Ramón Serrano Suñer, *Entre el silencio y la propaganda, la historia como fue: Memorias* (Barcelona, 1977), pp. 328–9. Franco's brother, Nicolás, told the Portuguese Prime Minister, Oliveira Salazar, on 13 July 1940, that the Caudillo had considered the war lost by England ever since Dunkirk. (Ministerio de negócios estrangeiros, *Dez Anos de política externa (1936–1947): A nação portuguesa e a segunda guerra mundial* (D.A.P.E., VII (Lisbon, 1971), 252).
37 Hoare to Halifax, 11 June 1940, Halifax Papers, FO 800/323.
38 CAB 65/7, W.M. 164(40)10. Hoare's telegram No. 316, 11 June 1940, (FO 371/24514, C 6738/113/41) was being reported to the War Cabinet.
39 An English translation of the Spanish decree of non-belligerency is contained in F.R.U.S. *1940*, II (Washington, D.C., 1957), 797. Franco defined non-belligerency, on one occasion, as 'a state of more definite sympathy towards Italy and a wide awake attitude' (ibid., p. 888). Franco had resolved to declare Spain to be in a state of non-belligerency, on being directly requested by Mussolini to afford moral and economic solidarity to a belligerent Italy and indirectly prompted by Ciano to abandon neutrality for non-belligerency. (Mussolini to Franco, 9 June 1940, Ministerio degli Affair Esteri, *I Documenti diplomatici italiani* (D.D.I.), Series IX, IV (Rome), 620; Franco to Mussolini, 10 June 1940, p. 630; D.D.I., Series IX, V, 6). See also, Eccles (ed.), *By safe hand*, p. 126, where the M.E.W. official notes the explanation given to him in Lisbon by Spain's Ambassador there, Franco's brother Nicolás, of the meaning of this new international status: 'Nicolás Franco asserted that they meant nothing more by non-belligerent than they had previously meant by neutral, the new phrase was used to please the Axis and the extreme *Falangistas* who were looking for an excuse to throw over the government. General Franco was as firmly determined as ever not to have a shot fired on Spanish soil.'
40 Hoare to Halifax, 11 June 1940, Halifax papers, FO 800/323.
41 Enclosure with Hoare to Halifax, 20 June 1940, Halifax Papers, FO 800/323; Hoare's dispatch no. 299, 11 July 1940, FO 371/24508, C 7817/40/41. Copy in Templewood Papers, XIII, 20.
42 FO 371 24516, C 8045/113/41.
43 Sir Maurice Peterson, *Both sides of the curtain* (London, 1950), pp. 229–30.

44 FO 371/24516, C 8443/113/41.
45 FO 371/24511, C 9159/75/41. Hoare had a conversation with Orgaz on 16 July 1940, and reported to Halifax thus, about the latter: 'Almost every word he said to me showed his desire to keep Spain out of the war.' Hoare to Halifax, 16 July 1940, Halifax papers, FO 800/323.
46 D.G.F.P., Series D, X (London, 1957), 463–4.
47 FO 371/24515, C 7281/113/41.
48 FO 371/24514, C 6738/113/41.
49 FO 371/24515, C 7281/113/41; FO 371/24510, C 6032/75/41. Hoare told Franco at his interview that the British Government wished to support and strengthen the Spanish Government, as it appeared to want to keep out of the war, and to improve Anglo-Spanish relations.
50 CAB 65/7, WM 178(40)4.
51 FO 371/24516, C 7580/113/41; Hoare to Beaverbrook, 5 July 1940, Templewood Papers, XIII, 17; Templewood, *Ambassador*, pp. 52–3; CAB 65/8, WM 193(40)4.
52 Hoare to Halifax, 1 July 1940, Halifax papers, FO 800/323; also Hoare to Halifax, 5 July 1940, ibid.; CAB 65/8, WM 205(40)3.
53 D.G.F.P., Series D, X, 97–8.
54 FO 371/24514, C 6738/113/41; On Yagüe and the domestic political scene in Spain, see Stanley G. Payne, *Falange: a history of Spanish fascism* (Stanford, 1961), 1967 edn., pp. 213–14.
55 CAB 80/14, C.O.S. (40)545.
56 Hoare to Chamberlain, 30 July 1940, Templewood Papers, XIII, 2; D.A.P.E., VII, 336–7.
57 FO 371/24514, C 6538/113/41; FO 371/24501, C 6938/30/41; Medlicott, *Economic blockade*, I, 513; Eccles (ed.), *By safe hand*, pp. 110–13, 125–6.
58 CAB 65/8, WM 216(40)1.
59 Hoare to Churchill, 22 July 1940, PREM 4/21/1.
60 The phrase is, of course, Gerald Brenan's. See his *The Spanish labyrinth* (Cambridge, 1943).
61 FO 371/24516, C 8045/113/41.
62 Halifax to Hoare, 30 July 1940, Templewood Papers, XIII, 20.
63 CAB 79/6, C.O.S. (40) 251st Mtg., Min. 5; FO 371/24516, C 8045/113/41.
64 Hoare to Beaverbrook, 7 August 1940, Templewood Papers, XIII, 17.
65 Charles R. Halstead in his article, 'Consistent and total peril from every side: Portugal and its 1940 protocol with Spain', *Iberian studies* (1974), 15–29, argues that Portuguese assent to Spanish freedom of action concerning Gibraltar was only implicit (ibid., p. 19 and note 76). The text of the Protocol, which is to be found in D.A.P.E., VII, 323–5, in Portuguese and Spanish, certainly contains no reference to Gibraltar. However, Beigbeder told the German Ambassador in Madrid that the written Protocol had been accompanied by 'a secret oral agreement . . . [by which] . . . Portugal would give Spain an entirely free hand for an attack on Gibraltar' (D.G.F.P., Series D, X, 515). Given the natural temptation for the Spanish Foreign Minister to interpret, in a form acceptable to the Germans, Spain's concord with Britain's 'oldest ally', Halstead's argument that the understanding on the issue was merely tacit, may well be a more accurate assessment of the nature of the Hispano–Portuguese exchange. See also, Halstead, 'Consistent and total

peril', 20 and note 106; D.G.F.P., Series D, X, 225; and D.A.P.E., VII, 294–5, 297, 301–2. On the Treaty itself, see Charles R. Halstead, 'Peninsular purpose: Portugal and its 1939 Treaty of Friendship and Non-Aggression with Spain', *Il politico*, XLV (1980), 287–311.

66 D.G.F.P. Series D, X, 514–15.
67 Hoare to Sir Walter Layton, 4 July 1940, Templewood Papers, XIII, 2.
68 See, e.g., Hoare's dispatch No. 299, 11 July 1940, FO 371/24508, C 7817/40/41.
69 Halifax to Hoare, 17 July 1940, Templewood Papers, XIII, 20.
70 Dalton Papers, diary 24, 16 May 1941; Lord Harvey of Tasburgh diaries, 15 November 1942, British Library Add. Mss. 56399. The only revealing documentary evidence on this problem which I have discovered is contained in the foregoing references, and in note 72, but there are tantalisingly vague allusions in the following: Hoare to Halifax, 7 June 1940, Halifax papers, FO 800/323; Hoare to Beaverbrook, 21 June 1940, Templewood Papers, XIII, 17; Halifax to Hoare, 11, 19 June 1940, Halifax papers FO 800/323; Hillgarth to Churchill, 21 June 1940, PREM, 4/21/2A; Hoare to Churchill, 12, 27 June 1940, Templewood Papers, XIII, 16; Hoare to Chamberlain, 6 June 1940, Templewood Papers, XIII, 17; Hoare to Eden, 24 December 1940, Eden to Hoare, 3 January 1941, Templewood Papers, XIII, 21; Hoare to Brendan Bracken, 6 June 1940, Templewood Papers, XIII, 17. See, also, Donald McLachlan, *Room 39: naval intelligence in action, 1939–45* (London, 1968), pp. 203–4 and Nigel West, *MI6: British secret intelligence service operations, 1909–45* (London, 1983), pp. 135, 184, 216–17.
71 PREM 4/32/7.
72 It was the Military Attaché at the British Embassy in Madrid during the war, Brigadier W. W. T. Torr, who reached this retrospective judgement in a note on the Chief of the German Abwehr, Admiral Canaris, which is in the Templewood Papers at XXIII: (B) 3. The note is unsigned and undated, but its authorship may be deduced from Hoare to Torr, 17 March 1958, Templewood Papers, XXIII, 3.
73 See, e.g., Dalton papers, diary 24, 16 May 1941, and p. 22b in chapter nine.
74 Hoare to Beaverbrook, 5 July 1940, Templewood Papers, XIII, 17.
75 Ramón Garriga, *La España de Franco: las relaciones secretas con Hitler* (Buenos Aires, 1965), 1970 edn. (Puebla, Mexico), pp. 87–9; Templewood, *Ambassador*, pp. 54–5.
76 Trythall, *Franco*, p. 158.
77 Templewood, *Ambassador*, pp. 103–4; *Arriba*, 13 March 1941; 370 H. C. DEB, 5s., cols. 973–4.
78 Templewood, *Ambassador*, pp. 56–7.
79 FO 371/24511, C 8633, C 8526, C 8993/75/41.
80 FO 371/24511, C 8526/75/41.
81 Intro., H. R. Trevor-Roper, *Hitler's table talk: his private conversations* (London, 1953), 1973 edn., p. 694.
82 Sir Llewellyn Woodward, *British foreign policy in the Second World War* (5 vols., London, 1970–6), I (1970), 434; Report on Gibraltar, 6 August 1940, PREM 3/199; FO 371/26897, C 4642/33/41.
83 Brian Crozier, *Franco: a biographical history* (London, 1967), p. 314;

Cowling, *Impact of Hitler*, pp. 165, 167, 340; Alba's dispatch no. 545, 20 May 1940, legajo R. 985, E.16, M.A.E.

84 Hoare to Halifax, 15 August 1940, Templewood Papers, XIII, 20; CAB 66/11, W.P. (40) 362, appendix 1, para. 22.

85 See, e.g., Hoare to Halifax, 16 July 1940, Halifax Papers, FO 800 323; Hoare to Halifax, 15 August 1940, Templewood Papers, XIII, 20.

86 West, *MI6*, pp. 109, 135, 184, 216.

87 Ibid., p. 184; Kim Philby, *My silent war* (London, 1968), 1969 edn., pp. 57–8.

88 J. C. Masterman, *The double-cross system in the war of 1939 to 1945* (New Haven and London, 1972), pp. 57–8, 76, 92–3, 99, 113.

89 David Stafford, *Britain and European resistance, 1940–1945: a survey of the special operations executive with documents* (London, 1980), pp. 55–6; Richard Harris Smith, *O.S.S.: The secret history of America's first central intelligence agency* (Berkeley, 1972), 1981 edn., p. 77.

90 PREM 4/21/2A.

91 Nigel West, *MI5: British security service operations, 1909–1945* (London, 1981), 1983 edn., p. 368.

92 McLachlan, *Room 39*, p. 190; Patrick Beesly, *Very Special Admiral: the life of Admiral J. H. Godfey, CB* (London, 1980), pp. 143–4; Burdick, ' "Moro" ', 283.

93 Burdick, ' "Moro" ', 280. However, that Hillgarth could also act more forcefully against German covert operations is demonstrated by his response to the Nazi network which maintained a close surveillance of the Strait of Gibraltar. Hillgarth employed native Spaniards, organised and paid by British sources in Gibraltar, to disrupt the German observation operation by direct action. This arrangement absolved the Naval Attaché of any responsibility for these agents' activities if they were discovered by the Spanish authorities (McLachlan, *Room 39*, pp. 195–6).

94 See also, M. R. D. Foot and J. M. Langley, *MI9: escape and evasion: 1939–1945* (London, 1979), pp. 44, 76–7; J. M. Langley, *Fight another day* (London, 1974), p. 141.

95 Hoare to Halifax, 26 June 1940, Halifax papers, FO 800/323.

96 Ibid. It is interesting to note that although Hoare gave a lengthy extract from this letter in his memoirs (*Ambassador*, pp. 36–9), he omitted the crucial parts of it expressing his view that the Franco government had to be sustained, particularly neglecting to include the passage advocating that Britain should meet the former's claims over Moroccan Zones. For, considerations of possible embarrassment in post-war Anglo-French relations aside, Hoare is throughout his book anxious to minimise the extent to which he counselled support for Franco during the initial phase of his mission. Hoare's memoirs, which were published in 1946, should be viewed, in part, as both an attempt to lay the ghost of appeasement which haunted his public reputation and as a shot in his campaign to engineer the restoration of the monarchy in Spain, and the elimination from power of General Franco, for the post-war period.

97 CAB 66/9, W.P. (40)259; Arnold and Veronica M. Toynbee (eds.), *The war and the neutrals (Survey of International Affairs, 1939–1946)*, (London, 1956), pp. 21–2, 27.

98 Halifax to Hoare, 30 July 1940, Templewood Papers, XIII, 20; Dalton

Papers, diary 23, July 1940; Dilks (ed.) *Cadogan diaries*, p. 315; FO 371/ 25178, W 9135/5114/49.

99 Medlicott, *Economic blockade*, I, 513–15; FO 371/24514, C 6538/113/ 41; FO 371/24501, C 6938/30/41; Eccles (ed.), *By safe hand*, pp. 103–4, 110–13, 125–6, 141.

100 Donald S. Detwiler, *Hitler, Franco und Gibraltar: Die Frage des spanischen Eintritts in den Zweiten Weltkrieg* (Wiesbaden, 1962), p. 26. See, also, Detwiler's article, 'Spain and the Second World War', *Review of Politics*, 33 (1971), 41–2.

101 *Arriba*, 18 July 1940. My translation: the translation in FO 371/24508, C 7778/40/41, is so free as to be inaccurate.

102 Alba's dispatch no. 776, 22 July 1940, legajo R. 985, E.8, M.A.E.; Detwiler, *Hitler, Franco und Gibraltar*, p. 26. Alba's dispatch was apparently given by the Spanish Minister for Foreign Affairs to the Germans, as Beigbeder had promised to do with such reports, since the Germans were anxious for, and short of, news from Britain. Alba's dispatches had a wider circulation than even the Spaniards knew, for they were regularly read by the British secret service who surreptitiously opened, and inspected, the contents of the Spanish diplomatic bag, while it was *en route* between London and Madrid. Tampering with the diplomatic bags of all the neutral states was a common enough espionage practice of British wartime intelligence, but Alba's diplomatic communications posed a particular and, indeed, insoluble problem for the Iberian sub-section of S.I.S.'s section V, as the then sub-section chief, Kim Philby has admitted:

> We had regular access to the Spanish diplomatic bag, and from it learnt that Alba periodically sent to Madrid despatches on the British political scene of quite exceptional quality. As we had no doubt that the Spanish Foreign Ministry would make them available to their German allies, these despatches represented a really serious leakage. Yet there was nothing that could be done. There was no evidence that the Duke had obtained his information improperly. He simply moved with people in the know and reported what they said, with shrewd commentaries of his own. For some time, MI5 toyed with the idea of using him as a channel for deception. But his informants were just too high up. They included such people as Brendan Bracken, Beaverbrook, even Churchill himself; they could scarcely stoop to trickery with a grandee of Spain. So there we had to leave it, cherishing a single hope. Alba's reports maintained a tone wholly friendly to Britain. It was possible that Hitler would dismiss him as an incurable Anglophile. After all he was Duke of Berwick too.' (Philby, *My silent war*, pp. 60–1, 91.)

103 363 H.C., DEB 5s. cols. 1209–10.
104 CAB 65/8, WM 202 (40) 3.
105 Medlicott, *Economic blockade*, I, 535; Herbert Feis, *The Spanish story: Franco and the nations at war* (New York, 1948), 1966 edn., pp. 37–46; FO 837/716, S 4/20; Bert Allan Watson, *United States–Spanish Relations, 1939–1946*, unpublished Ph.D., (The George Washington University, Washington, D.C., 1971), pp. 45–7.
106 Templewood, *Ambassador*, pp. 48–9.
107 Hoare to E. M. Thomson, 24 September 1940, Templewood Papers, XIII, 2. See also, Hoare to Sir Clive Liddell, 22 July 1940, ibid.

108 Aznar's article in *Arriba*, 31 May 1940, was entitled 'Politíca de Inglaterra y España, Gibraltar, Honor y Deber de los Españoles'; FO 371/24514, C 6385/113/41; Detwiler, *Hitler, Franco und Gibraltar*, p. 18, quoting a report of the German Ambassador, von Stohrer, of 6 May 1940, to Berlin.

109 *Arriba*, 31 May 1940.

110 PREM 3/199.

111 Woodward, *British foreign policy*, I, 436. I have been forced to rely on Woodward's account of the Cabinet meeting (W.M. 171 (40)5), as the official record is, at present, not open to research.

112 Ibid., p. 436.

113 PREM 3/199.

114 Ibid.

115 Ibid.

116 Ibid.

117 The text of the minute was recorded in Hansard, at H.C. DEB. 5s, vol. 527. col. 2290. Churchill had already published the substance of this minute in his *Their finest hour*, American edn., p. 640. For reports on the Spanish allegations, see *The Times*, 22 February, 17 May 1954.

118 PREM 3/199.

119 Ibid.

120 Halifax to Hoare, 26 September 1940, Templewood Papers, XIII, 20; FO 371/24512, C 10486/75/41; FO 371/26906, C 4508/46/41. The Spanish Ambassador in London, the Duke of Alba, reported to Madrid on 8 July 1940, that the British Parliamentary Under-Secretary of State for Foreign Affairs, R. A. Butler, had assured him a few days earlier that England was prepared 'to consider later all Spain's problems and aspirations, including that of Gibraltar' (Alba's dispatch No. 719, 8 July 1940, legajo R. 985, E.8, M.A.E.). See, also, R. Rodríguez-Moñino Soriano, *La misión diplomática del XVII Duque de Alba en la Embajada de España en Londres* (Valencia, 1971), p. 63).

121 *The Times*, 22 May 1954.

122 Charles R. Halstead, 'Un "Africain" Méconnu: le Colonel Juan Beigbeder', *Revue d'Histoire de la Deuxième Guerre Mondiale*, 21 (1971), 32–3. He also quotes Franco as making the following statement: 'I could only, with difficulty, understand my own reactions, or understand those of my companions-in-arms without taking account of Africa.' (p. 33.)

123 Serrano Suñer, *Memorias*, p. 285.

124 Templewood, *Ambassador*, p. 50; Templewood Papers, XIII, 12. For an evaluation of Beigbeder's performance as *franquista* High Commissioner in Spanish Morocco, see Charles R. Halstead, 'A "somewhat machiavellian" face: Colonel Juan Beigbeder as High Commissioner in Spanish Morocco, 1937–39', *The Historian*, 37 (1974), no. 1, pp. 46–66; Eccles (ed.), *By safe hand*, p. 75.

125 D.D.I., 9th Series, V, 33–4.

126 Halstead, 'Un "Africain",' pp. 42–3, 57; FO 371/24515, C 7281/113/41; F. Charles-Roux, *Cinq mois tragiques aux affaires étrangères (21 mai–1 novembre 1940)* (Paris, 1949), pp. 224–47. The Spanish historical claim to a greater share of Morocco was based on the fact that the zone eventually coming under Spanish 'supervision' and 'protection' by the

Franco-Spanish Treaty of 1912 was substantially less than that originally allocated to Spain under both the proposed Franco-Spanish treaty of 1902 and the secret Franco-Spanish agreement of 1904. However, the Spanish had only been drawn very reluctantly into a Moroccan commitment by the vigour of French expansion there (Stanley G. Payne, *Politics and the military in modern Spain* (Stanford, 1967), pp. 102–15; Crozier, *Franco*, p. 38).

127 Saña, *El Franquismo*, pp. 168–70.

128 Templewood, *Ambassador*, pp. 51–2; CAB 65/7, WM 151 (40)3, WM 152 (40)4, WM 166(40)8; FO 371/24514, C 6738/113/41; Halstead, 'Un Africain', pp. 41–2; D.D.I. 9th Series, V, 32–3.

129 Halifax to Hoare, 8 July 1940, Templewood Papers, XIII, 20. Cadogan, Permanent Under-Secretary of State for Foreign Affairs, argued, in a minute of 7 July 1940, to Lord Halifax that Britain should not encourage Spanish encroachment in French Morocco, whilst it still entertained hopes of a Gaullist resistance movement emerging there (FO 800/323).

130 Hoare to Beaverbrook, 23 July 1940, Templewood Papers, XIII, 20. Beaverbrook had given tangible expression to his belief in Hoare's political merits by presenting him with three cheques to the total of £6,000 between November 1938 and November 1939, to relieve the latter's financial worries (A. J. P. Taylor, *Beaverbrook* (London, 1972), 1974 edn., pp. 498–9, 501–2. See also, Cross, *Hoare*, pp. 291–3; Beaverbrook to Hoare, 22 November 1938, Templewood Papers, X, 3; Hoare to Beaverbrook, 29 May 1940, Beaverbrook Papers, C/308). However, Beaverbrook was neither convinced by Hoare's letter, nor by Halifax's Cabinet contribution (referred to in note 132) of the desirability of British involvement in the dismemberment of French North Africa. 'Everything', he wrote to Hoare, 'depends on . . . our future relations with the French . . . The situation is too complex and too fluid.' (Beaverbrook to Hoare, 29 July 1940, ibid.).

131 Eccles (ed.), *By safe hand*, p. 156.

132 CAB 65/8, WM 211(40)3.

133 FO 371/24453, C 9920/7277/28.

134 Hoare's dispatch no. 407, 13 September 1940, Templewood Papers, XIII, 20.

135 D.G.F.P., Series D, X, 99, footnote 1.

136 Dionisio Ridruejo, *Casi unas memorias* (Barcelona, 1976), p. 214.

137 The phrase is Mussolini's, in Mussolini to Franco, 25 August 1940, D.G.F.P., Series D, X, 542.

138 Templewood Papers, XIII, 2 (Hoare's dispatch no. 407 of 13 September 1940).

139 D.G.F.P., Series D, X, 99–100. The Spanish were still seeking such a reduction in August (515). See also, D.D.I., 9th Series, X, 295, 576–7.

140 Robert O. Paxton, *Vichy France, Old Guard and New Order, 1940–1944* (London, 1972), p. 81. According to Portugal's Prime Minister, Oliveira Salazar, Serrano Suñer had also urged Franco to occupy French Moroccan cities at the same time as Tangier, in June 1940, and wanted a forward policy in Africa when France's defeat became apparent (D.A.P.E., VII, 434, 453).

141 D.G.F.P., Series D, IX, 526, note 2; D.G.F.P. Series D, X, 160.

142 Franco to Mussolini, 15 August 1940, D.G.F.P., Series D, X, 484–6. Mussolini to Franco, 25 August 1940, 542.
143 Templewood Papers, XIII, 20, (Hoare's dispatch no. 407 of 13 September 1940). See, also, FO 371/24453, C 9920/7277/28; D.D.I., 9th Series, V, 557–8; and Dispatch no. 64 of the Conde de Artaza (Spanish Consul in Newcastle-upon-Tyne), 6 September 1940, legajo R.5165, E 10, M.A.E.
144 CAB 80/56 C.O.S. (40)3(o), Annex I. See also, J. R. M. Butler *Grand Strategy*, II (London, 1957), 313.
145 Harvey diaries, 8 September 1940, Add. 56397.
146 Hoare to Churchill, 27 August 1940, Templewood Papers, XIII, 16. On the same day Beigbeder 'once again showed his great anxiety' about Morocco in conversation with Hoare (FO 371/24516, C 9342/113/41).
147 Templewood Papers, XIII, 16. See, also, D.A.P.E., VII, 411.
148 Hoare to Halifax, 16 September 1940, Halifax Papers, FO 800/323; FO 371/24511, C 10330/75/41. See too, the conversation between the Duke of Alba and R. A. Butler, 26 September 1940, FO 371/24512, C 10258/75/41. See also, FO 371/24516, C 9648/113/41, and FO 371/24511, C 9913/75/41. Salazar also advised the Portuguese Ambassador in London, on 21 September 1940, that a British-inspired Moroccan revolt would embroil them in hostilities with the Spaniards. His warning was relayed to Halifax on 24 September (D.A.P.E., VII, 434–5, 451–4).
149 CAB 66/12, W.P. (40)382. See also, Hillgarth's 12 September report to the Director of Naval Intelligence, FO 371/24516, C 10146/113/41. Captain Hillgarth confirmed that he had discussed the note for Churchill with Hoare before dispatching it, in my interview with him on 27 January 1977.
150 Arthur Marder, *Operation 'Menace': the Dakar expedition and the Dudley North affair* (London, 1976), pp. 62–3; CAB 84/18, J.P. 430(40); PREM 3/431, C.O.S. (40)696; PREM 3/431, C.O.S. (40)3(o); PREM 7/3.
151 CAB 84/19, J.P. (40)463.
152 Ibid.
153 Churchill, *Their finest hour*, American edn., p. 487.
154 FO 371/24511, C 10372/75/41. See, also, D.A.P.E., VII, 453–4, 467. Serrano Suñer told the Germans of this British move which he interpreted as indicating 'visible weakness on the part of England and possibly even the beginning of an inclination towards peace' (D.G.F.P. Series D, XI, 182).
155 FO 371/24511, C 10372/15/41; PREM 4/21/2A. See also, F.R.U.S., 1940, II, 810.
156 Eccles (ed.), *By safe hand*, p. 157.
157 Halifax to Hoare, 27 August 1940, Templewood Papers, XIII, 20; Templewood Papers, XXIII, 1.

3. Opposition

1 Dilks (ed.), *Cadogan diaries*, p. 334.
2 Quoted by Watkins, *Britain divided*, p. 118.
3 Halifax to Hoare, 24 September 1940, FO 371/24510, C 6473/75/41.
4 364 H.C. DEB. 5s, cols. 1199–1200.
5 FO 371/24511, C 9159/75/41; Hoare to Beaverbrook, 6 September 1940, Templewood Papers, XIII, 17. For an example of Spanish reaction to, and

use of, this article, see the *Arriba* editorial, 'A Cara Descubierta', 4 September 1940.

6 FO 371/24511, C 9159/75/41; Hoare to Halifax, 12 September 1940, Templewood Papers, XIII, 20; Hoare to Halifax, 30 July 1940, FO 371/ 24510, C 6473/75/41. As early as 21 and 22 June 1940, Hoare felt constrained to deny to both Franco and Beigbeder that Britain was plotting to overthrow their government (FO 371/24515, C 7281/113/41).

7 PREM 4/21/2A; FO 371/24511, C 9159/75/41; FO 371/24512, C 10573/ 75/41; Hickleton Papers, A7.8.6: Halifax Diary, 23 October 1940. See, also, Sonia Orwell and Ian Angus (eds.), *The collected essays, journalism and letters of George Orwell* (4 vols., London, 1968), II, *My country right or left, 1940–1943,* 1970 edn., 429, War-time diary: 1940, 23 November.

8 Halifax to Sinclair, 29 July 1940, PREM 4/21/2A; Halifax to Hoare, 24 September 1940, FO 371/24510, C 6473/75/41. See also, Sinclair to Halifax, 30 July 1940, PREM 4/21/2A.

9 Hoare to E. J. Robertson (of the *Daily Express*), 27 July 1940, Templewood Papers, XIII, 2.

10 Orwell and Angus (eds.), *Essays,* II, 402, War-time diary: 1940, 24 June.

11 *News Chronicle,* 30 September 1940.

12 Harold J. Laski, *Where do we go from here? an essay in interpretation* (Harmondsworth, 1940), pp. 38–9.

13 FO 371/24511, C 10117/75/41.

14 (London, 1940), pp. 115, 117–18.

15 365 H.C. DEB 5s, col. 1304. For the significance of the demand for a declaration of war aims and the people's war concept in the context of the apparently general swing leftwards in British public opinion after Dunkirk, see Paul Addison, *The road to 1945, British politics and the Second World War* (London, 1975), 1977 edn., pp. 103–63.

16 Eccles (ed.), *By safe hand,* p. 139.

17 John Colville, *Footprints in time* (London, 1976), p. 149.

18 Dilks (ed.), *Cadogan diaries,* p. 338.

19 Forrest's article was entitled 'The Spanish people are our allies'. On 1 October 1941, the Labour M.P., J. C. Wedgwood, sought in the course of parliamentary questioning to secure British intervention with the Vichy French Government over the plight of former members of the International Brigades who had been interned in France. He justified his case for British concern on 'the fact that these International Brigades fought for our cause' (374 H.C. DEB 5s, cols. 554–5).

20 *100,000,000 allies,* p. 35.

21 (London, 1940), p. 120.

22 Attlee to Halifax, 30 October 1940, Halifax Papers, FO 800/323. See also, Harvey diaries, 24 November 1940, Add. 56397.

23 Hoare to Sir Walter Layton (of the *News Chronicle*), 4 July 1940, Templewood Papers, XIII, 2.

24 Paul Addison, *The road to 1945,* 1977 edn., pp. 121–6.

25 Joseph P. Lash, *Roosevelt and Churchill, 1939–1941: the partnership that saved the west* (London, 1977), pp. 280–1.

26 Edwards, *British government,* p. 199; Hugh Dalton, *The fateful years: memoirs, 1931–1945* (London, 1957), pp. 98–100.

27 Butler to Hoare, 20 July 1940, Templewood Papers, XIII, 17.

28 Alba to Beigbeder, 27 August 1940, legajo R. 985, E. 12, M.A.E.
29 Hoare to Halifax, 10 September 1940, Halifax Papers, FO 800/323; FO 371/24527, C 7501/9501/41; FO 371/24511, C 8570/75/41; Hoare to Halifax, 30 July 1940, FO 371/24510, C 6473/75/41; Hoare to Halifax, 12 September 1940, FO 371/24511, C 10117/75/41; Dalton Papers, diary 23, 2 July 1940; CAB 65/8, WM 191(40)7; PREM 4/21/2A; PREM 7/2: Desmond Morton's minute to the Prime Minister, 9 August 1940.
30 This account of the July effort to induce Negrín to agree to leave Britain is based on the following: CAB 65/8, WM 191 (40) 7, WM 215 (40) 4; Halifax to Hoare, 17, 30 July 1940, Templewood Papers, XIII, 20; FO 371/24527, C 7501/7501/41; Dalton Papers, diary 23, 26 July 1940.
31 FO 371/24511, C 10117/75/41.
32 FO 371/24512, C 11460/G; FO 371/24508, C 11460/40/41.
33 Attlee to Halifax, 30 October 1940, Halifax Papers, FO 800/323.
34 CAB 65/10, WM 281 (40) 6. See also, Halifax to Dalton and Duff Cooper, 31 October 1940, FO 371/24508, C 11460/40/41 and Duff Cooper to Halifax, 4 November 1940, ibid.
35 CAB 65/10, WM 285 (40) 8; *The week*, no. 393, 20 November 1940.
36 FO 371/24513, C 12589/75/41.
37 Halifax to Hoare, 21 December 1940, Templewood Papers, XIII, 20.
38 365 H.C. DEB 5s, col. 1954.
39 Phillip Noel-Baker to Cadogan, 9 December 1940, FO 371/24512, C 1172/75/41.
40 See, e.g., FO 371/24513, C 12472/75/41.
41 Halifax to Hoare, 21 December 1940, Templewood Papers, XIII, 20.
42 Hickleton Papers, A7.8.6: Halifax diary, 1 November 1940.
43 Dalton Papers, Miscellaneous III (1929–40).
44 Dalton Papers, diary 23, 24 October 1940; Dalton Papers, diary 22, 16 May 1940.
45 Dalton to David Eccles, 27 August 1940, Halifax Papers, FO 800/323. This letter ended up in Halifax's hands because Hoare passed it on to the Foreign Secretary, protesting at the attitude contained therein, with an admonition not to let Dalton know that he had done so. Hoare's covering letter to Halifax included the following passage: 'You will see in the letter that he sneers at my efforts with the Spanish press as if I were the controller of the press here, whilst the last paragraph looks as if he was running a policy diametrically opposed to the line agreed with the Chiefs of Staff and the War Cabinet.' (Hoare to Halifax, 3 September 1940, Halifax Papers, FO 800/323.)
46 Although Dalton also admitted that he liked to tease Eccles. Dalton Papers, diary 23, 1 December 1940.
47 Sir John Lomax, *The diplomatic smuggler* (London, 1965), pp. 99, 108.
48 Eccles (ed.), *By safe hand*, pp. 15–16, 141.
49 Hillgarth's memorandum for Hoare, 2 June 1940, Templewood Papers, XIII, 2.
50 Hoare to Halifax, 16 July 1940, Halifax Papers, FO 800/323; Dalton was highly amused at Hoare's self-congratulatory tone in this 'scream of a letter' which Halifax had passed on to him (Dalton Papers, diary 23, 28 July 1940).
51 CAB 66/9, W.P. (40) 259; CAB 65/8, WM 202 (40) 3. Hoare did, however, object to the reversal of priorities suggested by Dalton in his policy,

which was to inform the Spaniards that they would be subject, along with the rest of the Western European seaboard, to a British blockade, but then to promise them reasonable quotas of imports and British help in filling the permitted rations. Hoare wanted to assure the Spanish Government of adequate supplies first, and then to seek reciprocal Spanish commitments to facilitate Britain's endeavour to deny materials to the Axis war effort (FO 371/25178, W 9109/5114/49; Hoare to Halifax, 16 July 1940, Halifax Papers, FO 800/323).

52 Hoare to Halifax, 16 July 1940, Halifax Papers, FO 800/323.
53 Hoare to Halifax, 23 July 1940, Templewood Papers, XIII, 20. See also Hoare to Chamberlain, 9 September 1940, Templewood Papers, XIII, 17.
54 Dalton Papers, Miscellaneous III, 1929–40. See also Dalton Papers, diary 23 for 31 August 1940. One of the M.E.W. spokesmen at an inter-departmental meeting on economic policy towards Spain, held on 20 June 1940, declared that his Ministry 'wanted at all costs to avoid a repetition of the Italian episode, and to prevent the building up of Spain's war potential' (FO 371/25178, W 9109/5114/49).
55 See, for example, Hoare to Halifax, 23 July 1940, Templewood Papers, XIII, 20. David Eccles was equally anxious to refute any assimilation of the Italian and Spanish cases. He informed his Ministry as follows: 'The present attitude of Spain towards the war is different from that of Italy in September last. Mussolini always wanted to fight on the side of Germany, Franco and his Generals do not. In the first case the policy of appeasement was a shockingly bad bet, that no punter of experience would have taken, in the second it is a sound proposition because horse and jockey want to win. I can say this now because I recorded this view on 10 September, 1939.' (Note on his Madrid visit by David Eccles, enclosed with his letter to Charles Stirling, M.E.W., 17 July 1940, FO 837/724, T.4/1, vol. I.) See, also, Eccles (ed.), *By safe hand*, p. 14.
56 Hoare to Halifax, 15 August 1940, FO 371/24508, C 8761/40/41.
57 Medlicott, *Economic blockade*, I, p. 530.
58 See, for example, Hoare to Halifax, 8 August 1940, Halifax Papers, FO 800/323; Hoare to Halifax, 12 August 1940, Templewood Papers, XIII, 20; Hoare to Halifax, 30 August 1940, Templewood Papers, XIII, 20; Hoare to Halifax, 3 September 1940, Halifax Papers, FO 800/323; FO 371/24516, C 9776/113/41.
59 FO 371/23508, C 8761/40/41.
60 Dalton Papers, diary 23, for 31 August 1940.
61 Ibid., 25 July 1940; Hoare to Halifax, 3 September 1940, Halifax Papers, FO 800/323.
62 Halifax to Hoare, 26 September 1940, Templewood Papers, XIII, 20.
63 Halifax to Dalton, 20 August 1940, FO 837/719, T. 4/14, I; Dalton to Halifax, 22 August 1940, ibid.; Dalton to Halifax, 1 September 1940, ibid.; Halifax to Dalton, 4 September 1940, ibid.; Dalton to Halifax, 5 September 1940, ibid.; Halifax to Dalton, 30 September 1940, ibid.; Dalton to Halifax, 4 October 1940, ibid.; Dalton Papers, diary 23, 28 July 1940.
64 Halifax to Hoare, 6 September 1940, Halifax Papers, FO 800/323. See, also, Halifax to Hoare, 23 August 1940, Templewood Papers, XIII, 20: We are watching the Ministry of Economic Warfare very jealously and shall do our best to prevent them making things too difficult for you. It is a physical effort

for Dalton to keep his hands off any ship on which he can lay them but he has not really, I think, behaved too badly over the particular concessions for which at your insistence I have pressed him.

65 Cadogan (writing on behalf of Halifax) to Hoare, 13 September 1940, Templewood Papers, XIII, 17.
66 Ibid., and Halifax to Hoare, 6 September 1940, Halifax Papers, FO 800/323.
67 FO 837/719, T. 4/14, vol. I.
68 The foregoing account is based on the following: FO 837/716, S 4/20, T. 4/291, vol. I; FO 837/726, T. 4/291, vol. II; FO 837/728, T.4/291, vol. III; Hoare to Halifax, 23 July 1940, Templewood Papers, XIII, 20; Halifax to Hoare, 27 August 1940, ibid.; FO 371/24508, C 876/40/41; Hoare to Halifax, 30 September 1940, Halifax Papers, FO 800/323; Hoare to Halifax, 6 September 1940, ibid.; Hoare to Chamberlain, 9 September 1940, Templewood Papers, XIII, 17; Dalton Papers, diary 23, 26 July 1940; Halifax to Hoare, 26 September 1940, Templewood Papers, XIII, 20; 'Annual Report: Spain', 1940–1, Annex B, Templewood Papers, XIII, 20; legajo R.2243, E.33, M.A.E.; legajo R.2246, E.56, E.75, M.A.E. Halifax to Hoare, 26 September 1940, Templewood Papers, XIII, 20, contains the following: 'the work that Eccles and Turner have been doing has been most useful not only at your end but also for its cumulative effect on Dalton's mind'. See, also, Medlicott, *Economic blockade*, I, pp. 534–8 and Eccles (ed.), *By safe hand*, p. 148.
69 Dalton Papers, Miscellaneous III.
70 FO 837/719, T. 4/14, vol. I.
71 Hoare to Halifax, 1 November 1940, Templewood Papers, XIII, 20.
72 CAB 66/11, W.P. (40) 362.
73 CAB 69/1, D.O. (40) 34th Mtg., Min. 1.
74 Dean Acheson, *Present at the creation: my years in the State Department* (London, 1970), p. 53.
75 Beaverbrook to Hoare, 5 September 1940, Templewood Papers, XIII, 17.
76 Halifax to Hoare, 17 July, 30 July, 15 August 1940, Templewood Papers, XIII, 20.
77 Churchill's personal minute of 29 September 1940, to Halifax, Halifax Papers, FO 800/323.
78 Lomax, *Diplomatic smuggler*, p. 76.
79 Dalton, *Fateful years*, pp. 96–7; Dalton Papers, diary 24, 26 February 1941.
80 Reviewing the response of some British governmental figures to Hoare's diplomatic endeavour in Madrid, near the end of 1940, Halifax noted that 'Winston has been very good about it' (Halifax to Hoare, 21 December 1940, Templewood Papers, XIII, 20).
81 The description of Churchill as a 'child of genius' occurred to many who encountered him. See, e.g., Dalton Papers, diary 23, 3 September 1940 and Hickleton Papers, A. 7.8.4, Halifax diary: 19 June 1940.
82 Dilks (ed.), *Cadogan diaries*, p. 54. See also, Harvey diaries, 15 January 1941, Add. 56397.
83 Halifax in conversation with Dalton, Dalton Papers, diary 23, 18 December 1940.

84 CAB 65/7, WM 178 (40) 4.
85 CAB 79/5, C.O.S. (40) 184th. Mtg., Min. 1, C.O.S. (40) 203rd. Mtg., Min.
    1 and Annex, C.O.S. (40) 218th Mtg., Min. 2; CAB 80/13, C.O.S. (40) 465
    (J.P.); CAB 80/14, C.O.S. (40) 501 (J.P.); CAB 66/9, W.P. (40) 265; Major-
    General Ismay's minute for the Prime Minister, 12 July 1940, PREM 3/
    361/1; D.O. (40) 46th Mtg., Min. 1, PREM 3/361/6A.
86 CAB 79/5, C.O.S. (40) 218th Mtg., Min. 2; CAB 66/9, W.P. (40) 265; S. W.
    Roskill, *The war at sea, 1939–1945* (3 vols., H.M.S.O., London, 1954–
    61), *History of the Second World War, United Kingdom Military Series*,
    edited by J. R. M. Butler, I (1954), 1976 edn., pp. 272–3.
87 CAB 80/13, C.O.S. (40) 465 (J.P.), C.O.S. (40) 474 (J.P.); CAB 80/14,
    C.O.S. (40) 501 (J.P.); CAB 79/5, C.O.S. (40) 203rd, Mtg., Min. 1 and
    Annex; CAB 66/9, W.P. (40) 265; Ismay's minute for the Prime Minister,
    12 July 1940, PREM, 3/361/1; CAB 66/10, W.P. (40) 277.
88 CAB 79/5, C.O.S. (40) 184th Mtg., Min. 1, C.O.S. (40) 218th Mtg., Min. 2;
    CAB 80/13, C.O.S. (40) 465 (J.P.); CAB 80/14, C.O.S. (40) 501 (J.P.);
    C.O.S. (40) 545 (J.P.); C.O.S. (40) 546 (J.P.); C.O.S. (40) 543; CAB 66/9,
    W.P. (40) 265.
89 For a review of 'The official British attitude to the Anglo-Portuguese
    alliance, 1910–1945' see Glyn A. Stone's article in the *J.C.H.*, 10 (1975),
    729–46. Stone stresses that the main value of this almost 600-year-old
    alliance, from the British viewpoint, lay particularly in the measure of
    assurance which it brought that the strategically-placed Portuguese
    Atlantic Islands would not fall into hostile hands.
90 Churchill, *Their finest hour*, p. 625.
91 CAB 65/14, WM 209 (40) 7, Confidential Annex.
92 Churchill's personal minute to Halifax, 24 July 1940, FO 371/24515, C
    7429/113/41.
93 My translation from the Portuguese and Spanish texts of the Additional
    Protocol contained in D.A.P.E., VII, 323–5.
94 FO 371/24494, C 10637, C 13107/4066/36.
95 Ibid.
96 D.A.P.E., VII, 251.
97 Halifax's advice was recorded by Dalton after a conversation: Dalton
    Papers, diary 23, 14 November 1940.
98 Halifax's personal minute to Churchill, 31 July 1940, PREM 3/361/1.
    The minutes on the question drawn up by members of the Foreign Office
    were forwarded in transcript with Halifax's 31 July minute and are
    located in PREM 3/361/1, originals in FO 371/24515, C 7429/113/41.
    Halifax had been quick to point out to Churchill, as early as 9 July, the
    political disadvantages – though, without referring to the negative
    impact upon Spain – of a premature *coup de main* against the Port-
    uguese Atlantic Islands, when apprised of the Chiefs of Staff's project for
    a preventive action, if active Spanish hostility seemed imminent.
    (Halifax's personal minute to Churchill, 9 July 1940, PREM 3/361/1.)
    Churchill agreed then that nothing should be done 'without a Cabinet
    decision' (ibid.).
99 For a subsequent commentator's positive assessment of Churchill's
    interventionism, see Patrick Cosgrave, *Churchill at war*, I, *Alone*,
    1939–40 (London, 1974), pp. 338–9. For a negative contemporary reac-

tion see a letter Lord Hankey – Britain's perennial bureaucrat – wrote, but did not send, to Hoare, because he decided it was too indiscreet: 11 November 1941, Hankey Papers, 4/32, and Hankey diary: 1/7, 28 April, 2 May, 6 May, 13 June 1941.

100 Hickleton Papers, A 7.8.4, Halifax diary: 30 May 1940.
101 See e.g., Colville, *Footprints in time*, p. 90.
102 CAB 79/11, C.O.S. (41) 147th Mtg., Min. 2; Lord Leathers' personal minute to Churchill, 18 September 1941, and Churchill's written comment thereupon, which was communicated to the Minister of War Transport, on 20 September 1941, PREM 3/361/1.

4. The Spanish scene

1 Hans-Adolf Jacobsen (ed.), *Generaloberst Halder, Kriegstagebuch, tägliche Aufzeichnungen des Chefs des Generalstabes des Heeres* (3 vols., Stuttgart, 1962–4), II, *Von der geplanten Landung in England bis zum Beginn des Ostfeldzuges* (1.7.1940–21.6.1941) (1963), 124.
2 Payne, *Falange*, p. 169.
3 CAB 66/12, W.P. (40) 382.
4 Thomas J. Hamilton, *Appeasement's child: the Franco regime in Spain* (London, 1943), pp. 78–80.
5 D.G.F.P., Series D, X, 99. Shortly before his recall from the French Embassy in Madrid to a doomed France, Marshal Pétain commented to United States Ambassador Weddell on the 'three-cornered fight', in progress in Spain, between the Requetés (Carlist militia), the Falange and the Generals. (Roosevelt Papers, President's Secretary's File: Spain: 1940).
6 D.G.F.P., Series D, X, 99; CAB 66/12, W.P. (40) 382.
7 Memorandum by the Royal Institute of International Affairs, of 28 November 1939, on 'The balance of forces in Spain', Templewood Papers, XIII, 1A; Payne, *Politics and the military*, pp. 427, 429.
8 Fred Taylor (ed.), *The Goebbels diaries 1939–1941* (London, 1982), pp. 162, 164.
9 Ibid., p. 160.
10 Halstead, 'A "somewhat Machiavellian" face', 65; D.G.F.P., Series D, X, 99. See also, ibid., 224, where von Stohrer speaks of the 'great tension' between Beigbeder and Serrano Suñer.
11 See, for instance, Hoare to Halifax, 6 Septemberr 1940, Halifax Papers, FO 800/323; Hoare's dispatch no. 395, 5 September 1940, Templewood Papers, XIII, 20; Hoare's dispatch no. 299, 11 July 1940, FO 371/24508, C 7817/40/41.
12 FO 371/49663, Z 11696/11696/41; Hoare's memorandum of 24 September 1940, PREM 4/21/1; Serrano Suñer, *Entre Hendaya y Gibraltar*, pp. 234, 246–8; idem, *Memorias*, p. 288. Serrano Suñer claims, in the latter volume of memoirs, that his belief in the certainty of a German victory was based, chiefly, on Franco's opinions whom he considered 'an infallible oracle on military questions'. Serrano Suñer maintains here, too, that despite 'believing blindly' in the coming German success, Franco and he were aware that the war would be long (*Memorias*). However, Beigbeder's contemporary assertion that Serrano Suñer was in

the vanguard of those expecting a speedy German success, seems a more likely reflection of the latter's attitude at that time. (Hoare's memorandum of 24 September 1940, PREM 4/21/1.) A conviction that the triumph of German arms was imminent was a logical complement to the view that such an eventuality was inevitable. Moreover, in a post-war conversation with a British diplomatic official, Serrano Suñer admitted that he – and most other Spaniards – operated after the fall of France, on the assumption that they were 'in sight of a German triumph' (FO 371/49663, Z 11696/11696/41). Serrano Suñer also impressed the Portuguese Ambassador, Pereira, as being convinced, after the fall of France, that the defeat of England was an 'accomplished fact'. (Pedro Theotonio Pereira, *Memórias* (Lisbon, 1973), II, 223, 227). See also, Heleno Saña, *El Franquismo sin mitos: conversaciones con Serrano Suñer* (Barcelona, 1982), p. 170.

13 Hoare to Halifax, 30 July 1940, FO 371/24510, C 6473/75/41. Beigbeder actually showed Alba's report to Hoare. Alba's dispatch no. 776, 22 July 1940, legajo R. 985, E. 8, M.A.E.

14 Halstead, 'Un "Africain" méconnu', 48; Pereira, *Memórias*, II, 222. On 10 August 1940, Beigbeder told the Portuguese Ambassador that he thought 'the war was going to be long' (D.A.P.E., VII, 358).

15 See, e.g., Gascoigne's telegram from Tangier, 11 July 1940, FO 794/19.

16 FO 371/24511, C 8526/75/41.

17 D.G.F.P., Series D, X, 514.

18 FO 371/24516, C 9648/113/41.

19 Hoare to Halifax, 6 September 1940, Halifax Papers, FO/800 323; Templewood, *Ambassador*, 66–7.

20 Crozier, *Franco*, pp. 417, 551, note 8. Serrano Suñer describes Beigbeder, in his *Memorias*, as a 'strange and singular person ... capable of a thousand insanities' (p. 266).

21 Hoare to Churchill, 27 August 1940, Templewood Papers, XIII, 16. Franco himself bore witness, in conversation with his cousin in January 1955, to the 'great friendship' shared by Beigbeder and Hoare, remarking that the former addressed the latter as 'Brother Samuel' (Franco Salgado-Araujo, *Mis conversaciones*, p. 67).

22 Hoare to Churchill, 27 August 1940, Templewood Papers, XIII, 16. See, also, Hoare's early July assessment of Beigbeder in FO 371/24508, C 7817/40/41.

23 Hoare's dispatch no. 395, 5 September 1940, Templewood Papers, XIII, 20.

24 Hoare to Halifax, 20 September 1940, Halifax Papers, FO 800/323.

25 Charles-Roux, *Cinq mois tragiques*, p. 242.

26 FO 371/24508, C 7817/40/41; FO 371/24510, C 6032/75/41.

27 See e.g., Halder, *Kriegstagebuch*, II, 79 (27 August 1940): '... Suñer der aber mehr italienisch gesinnt ist als deutsch', (Admiral Canaris in conversation with Halder); D.G.F.P., Series D, X, 98. The Duke of Alba also told R. A. Butler, on 12 October 1940, that Serrano Suñer was 'more pro-Italian than pro-German' (FO 371/24512, C 10892/75/41).

28 Templewood, *Ambassador*, pp. 57–8.

29 R.I.I.A. Memorandum on 'The balance of forces in Spain', Templewood Papers, XIII, 1a; Payne, *Falange*, pp. 160–1.

30 See, e.g. D.G.F.P., Series D, III, 848; Detwiler, *Hitler, Franco und Gibraltar*, p. 153. For the British (presumably Hoare's) vituperative view of Serrano Suñer's political effectiveness consult the 'Annual Report: Spain', 1940–1, Templewood Papers, XIII, 20, where the Spanish Minister is described as 'deliberately ill-mannered, spitefully feminine, small-minded, fanatical, impetuous and desperately ill'.

31 Detwiler, *Hitler, Franco und Gibraltar*, p. 153; D.G.F.P., Series D, X, 97; XI, 40.

32 Walter Maxwell Scott to Halifax, 14 August 1939, Halifax Papers, FO 800/323; Detwiler, *Hitler, Franco und Gibraltar*, p. 153; D.G.F.P., Series D, X, 97; XI, 40; Payne, *Politics and the military*, p. 429; Saña, *El Franquismo*, p. 78.

33 Halder, *Kriegstagebuch*, II, 159; cf. FO 371/24509 C 13170/40/41, where a British official describes Serrano Suñer as 'the best hated man in Spain'.

34 Payne, *Falange*, pp. 227–31.

35 See, e.g., FO 371/26939, C 4400, C 4369, C 6882/222/41; FO 371/26905, C 4802/46/41.

36 CAB 66/12, W.P. (40) 382.

37 Halder, *Kriegstagebuch*, II, 79, 159.

38 FO 371/24516, C 8442/113/41.

39 FO 371/24508, C 10874/40/41; Hoare to Halifax, 1 October 1940, Halifax Papers, FO 800/323.

40 Hoare's dispatch no. 187, 12 May 1941, FO 371/26897, C 5225/33/41.

41 FO 371/24508, C 7817/40/41.

42 Quoted by *The Times*, 3 October 1940.

43 FO 371/24513, C 10188/112/41. By November 1940, the Ministry of Agriculture was informing the German Embassy that their most recent estimate of the Spanish harvest was 2,300,000 tons which, with 500,000 tons reserved for seed grain and 550,000 tons retained by the grain farmers for their domestic needs, would leave a deficit of 1,250,000 tons (D.G.F.P., Series D, XI, 574). By April 1941, the British were informed by the Spanish Director General of Agriculture that the harvest for 1940 had amounted to 2,161,284 tons (FO 837/738F, T 4/264: 'Report on Wheat Situation in Spain' enclosed with H. Ellis-Rees to C. N. Stirling, 15 April 1941).

44 FO 371/24513, C 13108/75/41; David Avery, *Not on Queen Victoria's birthday: the story of the Río Tinto mines* (London, 1974), p. 383; FO 371/24509, C 12016/40/41; FO 371/24513, C 13604/75/41.

45 FO 371/24509, C 12016/40/41.

46 Lomax, *Diplomatic smuggler*, p. 67; FO 837/738F, T. 4/264.

47 FO 371/24509, C 11811/40/41.

48 FO 371/24509, C 12016/40/41.

49 D.G.F.P., Series D, XI, 848; Hoare to C. G. Lang, Archbishop of Canterbury, 30 December 1940, Templewood Papers, XIII, 2; FO 371/24506, C 13776/30/41.

50 Burdick, *Germany's military strategy*, p. 110.

51 D.G.F.P., Series D, XI, 848; F.R.U.S., 1940, II, 842; FO 371/24513, C 1289/112/41.

52 Avery, *Not on Queen Victoria's birthday*, p. 383.

53 Larry Collins and Dominique Lapierre, *Or I'll dress you in mourning: the extraordinary rise of El Cordobés* (London, 1969), 1973 edn., p. 103. The scope of the human tragedy may be indicated by quoting the passage preceding the sentence cited in the text:

> You can never understand if you've never been hungry. The hunger we had in those days after the war – sometimes even now I cry when I think about it. Then that was all you could do for it, cry. You cried when you went to bed at night because there was nothing for you to eat, and you cried in the morning when you got up because there was still nothing to eat. Your stomach hurt so much you couldn't stand up straight. People fell down and died, just like that, in the streets ... then. You could see them lying there with their bellies all swollen up. They died because they had nothing to eat, but their stomachs were all swollen up as though they'd eaten too much (pp. 102–3).

See also pp. 100–2; Ronald Fraser, *In hiding: the life of Manuel Cortés* (London, 1972), pp. 24–5; *The Pueblo: a mountain village on the Costa del Sol* (London, 1973), p. 77.

54 FO 371/24509, C 12016/40/41. See also, Raymond Carr and Juan Pablo Fusi Aizpurua, *Spain: dictatorship to democracy* (London, 1979), pp. 49–50.

55 *The Times*, 1 February 1941.

56 D.G.F.P., Series D, XI, 575.

57 Stanley G. Payne, *Franco's Spain* (London, 1968), p. 58. See also, Josep Fontana and Jordi Nadal, 'Spain, 1914–1970', in Carlo M. Cipolla (ed.), *The Fontana economic history of Europe*, vol. 6, *Contemporary economies*, Part Two (London, 1976), pp. 504–5.

58 FO 371/24516, C 9648/113/41.

59 FO 371/24509, C 12016/40/41.

60 FO 371/24513, C 13604/75/41.

61 FO 371/24509, C 12016/40/41.

62 FO 371/24509, C 11811/40/41.

63 FO 371/24509, C 12016/40/41.

64 Eccles (ed.), *By safe hand*, p. 149.

65 Hamilton, *Appeasement's child*, pp. 130–1.

66 *The Times*, 31 December 1940.

67 Hamilton, *Appeasement's child*, p. 119; 'Report on wheat situation in Spain', enclosed with Ellis Rees to Stirling, 15 April 1941, FO 837/738F, T 4/264.

68 Carr and Fusi, *Spain*, p. 50; Avery, *Not on Queen Victoria's birthday*, p. 383; *The Times*, 31 December 1940; 'Report on wheat situation in Spain', enclosed with Ellis Rees to Stirling, 15 April 1941, FO 837/738F, T 3/264; Collins and Lapierre, *El Cordobés*, pp. 98, 100–1.

69 D.G.F.P., Series D, IX, 605.

70 See, for instance, D.G.F.P., Series D, X, 445, 463, 562, and Series D, XI, 575–6.

71 D.G.F.P., Series D, XI, 39.

72 Walter Schellenberg, *The Schellenberg memoirs* (London, 1956), pp. 134–5.

73 Halder, *Kriegstagebuch*, II, 79.

74 D.G.F.P., Series D, IX, 621; and Series D, X, 443, 499–500, 521, 561.

75 See, for instance, George Hills, *Franco: the man and his nation* (London, 1967), pp. 343–51, and Crozier, *Franco*, pp. 313–14. Trythall, too, argues that Franco's enthusiasm for entering the war had evaporated, by July 1940 (Trythall, *Franco*, pp. 164–7).

76 Lomax, *Diplomatic smuggler*, pp. 103–4.

77 Peterson, *Both sides of the curtain*, pp. 229–30. Peterson's expression of the view, in his post-war memoirs, that Spain's internal weakness ensured its neutrality irrespective of British diplomatic endeavour, was hardly unconnected with his bitterness at being removed from the Madrid Embassy, and his consequent reluctance to acknowledge any possible contribution made by his successor to the maintenance of Spanish non-belligerency. From his wartime post, as Controller of Overseas Publicity at the Ministry of Information, Peterson could never resist sniping at the official conduct of policy towards Spain whenever he was consulted over its routine implementation.

78 McLachlan, *Room 39*, p. 193.

79 Eccles (ed.), *By safe hand*, pp. 102–3.

80 Serrano Suñer, *Memorias*, p. 348.

5. Strategic diplomacy: Septembe–October, 1940

1 Hans Umbreit, 'Die Rückkehr zu einer indirekten Strategie gegen England', in *Das Deutsche Reich und der Zweite Weltkrieg*, II, Hans Umbreit, Klaus A. Maier, Horst Rohde, Bernd Stegemann, (eds.), *Die Errichtung der Hegemonie auf dem europäischen Kontinent* (Stuttgart, 1979), p. 409; MacGregor Knox, *Mussolini unleashed, 1939–1941: politics and strategy in fascist Italy's last war* (Cambridge, 1982), pp. 181–2; Gerhard L. Weinberg, *World in the balance: behind the scenes of World War II*, (London, 1981), pp. 16–17.

2 Umbreit, 'Die Rückkehr', pp. 409–10.

3 Ibid., p. 412.

4 D.G.F.P., Series D, X, 396.

5 Halder, *Kriegstagebuch*, II, 79; F.C.N.A., p. 134.

6 D.G.F.P., Series D, X, 514; Percy E. Schramm (ed.), *Kriegstagebuch des Oberkommandos der Wehrmacht (Wehrmachtführungsstab)* (4 vols., Frankfurt am Main, 1961–5), I, Hans-Adolf Jacobsen (ed.), *1 August 1940–31 December 1941* (1965), p. 48.

7 D.G.F.P., Series D, X, 97–8, 349; XI, 38, 40; Halder, *Kreigstagebuch*, II, 79.

8 FO 371/24516, C 9648/113/41.

9 Herbert Feis, *The Spanish Story: Franco and the nations at war*, pp. 57–8.

10 FO 371/24516, C 10395/113/41. Indeed, on Serrano Suñer's return to Madrid, he was informed by the German security service that one of the Spaniard's junior secretaries, Latre, who had accompanied him on the trip to Berlin, was spying for the British Embassy. However, another more senior member of Serrano Suñer's entourage in Berlin, Dionisio Ridruejo, did not consider this fact to be a major breach of security since 'the complaints of the principal negotiator were much more abundant than his revelations' during their time in Berlin (Dionisio Ridruejo, *Casi unas memorias* (Barcelona, 1976), p. 216).

11 Richthofen diary, cited by Burdick, *Germany's military strategy and Spain*, p. 43.
12 FO 371/24516, C 10395/113/41.
13 D.G.F.P., Series D, X, 463–4.
14 Interview with Charles Favrel, *Paris-Presse*, 26 October 1945, FO 371/ 49663, Z 13272/11696/41. The British Embassy in Madrid was informed, at the time of the publication of the interview that Serrano Suñer, called to account by Franco over it, was obliged to repudiate its authenticity. Serrano Suñer, however, had personally admitted that the interview was genuine in the presence of a member of the British Embassy (ibid.). The assessment of the Favrel interview contained in Serrano Suñer's first volume of memoirs, *Entre Hendaya y Gibraltar*, published in May 1947, is rather ambiguous:

> Without my authorisation, without (my) knowing about his work, or much less correcting it, he published a few articles in which there are many things from amongst those which I said to him, although, almost always, with neither the nuances nor the chiaroscuro of my words which he could pick up (only) with great difficulty; with an infinity of errors, sometimes doubtless involuntary, but at others with deliberate distortions (p. 323).

15 Saña, *El Franquismo*, p. 170.
16 *Arriba*, 17 September 1940.
17 Ibid.
18 Serrano Suñer, *Memorias*, p. 285.
19 Ibid., p. 322.
20 Glen T. Harper, *German Economic Policy in Spain during the Spanish Civil War 1936–1939* (Paris, 1967), passim; D.G.F.P., Series D XI, 90, 155, 172–3, 183–4, 213–15, 251, 329–30, 380, 582; Franco to Serrano Suñer, 21 September 1940, in Serrano Suñer, *Memorias*, p. 337.
   In conversation with Italian Foreign Minister Ciano, on 28 September 1940, Hitler expressed his resentment at the disdainful tone adopted by the Spaniards towards the German claim for repayment for their aid during the civil war: 'When now the Germans demand the payment of the 400 million debt incurred during the Spanish Civil War, this is often interpreted by the Spanish as a tactless confusing of economic and idealistic considerations, and as a German, one feels toward the Spanish almost like a Jew, who wants to make business out of the holiest possessions of mankind.' (D.G.F.P., Series D, XI, 213). Hitler spoke in almost identical terms to Mussolini, on 4 October 1940 (Ibid., 251).
21 Franco to Serrano Suñer, 23 September 1940, in Serrano Suñer, *Memorias*, p. 342.
22 Ibid., pp. 341–2; also p. 343, Franco to Serrano Suñer, 24 September 1940.
23 Ibid., p. 340, Franco to Serrano Suñer, 21 September 1940.
24 This ambivalence in Spanish policy may also, of course, have been due to Franco's unwillingness to reveal his real diplomatic intentions to others in government, or to a desire to disguise that intent, or even to sheer lack of centralised administrative direction.
25 See, e.g., D.G.F.P., Series D, XI, 86, 96–7.
26 FO 371/24516, C 10395/113/41.
27 Ibid.; cf. D.G.F.P., Series D, XI, 90.
28 D.G.F.P., Series D, XI, 90, 97.

29 Ibid., 106–7.
30 Ibid., 84–5, 96–7, 100–101, 118, 135, 168–72, 201–3. In conversation with Mussolini in Florence, on 28 October 1940, Hitler told him that Spain's territorial demands also included French Catalonia and 'an enlargement of Spanish Guinea' (ibid., 420).
31 Muggeridge (ed.), *Ciano's diary*, p. 295.
32 Franco to Serrano Suñer, 21 September 1940, in Serrano Suñer, *Memorias*, p. 335.
33 D.G.F.P., Series D, XI, 168; Franco to Hitler, 22 September 1940, ibid., 153.
34 Ibid., 155.
35 Ibid., 171–2. See also, ibid., 183–4.
36 Ibid., 90, 172–3, 183–4, 214–19. See also, ibid., 581–2. Hoare, along with Brendan Bracken, had hit upon the idea of transferring control of the massive Río Tinto enterprise from its British owners to Spanish capitalists. On his arrival in Madrid, he had been reminded by shouting demonstrators that not only Gibraltar but also Río Tinto was Spanish. However, a British approach does not seem to have been made to the Spanish Government until the summer of 1941 and, even then, the Spaniards could not agree on terms with the company. The Spanish takeover did not in fact, occur until long after the Second World War (Hoare to R. A. Butler, 22 June 1940, Templewood Papers, XIII, 17; Avery, *Not on Queen Victoria's Birthday*, p. 385).
37 Franco to Serrano Suñer, 21 September 1940, in Serrano Suñer, *Memorias*, pp. 335–7.
38 Ibid., pp. 334–5; also p. 341–2, Franco to Serrano Suñer, 23 September 1940.
39 Ibid., pp. 331, 335, 338, 342.
40 D.G.F.P., Series D, XI, 169, 197–200.
41 Ibid., 98.
42 Serrano Suñer, *Entre Hendaya y Gibraltar*, p. 265.
43 Ibid., p. 284.
44 Franco to Serrano Suñer, 21 September 1940, in Serrano Suñer, *Memorias*, p. 338.
45 D.A.P.E., VII, 519.
46 Halder, *Kriegstagebuch*, II, 100.
47 Ibid., p. 124.
48 Knox, *Mussolini unleashed*, pp. 183–4.
49 D.G.F.P., Series D, XI, 104. See also, ibid., 373–4.
50 Ibid., 212–13.
51 Ibid., 212, 251–3, 374–9, 415, 603–4.
52 Norman Rich, *Hitler's War Aims* (2 vols., London, 1973–4), I (1973), 168–71. See also, Martin van Creveld, *Hitler's Strategy, 1940–41: The Balkan Clue* (London, 1973), pp. 33–4.
53 Muggeridge (ed.), *Ciano's diplomatic papers* (London, 1948), pp. 424–5. Actually, Mussolini's own attitude towards Spain's recruitment into the Axis was far from enthusiastic during the crucial months of September–October 1940, when the Germans broached the topic with him. (D.G.F.P., Series D, XI, 121, 214, 256, 333.) Von Weizsäcker was under the impression, by 25 October, that Mussolini was 'very unequivocal'

about not wanting Spain to be too close to the Axis 'for the present' *Die Weizsäcker-Papiere, 1933–1950*, L. E. Hill ed., Frankfurt, 1974, p. 221). The Duce, doubtless, wanted to preserve his privileged place as Hitler's foremost ally without any competition from Franco (van Creveld, *Hitler's Strategy*, p. 46). Again, Franco's and Mussolini's territorial designs on French North Africa were not readily compatible.

54 D.G.F.P., Series D, XI, 598–9; Hitler to Mussolini, 20 November 1940, ibid., 641; van Creveld, *Hitler's strategy*, pp. 57–60, 73, 82–4, 92–4.

55 Woodward, *British foreign policy*, I, 437. The original Cabinet paper, W.P. (40) 394 is closed to research, at present.

56 Halifax to Hoare, 26 September 1940, Templewood Papers, XIII, 20.

57 Woodward, *British foreign policy*, I, 437–8.

58 Hoare's memorandum, of 24 September 1940, PREM 4/21/1 and Halifax Papers, FO 800/323, copy in Templewood Papers, XIII, 20. This memorandum as printed in Hoare's *Ambassador on Special Mission*, pp. 67–71 is wrongly dated 27 September 1940. Hoare also excised from the version published in his memoirs, *inter alia*, the explicit declaration of Beigbeder's ambitions of territorial expansion at the expense of French Morocco, and omitted to mention his own support for the Minister's aspirations.

59 Ibid.

60 Hoare to Halifax, 23 September 1940, Halifax Papers, FO 800/323.

61 Halifax to Churchill, 28 September 1940, PREM 4/21/1.

62 Churchill's personal minute to Halifax, 29 September 1940, Halifax Papers, FO 800/323, copy in PREM 4/21/1.

63 The official record of the Cabinet meeting is closed to research at present, but the conclusions reached in the text are based on the following: Woodward's summary of its decisions, *British foreign policy*, I, 438 and Dalton's account in Dalton Papers, diary 23, 2 October 1940. See also, Halifax's personal telegram to Hoare, 5 October 1940 (No. 836), FO 371/24503, C 10661/30/41, copy in FO 837/719, T. 4/14, vol. 1, which was co-drafted by experts of the Foreign Office and the Ministry of Economic Warfare; Dalton to Halifax, 4 October 1940, FO 837 719, T. 4/14, vol. I; Eccles to Halifax 8 October 1940, FO 371/24503, C 10661/30/41; Hoare to Dalton, 10 October 1940, Templewood Papers, XIII, 17; Dalton Papers, Miscellaneous III; Hickleton Papers, A7.8.5: Halifax diary, 2 October 1940; Eccles (ed.), *By safe hand*, p. 163.

64 CAB 65/9, WM 266(40)7, WM 267(40)3.

65 FO 371/24512, C 10486/75/41.

66 Ibid. See, also, FO 371/26962, C 12048/1051/41.

67 FO 371/24512, C 10797/75/41; Dalton Papers, diary 23, 9 October 1940.

68 FO 371/24517, C 10639/113/41.

69 FO 371/24512, C 10486/75/41.

70 365 H. C. DEB, 5s, col. 302; Alba's telegram No. 586, 9 October 1940, legajo R. 985, E.6., M.A.E.

71 FO 371/24512, C 10892/75/41.

72 Cited by *The Times*, 18 October 1940.

73 CAB 65/9, WM 273(40)8.

74 Ibid.

75 FO 371/24516, C 10395/113/41.
76 Serrano Suñer, *Entre Hendaya y Gibraltar*, p. 266; D.G.F.P., Series D, XI, 258. The Vichy French Foreign Minister, Paul Baudouin, was also told by his Ambassador in Madrid that there had been a German demand for Beigbeder's removal from the Ministry of Foreign Affairs: '. . . Colonel Beigbeder's position seems in danger for it appears that Chancellor Hitler called for his dismissal after Serrano Suñer's visit to Berlin'. (*The private diaries of Paul Baudouin* (London, 1948), p. 257, 16 October 1940.) See also, Franco Salgado-Araujo, *Mis conversaciones privadas*, p. 12.
77 Hoare's memorandum of 18 October 1940, containing his reflections on, and reactions to, Beigbeder's fall from office was circulated amongst the War Cabinet by Halifax. There are copies of it in PREM 4/21/1, FO 371/24508, C 11259/40/41 and Templewood Papers, XIII, 20.
78 FO 371/24514, C 6738/113/41. See, also, D.A.P.E., VII, 337, where Pereira speaks of 'a certain indiscretion' as 'peculiar' to Beigbeder.
79 Walter Maxwell Scott to Halifax, 14 August 1939, Halifax Papers, FO 800/323.
80 FO 371/24517, C 10639/113/41.
81 Thus, Lord Halifax informed the War Cabinet on Monday, 21 October 1940, that General Franco, meeting with Hoare, 'had been at pains to explain that the ministerial changes meant no change in policy' (CAB 65/9, WM 274(40)3; FO 371 C 11166/30/41).
82 Hoare's 18 October 1940 memorandum, copies in: PREM 4/21/1; FO 371/24508, C 11259/40/41; Templewood Papers, XIII, 20.
83 Ibid., CAB 65/9, WM 274(40) 3.
84 Hoare's 18 October 1940, memorandum, copies in: PREM 4/21/1, FO 371 24508, C 11259/40/41, Templewood Papers, XIII, 20; Eccles (ed.), *By safe hand*, p. 171.
85 FO 371/24517, C 11790/113/41; FO 371/24508, C 11573/40/41.
86 Muggeridge (ed.), *Ciano's diplomatic papers*, P. 402.
87 Serrano Suñer, *Memorias*, pp. 300–1; D.G.F.P. Series D, XI, 466.
88 D.G.F.P., Series D, XI, 375–7, 383, 466.
89 Ibid., 374.
90 Ibid., 379.
91 Serrano Suñer, *Memorias*, p. 299. Franco's declaration, as recorded by Serrano Suñer, that Spain would not enter the war 'now' unless the Germans promised solid territorial gain in advance, may seem to imply that the Caudillo was still actively considering belligerency in the near future as late as the Hendaye conference. However, Serrano Suñer's general account of his leader's attitude and stance at that meeting contradicts this inference. The whole weight of evidence adduced in this chapter, also conflicts with the notion that Franco was still contemplating rushing into the war on Germany's side then. One may, perhaps, conclude that the adverb merely slipped into Serrano Suñer's recollection of his chief's statement.
92 D.G.F.P., Series D, XI, 420.
93 Serrano Suñer, *Memorias*, pp. 300–1. Franco expressed his anger and disgust at having to bow to German pressure in signing a protocol of alliance with the Axis, by cryptically remarking that 'it is necessary to have patience: today we are an anvil, tomorrow we will be a hammer' (ibid., p. 301).

94 D.G.F.P., Series D, XI, 466.
95 Ibid., 402. See also, 380, 383.
96 Franco to Hitler, 30 October 1940, in Serrano Suñer, *Memorias*, p. 304.
97 D.G.F.P., Series D., XI, 466.
98 Ibid., 415.
99 Hill (ed.), *Die Weizsäcker Papiere*, p. 218.
100 Burdick, *Germany's military strategy*, p. 63; D.G.F.P., Series D, XI, 452.
101 D.G.F.P., Series D, XI, 603.
102 Ibid.; R. T. Thomas, *Britain and Vichy: The dilemma of Anglo-French Relations, 1940–42* (London, 1979), p. 33.
103 Message from Beigbeder to Hoare, enclosed with Hoare to Halifax, 30 October 1940, Halifax Papers, FO 800/323.
   Beigbeder's information, too, tends to support the interpretation that at this time Hitler was not trying to get Spain into the war urgently (Spanish belligerency only becoming vital with the Italian disaster in Greece). He informed Hoare that 'Germany does not seem to be in a hurry for Spain to come into the war as her ally' (ibid.).
   The Portuguese did get wind of the Secret Protocol of Alliance between Spain, Germany and Italy (D.A.P.E., VII, 529).
104 FO 371/24517, C 12085/113/41; F.R.U.S., 1940, II, 802.
105 CAB 66/14, W.P. (40) 488; CAB 80/56, C.O.S. (41) 31 (o).
106 FO 371/24508, C 11460/40/41.
107 Ibid., Hoare to Halifax, 29 October 1940, enclosing a message from Beigbeder to Hoare, Halifax Papers, FO 800/323; Hoare to Halifax, 30 October 1940, enclosing a message from Beigbeder to Hoare, ibid.; Hoare to Halifax, 4 November 1940, ibid.; FO 371/24517, C 12295/113/41; Hoare to Churchill, 22 October 1940, Templewood Papers, XIII, 16.
108 FO 371/24508, C 11460/40/41.
109 CAB 80/56, D.O. (40) 37th Mtg., Min. 4.
110 PREM 3/405/1; CAB 80/106, C.O.S. (40) 30 (o) (J.P.). The paper was issued for the personal use of the Prime Minister. Churchill did not react kindly to the way in which the Joint Planning Staff regularly proved the impracticability of his successive, pet projects, and dubbed it 'the whole machinery of negation' (Sir John Wheeler-Bennett (ed.), *Action this day, working with Churchill* (London, 1968), pp. 195–6).
111 CAB 79/55, C.O.S. (40) 25th Mtg., Min. 1 (o).
112 FO 371/24517, C 12295/113/41.
113 Ibid.
114 Payne, *Politics and the Military*, p. 427.
115 Hoare to Halifax, 29 October 1940, Halifax Papers, FO 800/323, includes the following statement by the Ambassador: 'The big issue for London is whether or not it is possible to assist a Spanish national movement in the south of Spain. If it is, Beigbeder can be extremely useful. He is a great figure among the Moors and assuming that Muñoz Grandes is left in military command of Andalusia, he will have great influence with the Spanish Army.'
116 FO 371/24517, C 11145/113/41.
117 CAB 66/12, W.P. (40) 382.
118 FO 371/24508, C 11573/40/41.
119 FO 371/24512, C 11632/75/41.
120 FO 371/24509, C 12266/40/41. Hoare's telegram to the Foreign Office

recording the 'Chief of Staff's' declarations did not identify the General, but I assume that it was General Carlos Martínez Campos, Chief of Staff of the Army, rather than General Francisco Martín Moreno, Chief of the Supreme General Staff of the armed services.

121 FO 371/24509, C 13128/40/41; Eccles (ed.), *By safe hand*, p. 197.
122 FO 371/24509, C 13170/40/41. See also, D.A.P.E., VIII (Lisbon, 1973), 78.
123 See, e.g., PREM 4/21/2A; Gerald R. Kleinfeld and Lewis A. Tambs, *Hitler's Spanish legion: the Blue Division in Russia* (Carbondale, 1979), pp. 192–7, 228, 321–7, 311–13; and Norman Rich, *Hitler's war aims*, II (London, 1974), 403.
124 D.G.F.P., Series D, XI, 849.
125 CAB 66/12, W.P. (40) 382.
126 FO 371/24509, C 13170/40/41.
127 FO 371/24509 C 12266/40/41.
128 D.G.F.P., Series D, XI, 824–5.

6. Economic diplomacy: September–December, 1940

1 Cited by *The Times*, 18 October 1940.
2 *Arriba*, 19 October 1940; FO 371/24508, C 11493/40/41.
3 FO 371/24508, C 11493/40/41.
4 Churchill to Cardinal Hinsley, 3 November 1940, PREM 4/21/2A. This letter was almost entirely a draft by other hands which the Prime Minister accepted.
5 D.G.F.P., Series D, XI, 330–1.
6 Serrano Suñer, *Memorias*, p. 316, citing an article, 'Fue Pétain que nos salvo de la guerra', by Joaquín Satrústegui (*A.B.C.*, 26 May 1976).
7 D.G.F.P., Series D, IX, 605.
8 Feis, *Spanish Story*, p. 77.
9 D.G.F.P., Series D, X, 561, footnote 2. Italy was in no position to aid Spain economically either, due to the poor Italian harvest of 1940, as Mussolini explained to Serrano Suñer in Rome, on 1 October (D.D.I., 9th Series, V, 639).
10 D.G.F.P., Series D, XI, 106, 154.
11 Ibid., 598–9, 606, 641; van Creveld, *Hitler's strategy*, pp. 82–4; Rich, *Hitler's war aims*, I, 171–3; H. R. Trevor-Roper (ed.), *Hitler's war directives, 1939–1945* (London, 1964), 1966 edition, pp. 81–7.
12 Muggeridge (ed.), *Ciano's diplomatic papers*, pp. 408–9. See, also, D.G.F.P., Series D, XI, 606–7.
13 D.A.P.E., VII, 580.
14 Serrano Suñer, *Entre Hendaya y Gibraltar*, pp. 323–4; idem, *Memorias*, p. 306; D.G.F.P., Series D, XI, 599, 602, 605, 619–22.
15 D.G.F.P., Series D, XI, 602–5.
16 Ibid., 600–1, 619–20, 623; Serrano Suñer, *Entre Hendaya y Gibraltar*, p. 328.

In the course of Germany's attempt in early 1941 to entice Spain into the war, the bait of prior economic help in return for the surrender of Spain's freedom to decide when – and, so, if – to fight – was dangled again before Franco: 'If Spain entrusts to the Axis the determination of the date of Spain's entry into the war, Germany, as a preliminary service, is ready to make available to Spain before entry into the war . . . 100,000 tons of grain . . . and to supply further aid shipments out of German reserve stocks after entry into the war . . .' (D.G.F.P., Series D, XI, 1184).

Serrano Suñer's contention that he delivered at Berchtesgaden 'the most concrete and dramatic' of Spain's negative replies to Germany's demands that it enter the war or, at least, let German troops cross its territory (*Memorias*, p. 307) is not supported by either the contemporary German documents nor his own earlier account in *Entre Hendaya y Gibraltar*, pp. 325–39. The version of the Obersalzberg and Berchtesgaden meetings contained in the latter work is, for the most part, accurate, but it does fail to highlight the fact that the Germans demanded the right, which Serrano Suñer did not explicitly refuse, to determine the moment of Spain's entry into the war, in return for German economic aid.

Serrano Suñer's assertion that he gave Hitler a flat 'no' at the Berghof talk is also, of course, contradicted by the whole subsequent development of Hispano-German relations, up to the following 7 December, when Franco did definitively refuse to involve Spain in the war for the foreseeable future.

17 D.G.F.P., Series D, XI, 705.
18 Ibid., 739.
19 FO 371/26904, C 1620/46/41.
20 FO 371/24513, C 10188/112/41; FO 837/718, T. 4/264, vol. 1.
21 F.R.U.S., 1940, II, 805–8. A dispatch from David Eccles to Lord Drogheda, Joint Director in the Ministry of Economic Warfare, of 24 September 1940, seems to indicate that it was Eccles who suggested to the Spaniards the idea of seeking a loan from the United States (FO 837/719, T. 4/14, vol. I). See also, Eccles (ed.), *By safe hand*, p. 152.
22 FO 371/24513, C 9827/112/41.
23 Feis, *Spanish story*, pp. 57—8; F.R.U.S., 1940, II, 808–10; Cordell Hull, *The memoirs of Cordell Hull* (2 vols., London, 1948), I, 875.
24 FO 371/24513, C 10107/112/41, C 10188/112/41.
25 F.R.U.S., 1940, II, 810–17; Dalton Papers, diary 23, 7 October 1940; Hull, *Memoirs*, I, 875–6.
26 Feis, *Spanish story*, pp. 60–1; Allan Watson, *United States–Spanish relations*, p. 51.
27 Feis, *Spanish story*, pp. 61–2.
28 Ibid., pp. 65–6, 99; F.R.U.S., 1940, II, 822–3.
29 Sumner Welles to Roosevelt, 28 October 1940, Roosevelt Papers, File 307-A.
30 F.R.U.S., 1940, II, 824; Feis, *Spanish story*, p. 100.
31 F.R.U.S., 1940, II, 825–31; Charles R. Halstead, 'Diligent diplomat: Alexander W. Weddell as American Ambassador to Spain, 1939–1942', *The Virginia Magazine of History and Biography*, 82 (1974), no. 1, 19. See also, Decimal Files, Department of State (D.F.D.S.) National Archives, Washington, D.C., 852. 00/9536.
32 FO 371/24513, C 12249/112/41. He also declared that he alone favoured a trial policy. If so, he was a rather faint-hearted advocate: cf. his letter of 28 October to Roosevelt cited in the text above. See also, Harold. L. Ickes, *The secret diary of Harold L. Ickes*, III, *The lowering clouds, 1939–41* (London, 1955), 372–3.

33 F.R.U.S., 1940, II, 837.
34 Ibid., 821.
35 FO 371/24508, C 11493/40/41.
36 FO 371/24508, C 11573/40/41.
37 FO 371/24512, C 11615/75/41.
38 FO 371/24517, C 12075/113/41.
39 F.R.U.S, 1940, II, 834.
40 See, e.g., ibid., 828–9.
41 See, e.g., CAB 66/13, W.P. (40) 460, Annex; Hoare to Halifax, 8 November 1940, Halifax Papers, FO 800/323; Fred L. Israel (ed.), *The war diary of Breckinridge Long* (Lincoln, Nebraska, 1966), pp. 153–4, 162.
42 Cited by Lash, *Roosevelt and Churchill*, p. 214 and James MacGregor Burns, *Roosevelt: the lion and the fox, 1882–1940* (New York, 1956), p. 441.
43 F.R.U.S., 1940, II, 831–2; FO 371/24505, C 11573/40/41. Interestingly, Foreign Office telegram No. 2963 of 7 November 1940, to Butler, had advised the British Chargé d'Affaires in Washington, that the 'United States Government will no doubt themselves decide whether they wish to ask for any assurances beyond those already received from the Spanish Government in connection with these negotiations and if so what these assurances should be'. Butler, however, in the *aide-mémoire* which he left with the State Deparment, on 9 November, during a conversation with Sumner Welles, argued against seeking further such assurances, along the lines described in the text. In so doing, he was following the advice on this point contained in Hoare's telegram No. 947, 2 November 1940, to the Foreign Office, the major recommendations of which were generally accepted by the British Government, as Butler was informed (ibid.).
44 F.R.U.S., 1940, II, 833. See, also, Feis, *Spanish story*, p. 102; Harvey diaries, 11 November 1940, Add. 56397.
45 Medlicott, *Economic blockade*, I, 541.
46 FO 371/24513, C 12249/112/41.
47 FO 371/24505, C 12501/30/41. See, also, Eccles (ed.), *By safe hand*, p. 195.
48 FO 371/24513, C 12249/112/41; CAB 65/10, WM 291 (40) 3; F.R.U.S., 1940, II, 836.
49 FO 837/724, T., 4/1, vol. I; F.R.U.S, 1940, II, 836.
50 F.R.U.S., 1940, II, 839.
51 Eccles (ed.), *By safe hand*, p. 205.
52 CAB 66/13, W.P. (40), 460, Annexes I and II; FO 371/24505, C 12495/30/41.
53 CAB 80/23, C.O.S. (40), 965; CAB 66/13, W.P. (40) 460; CAB 65/10, WM 295 (40), 6; CAB 79/7, C.O.S. (40) 398th Mtg., Min. 2, C.O.S. (40) 299th Mtg., Min. 2; FO 371/23409, C 12866/40/41.
54 'Former Naval Person' to President Roosevelt, 23 November 1940, PREM 3/468.
55 FO 371/24505, C 12495/30/41; CAB 66/13, W.P. (40) 460, Annex I.
56 For an instance of Eccles' espousal of the policy of economic help to Spain, see Eccles to Lord Drogheda, 24 September 1940, FO 837/719, T. 4/14, vol. I.

57 Dalton's minute, 26 November 1940, FO 837/730, T. 4/76, vol. I.
58 FO 371/24505, C 12870, C 12939/30/41; FO 837/730, T. 4/76, vol. I;
   Eccles to Hoare, 30 November, 1940, Templewood Papers, XIII, 2. See
   also, Eccles (ed.), *By safe hand*, pp. 206–7.
59 FO 371/23513, C 12745/112/41; FO 371/24505, C 12939/30/41; R. M.
   Makins to S. D. Waley (of the Treasury), 28 November 1940, FO 837/
   730, T. 4/76, vol. I.
60 FO 837/730, T. 4/76, vol. I; FO 371/24513, C 12813/75/41.
61 F.R.U.S., 1940, II, 837–8.
62 Ibid., 838; Hull, *Memoirs*, I, 878; CAB 65/10, W.M. 298 (40) 3.
63 FO 371/23513, C 12745/112/41; Hull, *Memoirs*, I, 878–9.
64 FO 371/23513, C 12745/112/41; Hull, *Memoirs*, I, 879.
65 F.R.U.S., 1940, II, 839–43; Feis, *Spanish story*, p. 105.
66 FO 371/24513, C 12905/112/41.
67 Watson, *United States–Spanish relations*, p. 56.
68 FO 371/24513, C 12905/112/41.
69 F.R.U.S., 1940, II, 845–7. See, also, Watson, *United States–Spanish
   relations*, pp. 341–3 and the *Arriba* editorials of 16 October, 17, 19, 20
   November and 5 December 1940.
70 Feis, *Spanish story*, p. 106.
71 Ibid.; F.R.U.S., 1940, II, 848–50; cf. the State Department's
   memorandum of 16 December 1940, for the President: Roosevelt
   Papers, President Secretary's File: Spain. The text of the State Department's telegram no. 350, of 19 December 1940, to Weddell became
   known to Germany's Ambassador von Stohrer, but he was inclined to
   explain it away (D.G.F.P., Series D, XI, 975–6). See, also, D.G.F.P., Series
   D, XI, 601.
72 F.R.U.S., 1940, II, 850–1.
73 Allan Watson, *United States–Spanish relations*, pp. 58–9; Feis, *Spanish
   Story*, p. 107; Theodore A. Wilson, *The first summit, Roosevelt and
   Churchill at Placentia Bay, 1941* (London, 1970), pp. 35–6.
74 Feis, *Spanish story*, p. 107.
75 Hull, *Memoirs*, I, 881.
76 F.R.U.S., 1940, II, 851–3; Hull, *Memoirs*, I, 880–1.
77 F.R.U.S., 1940, II, 854; Feis, *Spanish story*, p. 108.
78 President Roosevelt to 'Former Naval Person', 31 December 1940,
   PREM 3/469.
79 CAB 65/17, WM 1(41) 3; 'Former Naval Person' to President Roosevelt,
   3 January 1941, PREM 3/469; Dalton Papers, diary 24, 2 January 1941.
80 Thomas, *Britain and Vichy*, pp. 56–7, 66–8, 94–117.
81 See, e.g., Hoare to Halifax, 20 September 1940, Halifax Papers, FO 800/
   323; Halifax to Hoare, 26 September 1940, Templewood Papers, XIII, 20;
   Hoare to Halifax, 1 October 1940, Halifax Papers, FO 800/323; Hoare to
   Halifax, 25 October 1940, Halifax Papers, FO 800/323; Hoare to Halifax,
   1 November 1940, Halifax Papers, FO 800/323; Hoare to Halifax, 8
   November 1940, Halifax Papers, FO 800/323; relevant passage is also in
   CAB 66/13, W.P. (40) 442; Halifax to Hoare, 29 November 1940,
   Templewood Papers, XIII, 20; R. T. Thomas, *Britain and Vichy, the
   dilemma of Anglo-French relations 1940–42* (London, 1979), pp. 68,
   73–4.

82 CAB 66/13, W.P. (40) 448.
83 Thomas, *Britain and Vichy,* p. 82.
84 FO 371/24513, C 12854/75/41.
85 FO 837/730, T. 4/76, vol. I; FO 371/24453, C 13103/5847/28; Eccles to Hoare, 3 December 1940, Templewood Papers, XIII, 2.
86 James Leutze (ed.), *The London Observer: the Journal of General Raymond E. Lee, 1940–1041* (London, 1972), p. 154.
87 FO 837/730, T. 4/76, vol. I.
88 Quoted by Detwiler, *Hitler, Franco und Gibraltar,* p. 86.
89 Medlicott, *The economic blockade,* I, 545. There were critics of the barter agreement between Britain, Morocco and Spain, within British Government circles. They felt that Hoare, in his anxiety to appease the Spaniards, had made major economic concessions, at Britain's expense, which could only result in Franco's Spain reaping significant political credit amongst the Moroccans (Harvey Diaries, 15 November 1940, Add. 56397).
90 Medlicott, *Economic blockade,* I, 542.
91 Hoare to Halifax, 5 December 1940, Halifax Papers, FO 800/323; *The Times,* 16 September, 19 October 1940; F.R.U.S, 1940, II, 837; Payne, *Falange,* pp. 207, 295.
92 FO 837/730, T. 4/76, vol. I.
93 FO 371/24513, C 13361/75/41.
94 Ibid.; FO 371/24453, C 13205/5847/28.

7. The Tangier crisis

1 D.G.F.P., Series D, XI, 725, 739–41.
2 Jacobsen (ed.), *Kriegstagebuch des OKW,* I, 196; Burdick, *Germany's military strategy,* pp. 97–8.
3 Rich, *Hitler's war aims,* I, 171–73; D.G.F.P., Series D, XI, 598–9, 639–41, 790–1, van Creveld, *Hitler's strategy,* p. 83.
4 Trevor-Roper, (ed.), *Hitler's war directives,* pp. 81–7, also in D.G.F.P., Series D, XI, 527–31. For the evolution of German strategy towards Spain, in general, and of Operation 'Felix', in particular, see Burdick's *Germany's military strategy,* pp. 17–95.
5 Heinz Höhne, *Canaris* (London, 1979), pp. 437–8.
6 Detwiler, *Hitler, Franco und Gibraltar,* pp. 84–8, 151, 169–71; idem, 'Spain and the Axis during the Second World War', *Review of Politics,* 31 (1971), 48; Léon Papeleux, *L'amiral Canaris: entre Franco et Hitler* (Tournai, 1977), pp. 138–40, 145.
7 Papeleux, *L'amiral Canaris,* p. 140.
8 D.G.F.P., Series D, XI, 816–17, 852–3.
9 F.C.N.A., p. 167; Trevor-Roper (ed.), *Hitler's war directives,* p. 87.
10 Burdick, *Germany's military strategy,* pp. 115–16.
11 Ewan Butler, *Mason-Mac: the life of Lieutenant-General Sir Noel Mason-Macfarlane* (London, 1972), p. 127.
12 Barry A. Leach, *German strategy against Russia, 1939–1941* (Oxford and London, 1973), p. 76.
13 D.G.F.P., Series D, XI, 850.
14 Ibid., 817; F.C.N.A., p. 171.

15 D.G.F.P., Series D, XI, 853.
16 Hill (ed.), *Die Weizsäcker-Papiere*, pp. 228, 235.
17 FO 371/24453, C 13218/5847/28; *The Times*, 5, 15 November 1940; Graham H. Stuart, *The international city of Tangier* (Stanford, second edition, 1955), pp. 73–108, 201–48. An English translation of Yuste's decree is printed in F.R.U.S, 1940, III, 786.
18 CAB 65/10, WM 285(40) 6.
19 *The Times*, 15 November 1940.
20 365. H.C. DEB. 53, cols. 1679.
21 Ibid.
22 FO 371/24453, C 12954/5847/28.
23 FO 371/24453, C 13296/5847/28. An English translation of this 'decree law of the Chief of State' is printed in F.R.U.S, 1940, III, 786.
24 FO 371/24453, C 13296/5847/28.
25 FO 371/24453, C 13004/5847/28.
26 FO 371/24453, C 13056/5847/28.
27 Ibid., CAB 65/10, WM 300(40)4.
28 FO 371/24453, C 13103/5847/28.
29 367 H.C. DEB, 5s., cols. 507–9.
30 FO 371/24453, C 13205/5847/28.
31 Ibid.
32 367 H.C. DEB. 5s. cols. 885–7.
33 FO 371/24505, C 13317/30/41; FO 837/730, T. 4/76 vol. 1. Hoare also summarised his 11 December interview with Serrano Suñer in his 15 December telegram, No. 1239, in FO 371/24513, C 13428/75/41.
34 FO 371/24513, C 13372/75/41; FO 371/24513, C 13317/75/41. Serrano Suñer had implied, in his 11 December interview with Hoare, that there would be a dismissal of British officials from the Tangerine International Administration, by promising that 'all British officials who may lose their posts will be fully indemnified' (FO 371/24505, C 13317/30/41). Hoare, however, neglected to send word of this immediately to London, dispatching a telegram only on 12 December, which was further delayed *en route*. It arrived in London about the same time as the crisis occasioned by the removal of the British officials in Tangier broke (ibid.; FO 371/24513, C 13317/75/41).
35 FO 371/24513, C 13317/75/41; Dilks (ed.), *Cadogan diaries*, p. 340. Butler, who shouldered the burden of defending the Government's position over Tangier in the House of Commons, gave expression to his annoyance over the affair of the Italian submarines, in a minute of 17 December 1940:

> I find the position of the Tangier submarines very unsatisfactory. Why, if I am told that they are unseaworthy do they go to sea? If they do go to sea, why are they not stopped by the Navy? We are always being blamed for the gross defects of Naval intelligence . . . It is difficult to defend in the House (a) false information, (b) inaction . . . (FO 371/24520, C 13635/334/41).

See also, FO 371/24513, C 13361/75/41.

Churchill, too, had queried his Foreign Secretary, on 4 December, as to whether 'the abuse of neutrality implied in the retention of these submarines' at Tangier did not require 'a stronger line' (Prime Minister's

Personal Minute to Halifax, 4 December 1940, FO 371/24520, C 13048/
334/41). Halifax, in reply, accepted that in the absence of satisfactory
action in the near future by Spain, 'we must reserve our entire liberty of
action' towards the Italian warships (Halifax's minute to Churchill, 5
December 1940, ibid.).

Vansittart had called, on 12 December, for a tougher line towards
Spain 'all around' because of its 'entirely unneutral' attitude over the
Italian submarines at Tangier. He even questioned whether the Royal
Navy should not 'be prepared to go in and sink them for keeps?' The
minute in which Vansittart made these points was, apparently, drafted
by the Admiralty. The plea for consideration of direct action – but not
that for a stiffer general line towards Spain – was, of course, superseded
by the departure of the Italian submarines from Tangier on 13 December
(ibid.). See also, FO 371/24505, C 13317/30/41.

36 Hoare's telegram No. 1236, 14 December 1940, Avon Papers, FO
954/27A.
37 Orwell and Angus (eds.), *Collected essays*, II, War-time diary: 1940, 25
October, 429.
38 William L. Langer and S. Everett Gleason, *The world crisis and American foreign policy* (2 vols., New York, 1952–3), II, *The undeclared war,
1940–1941* (1953), 1968 edn., 65. See also, Leutze (ed.), *London
Observer*, p. 41.
39 CAB 80/56, C.O.S. (40) 798; L. C. Hollis to W. Strang, 31 October 1940,
FO 371/24494, C 10637/4066/36, copy in CAB 21/1489, s. 50/61; C.O.S.
(40) 54 (o) (J.P.) in FO 371/26809, C 115/115/36; Roskill, *War at sea*, I,
273.
40 L. C. Hollis to W. Strang, 31 October 1940, FO 371/24494, C 10637/
4066/36, copy in CAB 21/1489, s. 50/61; Strang to Hollis, 9 November
1940, FO 371/24494, C 10637/4066/36.
41 CAB 79/55, C.O.S. (40) 23 (o); CAB 80/106, C.O.S. (40) 29 (o) (J.P.).
42 CAB 79/7, C.O.S. (40) 384th Mtg., Min. 2.
43 F.C.N.A., p. 142.
44 Ibid., pp. 146–7; Burdick, *Germany's military strategy*, p. 64.
45 F.C.N.A., pp. 147–8.
46 Burdick, *Germany's military strategy*, p. 65.
47 Trevor-Roper (ed.), *Hitler's war directives*, pp. 81–7; D.G.F.P., Series D,
XI, 527–31.
48 F.C.N.A., pp. 152–3; Burdick, *Germany's military strategy*, p. 75.
49 Burdick, *Germany's Military Strategy*, p. 101.
50 CAB 79/9, C.O.S. (40) 385th Mtg., Min. 1. The Chiefs of Staff also
expressed their reawakened reservations over a preventive seizure of the
islands by requesting a new plan for carrying out 'Brisk' against German-
occupied Azores (ibid.). This report, when completed, reached no clear-
cut conclusions. It stated that there would be a better chance of retaking
the cable station at Horta, than the harbour of Ponta del Gada and that
much would depend on the effectiveness of naval gun-fire against the
Islands' defences (CAB 80/106, C.O.S. (40) 37 (o) J.P.).
51 C.A.B. 122/044, C.O.S. (40) 22 (o).
52 ADM 199/1931.
53 D.O. (40) 46th Mtg., Min. 1, copy in PREM 3, 361/6A.

54 CAB 79/55, C.O.S. (40) 29 (o).
55 CAB 84/24, J.P. (40) 733; CAB 80/23, C.O.S. (40) 987 (J.P.); CAB 80/56, C.O.S. (40) 29 (o) (Draft). The Joint Planning Staff closed their report with an emphatic counsel of prudence: 'Our study of this problem which brings into relief the difficulties with which we shall be faced if the Germans move into Spain, clearly shows the vital importance of doing all we can to ensure that Spain remains friendly and prepared to invite our assistance against German aggression.' (CAB 84/24, J.P. (40) 733).
56 FO 371/24494, C 10637/4066/36. The telegram also frankly and concisely acknowledged Britain's strategic predicament concerning the Atlantic Islands: '. . . the dilemma is that by occupying the Azores, we may apart from incurring Portuguese hostility, bring Spain into the war against us, but that, on the other hand, if we do not act, we may be forestalled and still have Spain and Portugal in the war against us, and so in the end get nothing'.
57 FO 371/24494, C 13107/4066/36.
58 Dilks (ed.), *Cadogan Diaries*, p. 339. The other Foreign Office men who participated in the 13 December talk, were Acting Assistant Under-Secretary of State, William Strang, and Acting First Secretary, Frank Roberts.
59 CAB 79/55, C.O.S. (40) 29 (o); Churchill's personal minute of 1 December 1940, to General Ismay for Chiefs of Staff Committee, PREM 3/361/6A.
60 Dalton Papers, diary 23, 17 December 1940.
61 Alba's dispatch No. 1126, 9 December 1940: Alba papers, Caja 1[A], No. 5; legajo R. 985, E.8, M.A.E.
62 CAB 80/24, C.O.S. (40) 1040 (J.I.C.), also Paper J.I.C. (40) 417.
63 F. H. Hinsley, E. E. Thomas, C. F. G. Ransom, R. C. Knight, *British intelligence in the Second World War; its influence on strategy and operations* (3 vols., London, 1979–), I, 257.
64 Dilks (ed.), *Cadogan diaries*, p. 340.
65 Ibid., p. 340.
66 FO 371/24494, C 13107/4066/36; CAB 79/55, C.O.S. (40) 33 (o); Roskill, *War at sea*, I, 273.
67 CAB 80/24, C.O.S., (40) 1040.
68 CAB 79/55, C.O.S. (40) 32 (o). The C.I.G.S., General Dill, was absent from this meeting and the Chequers one. His place was taken by the Vice-C.I.G.S., Lieutenant-General Haining.
69 CAB 79/55, C.O.S. (40) 33 (o).
70 Ibid.
71 Dilks (ed.), *Cadogan diaries*, p. 340.
72 CAB 79/55, C.O.S. (40) 33 (o).
73 Ibid.
74 Ibid.
75 Ronald Tree, *When the moon was high: memoirs of peace and war, 1897–1942* (London, 1975), p. 136, quoting the diary of Churchill's then Private Secretary, John Colville, for 15 December 1940.
76 CAB 79/55, C.O.S. (40) 33 (o).
77 CAB 80/56. C.O.S. (40) 32 (o).

78 CAB 69/1, D.O. (40) 50th Mtg.
79 CAB 84/25, J.P. (40) 800 (o).
80 D.G.F.P., Series D, XI, 465.
81 Ibid., 967–9.
82 *Arriba*, 23 November 1940.
83 Ibid., 2 January 1941, reporting Serrano Suñer's interview with the weekly, *Haz*.
84 FO 371/24453, C 129541/584/28 (see also, C 12419 and C 12433); D.G.F.P., Series D, XI, 604.
85 D.G.F.P., Series D, XI, 86, 602.
86 FO 371/24453, C 13103/5847/28.
87 Eccles (ed.), *By safe hand*, p. 192. See also, pp. 208–9.
88 FO 371/24529, C 13554/13554/41; FO 371/24513, C 13428/75/41.
89 CAB 65/10, WM 306 (40) 5; CAB 65/16, WM 306 (40) 3, Confidential Annex; FO 371/24513, C 13428/75/41; Dilks (ed.), *Cadogan diaries*, p. 341.
90 Halifax to Hoare, 21 December 1940, Templewood Papers, XIII, 20. Cf. the last paragraph added by Halifax himself to telegram No. 1338, of 22 December, to Hoare: 'On general question you will appreciate that anxious as we are to do the best we can over Tangier, and to make the most of any levers we possess to influence Spanish Government, Cabinet continues to attach first importance to keeping Spain out of the war.' (This was actually sent as a separate telegram, No. 1339, of 22 December 1940. Both telegrams are in FO 371/24529, C 13601/13542/41).
91 FO 371/24513, C 13428/75/41.
92 FO 371/24529, C 13899/13542/41.
93 367 H.C. DEB. 5s. cols. 1411–22.
94 FO 371/24529, C 13601/13542/41.
95 Hoare to Halifax, 18 December 1940, Templewood Papers XIII, 20; CAB 66/14, W.P. (40) 488. See, also, Eccles (ed.), *By safe hand*, pp. 208–9.
96 FO 371/24506, C 13633/30/41.
97 Halifax to Hoare, 21 December 1940, Templewood Papers, XIII, 20. Halifax was here merely adopting almost word for word Cadogan's argument, in a minute occasioned by Hoare's request for permission to facilitate (four) shiploads of wheat, at his own discretion (FO 371/24506, C 13633/30/41).
98 Hoare to Halifax, 20 December 1940, Halifax Papers, FO 800/323.
99 Lord Cranborne to Halifax, 1 December 1940, Halifax Papers, FO 800/323.
100 Halifax to Cranborne, 5 December 1940, Halifax Papers, FO 800/323.
101 Halifax to Hoare, 21 December 1940, Templewood Papers, XIII, 20.
102 See, e.g., Hoare to Eden, 31 December 1940, Templewood Papers, XIII, 21, and Hoare to J. L. Garvin, 30 December, Templewood Papers, XIII, 2.
103 Hoare to Eden, 24 December 1940, Templewood Papers, XIII, 21.
104 Nigel Nicolson (ed.), *Harold Nicolson, diaries and letters, 1939–45* (London, 1967), 1970 edn., pp. 51, 61; FO 371/24609, C 1651/46/41; Harvey diaries, 15 January 1941, Add. 56397.
105 FO 371/24506, C 13776/30/41.
106 FO 371/26904, C 49/46/41.

107 Ibid.; John Harvey (ed.), *The war diaries of Oliver Harvey, 1941–1945* (London, 1978), p. 21.

108 FO 371/24513, C 13907/75/41.

109 FO 371/26924, C 294/108/41.

110 This account of the late December 1940–January 1941 negotiations is based on the following: FO 371/24513, C 13428/75/41; FO 371/26892, C 303/13/41, C 13/13/41, C 268/13/41, C 138/13/41, C 355/13/41, C 588/ 13/41, C 607/13/41, C 66/13/41, C 1384/13/41, C 894/13/41, C 913/13/ 41, C 1088/13/41; CAB 65/17, WM 4 (41) 2; Hoare to Eden, 31 December 1940, Hoare's dispatch No. 16, of 11 January 1941, Hoare to Eden, 22 January 1941, Templewood Papers, XIII, 21.

111 Hoare to R. A. Butler, 15 January 1941, Templewood Papers, XIII, 18.

112 Hoare to Bracken, 6 January 1941, Templewood Papers, XIII, 18. See also, FO 371/26939, C 232/222/41.

113 FO 371/26892, C 13/13/41.

114 FO 371/26892, C 138/13/41; CAB 65/17, WM 2 (41) 3.

115 Dusko Popov, *Spy/Counterspy* (London, 1974), 1976 edn., pp. 62–4, 66–8.

116 Major-General Sir Kenneth Strong, *Men of intelligence: a study of the roles and decisions of Chiefs of Intelligence from World War I to the present day* (London, 1970), p. 119.

117 C.O.S. (40) 54 (o) (J.P.), copy in FO 371/26809, C 115/115/36; L. C. Hollis to R. M. Makins, 3 January 1941, ibid.
    The Foreign Office reaction to the news that Britain was not going to take any precipitate action against the Azores was generally one of relieved welcome, but Eden's feelings were mixed: 'I think this estimate of Spanish opinion optimistic but the decision is what matters and I cordially endorse it.' (ibid.)

118 CAB 80/25, C.O.S. (41) 23; CAB 79/8, C.O.S. (41) 28th Mtg., Min. 1, Annex.

119 Attlee's minute to Churchill, 7 January 1941, Attlee Papers, 2/2.

120 FO 371/26904, C 460/46/41; Eden to Hoare, 15 January 1941, Avon Papers, FO 954/27A.

121 CAB 80/56, C.O.S. (41) 2 (o). Churchill reprints his minute to the Chiefs of Staff in his *The grand alliance*, American edn. (Boston, 1950), pp. 5–11, omitting, however, the reference to operations 'Brisk' and 'Shrapnel'. Again, no doubt, he was anxious to avoid revealing that the British response, at this stage of the war, to a German incursion into Spain, would have been the seizure of bases in the Portuguese Atlantic Islands.

122 CAB 69/18, D.O. (41) 3rd Mtg., Min. 1, Confidential Annex.

123 PREM 3/186A/5.

124 Hoare to Churchill, 11 January 1941, Templewood Papers XIII, 16; PREM 3/317/1.

125 PREM 4/21/1; FO 371/26904, C 460/46/41.

126 FO 371/26962, C 1051/1051/41, C 1685/1051/41; FO 371/26939, C 1679/222/41; FO 371/26893, C 1188/13/41; FO 371/26904, C 1192/46/41.

127 PREM 3/186A/5.

128 Ibid. See, also, Hickleton Papers, A7.8.6.: Halifax diary, 28 October

1940; Thomas, *Britain and Vichy*, pp. 82–7; Elisabeth Barker, *Churchill and Eden at war* (London, 1978), pp. 36–8.

129 CAB 69/2, D.O. (41), 1st Mtg., Min. 1; CAB 79/8, C.O.S. (41) 15th Mtg., Mins. 4 and 6; CAB 84/26, J.P. (41) 29 (s) and (o); CAB 84/27, J.P. (41) 71; CAB 84/27, J.P. (41) 81 (o) and (s); CAB 84/27, J.P. (41) 84.

130 CAB 80/56, C.O.S. (41) 31 (o); CAB 79/9, C.O.S. (41) 46th Mtg., Min. 5.

131 FO 371/26945, C 2065/306/41. Hoare may not have been as absolutely hopeful of Spanish resistance to a German incursion emerging, as he appeared in his reports to London. For, in conversation with the Portuguese Pereira in Madrid, on 20 February 1941, he conceded that it was 'too early to count on serious resistance on the part of the Spaniards against a German invasion' but he believed that 'the spirit of opposition' was growing stronger all the time (D.A.P.E., VIII, 120).

132 FO 371/26945, C 1280/306/41; FO 371/26939, C 560/222/41; FO 371/26939, C 232/222/41; FO 371/26945, C 1050/306/41; D.A.P.E., VIII, 135.

133 FO 371/26904, C 986/46/41; FO 371/26945, C 2065/306/41. See, also, FO 371/26904, C 1172/46/41; FO 371/26939, C 1679/222/41; FO 371/26939, C 1580/222/41.

134 FO 371/26945, C 2420/306/41; cf. FO 371/26945, C 1975/306/41.

135 D.G.F.P., Series D, XI, 1140; cf., also, ibid., XII, *February 1, 1941–June 22, 1941* (London, 1962), 36–7.

136 D.A.P.E., VIII, 84.

137 Jacobsen (ed.), *Kriegstagebuch des OKW*, I, 229.

138 D.G.F.P., Series D, XI, 913.

139 Ibid., 991–2.

140 Ibid., 1058; Jacobsen (ed.), *Kriegstagebuch des OKW*, I, 256.

141 Muggeridge (ed.), *Ciano's diplomatic papers*, p. 418.

142 Ibid., pp. 419–20; Muggeridge, *Ciano's diary*, p. 330.

143 D.G.F.P., Series D, XI, 1157–8, 1140–3, 1170– 1, 1173–5, 1183–4, 1217–18, 1222–3; ibid., XII, 37–42.
      It is unclear whether von Stohrer delivered this warning to the Caudillo, as the Ambassador asked for it to be rephrased so as to remove the innuendo that Germany, itself, was threatening Spain. However, the German Foreign Ministry's reply to his request has not been found. (Ibid., Series D., XI, 1157–8, 1171.)

144 Ibid., Series D, XI, 1173–5, 1188–91, 1208–10, 1222–3; ibid., XII, 30, 51–3, 78–9. See, also, D.A.P.E., VIII, 91.

145 Muggeridge (ed.), *Ciano's diplomatic papers*, pp. 421–30.

146 D.G.F.P., Series D, XII, 96–7, 131–2.

147 Ibid., 37–42.

148 Ibid., 176–8.

149 Ibid., 359. Franco had commented in his letter, of 21 September 1940, to Serrano Suñer, when the latter was in Berlin, on Hitler's contention that the closure of the Strait of Gibraltar 'would resolve by itself the question of North Africa and the Mediterranean'. For, he pointed out to his minister, Gibraltar was a 'necessary condition for the liberation of the Mediterranean' but not a sufficient one, since there was 'another door and (there were) other bases in the Eastern Mediterranean' (Serrano Suñer, *Memorias*, p. 340).

In a letter to Hitler the following day, Franco had brought this point to the Führer's attention: 'Obviously freedom of movement in the western Mediterranean is dependent upon Italian success in Alexandria and Suez . . .' (D.G.F.P., Series D, XI, 155).

Von Stohrer also reported, on 29 November 1940, that when Serrano Suñer relayed to him the Caudillo's views on Spanish belligerency, in the aftermath of the Berchtesgaden talks between the Spanish Foreign Minister and Hitler, they included the following one: 'Franco is of the opinion that simultaneously with the G(ibraltar)-action another action should be carried out in the eastern Mediterranean for the purpose of closing the Suez Canal.' Serrano Suñer also admitted to the German Ambassador, then, that the Spaniards were afraid that British pressure on them, if they joined the fight, would be 'too strong unless the English fleet and other military means in the Mediterranean (were) partly tied down in the eastern theatre of war' (ibid., 740).

150 CAB 80/56, C.O.S. (41) 31 (o); CAB 79/9, C.O.S. (41) 46th Mtg., Min. 5.
151 PREM 3/317/3.
152 FO 371/26909, C 584/71/41; Medlicott, *Economic blockade*, I, 542; FO 371/26910, C 926/71/41.
153 Serrano Suñer, *Entre Hendaya y Gibraltar*, p. 330. See, also, FO 371/26896, C 433/33/41.
154 FO 371/26960, C 919/919/41.
155 FO 371/26909, C 584/71/41; Medlicott, *Economic blockade*, I, 543. See, also, FO 371/26904, C 1192/46/41.
156 D.A.P.E., VIII, 70–1.
157 Ibid., 72–3.
158 FO 371/28372, Z 380/132/17; Dilks (ed.), *Cadogan diaries*, p. 350.
159 FO 371/26960, C 919/919/41.
160 Dalton Papers, diary 24, 28 January 1941.
161 FO 371/26892, C 913/13/41.
162 CAB 65/17, WM 12 (41) 2; CAB 66/14, W.P. (41) 21.
163 CAB 65/17, WM 13 (41) 6.
164 FO 371/26892, C 1088/13/41.
165 PREM 3/317/3.
166 FO 371/26892, C 1088/13/41; FO 371/26893, C 1716/13/41, C 1863/13/41, C 2097/13/41.

8. The limits of attraction

1 FO 371/26910, C 926/71/41. According to Glen Barclay (*Struggle for a continent, the diplomatic history of South America, 1917–1945* (London, 1971), p. 155) Spain and Argentina had concluded a huge barter deal to the value of $4,150,000, which involved, at first, the sale of 350,000 tons of Argentinian corn, which was followed by a further shipment of 500,000 tons of wheat and 1,500 tons of meat. Ricardo de la Cierva gives the wheat total as 500,000 tons (*Historia del Franquismo, I, orígines y configuración (1939–45)* (Barcelona, 1975), p. 217). The deal also included 120,000 bales of cotton (ibid., and FO 371/26910, C 926/71/41). See also, Viñas, *et al.*, *Política comercial exterior*, I, 367–8.

2 FO 371/26910, C 926/71/41.
3 FO 371/26904, C 1027/46/41; Hoare to Eden, 4 February 1941, Templewood Papers, XIII, 21.
4 FO 371/26910, C 1027/46/41.
5 Eden to Hoare, 11 February 1941, Avon Papers, FO 954/27A. See also, Roger Makins's minute, of 8 February 1941, ibid.
6 FO 371/26910, C 1437/71/41; FO 837/738E, T. 4/76.
7 FO 371/26910, C 1437/71/41. See also, Oliver Harvey's note for Eden, 24 August 1941, Harvey Papers, Add. 56402.
8 FO 371/26910, C 1684/71/41.
9 FO 371/26910, C 1608/71/41.
10 FO 371/26910, C 1473/71/41; FO 371/26892, C 1088/13/41.
11 Templewood Papers, XIII, 12.
12 No. 2, 17 February 1941, FO 371/26904, C 1651/46/41.
13 Ibid.; FO 371/26945, C 1617/306/41.
14 FO 371/26904, C 1787/46/41.
15 Hoare to R. A. Butler, 25 February 1941, Templewood Papers, XIII, 18.
16 FO 371/26904, C 1787/46/41.
17 FO 371/26939, C 1713, C 1714/222/41; Hoare to Churchill, 18 February 1941, Templewood Papers, XIII, 16. See also, Hoare to Beaverbrook, 19 February 1941, Templewood Papers, XIII, 18; Hoare to R. A. Butler, 25 February 1941, ibid. and FO 371/26911, C 2085/71/41.
18 FO 371/26912, C 2767/71/41.
19 FO 371/26945, C 2065/306/41.
20 Ibid.
21 FO 371/26913, C 3753/71/41.
22 FO 371/26912, C 3013, C 3135/71/41.
23 FO 371/26912, C 2892/71/41; CAB 65/18, WM 31 (41) 3; FO 371/26913, C 3456, C 3753/71/41.
24 Eden's minute to Churchill, 19 April 1941, FO 371/26913, C 4167/71/41; FO 371/26913, C 3440, C 3715/71/41.
25 FO 371/26913, C 4167/71/41.
26 FO 371/26932, C 3319/163/41; *Arriba*, 1 April 1941.
27 Medlicott, *Economic blockade*, I, 545.
28 FO 371/26924, C 2614/108/41.
29 FO 371/26924, C 2519/108/41. The British request was communicated to the State Department, on 20 March 1941. However, Lord Halifax, then of course British Ambassador to the United States, omitted any mention of a specific figure for the suggested credit from the message which he gave to Sumner Welles detailing the British proposals (F.R.U.S., 1941, II (Department of State, Washington, 1959), 886–7).
30 F.R.U.S., 1941, II, 882.
31 Ibid., 880–1, 885.
32 Feis, *Spanish story*, p. 109.
33 FO 371/26924, C 3629/108/41. See, also, FO 371/26924, C 3134/108/41.
34 FO 371/26924, C 3629, C 4002/108/41; Medlicott, *Economic blockade*, I, 546.
35 Dalton was not at all keen on Eccles undertaking this assignment to Washington and only agreed to let Eccles go on this temporary mission in return for getting Noel Hall accepted as permanent representative of

the Ministry of Economic Warfare in the British Embassy in Washington (FO 371/26924, C 2614/108/41; W. N. Medlicott, *The economic blockade*, II (London, 1959), 28). See also, Eccles (ed.), *By safe hand*, pp. 239, 245.

36 FO 371/26924, C 4151/108/41. The proposal to send the Spaniards substitute oils was not welcome to Dalton, who had imposed an embargo on all vegetable oil and animal fat imports into Spain, in retaliation for the Spaniards' promise to export 16,000 tons of olive oil to the Axis. It took the outbreak of a typhus epidemic in Spain, and an intervention by Churchill, before the Minister of Economic Warfare could be persuaded, in late April 1941, to allow 3,000 tons of tallow and 1,500 tons of palm oil for the making of soap, through the blockade. But he remained adamant that edible oils could not be let into Spain because of the 'internal political situation' in Britain (Medlicott, *Economic blockade*, I, 534–4; FO 371/26924, C 3629/108/41).

R. A. Butler acknowledged to his Foreign Office colleagues, on 28 April 1941, that the parliamentary position over Spain was 'not good' but also commented that the 'real political difficulty' was 'to hold Dalton and avoid a fissure between the F.O. and M.E.W.'. (FO 371/26924, C 4151/108/41.) Butler wrote to Dalton, the same day, to wean him from his intransigent position: 'We are particularly anxious not to miss an opportunity of concerting policy in regard to Spain with the U.S. Government. We shall need U.S. support whichever way the cat jumps in Spain. There is little more that we alone can do to revive the wilting plant of Spanish resistance to German pressure, but by refusing to agree to the U.S. appeal we can, in fact, introduce grit rather than lubricant into the machinery of Anglo-American co-operation' (ibid.). Dalton let himself be persuaded yet again (FO 371/26924, C 4309/108/41).

37 FO 371/26924, C 4427/108/41.
38 F.R.U.S., 1941, II, 887–8.
39 Ibid., 887–90; *Actes et documents du Saint Siège Relatifs à la 2e Guerre Mondiale*, V, *Le Saint Siège et la Guerre Mondiale, juillet, 1941–octobre, 1942* (Vatican City, 1969), 149; FO 371/26924, C 4044/108/41; D.G.F.P., Series D, XII, 591; Charles R. Halstead, 'The dispute between Ramón Serrano Suñer and Alexander Weddell', *Rivista di Studi Politici Internazionali*, luglio–settembre 1974, No. 3, 449–54.
40 F.R.U.S., 1941, II, 890.
41 Ibid., 891.
42 Feis, *Spanish story*, p. 131.
43 F.R.U.S., 1941, II, 893–4.
44 Ibid., 895–7; also 1940, II, 850.
45 Ibid., 1941, II, 903.
46 Ibid., 904–6.
47 Weddell's telegram, no. 550, 15 June 1941, to Hull, D.F.D.S., 740.0011, EW 1939/11470; Halstead, 'The dispute', 457–8; FO 371/26925, C 6692/108/41.
48 FO 371/26925, C 6692/108/41. Halifax reported to the Foreign Office, on 10 July 1941, that Welles had authorised Weddell to renew the American offer of economic aid when he saw Franco, but nothing came of this as is noted below (FO 371/26925, C 7685/108/41).

49 FO 371/26925, C 7521, C 7685/108/41; Hoare to Eden, 24 April 1941, Templewood Papers, XIII, 21.
50 F.R.U.S., 1941, II, 908.
51 Halstead, 'The dispute', 454–5; Weddell to Serrano Suñer, 15 May 1941, D.F.D.S., 740.0011, EW 1939/13012.
52 Halstead, 'The dispute', 450. Halstead records that junior Spanish officials told American Embassy officials that they attributed such German censorship of Spanish mail to the misdirection of letters to German-occupied France (457).
53 Ibid., 468; Halstead, 'Diligent diplomat', 31.
54 FO 371/26925, C 6616/108/41; F.R.U.S., 1941, II, 907.
55 D.G.F.P., Series D, XII, 942–3, 949–50. See, also, Muggeridge (ed.), *Ciano's diplomatic papers*, p. 442.
56 Muggeridge (ed.), *Ciano's diary*, p. 352.
57 Muggeridge (ed.), *Ciano's diplomatic papers*, pp. 443–4. On the previous 4 May, Ciano had also written to Serrano Suñer, on Mussolini's instructions, in similar, but rather less urgent terms: 'You know how much the Duce and Italy have respected and still respect Spain's complete independence in deciding on its attitude towards the conflict. You alone can judge how much it is possible to do for the good of your country and when it can be done. But it is certain that Spain can have no other place than at the side of Italy and Germany, and past as well as future events are destined to make this union ever more intimate and effective. The great new destiny of Spain is to be found in the certain victory of the Totalitarian States' (ibid., and Muggeridge (ed.), *Ciano's diary*, p. 339).
58 D.G.F.P., Series D, XII, 1007–8.
59 FO 371/26925, C 6616/108/4.
60 FO 371/26906, C 7752/46/41.
61 D.G.F.P., Series D, XIII, *June 23–December 11, 1941* (London, 1964), 444–5. It is interesting to note that the British could appreciate that the Spanish press had to pay public lip-service to Germany. David Eccles tried to impress this point upon Norman Davis, Chairman of the American Red Cross, in a letter of 19 May 1941: 'It would be a mistake to insist on a major change in the enemy controlled press (in Spain), which is an exhaust pipe that allows Spain to blow off the pressure of German steam, and to appear pro-Axis, a necessary disguise until we can promise our friends adequate military assistance to oppose the German Army' (Eccles (ed.), *By safe hand*, p. 272).
62 D.G.F.P., Series D, XIII, 445–6.
63 Feis, *Spanish story*, pp. 133–4.
64 FO 371/26925, C 7434/108/41.
65 Feis, *Spanish Story*, p. 138.
66 PREM 4/21/1; Cárdenas's dispatch No. 289, 22 July 1941, legajo R. 1448, E. 3, M.A.E.
67 PREM, 4/21/1.
68 Feis, *Spanish story*, p. 138; Medlicott, *Economic blockade*, II, p. 287.
69 Feis, *Spanish story*, p. 139.
70 Ibid., pp. 139, 141–4.
71 Allan Watson, *United States–Spanish relations*, pp. 83–4.
72 F.R.U.S., 1941, II, 915–16.
73 Ibid., 914.

74 Halstead, 'The dispute', 465–6; F.R.U.S., 1941, II, 917–19, 921, 923–4; FO 371/26926, C 10859/108/41.
75 F.R.U.S., 1941, II, 924–5; FO 371/26926, C 10946/108/41.
76 F.R.U.S., 1941, II, 925.
77 Ibid., 923.
78 Ibid., 928–9.
79 FO 371/26926, C 11688/108/41.
80 Feis, *Spanish story*, p. 141; Medlicott, *Economic blockade*, II, 41. The purpose of the Economic Defense Board was defined in Article I of the Presidential Order, of 30 July 1941, establishing it:
    the conduct, in the interest of national defense, of international economic activities including those relating to exports, imports, the acquisition and disposition of materials and commodities from foreign countries including preclusive buying, transactions in foreign exchange and foreign-owned or foreign-controlled property, international investments and extensions of credit, shipping and transportation of goods among countries, the international aspects of patents, international communications pertaining to commerce, and other foreign economic matters (Medlicott, *Economic blockade*, II, 42).
81 Feis, *Spanish story*, p. 141; F.R.U.S., 1941, II, 929–30; FO 371/26926, C 1120/108/41.
82 FO 371/26926, C 11464/108/41; F.R.U.S., 1941, II, 930–1.
83 D.G.F.P., Series D, XIII, 168–9, 628–30, 647–8.
84 Burdick, 'Moro', 256–84.
85 Ibid., 272.
86 D.G.F.P., Series D, XI, 787–8. See also, ibid., 445.
87 Burdick, 'Moro', 280.
88 F.R.U.S., 1941, II, 930.
89 Hull, *Memoirs*, II, 1188.
90 Allan Watson, *United States–Spanish relations*, pp. 86–7; FO 371/26926, C 11688/108/41.
91 Feis, *Spanish story*, p. 148; FO 837/744, T. 4/291, vol. I.
92 Feis, *Spanish story*, p. 148; FO 371/26926, C 11688/108/41.
93 FO 837/744, T. 4/291, vol. I.
94 FO 371/26926, C 11688/108/41.
95 Feis, *Spanish story*, pp. 142, 148–9.
96 FO 837/735, T. 4/76; FO 371/26926, C 13957/108/41.
97 Feis, *Spanish story*, pp. 150–1; FO 371/26926, C 14031/108/41; Medlicott, *Economic blockade*, II, 293; Hull, *Memoirs*, II, 1189.
98 Feis, *Spanish story*, pp. 151–2.
99 Medlicott, *Economic blockade*, II, 288.
100 PREM 4/21/2A; FO 837/735, T. 4/76; Feis, *Spanish story*, p. 152; Hull, *Memoirs*, II, 1189. See also, FO 837/744, T. 4/291, vol. I.
101 PREM 4/21/2A.
102 Feis, *Spanish story*, pp. 151–4; Hull, *Memoirs*, II, 1189.
103 Medlicott, *Economic blockade*, II, 294. See also, Hoare to David Eccles, 16 January 1942, in Eccles (ed.), *By safe hand*, p. 330, where he describes the American *aide-mémoire*, even as modified, as 'a most unsatisfactory document' and faults the U.S. Government for its failure to grasp that the 'real justification for supplying Spain with the necessities of life is not . . . economic but strategic.'
104 Hull, *Memoirs*, II, 1189–90.

105 Feis, *Spanish story*, p. 177; Medlicott, *Economic blockade*, II, 303.
106 Medlicott, *Economic blockade*, II, 291, 308–13.
107 Ibid., 557.
108 Feis, *Spanish story*, p. 196.
109 Ibid., pp. 230–54; Medlicott, *Economic blockade*, II, 557–76; Woodward, *British foreign policy in the Second World War*, IV (London, 1975), 18–28; Barker, *Churchill and Eden*, pp. 158–60.
110 Medlicott, *Economic blockade*, II, 574–5; Woodward, *British foreign policy*, IV, 25–6.
111 FO 371/26915, C 7619/71/41.
112 Medlicott, *Economic blockade*, I, 548; CAB 79/55, C.O.S. (41) 23rd Mtg., Min. 2 (o), Appendix A, Annex 1; Eccles (ed.), *By safe hand*, p. 301.
113 Medlicott, *Economic blockade*, I, 548.
114 Ibid., II, 310, 312.
115 Ibid., I, 548.
116 Ibid.
117 Ibid., II, 285.
118 David L. Gordon and Royden Dangerfield, *The hidden weapon: the story of economic warfare* (New York, 1947), pp. 100–20; Feis, *Spanish story*, pp. 261–2; Medlicott, *Economic blockade*, II, 305–8, 323-36, 591–610, 656–9.
119 Viñas, *et al.*, *Política comercial exterior*, I, 368; Barclay, *Struggle for a continent*, p. 118. 'See also, FO 371/26918, C 11198/71/41; Fontana and Nadal, 'Spain', p. 505.
120 'Annual Report: Spain', copy in Templewood Papers, XIII, 20.
121 FO 837/738A, T. 4/3.
122 Ibid., Malcolm Thomson to J. W. Nicholls, 14 March 1941.
123 FO 837/738A, T. 4/3.
124 FO 371/26891, C 8935/3/41.
125 FO 371/26898, C 11402/33/41.
126 FO 371/26891, C 9527/3/41.
127 FO 371/26899, C 13046/33/41.
128 FO 371/26939, C 5110/222/41.
129 Paxton, *Vichy France*, pp. 116–20.
130 FO 371/26939, C 5110/222/41.
131 FO 371/26890, C 6255/3/41.
132 *The Times*, 20, 21 May, 1949.
133 Crozier, *Franco*, p. 358.
134 466 H.C. DEB. 5s. cols. 188–90.
135 Serrano Suñer, *Entre Hendaya y Gibraltar*, pp. 301–2; *The Times*, 20 May 1949.
136 CAB 69/2, D.O. (41) 64th Mtg.
137 FO 371/26962, C 12048/1051/41.
138 Ibid.
139 Ibid.
140 CAB 69/3, D.O. (41) 25; FO 371/26932, C 12048/1051/ 41.
141 Paxton, *Vichy France*, pp. 124–5. Paxton notes that the German initiative which secured Weygand's dismissal was encouraged by the latter's rival in the Vichy regime, Admiral Darlan (p. 125).
142 FO 371/26940, C 13672/222/41.

143 Serrano Suñer, *Memorias*, pp. 357–8.
144 CAB 79/9, C.O.S. (41) 61st. Mtg., Min. 6.
145 CAB 79/9, J.P. (41) 142; FO 371/26904, C 1787/46/41.
146 CAB 80/57, C.O.S. (41) 46 (o); CAB 79/9, C.O.S. (41) 78th Mtg., Min. 7, 79th Mtg., Min. 6, 82nd. Mtg., Min. 8.
147 FO 371/26939, C 2328/222/41; PREM 3/405/6.
148 Churchill's minute to General Ismay, for the Chiefs of Staff Committee, 10 March 1941: CAB 80/57, C.O.S. (41) 59 (o).
149 CAB 80/57, C.O.S. (41) 57 (o); PREM 3/405/6.
150 Churchill's minute to General Ismay for the Chiefs of Staff: CAB 80/57, C.O.S. (41) (o); PREM 3/405/6.
151 FO 371/26939, C 2328/222/41; PREM 3/405/6.
152 The British, however, did secure some evidence which seemed to prove that the Carlist Requetés would resist, passively or actively, a German entry into Spain, by force or by invitation, notwithstanding the Nazi victories of April–May 1941. See FO 371/26945, C 4170/306/41; FO 371/26898, C 11381/33/41.
153 FO 371/26946, C 6722/306/41; Hoare to Eden, 30 May 1941, with enclosure, Templewood Papers, XIII, 21; see also, Hoare to Eden, 4 June 1941, with enclosures.
154 FO 371/26945, C 5867/306/41.
155 FO 371/26899, C 12056/33/41.
156 FO 371/26891, C 8744/3/41.
157 Hillgarth to Churchill, 12 August 1941, PREM 4/21/1. See also, FO 371/26891, C 9154/3/41.
158 FO 371/26898, C 11957/33/41; Pedro Sainz Rodríguez, *Testimonio y Recuerdos* (Barcelona, 1978), pp. 275, 278.
159 FO 371/26899, C 13886/33/41.
160 D.G.F.P., Series D, XII, 615. See also 774.
161 Ibid., XIII, 631
162 Serrano Suñer, *Memorias*, pp. 288, 329.
163 FO 371/26898, C 11958/33/41.
164 FO 371/26939, C 6021/222/41.
165 FO 371/26898, C 10618, C 10758, C 11040, C 11367/33/41.
166 FO 371/26898, C 11958/33/41. See also, Eden to Hoare, 11 September 1941, Avon Papers, FO 954/27A and M. S. Williams's minute, of 28 August 1941.
167 W.P. (41) 266, copy in FO 371/26899, C 12056/33/41.
168 FO 371/26899, C 13225/33/41.
169 D.G.F.P., Series D, XII, 774, 796; see also, 930.
170 Hoare to Eden, 13 May 1942, Templewood Papers, XIII, 22; Hoare's dispatch no. 151, 14 May 1942, ibid.; Eden to Hoare, 3 June 1942, ibid.; Hoare to Eden, 12 June 1942, ibid.; Hoare's dispatch no. 215, 1 July 1942, enclosing a copy of a letter from General Aranda to Don Juan, of 25 June 1942, ibid; Hoare's dispatch no. 222, 7 July 1942, ibid.; Harris Smith, *O.S.S.*, pp. 78–82.
171 Klaus-Jörg Ruhl, *Spanien im Zweiten Weltkrieg: Franco, die Falange und das 'Dritte Reich'* (Hamburg, 1975), pp. 402–3.
172 FO 371/26891, C 8773, C 9154/3/41; Eden's comment, of 19 August 1941, on Hillgarth to Churchill, 12 August 1941, PREM 4/21/1; FO 371/

26898, C 9804, C 9976, C 11958/33/41; FO 371/26899, C 12056, C 12361, C 13057, C 14065/33/41.
173 FO 371/26945, C 4170/306/41; FO 371/26899, C 12972/33/41. See also, Harvey diaries, 7 August 1941, Add. 56398.
174 D.G.F.P., Series D, XII, 613; FO 371/26898, C 11234/33/41; FO 371/26899, C 12972/33/41.
175 FO 371/26891, C 8773/3/41; FO 371/26898, C 11367/33/41.
176 Payne, *Politics and the military*, pp. 429–30; de la Cierva, *Historia del Franquismo*, I, 203–7. See also, e.g., José María Gil Robles, *La Monarquía por la que yo luché: páginas de un diario (1941–1954)* (Madrid, 1976), p.17.
177 De la Cierva, *Historia del Franquismo*, I, 211.
178 Serrano Suñer, *Memorias*, p. 201.

9. The exhaustion of diplomacy

1 FO 371/26905, C 4802/46/41. See also, FO 371/26939, C 4369/222/41.
2 FO 371/26905, C 4802/46/41. See also, FO 371/26945, C 3772/306/41.
3 Dilks (ed.), *Cadogan diaries*, pp. 372–5, 380–1; Leutze (ed.), *The London Observer*, p. 251.
   Cadogan may have somewhat been unfair to include Churchill, for all his renowned impetuosity, in his strictures on his political chiefs' alleged commitment to forward action, for its own sake. For, Churchill could realise that patience was a primary virtue for successful diplomacy, a point which he sought to impress upon Cadogan, in June 1945: 'It always seems to me that so much of diplomacy consists of waiting ... There should be intervals.' Again, the Prime Minister reproved another British diplomat, in February 1944, for 'this extraordinary itch to be doing something every day' (Barker, *Churchill and Eden*, p. 25).
4 Dilks (ed.), *Cadogan diaries*, p. 376.
5 Ibid., pp. 378, 381–2.
6 FO 371/26939, C 4191, C 4369, C 4400/222/41; FO 371/26945, C 4004, C 4505/306/41; FO 371/26905, C 4802/46/41; CAB 65/18, WM 42 (41) 3; Dalton Papers, diary 24, 23 April 1941.
7 FO 371/26939, C 4918/222/41.
8 FO 371/26945, C 3772/306/41; FO 371/26939, C 4400, C 4369, C 6555/222/41; Hoare to Hankey, 28 April 1941, Templewood Papers, XIII, 18; FO 371/26940, C 7192/222/41; Hoare's dispatch No. 187, 12 May 1941, Templewood Papers, XIII, 21.
9 Hoare to Eden, 30 May 1941, Templewood Papers, XIII, 21.
10 CAB 79/12, C.O.S. (41) 213th Mtg., Min. 3 and J.P. (41) 444; Butler, *Grand Strategy*, II, 547–70.
11 CAB 79/12, J.P. (41) 444; J. M. A. Gwyer, *Grand strategy*, III, June 1941–August 1942, Part I (London, 1964), 7.
12 D.G.F.P., Series D, XII, 711. The authenticity of this report of Serrano Suñer's utterances is confirmed by the fact that the informant recorded the Foreign Minister as also, characteristically, stating the following: 'Spain's entry into the war would be greatly facilitated if Spain knew

what she had to gain. The assurances she has had from Germany thus far (Hendaye) are too vague' (ibid.).

13 Ibid., 929.
14 Ibid.
15 Churchill's minute to Chiefs of Staff Committee, Sir Alexander Cadogan and R. A. Butler, 22 March 1941, PREM 3/361/1, copy in CAB 79/55, C.O.S. (41) 7th Mtg. (o), as Annex II. See also, Churchill's minute to the First Lord of the Admiralty, 21 March 1941, ADM 199/1933 and Dilks (ed.), *Cadogan diaries*, p. 365.
16 Chiefs of Staff minute to Prime Minister, 23 March 1941, PREM 3/361/1, copy in CAB 79/55, C.O.S. (41) 7th Mtg. (o), Annex I. See also, CAB 80/27, C.O.S. (40) 201 and CAB 21/1489.
17 CAB 79/55, C.O.S. (41) 6th Mtg. (o); FO 371/26896, C 2817/33/41; CAB 79/10, C.O.S. (41) 105th Mtg.
18 Chiefs of Staff minute to Prime Minister, 23 March 1941, PREM 3/361/1, copy in CAB 79/55, C.O.S. (41) 7th Mtg. (o), as Annex I.
19 Churchill's minute to General Ismay for Chiefs of Staff Committee, 24 March 1941, PREM 3/361/1. Churchill also contended that the rerouting of all Atlantic traffic to the west 'would be a supreme admission of failure and defeat at sea' (ibid.).
20 CAB 79/55, C.O.S. (41) 8th Mtg. (o).
21 I have been unable to find any trace of the further review of this problem, scheduled for 26 March 1941, in the available Cabinet archives, but it may be contained in CAB 79/75, C.O.S. (41) 9th Mtg. (o), the record of which is closed until 1992. The Chiefs of Staff meeting, at 10.30 a.m. on 26 March, recorded in CAB 79/10 C.O.S. (41) 109th Mtg., did not discuss a preventive move against the Portuguese Islands, nor did Churchill attend it.
22 On 25 July 1941, the then Vice Chief of the Imperial General Staff, General Pownall, confided to his diary the trouble which Churchill caused his strategic advisers: 'One of the main battles here is to try and keep Winston on the rails, and he is terribly apt to go off at a tangent.' Bond (ed.), *Chief of Staff*, II, 33.
23 Churchill's personal minute to Chiefs of Staff, Cadogan and R. A. Butler, 22 March 1941, PREM 3/361/1 and copy in CAB 79/55, C.O.S. (41) 7th Mtg. (o), as Annex II. See also, Churchill's draft of a 'Former Naval Person' telegram to Roosevelt, of 22 March 1941, PREM 3/469.
24 As a result of their talk with Churchill, on 24 March, the Chiefs of Staff had directed, on the following day, that a plan for the capture of the Canary Islands against Spanish opposition be drawn up (CAB 79/10, C.O.S. (40) 108th Mtg., Min. 7).
25 CAB 79/11, C.O.S. (41) 143rd Mtg., Min. 9. Cavendish-Bentinck added, however, that there were 'no indications yet of extensive German troop movements towards the Spanish frontier' (ibid.).

Cavendish-Bentinck and Davidson, both members of the Joint Intelligence Sub-Committee had had a 'wrangle' at the Chiefs of Staff Committee meeting, on 1 April 1941, over the Director of Military Intelligence's assertions that the Germans would move into Spain, before 1 June, and that they would not attack Russia. The Foreign Office man had contradicted him on both counts. As a result, the J.I.C. instituted the practice of holding a preliminary meeting to reach an agreed view, before their regular weekly Tuesday session with the Chiefs of Staff. Cavendish-Bentinck described Davidson's stance at the Joint Intelligence Committee's preliminary meeting on 20 June, thus: '... the D.M.I. again trotted out this ridiculous theory that the Germans are about to move into Spain, which is unsupported by any material indications. However, we did not pass on Major General Davidson's views on Spain to the Chiefs of Staff.' (FO 371/26946, C 6874/306/41). It is interesting to note that the strategic outlook, in late April 1941, was so bleak that Cavendich-Bentinck did not dissent from Davidson's prediction of an early German entry into Spain at the Chiefs of Staff meeting, on 22 April. Presumably, this opinion had been settled by prior discussion, too, amongst the members of the J.I.C.

26 Dilks (ed.), *Cadogan diaries*, pp. 373–4.
27 FO 371/26945, C 4131/306/41. However, see also, Morton's minute, of 28 April 1941, to the Prime Minister, where Hillgarth on a visit to London reported Hoare's view, communicated to the Naval Attaché six days before, that Spain would not adhere to the Axis or 'voluntarily permit the passage of German troops' as long as the British held Egypt, notwithstanding their other recent military reverses in the Eastern Mediterranean (PREM 7/4).
28 CAB 79/11, C.O.S. (41) 145th Mtg., Min. 4.
29 CAB 79/11, C.O.S. (41) 144th Mtg., Min. 8.
30 J.P. (41) 313, copy attached in CAB 79/11, C.O.S. (41) 146th Mtg., Min. 4.
31 Ibid.; Roskill, *War at sea*, I, 380; J.P. (41) 326, copy in CAB 79/11, C.O.S. (41) 149th Mtg., Min. 2, as Annex I. The Joint Planners also recommended 'that the War Cabinet should be asked to approve operations to secure the Cape Verdes, and, if possible, attempts to carry out peaceful landings in the Azores and Madeira simultaneously' (J.P. (41) 313, copy attached in CAB 79/11, C.O.S. (41) 146th Mtg., Min. 4).
32 CAB 79/11, C.O.S. (41) 146th Mtg., Min. 4 and C.O.S. (41) 147th Mtg., Min. 2.
33 CAB 79/11, C.O.S. (41) 147th Mtg., Min. 2.
34 Ibid.
35 FO 371/26945, C 4505, C 4506/306/41; FO 371/26905, C 4609/46/41; CAB 79/11, C.O.S. (41) 152nd Mtg., Min. 4.
36 Foreign Office telegram to Washington, no. 2186, 24 April 1941, containing the text of 'Former Naval Person' to President Roosevelt telegram of 23 April 1941, PREM 3/469.
37 'Former Naval Person' to President Roosevelt, 29 April 1941, PREM 3/469.
38 President Roosevelt to 'Former Naval Person', 1 May 1941, PREM 3/469.
39 'Former Naval Person' to President Roosevelt, 3 May 1941, PREM 3/469. See also, Dilks (ed.), *Cadogan diaries*, p. 375.
40 President Roosevelt to 'Former Naval Person', 3 May 1941, PREM 3/469.
41 'Former Naval Person' to President Roosevelt, 14 May 1941, PREM 3/469.
42 Lash, *Roosevelt and Churchill*, p. 316; Langer and Gleason, *Undeclared war*, p. 369; Halifax's telegram, no. 2406 to Foreign Office, 28 May 1941,

PREM 3/469. In mid May Roosevelt was contemplating extending the Monroe Doctrine, in a message to Congress, to include all of West Africa, north of the equator, and the Spanish and Portuguese Islands. Hull dissuaded him from doing so on the grounds that such a declaration would both provoke the Germans into grabbing these territories and intensely antagonise American isolationists inside, and outside, Congress. (Hull, *Memoirs*, II, 959–60.)

Roosevelt, as a politician always sensitive to the currents of popular opinion, was probably influenced, too, by public press and political advocacy of a United States occupation of the Azores (Langer and Gleason, *Undeclared war*, p. 369; Hugh Kay, *Slazar and modern Portugal* (London, 1970), p. 162).

43 Lash, *Roosevelt and Churchill*, p. 325; Langer and Gleason, *Undeclared war*, p. 460. Roosevelt told Halifax that 'he had for political reasons felt bound to stress the importance of these islands (Azores and Cape Verdes) in his speech' (Halifax's telegram, no. 2406 to Foreign Office, 28 May 1941, PREM 3/469).

44 Halifax's telegram, no. 2406 to Foreign Office, 28 May 1941, PREM 3/469.

45 Lash, *Roosevelt and Churchill*, p. 341.

46 'Former Naval Person' to President Roosevelt, 29 May 1941, PREM 3/469; Foreign Office telegram no. 2930 to British Embassy, Washington, 30 May 1941, Avon Papers, FO 954/18A.

47 FO 371/26897, C 4627/33/41; Hoare's dispatch, no. 187, 12 May 1941, Templewood Papers, XIII, 21.

48 FO 371/26897, C 4627/33/41; de la Cierva, *Historia del Franquismo*, I, 214.

49 Hoare's dispatch, no 187, 12 May 1941, Templewood Papers, XIII, 21.

50 FO 371/26905, C 5143/46/41.

51 CAB 65/18, WM 49 (41) 3. See also, CAB 65/18, WM 47 (41) 4.

52 Eden to Hoare, 17 May 1941, FO 794/19; FO 371/26897, C 5018/33/41.

53 Hoare's telegram no. 711 to Eden, 10 May 1941, and Hoare to Eden, 15 May 1941, Avon Papers, FO 954/27A.

54 Dalton Papers, diary 24.

55 Payne, *Falange*, pp. 228–33; de la Cierva, *Historia del Franquismo*, I, 214–16.

56 FO 371/26897, C 5443/33/41.

57 Payne, *Falange*, pp. 229–31; de la Cierva, *Historia del Franquismo*, I, 216; Serrano Suñer, *Memorias*, p. 201; Fernando García Lahiguera. *Ramón Serrano Suñer: un documento para la historia* (Barcelona, 1983), pp. 189–93.

58 Serrano Suñer, *Memorias*, pp. 200–1; García Lahiguera, *Serrano Suñer*, p. 190.

59 CAB 69/2, D.O. (41) 27th Mtg.

60 CAB 69/2, D.O. (41) 28th Mtg., Min. 5. See also, Roger Makins's memorandum on 'The political implications of Operation "Puma" ', of 5 May 1941, and minutes attached thereat (Avon Papers, FO 954/18A).

61 CAB 69/2, D.O. (41) 28th Mtg., Min. 5.

62 CAB 69/2, D.O. (41) 40th Mtg., Min. 4; CAB 79/55, C.O.S. (41) 13th Mtg. (o); CAB 79/86, C.O.S. (41) 169th Mtg., Min. 1; CAB 79/11, C.O.S. (41) 186th Mtg., Min. 1 and 190th Mtg., Min. 2; L.C. Hollis's minutes to

Prime Minister, 26, 31 May 1941, PREM 3/361/1; J.P. (41) 431, attached to CAB 79/12, C.O.S. (41) 204th Mtg., Min. 3; CAB 79/12, C.O.S. (41) 207th Mtg., Min. 5.

63 J.P. (41) 444, attached to CAB 79/12, C.O.S. (41) 213th Mtg., Min. 3. See, also, CAB 80/58, C.O.S. (41) 109 (o).

64 Eden to Hoare, 28 June 1941, FO 794/19. See also, Eden's minute to Churchill, 8 July 1941, Avon Papers, FO 954/18A and Churchill, *Grand alliance*, American edn., pp. 142–3.

65 FO 371/26939, C 6929, C 6979/222/41.

66 Hoare to Eden, 2 July 1941, Templewood Papers, XIII, 21.

67 De la Cierva, *Historia del Franquismo*, I, 196; FO 371/26940, C 7260/222/41.

68 FO 371/26905, C 6947/46/41; Hoare's dispatch no. 253, 25 June 1941, Templewood Papers, XIII, 21.

69 FO 371/26905, C 7030, C 7133/46/41; FO 371/26906, C 7752/46/41; CAB 65/18, WM 63 (41) 2. Franco described the crowd who had attacked the British Embassy 'as mostly communists in disguise', in an interview with Hoare, on 28 June 1941 (FO 371/26906, C 7752/46/41).

Hoare wanted to adopt 'the strongest possible line', again, in December 1941, over a Spanish police 'blockade' of the press annexe to the British Embassy in Madrid, somewhat to the dismay of the Foreign Office. However, once again, this incident fizzled out without serious result (FO 371/26953, C 13718/484/41; FO 371/26907, C 13811, C 13816, C 13909, C 13954, C 13984, C 14001, C 14082/46/41).

70 FO 371/26940, C 7431/222/41.

71 FO 371/26940, C 7919/222/41. The Blue Division was created by order of the Spanish Army's Central Staff on 28 June 1941 (de la Cierva, *Historia del Franquismo*, I, 198).

72 Dionisio Ridruejo, *Los cuadernos de Rusia: diario* (Barcelona, 1978), pp. 9–10.

73 Serrano Suñer, *Entre Hendaya y Gibraltar*, p. 209.

74 D.G.F.P., Series D, XII, 1080–1; XIII, *June 23, 1941–December 11, 1941* (London, 1964), 16–17; Ruhl, *Spanien im Zweiten Weltkrieg*, p. 28; Kleinfeld and Tambs, *Hitler's Spanish Legion*, pp. 1–2.

75 Ruhl, *Spanien im Zweiten Weltkrieg*, p. 31; D.G.F.P., Series D, XII, 930; XIII, 39.

76 Translation of Franco's speech, of 17 July 1941, contained in PREM 4/21/1.

77 Harvey (ed.), *War diaries of Oliver Harvey*, p. 21; Harvey diaries, 18 July 1941, Add. 56398.

78 FO 371/26906, C 8104/46/41; Harvey Diaries, 18 July 1941, Add. 56398.

79 Harvey (ed.), *War diaries of Oliver Harvey*, pp. 21–2; Harvey diaries, 19 July 1941, Add. 56398.

80 CAB 66/17, W.P. (41) 174.

81 CAB 65/19, WM 72 (41), 4; CAB 66/17, W.P. (41) 174.

82 FO 371/26906, C 8032, C 8624/46/41; Medlicott, *Economic blockade*, II, 286.

83 CAB 69/8, D.O. (41) 52nd Mtg., Min. 4.

84 Dilks (ed.), *Cadogan diaries*, p. 393.

85 R. M. Makins's memorandum on 'Operation "PUMA"', 9 July 1941, and

attached minutes, Avon Papers, FO 954/18A. There was concern voiced within the Admiralty, too, about the vulnerability of the Canaries to aerial assault from French Moroccan and Spanish airfields. It was conceded that it was important to deny the strategic advantages possessed by the Canaries, to the Germans, but it was also doubted that Britain could ever exploit them because of the likely scale of German aerial attack on British naval bases there, from North Africa ('Remarks on C.O.S. (41) 20th Mtg. (o)' by H. M. Harwood, 26 July 1941, ADM 205/11, File No. 12).

Inadequacy of fighter defences does appear to have been a serious weakness in the British plan. Only one squadron of fighters, along with sixteen cased Hurricanes, for example, were provided for by the Joint Planners, in early June, for 'Puma', on the apparent assumption that French Moroccan airfields would not be used against British bases in the Canaries (J.P. (41) 431, copy attached in CAB 79/12, C.O.S. (41) 204th Mtg., Min. 3; J.P. (41) 313, copy attached in CAB 79/11, C.O.S. (41) 146th Mtg., Min. 4).

86 CAB 79/86, C.O.S. (41) 259th Mtg., Min. 3. Churchill's attitude as revealed at this meeting clearly contradicts the assertion by Woodward that the Prime Minister was 'less inclined than the Foreign Office to regard General Franco's speech as of major importance' (*British foreign policy*, I, 452). Not having consulted the records of the Defence Committee at all, and the Chiefs of Staff Committee only partially, as he explains in the foreword to the latter volume (p.v.), Woodward understandably misses the dramatic impact of Franco's speech on Britain's policy-makers.

87 CAB 65/23, WM 74 (41), Confidential Annex.

88 CAB 79/55, C.O.S. (41) 20th Mtg., (o); CAB 79/86, C.O.S. (41) 259th Mtg., Min. 3.

89 Gwyer, *Grand strategy*, III, Part I, 8; Roskill, *War at sea*, I, 380; CAB 79/13, C.O.S. (41) 264th Mtg., Min. 2.

90 CAB 79/55, C.O.S. (41) 23rd Mtg. (o), Min. 1; ADM 205/11, File No. 12; J.P. (41) 577, copy attached in CAB 79/13, C.O.S. (41) 257th Mtg., Min. 2; CAB 69/8, D.O. (41) 53rd Mtg., Min. 3, Confidential Annex.

91 Chiefs of Staff minute to Prime Minister, 29 July 1941, PREM 3/361/1, copy in CAB 79/55, C.O.S. (41) 23rd Mtg. (o) as appendix A.

92 Harvey (ed.), *War diaries of Oliver Harvey*, pp. 22–3; Harvey diaries, 22 (?23) July 1941, Add. 56398.

93 CAB 69/8, D.O. (41) 53rd Mtg., Min. 3, Confidential Annex; CAB 79/55, C.O.S. (41) 24th Mtg. (o).

94 CAB 79/13, C.O.S. (41) 273rd Mtg., Min. 3.

95 CAB 66/18, W.P. (41) 202, W.P. (41) 203; C.O.S. (R) 8, copy in PREM 3/485/5; F.R.U.S., 1941, I, 356–7; Harvey Diaries, 12 August 1941, Add. 56398.

96 C.O.S. (R) 6, copy in PREM 3/485/5.

97 Ibid.; CAB 66/18, W.P. (41) 202.

98 FO 371/26906, C 8491, C 8624/46/41. See also, Hoare to Hankey, 21 August 1941, Hankey Papers, 4/33; and Hoare to Eden, 2 August 1941, Templewood Papers, XIII, 21.

99 D.G.F.P., Series D, XIII, 223.

100 FO 371/49663, Z 11696/11696/41. The speech is wrongly placed in the year 1942 in the record of this conversation, but it seems clear that it was the 17 July 1941 discourse which was meant.
101 Eccles (ed.), *By safe hand*, p. 304.
102 Hoare to Beaverbrook, 6 August 1941, Templewood Papers, XIII, 18; FO 371/26906, C 8399/46/41. Actually, Hoare was probably not the only one to get wind of the projected British move against the Canaries for Franco revealed, in conversation with his cousin, after the war, his knowledge that 'the allies were on the point of violating our neutrality [by] invading the Canary Islands', a threat which worried him greatly. However, Franco did not specify whether it was sooner or later that he came to possess information of this planned operation (Franco Salgado-Araujo, *Mis conversaciones privadas*, p. 455).
103 Hillgarth to Churchill, 12 August 1941, PREM 4/21/1.
104 CAB 79/55, C.O.S. (41) 26th Mtg. (o).
105 Dill to Hoare, 26 August 1941, Templewood Papers, XIII, 18.
106 CAB 79/55, C.O.S. (41) 29th Mtg. (o), Min. 1, 28th Mtg. (o), 31st Mtg. (o); CAB 80/59, C.O.S. (41) 182 (o); Harvey diaries, 29 August 1941, Add. 56398.

Actually, Dill, who only two days earlier had written to Hoare to tell him of Torr's persuasive influence on the Chiefs of Staff, was the only one present at their 28 August meeting to point out the drawbacks of not carrying out 'Pilgrim' in September: '. . . if it were decided to postpone "Pilgrim" we should have to accept the disadvantage that the defences might grow steadily stronger. If in addition strong reinforcements were sent to the Island it might seriously prejudice the success of the operation.' (CAB 79/55, C.O.S. (41) 29th Mtg. (o), Min. 1).
107 Churchill's minute to Foreign Office, 25 July 1941, PREM 4/21/1.
108 Churchill's minute to Eden, 16 August 1941, PREM 4/21/1; FO 371/26907, C 9813/46/41; extract in FO 371/26907, C 9750/46/41. However, Churchill did conclude his minute with the following sentence: 'Meanwhile, however, preparations are going and should go forward' (PREM 4/21/1; FO 371/26907, C 9813/46/41).

The copies of the minute contained in the latter files both bear an original date, '7' August 1941, which has been scored through, and '16' placed above it. This may indicate that Churchill had read Franco's speech and changed his view of it, even before his August encounter with Roosevelt. This doubt about the date of Churchill's reinterpretation of Franco's discourse is significant because of the possible impact of his meeting with the President on his intention to execute 'Pilgrim'. If Churchill's mind had been moving away from launching the expedition before the meeting at Placentia Bay, the temptation of drawing the United States nearer active participation in the war, noted above, perhaps led him to consider seizing the Canaries, again. If that was the case, he changed his mind afterwards. On the other hand, all Churchill's doubts about the desirability of executing 'Pilgrim' may have arisen after the Atlantic meeting.
109 CAB 79/55, C.O.S. (41) 29th Mtg., (o), Min. 1. See also, Harvey (ed.), *War diaries of Oliver Harvey*, p. 36 and 'Former Naval Person' telegram no. T525, 28 August 1941, Avon Papers, FO 954/18A.

110 Bond (ed.), *Chief of Staff*, II, 34; Butler, *Grand Strategy*, III, pt. 2, p. 515.
111 Arthur Layton Funk, *The politics of Torch: the Allied landings and the Algiers 'putsch', 1942* (Lawrence, 1974), p. 95; Stephen E. Ambrose, *The supreme commander: the war years of General Dwight D. Eisenhower* (London, 1971), p. 94.
112 F. H. Hinsley, E. E. Thomas, C. F. G. Ransom, R. C. Knight, *British intelligence in the Second World War*, II (London, 1981), 468–72; FO 371/31289, C 10739/10738/41.
113 FO 371/31289, C 10739/10738/41.
114 FO 371/31289, C 10745/10738/G. See also, Dilks (ed.), *Cadogan diaries*, p. 478.
115 Michael Howard, *Grand strategy*, IV (London, 1972), 117–36; Ambrose, *Supreme commander*, pp. 86–96; Robert H. Ferrell (ed.), *The Eisenhower diaries* (New York, 1981), pp. 76–8.
116 Woodward, *British foreign policy*, IV, 11; Harvey diaries, 6 November 1942, Add. 56399. Both Serrano Suñer and General Varela had lost their government positions, on 2 September, in the political aftermath of a violent fracas between Carlists and Falangists on 16 August (Payne, *Falange*, pp. 234–6). Jordana, of course, was reappointed on 3 September 1942, to the ministry which he held before in 1938–9.
117 Carlton J. H. Hayes, *Wartime mission in Spain, 1942–1945* (New York, 1946), 1976 reprint (New York), pp. 90–1. Hayes replaced Weddell as U.S. Ambassador to Spain, on 2 May 1942 (ibid., p. 10).
118 Templewood, *Ambassador*, pp. 176–8.
119 Fernando Morán, *Una política exterior para España: una alternativa socialista* (Barcelona, 1980), p. 15.
120 Winston S. Churchill, *The Hinge of Fate*, American edn. (Boston, 1950), pp. 528, 541, 544, 596
121 Jordana to Alba, 27 November 1942, Alba Papers, Caja 2^A – No. 4.
122 Templewood, *Ambassador*, pp. 179–82.
123 Jordana to Alba, 27 November 1942, Alba Papers, Caja 2^A – No. 4.
124 *Akten zur deutschen Auswärtigen Politik*, Serie E, V, *1. Januar bis 30. April 1943* (Göttingen, 1978), 194; Kleinfeld and Tambs, *Hitler's Spanish legion*, pp. 306–10.

Conclusion

1 An extract from Adolf Hitler's memorandum on the Four Year Plan, August 1936 (Anthony Adamthwaite, *The lost peace: international relations in Europe, 1918–1939*, Documents of modern history series (London, 1980), p. 180.
2 Serrano Suñer, *Entre Hendaya y Gibraltar*, p. 296.
3 Trevor-Roper (ed.), *Hitler's table talk, 1941–44*, pp. 568–70; Rich, *Hitler's war aims*, II, 403–4.
4 Albert Speer, *Spandau: the secret diaries* (London, 1976), 1977 edn., pp. 183–4.
5 Templewood, *Ambassador*, p. 282.
6 Martin Wright, 'Why is there no International Theory?' in Herbert Butterfield and Martin Wight (eds.), *Diplomatic investigations: essays in the theory of international politics* (London, 1966), p. 33. Wight was

actually referring to international theory, which he defined as 'the theory of survival'. But, of course, survival is the focus of the practice, as much as the theory, of international relations.

7 Hitler to Franco, 6 February 1941, D.G.F.P., Series D, XII, 41.

8 Hoare's dispatch No. 274, 11 July 1941, copy in Templewood Papers, XIII, 21.

9 Cited by A. J. P. Taylor in 'Daddy, what was Winston Churchill?' in his *Essays in English history* (Harmondsworth, 1976), p. 298.

10 Memorandum by Lord Templewood on 'The Allied attitude towards the Franco Government', 16 October 1944, copies in FO 371/39671, C 14492/23/41 and CAB 66/88, W.P. (44) 665.

11 FO 371/39671, C 16544/23/41.

12 Muggeridge (ed.), *Ciano's diplomatic papers*, p. 291.

13 FO 371/39672, C 17266/23/41.

14 FO 371/39671, C 14492/23/41; CAB 66/88, W.P. (44) 665.

15 CAB 66/88, W.P. (44) 665.

16 FO 371/39671, C 13318/23/41.

17 Franco to Alba, 18 October 1944, CAB 66/59, W.P. (44) 735, Annex 11.

18 FO 371/39672, C 17007/23/41.

19 CAB 66/59, W.P. (44), 735.

20 Prime Minister's personal minute to Foreign Secretary, 11 December 1944, PREM 8/106.

21 Woodward, *British foreign policy*, IV, 30–1; CAB 66/57, W.P. (44), 22; CAB 66/58, W.P. (44) 665.

22 Prime Minister's personal minute to Foreign Secretary, 10 November 1944, FO 371/39671, C 16068/23/41.

23 CAB 65/48, WM 157 (44) 2.

24 Sir Llewellyn Woodward, *British foreign policy in the Second World War*, V, (London, 1976), 480–1.

25 Arthur P. Whitaker, *Spain and defense of the West: ally and liability* (New York, 1961), pp. 22–6; José Antonio Biescas and Manuel Tuñón de Lara, *España bajo la dictadura franquista, 1939–1975 (Historia de España* ed. by Manuel Tuñón de Lara, X) (Barcelona, 1980), p. 228; Edouard de Blaye, *Franco and the politics of Spain* (Harmondsworth, 1976), p. 163.

26 Whitaker, *Spain and defense*, pp. 30–1; de Blaye, *Franco*, pp. 169–71.

27 CAB 66/59, W.P. (44) 735; Hayes, *Wartime Mission*, p. 287.

28 Angel Viñas, *Los pactos secretos de Franco con Estados Unidos: bases, ayuda económica, recortes de soberanía* (Barcelona, 1981), pp. 26–7.

29 See, e.g., C. L. Sulzberger, *A long row of candles: memoirs and diaries (1934–1954)* (Toronto, 1969), pp. 419–20.

30 CAB 129/46, C.P. (51) 184, Annex B.

31 Viñas, *Los pactos*, pp. 53–4.

32 CAB 128/19, C.M. 49 (51) 5.

33 De Blaye, *Franco*, p. 172.

34 Viñas, *Los pactos*, p. 54; De Blaye, *Franco*, pp. 172–3.

35 Viñas, *Los pactos*, pp. 94–102.

36 Whitaker, *Spain and Defense*, pp. 44, 57–8; Angel Viñas, *et al., Política comercial exterior en Espana, (1931–1975)*, II (Madrid, 1979), 1256.

Bibliography

Unpublished Sources

Official Documents British Government Archives, Public Record Office.

Cabinet office
CAB 21 Registered Files.
CAB 65 War Cabinet Minutes.
CAB 66 War Cabinet Memoranda.
CAB 69 War Cabinet Defence Committee (Operations).
CAB 79 War Cabinet, Chiefs of Staff Commitee, Minutes of Meetings.
CAB 80 War Cabinet, Chiefs of Staff Committee, Memoranda.
CAB 81 War Cabinet, Chiefs of Staff Committees and Sub-Committees.
CAB 84 War Cabinet Joint Planning Committees.
CAB 107 War Cabinet, Co-ordination of departmental action in the event of war with certain countries.
CAB 122 British Joint Services Mission, Washington Office Files.
PREM 3 Operational Papers, Files of the Prime Minister's office kept at the War Cabinet offices dealing with defence and operational subjects.
PREM 4 Confiential Papers, Files of the Prime Minster's office kept at No. 10 Downing Street, dealing for the most part with civil and political matters.
PREM 8 Papers, 1944–5.

Admiralty
ADM 1 Admiralty and Secretariat Papers.
ADM 116 Admiralty and Secretariat Cases.
ADM 199 War of 1939–45, War History Cases.

Foreign office
FO 371 General Correspondence after 1906 Political.
FO 794 Private Office 'Individual' Files. Selected files of correspondence, etc., relating to ambassadors and senior diplomats.
FO 800 Private Collections of Various Ministers and Officials.

Ministry of Economic Warfare
FO 837 Ministry of Economic Warfare.

311

Private Documents

Alba Papers Palacio de Liria, Madrid.
Attlee Papers Churchill College, Cambridge.
Avon Papers FO 954, P.R.O.
Beaverbrook Papers House of Lords Record Office.
Dalton Papers British Library of Economics and Political Science, London School of Economics and Political Science.
Halifax Papers Two collections: (a) FO 800 309–28, P.R.O.; (b) Hickleton Papers (made available in York Public Library).
Hankey Papers Churchill College, Cambridge.
Lord Harvey of Tasburgh, diaries and papers British Library, London.
General Archive of Spain's Ministerio de Asuntos Exteriores Palacio de Santa Cruz, Madrid.
Phipps Papers Churchill College, Cambridge.
Roosevelt Papers Franklin D. Roosevelt Library, Hyde Park, New York. (The Library supplied me with xerox copies of the documents in this collection, relating to Spain, for the period 1940–1.)
Templewood Papers (Papers of Rt Hon. Sir Samuel Hoare, later Viscount Templewood). University Library, Cambridge.

Published Sources

Official documents

Actes et Documents du Saint Siège Relatifs à la 2e Guerre Mondiale. Vols. IV, V. Libreria Editrice Vaticana. Vatican City, 1967, 1969.
Dez Anos de Politíca Externa (1936–1947): A Naçao Portuguesa E A Segunda Guerra Mundial. Vols. VII, VIII. Ministério Dos Negócios Estrangeiros. Lisbon, 1971 and 1973.
I Documenti diplomatici italiani. 9th Series; Vols. IV, V. Ministero degli Affari Esteri. Rome, 1954.
Documents on British foreign policy 1919–1939. 2nd Series. Vols. XVII, XVIII, XIX. H.M.S.O. London, 1979, 1980, 1982.
Documents diplomatiques français, 2ᵉ Série (1936–39). Vols. III, IX, X. Ministère des affaires étrangères. Paris, 1966, 1974, 1976.
Documents on German Foreign Policy. Series D. Vols. III, IX, X, XI, XII, XIII. H.M.S.O. London, 1951, 1956, 1957, 1961, 1962, 1964; Series E; V, Gottingen, 1978.
Documents secrets du ministère des affaires étrangères d'Allemagne (1936–1943). Traduit du russe par Madeleine et Michel Eristov. Vol. III: *Espagne.* Paris, 1946.
Foreign Relations of the United States. 1938. Vol. I. Department of State, Washington, D.C., 1955.
Foreign Relations of the United States. 1940. Vols. II, III. Department of State, Washington, D.C., 1957.
Foreign Relations of the United States. 1941. Vols. I, II, III. Department of State, Washington, D.C., 1958–9.
'Führer Conferences on naval affairs', ed. H. G. Thursfield. *Brassey's Naval Annual.* London, 1948.
Hansard.

Hitler's war directives, 1939–1945. H. R. Trevor-Roper (ed.), London, 1964. 1966 edition.
Roosevelt and Churchill: their secret wartime correspondence. Francis L. Loewenheim, Harold D. Langley and Manfred Jonas (eds.). London, 1975.
The Spanish government and the Axis: official German documents. Department of State. Washington, D.C., 1946.

Diaries, Memoirs, etc.
Acheson, Dean *Present at the creation: my years in the State Department.* London, 1970.
Avon, The Earl of *The Eden memoirs,* vol. I *Facing the dictators.* London, 1962; vol. II, *The reckoning.* London, 1965.
Azaña, Manuel *Obras completas* vol. IV, *Memorias políticas y de guerra.* Mexico, 1968.
Azcárate, Pablo de *Mi embajada en Londres durante la guerra civil española.* Barcelona, 1976.
Baudouin, Paul *The private diaries of Paul Baudouin.* London, 1948.
Cadogan, Sir Alexander *The diaries of Sir Alexander Cadogan, 1938–1945.* David Dilks (ed.). London, 1971.
Charles-Roux, F. *Cinq mois tragiques aux affaires étrangères.* Paris, 1949.
Churchill, Winston, S. *The Second World War* vol. II, *Their finest hour.* American edn., Boston, 1949; vol. III, *The grand alliance.* American edn., Boston, 1950; vol. IV, *The hinge of fate.* American edn., Boston, 1950.
Ciano, Count Galeazzo *Ciano's diary, 1937–1938.* Malcolm Muggeridge (Introd.). London, 1952.
Ciano's diary, 1939–1943. Malcolm Muggeridge (ed.). London, 1947.
Ciano's diplomatic papers. Malcolm Muggeridge (ed.). London, 1948.
Colville, John *Footprints in time.* London, 1976.
Dalton, Hugh *The fateful years: memoirs, 1931–1945.* London, 1957.
Eccles, David (ed.). *By safe hand: letters of Sybil and David Eccles, 1939–42.* London, 1983.
Eisenhower, Dwight D. *The Eisenhower diaries.* Robert H. Ferrell (ed.). New York, 1981.
Franco Salgado-Araujo, Teniente General Francisco, *Mis conversaciones privadas con Franco.* Barcelona, 1976.
Mi vida junto a Franco. Barcelona, 1977.
Gil Robles, José María, *La Monarquía por la que yo luché: páginas de un diario (1941–1954).* Madrid, 1976.
Goebbels, Paul Josef *The Goebbels diaries, 1939–41.* Fred Taylor (ed.). London, 1982.
Halder, Generaloberst Franz *Kriegstagebuch: Tagliche Aufzeichungen des Chefs des Generalstabes des Heeres, 1939–1942,* 3 vols., vol. II, H.-A. Jacobsen (ed.). Stuttgart, 1963.
Harvey, Oliver *The diplomatic diaries of Oliver Harvey, 1937–1940.* London, 1970. John Harvey (ed.).
The war diaries of Oliver Harvey, 1941–1945. London, 1978.
Hayes, Carlton J. H. *Wartime mission in Spain, 1942–1945.* New York, 1946. 1976 reprint.
Hitler, Adolf *Hitler's table talk, 1941–44: his private conversations.* H. R. Trevor-Roper (ed.). 2nd edn., London, 1973.

Hull, Cordell *Memoirs*, 2 vols. London, 1949.

Ickes, Harold L. *The secret diary of Harold L. Ickes*, vol. III, *The lowering clouds, 1939–1941*. London, 1955.

Jacobsen, Hans-Adolf (ed.) *Kriegstagebuch des Oberkommandos der Wehrmacht*, vol. I, *1940–1941*. Frankfurt, 1965. 4 vol. series (1940–5), Percy E. Schramm (ed.).

Jones, Thomas *A diary with letters, 1931–1950*. London, 1954.

Kennedy, John *The business of war*. London, 1957.

Koltsov, Mijail *Diario de la guerra Española*. Madrid, 1978.

Langley, J. M. *Fight another day*. London, 1974.

Lee, Raymond E. *The London Observer: the journal of General Raymond E. Lee, 1940–1941*. James Leutze (ed.). London, 1972.

Liddell Hart, B. H. *The memoirs of Captain Liddell Hart*, vol. II. London, 1965.

Lockhart, Sir Robert Bruce *The diaries of Sir Robert Bruce Lockhart*, vol II, 1939–1965. Kenneth Young (ed.), London, 1980.

Lomax, Sir John *The diplomatic smuggler*. London, 1965.

Long, Breckinridge *The war diary of Breckinridge Long*. Fred L. Israel (ed.). Lincoln, Nebraska, 1966.

Maisky, Ivan *Spanish notebooks*. London, 1966.

Nicolson, Harold *Harold Nicolson: diaries and letters*, vol. I, 1930–9 (1969 edn,), vol. II, 1939–45 (1970 edn.), Nigel Nicholson (ed.). London.

Orwell, George *The collected essays, journalism and letters of George Orwell*, vol. II; *My country right or left, 1940–1943*. Sonia Orwell and Ian Angus (eds.). 4 vols., London, 1968. 1970 edn., Harmondsworth.

Pereira, Pedro Theotonio *Memórias*, vol. II. Lisbon, 1973.

Peterson, Sir Maurice *Both sides of the curtain*. London, 1950.

Philby, Kim *My silent war*. London, 1969 edn.

Piétri, Francois *Mes années d'Espagne*. Paris, 1954.

Popov, Dusko *Spy/counterspy*. London, 1974, 1976 edn.

Pownall, Sir Henry *Chiefs of staff: diaries of Lieutenant-General Sir Henry Pownall*, vol. I: *1933–40*. London, 1972. vol. II: *1940–1944*. Brian Bond (ed.). London, 1974.

Ridruejo, Dionisio *Casi unas memorias*. Barcelona, 1976.
     Los cuadernos de Rusia: diario. Barcelona, 1978.

Sainz Rodríguez, Pedro *Testimonio y Recuerdos*. Barcelona, 1978.

Schellenberg, Walter *The Schellenberg memoirs*. London, 1956.

Schmidt, Paul *Hitler's interpreter*. London, 1951.

Serrano Suñer, Ramón *Entre hendaya y Gibraltar*. 1973 edn., Barcelona.
     Memorias: entre el silencio y la propaganda, la historia como fue. Barcelona, 1977.

Speer, Albert *Spandau: the secret diaries*. London, 1977 edn.

Sulzberger, C. L. *A long row of candles: memoirs and diaries (1934–1954)*. Toronto, 1969.

Templewood, Viscount *Ambassador on special mission*. London, 1946.

Thompson, R. W. *Churchill and Morton: correspondence between Major Sir Desmond Morton and R. W. Thompson*. London, 1976.

Tree, Ronald *When the moon was high: memoirs of peace and war, 1897–1942*. London, 1975.

Wheeler-Bennett, Sir John (ed.) *Action this day: working with Churchill.* London, 1968.

Weizsäcker, Ernst von. *Die Weizsäcker-Papiere, 1933–1950.* Leonidas E. Hill (ed.). Frankfurt, 1974.

Books

Abella, Rafael *Por el imperio hacía díos: crónica de una posguerra.* Barcelona, 1978.

Abendroth, Hans-Henning *Hitler in der Spanischen Arena.* Paderborn, 1973.

Adamthwaite, Anthony *France and the coming of the Second World War, 1936–1939.* London., 1977.

Addison, Paul *The road to 1945, British politics and the Second World War.* London, 1977 edn.

Ambrose, Stephen E. *The supreme commander: the war years of General Dwight D. Eisenhower.* London, 1971.

Areilza, José María de *Embajadores sobre España.* Madrid, 1947.

Areilza, José María de and Castiella, Fernando María *Reivindicaciones de España,* Madrid, 2nd edn., 1941.

Avery, David *Not on Queen Victoria's birthday: the story of the Río Tinto mines.* London, 1974.

Barclay, Glen *Struggle for a continent: the diplomatic history of South America, 1917–45.* London, 1971.

Their finest hour. London, 1977.

Barker, Elisabeth *Churchill and Eden at war.* London, 1978.

Beesly, Patrick *Very special admiral: the life of Admiral J. H. Godfrey, C.B.* London, 1980.

Biescas, José Antonio and Tuñón de Lara, Manuel *España bajo la dictadura franquista (1939–1975).* Barcelona, 1980.

Birkinhead, Earl of *Halifax.* London, 1965.

Blaye, Edouard de *Franco and the politics of Spain.* Harmondsworth, Middlesex, 1976.

Brissaud, André *Canaris: la guerra Española y la segunda guerra mundial.* Barcelona, 1972.

Bullock, Alan *Hitler: a study in tyranny.* London, 1952. 1962 edn. Harmondsworth, Middlesex.

The life and times of Ernest Bevin, vol. I, *Trade Union leader, 1881–1940.* London, 1960.

Burdick, Charles B. *Germany's military strategy and Spain in World War II.* Syracuse, New York, 1968.

Burns, James MacGregor *Roosevelt: the lion and the fox, 1882–1942.* New York, 1956.

Roosevelt: the soldier of freedom, 1940–1945. New York, 1970.

Butler, Ewan *Mason-Mac: the life of Lieutenant-General Sir Noel Mason-Macfarlane.* London, 1972.

Butler, J. R. M. *Grand strategy,* vol. II, *September 1939–June 1941.* H.M.S.O., London, 1957; vol. III, *June 1941–August 1942.* London, 1964.

Cable, James *The Royal Navy and the Siege of Bilbao.* Cambridge, 1979.

Calvocoressi, Peter and Wint, Guy *Total war: causes and courses of the*

Second World War. London, 1972. 1974 edn., Harmondsworth, Middlesex.

Carr, Raymond *The Spanish tragedy: the civil war in perspective.* London, 1977.

Carr, Raymond and Fusi Aizpurua, Juan Pablo *Spain: dictatorship to democracy.* London, 1979.

Cierva, Ricardo de la *Historia del Franquismo,* vol. I, *orígines y configuración (1939–1945).* Barcelona, 1975.

Hendaya: punto final. Barcelona, 1981.

Collins, Larry and Lapiere, Dominique *Or I'll dress you in mourning: the extraordinary rise of El Cordobés.* London, 1968. 1969 edn., Frogmore, St Albans, Hertfordshire.

Colton, Joel *Léon Blum: Humanist in politics.* New York, 1966. 1974 edn., Cambridge, Mass.

Colvin, Ian *Canaris: chief of intelligence.* 1973 edn., Maidstone, Kent.

Cortada, James W. *Relaciones España – U.S.A., 1941–45.* Barcelona, 1973.

Cosgrave, Patrick *Churchill at war, I, Alone, 1939–40.* London, 1974.

Coverdale, John F. Italian intervention in the Spanish Civil War. Princeton, 1975.

Cowling, Maurice *The impact of Hitler: British politics and British policy, 1933–1940.* Cambridge and London, 1975.

Creveld, Martin van *Hitler's strategy, 1940–1941: the Balkan clue.* Cambridge and London,1973.

Cross, J. A. *Sir Samuel Hoare: a political biography.* London, 1977.

Crozier, Brian *Franco: a biographical history.* London, 1967.

Dankelmann, Otfried *Franco zwischen Hitler und den Westmächten.* Berlin, 1970.

Detwiler, Donald S. *Hitler, Franco und Gibraltar: die Frage des Spanischen Eintritts in den Zweiten Weltkrieg.* Wiesbaden, 1962.

Donoughue, Bernard, and Jones, G. W. *Herbert Morrison: portrait of a politician.* London, 1973.

Doussinague, José María *España Tenía Razón.* Madrid, 1949.

Duff, Charles *A key to victory: Spain.* London, 1940.

Dzelepy, E. N. *Franco, Hitler et les Alliés.* Brussels, 1961.

Edwards, Jill, *The British government and the Spanish Civil War, 1936–1939.* London, 1979.

Feiling, Keith *The life of Neville Chamberlain.* London, 1946.

Feis, Herbert *The Spanish story: Franco and the nations at war.* New York, 1948. 1966 edn.

Foot, Michael *Aneurin Bevan,* vol. I, 1897–1945. 2 vols., London, 1962, 1973; 1975 edn.

Foot, M. R. D. and Langley, J. M. *M19: Escape and evasion, 1939–1945.* London, 1979.

Fraser, Ronald *In hiding: the life of Manuel Cortés.* London, 1972.

The Pueblo: a mountain village on the Costa del Sol. London, 1973.

Funk, Arthur Layton *The politics of Torch: the allied landings and the Algiers Putsch, 1942.* Lawrence, 1974.

Gallo, Max *Spain under Franco: a history.* London, 1973.

García Lahiguera, Fernando *Ramón Serrano Suñer: un documento para la historia.* Barcelona, 1983.

Garriga, Ramón *La España de Franco: las relaciones secretas con Hitler.* 2nd edn., Puebla, Mexico, 1970.
Gibson, Ian *En busca de José Antonio.* Barcelona, 1980.
Gilbert, Martin *Winston S. Churchill,* vol. V, *1922–1939.* London, 1976.
Finest hour: Winston Churchill, 1939–1941. London, 1983.
Gordon, David L. and Dangerfield, Royden *The hidden weapon: the story of economic warfare.* New York, 1947.
Gwyer, J. M. A. *Grand strategy,* vol. III, *June 1941–August 1942,* Part I. H.M.S.O., London, 1964.
Hamilton, Thomas J. *Appeasement's child: the Franco regime in Spain.* London, 1943.
Harper, Glenn T. *German economic policy in Spain during the Spanish Civil War, 1936–1939.* Paris, 1967
Hillgruber, Andreas *Hitlers strategie: politik und kriegführung, 1940–1941.* Frankfurt, 1965.
Hills, George *Franco: the man and his nation.* London, 1967.
Rock of contention: a history of Gibraltar. London, 1974.
Hinsley, F. H. *Hitler's strategy.* Cambridge, 1951.
Hinsley, F. H., Thomas, E. E., Ransom, C. F. G., Knight, R. C. *British intelligence in the Second World War.* 3 vols. H.M.S.O. London, vol. I, 1979; vol. II, 1981.
Höhne, Heinz *Canaris.* London, 1979.
Howard, Michael *Grand strategy,* vol. IV, *August 1942–September 1943.* H.M.S.O., London, 1972.
Kay, Hugh *Salazar and modern Portugal.* London, 1970.
Kleinfeld, Gerald R. and Tambs, Lewis A. *Hitler's Spanish legion: the Blue Division in Russia.* Carbondale, 1979.
Knox, MacGregor *Mussolini unleashed, 1939–1941: politics and strategy in fascist Italy's last war.* Cambridge, 1982.
Langer, William L. *Our Vichy Gamble.* New York, 1947. 1966 edn.
Langer, William L. and Gleason, S. Everett *The world crisis and American foreign policy,* vol. I, *The challenge to isolation, 1937–1940.* New York, 1952; vol. II, *The undeclared war, 1940–1941.* New York, 1953.
Lash, Joseph P. *Roosevelt and Churchill, 1939–1941: the partnership that saved the west.* London, 1977.
Laski, Harold J. *Where do we go from here? an essay in interpretation.* Harmondsworth, 1940.
Leach, Barry A. *German strategy against Russia, 1939–1941.* Oxford and London, 1973.
Liddell Hart, B. H. *The defence of Britain.* London, 1939
Mack Smith, Denis *Mussolini's Roman empire.* London, 1976.
McLachlan, Donald *Room 39: naval intelligence in action, 1939–45.* London, 1968.
Masterman, J. C. *The double-cross system in the war of 1939 to 1945.* New Haven, 1972.
Medlicott, W. N. *The economic blockade,* vol. I. H.M.S.O., London, 1952; vol. II. H.M.S.O., London, 1959.
Monroe, Elizabeth *The Mediterranen in politics.* London, 1938.
Morales, Lezcano, Víctor *Historia de la no-beligerancia Española durante la segunda guerra mundial.* Las Palmas, 1980.

Morán, Fernando *Una política exterior para España: una alternativa socialista.* Barcelona, 1980.

Papeleux, Léon *L'Amiral Canaris: entre Franco et Hitler.* Tournai, 1977.

Parkinson, Roger *Blood, toil, tears and sweat: the war history from Dunkirk to Alemain, based on the War Cabinet Papers of 1940 to 1942.* London, 1973.

Paxton, Robert O. *Vichy France: Old Guard and New Order, 1940–1944.* London, 1972.

Payne, Stanley G. *Falange: a history of Spanish Fascism.* 1967 edn., Stanford.
Politics and the military in modern Spain. Stanford, 1967.
Franco's Spain. London, 1968.

Pelling, Henry *Britain and the Second World War.* London, 1970.

Pimlott, Ben *Labour and the Left in the 1930s.* Cambridge, 1977.

Pratt, Lawrence R. *East of Malta, west of Suez: Britain's Mediterranean crisis, 1936–1939.* Cambridge, 1975.

Proctor, Raymond *Agonía de un neutral (las relaciones hispanoalemanes durante la segunda guerra mundial y la división azul).* Madrid, 1972.

Puzzo, Dante A. *Spain and the Great Powers, 1936–1941.* New York. 1962. 1972 edn.

Rich, Norman *Hitler's war aims*, vol. I, *Ideology, the Nazi state, and the course of expansion.* London, 1973; vol. II, *The establishment of the New Order.* London, 1974.

Rodríguez-Moñino Soriano, Rafael *La misión diplomática del XVII duque de Alba: en la embajada de España en Londres (1937–1945).* Valencia, 1971.

Roskill, Captain S. W. *The war at sea, 1939–1945*, 3 vols., vol. I, *The defensive.* H.M.S.O., 1976 impression with amendments, London.

Ruhl, Klaus-Jörg *Spanien im Zweiten Weltkrieg: Franco, die Falange und das 'Dritte Reich'.* Hamburg, 1975.

Saña, Heleno *El Franquismo sin mitos: conversaciones con Serrano Suñer.* Barcelona, 1982.

'Scipio' *100,000,000 Allies – if we choose.* London, 1940.

Smith, Richard Harris *O.S.S.: the secret history of America's first central intelligence agency.* Berkeley, 1972, 1981 edn.

Southworth, Herbert Rutledge *El mito de la Cruzada de Franco.* Paris, 1963.
Antifalange: estudio crítico de 'Falange en la guerra de España: la unificación y Hedilla' de Maximiniano García Venero. Paris, 1967.

Stafford, David *Britain and European resistance 1940–1945.* London, 1980.

Strong, Sir Kenneth *Men of intelligence.* London, 1970.

Stuart, Graham H. *The international city of Tangier.* 2nd edn., Stanford, 1955.

Taylor, A. J. P. *Beaverbrook.* 1974 edn., Harmondsworth, Middlesex.

Taylor, A. J. P. (ed.), *Churchill: four faces and the man.* 1973 edn., Harmondsworth, Middlesex.

Thomas, Hugh *The Spanish Civil War.* 3rd edn., Harmondsworth, Middlesex, 1977.

Thomas, Hugh (ed.) *José Antonio Primo de Rivera: selected writings.* London, 1972.

Thomas, R. T. *Britain and Vichy: the dilemma of Anglo-French relations 1940–42.* London, 1979.

Toynbee, Arnold and Veronica (eds.) *The war and neutrals (survey of international affairs, 1939–1946).* London, 1956.
Traina, Richard P. *American diplomacy and the Spanish Civil War.* Bloomington, 1968.
Trythall, J. W. D. *Franco: a biography.* London, 1970.
Viñas, Angel *El oro de Moscú: alfa y omega de un mito franquista.* Barcelona, 1978.
  Los pactos secretos de Franco con Estados Unidos: bases, ayuda económica, recortes de soberanía. Barcelona, 1981.
Viñas, Angel et al. *Política comercial exterior en España (1931–1975),* 2 vols. Madrid, 1979.
Warner, Geoffrey *Pierre Laval and the eclipse of France.* London, 1968.
Watkins, K. W. *Britain divided: the effect of the Spanish Civil War on British political opinion.* London, 1963.
Weinberg, Gerhard L. *World in the balance: behind the scenes of World War II.* London, 1981.
Werth, Alexander *France and Munich: before and after the surrender.* London, 1939. 1969 edn., New York.
West, Nigel *MI5: British security service operations 1909–1945.* London, 1983, 1984 edn.
  MI6: British secret intelligence service operations, 1909–45. London, 1983.
Whitaker, Arthur P. *Spain and defense of the west: ally and liability.* New York, 1961.
Wilson, Theodore A. *The first summit: Roosevelt and Churchill at Placentia Bay, 1941.* London, 1970.
Woodward, Sir Llewellyn *British foreign policy in the Second World War,* vol. I, H.M.S.O., London, 1970; vol. IV, H.M.S.O., London, 1975; vol. V, H.M.S.O., London, 1976.
Wright, Gordon, *The ordeal of total war, 1939–1945.* New York, 1968.
Young, Robert J. *In command of France: French foreign policy and military planning, 1933–1940.* Cambridge, Mass., 1978.

Articles, Essays and Theses
Abendroth, Hans-Henning, 'Deutschlands Rolle im Spanischen Bürgerkrieg', in Manfred Funke (ed.), *Hitler, Deutschland und die Mächte.* Düsseldorf, 1978, pp. 471–88.
Allan Watson, Bert. *United States–Spanish relations, 1939–1946.* Unpublished Ph.D (The George Washington University), Washington, D.C., 1971.
Blinkhorn, Martin, 'Spain: "the Spanish problem" and the imperial myth', *Journal of Contemporary History,* XV (1980), 5–25.
Burdick, Charles B. ' "Moro": the resupply of German submarines in Spain, 1939–1942', *Central European History,* 10 (1970), 256–84.
Detwiler, Donald S. 'Spain and the Axis during the Second World War', *Review of Politics,* 31 (1971), 36–53.
Dreifort, John E. 'The French Popular Front and the Franco–Soviet Pact, 1936–37: a dilemma in foreign policy', *Journal of Contemporary History* (1976), 217–36.
Fontana, Josep and Nadal, Jordi 'Spain, 1914–1970, in Carlo M. Cipolla (ed.),

The Fontana economic history of Europe: vol. 6, *Contemporary economies.* Part II. London, 1976, pp. 460–529.

Halstead, Charles R. *Spain, the powers and the second world war.* Unpublished Ph.D. (University of Virginia), 1962.

'Un "Africain" Méconnu: Le Colonel Juan Beigbeder', *Revue d'Histoire de la Deuxième Guerre Mondiale,* vol. 21 (1971), no. 83, 31–60.

' "Consistent and total peril from every side": Portugal and its 1940 protocol with Spain', *Iberian Studies,* 3 (1974), 15–29.

'Diligent diplomat: Alexander W. Weddell as American Ambassador to Spain, 1939–1942', *The Virginia Magazine of History and Biography,* vol. 82 (1974), no. 1, 3–38.

'The dispute between Ramón Serrano Suñer and Alexander Weddell', *Rivista di Studi Politici Internazionali* (1974), no. 3, 445–71.

'A "somewhat Machiaevellian" face: Colonel Juan Beigbeder as High Commissioner in Spanish Morocco, 1937–1939', *The Historian,* 37 (1974), 46–66.

'Spanish foreign policy, 1936–1978' in James Cortada (ed.) *Spain in the twentieth-century world: essays on Spanish diplomacy, 1898–1978.* London, 1980.

'Peninsular purpose: Portugal and its 1939 Treaty of Friendship and Non-aggression with Spain', *Il Politico,* XLV (1980), 287–311.

Hamilton, Thomas J. 'Spanish dreams of empire', *Foreign Affairs,* 22 (1944), April, 458–68.

Harvey, Charles E. 'Politics and pyrites during the Spanish Civil War', *Economic History Review,* 31 (1978), 89–104.

Lammers, Donald, 'Fascism, communism and the Foreign Office, 1937–39', *Journal of Contemporary History,* 6 (1971), 66–86.

Niedhart, Gottfried 'British attitudes and policies towards the Soviet Union and international communism, 1933–9' in Wolfgang J. Mommsen and Lothar Kettenacker (eds.), *The fascist challenge and the policy of appeasement.* London, 1983, pp. 286–96.

Pike, David Winegate 'Franco and the Axis stigma', *Journal of Contemporary History,* 17, (1982), 369–407.

Ruhl, Klaus-Jörg 'L'alliance à distance: les relations économiques Germano–Espagnoles de 1936 à 1945', *Revue d'Histoire de la Deuxième Guerre Mondiale,* vol. 30 (1980) no. 118, 69–102.

Schnieder, Wolfgang 'Spanischer Bürgerkrieg und Vierjahresplan. Zur Struktur nazionalsozialistischer Aussenpolitik' in Wolfgang Schneider and Christof Dipper (eds.), *Der Spanische Bürgerkrieg in der internationalen politik (1936–1939).* Munich, 1976, pp. 162–90.

Southworth, Herbert 'The Falange: an analysis of Spain's fascist heritage' in Paul Preston (ed.), *Spain in crisis: the evolution and decline of the Franco regime.* Hassocks, Sussex, 1976, pp. 1–22.

Stafford, David 'The detonator concept: British strategy, SOE and European resistance after the fall of France', *Journal of Contemporary History,* 10 (1975), 185–217.

Stone, Glyn A. 'The official British attitude to the Anglo–Portuguese Alliance, 1910–45', *Journal of Contemporary History,* 10 (1975), 729–46.

'Britain, non-intervention and the Spanish Civil War', *European Studies Review,* 10 (1979), 129–49.

Taylor, A. J. P. 'Daddy, what was Winston Churchill?' in *Essays in English history*. Harmondsworth, Middlesex, 1976, pp. 295–307.

Umbreit, Hans 'Die Rückkehr zu einer indirekten Strategie gegen England', in Hans Umbreit, Klaus A. Maier, Horst Rohde and Bernd Stegeman (eds.), *Das Deutsche Reich und der Zweite Weltkreig*, II, *Die Errichtung der Hegemonie auf dem Europäischen Kontinent*. Stuttgart, 1979, 409–16.

Viñas, Angel 'La administración de la política económica exterior en España, 1936–1979', *Cuardernos Económicos de I.C.E.*, no. 13 (1980), 159–247.

Volkmann, Hans-Erich 'Die NS–Wirtschaft in Vorbereitung des Krieges' in H. E. Volkman, Wilhelm Deist, Manfred Messerschmidt and Wolfram Wette (eds.), *Das deutsche Reich und der Zweite Weltkrieg*, I, *Ursachen und Voraussetzungen der Deutschen Kriegspolitik*. Stuttgart, 1979, 177–368.

Wheeler, Douglas L. 'In the service of order: the Portuguese political police and the British, German and Spanish intelligence, 1932–1945', *Journal of Contemporary History*, 18 (1983), 1–25.

Wight, Martin 'Why is there no international theory?' in Herbert Butterfield and Martin Wight (eds.), *Diplomatic investigations: essays in the theory of international politics*. London, 1966, pp. 17–34.

Wilson, Robert R. 'Non-belligerency in relation to the terminology of neutrality', *American Journal of International Law*, 35 (1941), January, 121–3.

Woolberg, Robert Gale 'Spain as an African power', *Foreign Affairs*, 24 (1946), July, 723–35.

Newspapers
A.B.C. (Madrid).
Arriba (Madrid).
Daily Express (London).
Daily Herald (London).
Evening Standard (London).
News Chronicle (London).
New York Times (New York).
The Times (London).
The Week (London).

Interview with the late Captain Alan Hillgarth, R.N., on 27 January 1977.

Index